The collected works of Ruqaiya Hasan

Volume 5 Describing Language: Form and Function

Edited by Jonathan J. Webster and Carmel Cloran

Social order is not part of the 'nature of things', and it cannot be derived from 'the laws of nature'. Social order exists *only* as a product of human activity. No other ontological status may be ascribed to it without hopelessly obfuscating its empirical manifestations. Both in its genesis (social order is the result of part of human activity) and its existence in any instance of time (social order exists only and in so far as human activity continues to produce it) it is a human product.

P. L. Berger and T. Luckmann, *The Social Construction of Reality.* (1966: 70)

The Collected Works of Ruqaiya Hasan

Volume 5

Describing Language

Form and Function

Edited by Jonathan J. Webster and Carmel Cloran

SHEFFIELD UK   BRISTOL CT

Published by Equinox Publishing Ltd.
UK: Office 415, The Workstation, 15 Paternoster Row, Sheffield, South Yorkshire
       S1 2BX
USA: ISD, 70 Enterprise Drive, Bristol, CT 06010

www.equinoxpub.com

First published 2019

British Library Cataloging-in-Publication Data

A catalogue record for this book is available from the British Library

ISBN-13   978 1 90476 841 8 (hardback)
           978 1 90476 842 5 (paperback)
           978 1 78179 803 4 (ePDF)

Library of Congress Cataloging-in-Publication Data
Library of Congress Cataloging in Publication Control Number: 2004022853

Typeset by S.J.I. Services, New Delhi, India
Printed and bound by Lightning Source Inc. (La Vergne, TN), Lightning Source UK Ltd. (Milton Keynes), Lightning Source AU Pty. (Scoresby, Victoria)

Contents

Acknowledgements

1984   What kind of resource is language? *Australian Review of Applied Linguistics, 1, 1984.* Amsterdam: John Benjamins: 57–85 (29).

1987   Directions from structuralism. In *The Linguistics of Writing* edited by D. Attridge, A. Durant, N. Fabb, and C. McCabe. Manchester: Manchester University Press.

2014   Linguistic sign and the science of linguistics in Y. Fang and J. Webster (Eds). *Developing Systemic Functional Linguistics: Theory and Applications.* London: Equinox.

2012   A view of pragmatics in a social semiotic perspective. *Linguistics and the Human Sciences 5(3),* 251–279. February 2012

2013   Choice, system and realisation: Describing language as meaning potential. In. L. Fontaine, T. Bartlett, and G. O'Grady (Eds). *Systemic Functional Linguistics: Exploring Choice.* Cambridge: Cambridge University Press.

1987   The grammarian's dream: Lexis as most delicate grammar. In M. A. K. Halliday and R. P. Fawcett (Eds), *Recent Development in Systemic Linguistics, Vol 1.* London: Frances Pinter.

1985   Lending and borrowing: from grammar to lexis. In J. E. Clark (Ed.) *The Cultivated Australian: Festschrift in Honour of Arthur Delbridge.* Amsterdam: Helmut Buske.

1971   Syntax and semantics. In J. Morton (Ed.). *Biological and Social Factors in Psycholinguistics.* London: Logos.

2010   The meaning of not is not in not. In A. Mahboob and N. Knight (Eds). *Appliable Linguistics.* London: Continuum.

1970   The verb 'Be' in Urdu. In J. W. M. Verhaar (Ed.) *The Verb 'Be' and Its Synonyms.* Foundations of Language Supplementary Series 7.

Editor's preface

The opening section on *Language and Linguistics* begins with Hasan's *What kind of resource is language?* (1984), in which she argues a functional basis for the evolution of language. Originating out of 'the demands we make on it', whether trivial or 'enormously momentous', language both shapes and reinforces the intersubjective reality within which we live, work and play. Casual conversation between mother and child provides the environment within which Hasan explores how 'reality is spun out of language'. Besides being purposeful, speaking is also a potential. But this potentiality, as Hasan notes in *Directions from structuralism* (1987), 'is always limited by who we are, how others see us, what rights we enjoy, what obligations we carry.' In other words, the potentiality of the sign is actualized within a social context. In a more recent paper, *Linguistic sign and the science of linguistics* (2014), which Hasan herself described as 'a distant relative' of a plenary at the 10th Chinese National Conference of Functional Linguistics at Xiangxi Normal University in 2007, Hasan argues that that the appliability of Systemic Functional Linguistics derives from its ability to show how language works in context of situation. This ability, which as Hasan notes 'arises from the pursuit of a viable conception of the sign such as Saussure's to its logical end', renders SFL 'capable of being used to help solve any problem that implicates language in any social activity'. Taking issue with the more mainstream view of pragmatics that 'accept[s] the validity of competence as universal syntax', in 'A view of pragmatics in a social semiotic perspective' (2012), Hasan instead insists on attending to 'systemic features of the phenomena it seeks to describe even if as process/performance.' In Chapter Five, *Choice, system and realization: Describing language as meaning potential* (2013), Hasan explains that reference to 'choice' in SFL theory 'has no concern with individuality, freedom, will or all those other qualities that dictionaries assign to the act of choice'. Rather 'choice' is being used metaphorically to explicate 'the inner workings of language'.

Both chapters in the second section of this volume, *Lexicogrammatical Descriptions,* address the feasibility of 'an integrally inter-related level of form – a lexicogrammar' as opposed to 'the traditionally cherished sharp boundary between syntax and lexicon'. In Chapter Six, *The grammarian's dream: Lexis as most delicate grammar* (1987), Hasan takes a quote from Halliday – 'The grammarian's dream is … to turn the whole of linguistic form into grammar, hoping to show that lexis can be defined as "most delicate grammar"' (1961: 267) – as the basis for launching into her argument for 'an uninterrupted continuity between grammar and lexis'. In a Systemic-Functional model, the system networks are the grammar. Realizing the grammarian's dream of lexis as 'most delicate grammar' requires extending the delicacy of each of the four lexicogrammatical networks, each specified by one of the four metafunctions – experiential, logical, interpersonal and textual – 'so as to turn it into a device for the description and generation of units of form called "lexical item"'. As Hasan explains further in Chapter Seven, *Lending and borrowing: From grammar to lexis* (1985), the meaning of a lexical item is constructed by the grammar. Taking as her examples, the words 'lend' and 'borrow' and 'sell' and 'buy', Hasan shows that 'they mean what they mean because of the way they are used – because of the constructions in which they appear'.

The third section *On the Relations of Form and Meaning* discusses the hierarchic relation between semantics and the lexicogrammar, incorporating, as noted in the preceding chapters, both grammar and lexis. In Chapter Eight, *Syntax and semantics* (1971), as the title suggests, Hasan explores the relationship between meaning and form. The semantic level is dynamic, providing input to be mediated through the lexicogrammar before subsequently being realized as 'a string of meaningful noise'. The dominance of meaning both in daily life and over expression is further explored in Chapter Nine, *The meaning of 'not' is not in 'not'* (2011). The world turns on the exchange of meaning. It is 'the *raison d'être* for syntax and expression. Insisting on 'the centrality of meaning to human life', Hasan explores research across such human sciences as 'archaeological anthropology, neuroscience, psychology, sociology and last and most pertinent, one particular approach to the study of language, which treats linguistic meaning as the essence of humanity, viz., systemic functional linguistics.'

The final section presents *Brief Excursions into Urdu Grammar,* covering both transitivity choice in some Urdu clauses – Chapter Ten, *Some clause types in Urdu*; and the semantics of the Urdu verb *honaa/to be* – Chapter Eleven, *The verb 'Be' in Urdu* (1970).

Special thanks to two special people who have helped make this volume possible. Carmel Cloran, my co-editor for this volume, one of Professor Hasan's PhD students, assisted with editing the volume; and Professor Ruqaiya Hasan's sister, Zakia Sarwar, contributed her linguistic expertise in finalizing the final two chapters on Urdu.

Foreword

More than twenty years ago now, my colleagues and I interviewed our mentor and friend, the late Professor Ruqaiya Hasan, while we were in the process of editing the very first collection[1] of her works, a slim eight chapter volume of our favourite pieces which displayed the range of her interests rather than being a thematically coherent collection. During that interview, Hasan articulated the principle which guided her linguistic explorations: her sense of the existence of a continuity from the living of life right down to the morpheme. In essence, all her writing was concerned with the enactment of this principle and its investigation. As with all her writing, the papers in the present volume (the fifth of seven) demonstrate her pursuit of this principle.

From theoretical engagement with the great names of twentieth-century linguistics to fine-grained and detailed analyses of meaning, in all her academic endeavours – lectures, writings, interaction with students and colleagues – Ruqaiya Hasan brought a formidable intellect to bear on the problems with which she was concerned. As a teacher and mentor, she was inspirational and somewhat surprisingly forbearing of her students' attempts to express their understanding of unfamiliar concepts. Her writings – actually well-crafted essays – are not an easy read but they do greatly reward patience, persistence and repeated close readings. While still mourning her untimely passing, I am deeply grateful for the wonderful legacy she has left us of intelligent and principled application of linguistic theory and practice.

Carmel Cloran
Sydney
February 2018

Note

1   *Ways of Saying: Ways of Meaning: Selected Papers of Ruqaiya Hasan*, edited by C. Cloran, D. Butt and G. Williams, London: Cassell 1996.

I

LANGUAGE IN THE CONTEXT OF LIFE IN SOCIETY

1 What kind of resource is language? [1984]

It seems to me that there are some advantages in stating the title as I have done – in the form of a question. Of course, we all know that this is not a genuine question: it is just one of those tainted speech acts we are given to producing in everyday life. This speaker would not like the hearer(s) to provide an answer. In fact, if someone now started answering this question, I would be more than surprised; I would feel deprived. After all I have come here, prepared in my own humble way, to say something about what kind of resource I think language is. Nor do I think that by raising a question, I have run an enormous risk, since being familiar with conventions of behaviour at conferences, I feel justified in my belief that no one is going to steal my turn. But I realize (with hindsight to be frank) that there were good reasons for presenting the title as a question, rather than as a description. A descriptive title might have been *The kind of resource that Language is*, but that sounds altogether too final. I do not wish to take it upon myself to pronounce upon the kind of resource that language is. I simply wish to present an opinion: what I think is a possible answer to this question. Opinions are open to debate; they initiate a conversation in a manner that pronouncements may not. Naturally I do not wish to imply that the opinions I am about to offer are entirely my own: I am indebted to many scholars from whose work I have derived inspiration. It would be too tedious to mention all these names since the list is long; except for one – Michael Halliday, simply for the reason that he, if I am not mistaken, is the originator of the expression 'Language as a resource' (Halliday 1974a).

Let me now turn to the question that I have posed myself: what kind of resource is language? One way of approaching this question might be to try to enumerate the many ways in which language plays a crucial role in the life of a community: the uses to which we put language, from the humble everyday activities such as those of greeting friends, or entering into conversations motivated solely by 'sociability' (Goffman 1981) to those guided by a distinct purpose, be it that of buying a newspaper or buying petrol or the more awesome one of being interviewed for a job or a still more awesome one of educating the young: there is nowhere that language does not come in. In fact, it is not possible to present an exhaustive list of the range of uses for which we employ language. This is not a discovery made by linguists the other day; it is the commonsense perspective shared by most members of a community who have had the occasion, for some reason or other, consciously to think about it. I say 'for some reason or other consciously to think about it' simply because the ubiquity of language is such that we go about the business of living, making use of it and taking it for granted in much the same way as we take it for granted that eyes are for seeing and ears are for hearing. As the great Danish linguist, Hjelmslev, remarked: 'It is in the nature of language to be overlooked – to be a means and not an end' (Hjelmslev 1961). I mention this fairly obvious sense of the phrase 'language as a resource' simply as my way into asking some other questions. For example: Why is it possible for language to function as a means? How is it that language constructs an empire to which, virtually, no limits can be set? I am suggesting there is a chance that we might understand better what kind of resource language is by examining these questions rather than by the simple affirmation of the ubiquity of language. But, of course, to do justice to these questions, one must examine many aspects of language. That could take weeks, if not longer. So what I propose to do is to rush in where angels might fear to tread. I will declare that the reason language can be means to so many ends is because the ends were created largely by language. I am saying no more and no less than that a language is a shaper of reality for those who use it. I am aware that a claim of this kind, generally, does not go down well; at the least it engenders scepticism. However, I intend to stay with this claim, for I know of no better hypothesis for answering the questions I have just raised. Still, and particularly remembering the fate of Whorf, it appears necessary to expand on the claim that language is a shaper of reality.

The greatest problem that has arisen in regard to this claim derives from an assumption which I do not share – namely that there is one ultimate Reality, written with a capital R – a view which makes one cry out, in the words of Royce (1964) who expresses the attitude as follows:

> If you cannot convince me that there is some kind of knowable ultimate reality, or if you cannot convince me that there are certain absolute values by which I can live my life, I shall commit psychological

suicide. Either convince me that there is 'one truth' and one right way of doing things, or I shall conclude that everything is meaningless and I will not try any more.

The quest for ultimate reality rests upon assumptions about both the nature of the universe and the nature of the human mind, whereby it is assumed that there is one immutable ultimate reality and that human minds are innately fashioned to the perception of that reality. To use David Butt's phrase (1983), this is the hypothesis of the 'mirrorites'.

The rise of science and technology has created the illusion that such ultimate reality actually exists; and the reason we are being held back in our goal of discovering it is simply that we are bad behaviourists, or incurable empiricists (or whatever might be the academic term of abuse current at the time). To such an attitude, the thought is not daunting that the last century's cherished beliefs turn into this century's lamentable superstitions. Tracing the success of modern science to Galileo, Rorty (1981) chides 'modern philosophy' as follows:

> The tradition we call 'modern philosophy' asked itself 'How is it that science has had so much success? What is the secret of this success?' The various bad answers to these bad questions have been variations on a single charming but uncashable metaphor: namely, the new science discovered the language which nature itself uses. When Galileo said that the Book of Nature was written in the language of mathematics, he meant his new reductionistic, mathematical vocabulary didn't just *happen* to work, but that it worked *because* that was the way things *really* were. He meant that the vocabulary worked because it fitted the universe as a key fits a lock. (1981: 191–192)

Rorty argues that such bad answers to bad questions led to 'the neurotic Cartesian quest for certainty' (Rorty 1979: 161), to the triumph of 'pure reason' and to conceptions of the 'natural language of the mind'. He suggests that, instead of giving these answers

> We shall just say that Galileo had a good idea and Aristotle a less good idea; Galileo was using some terminology which helped, and Aristotle wasn't. Galileo's terminology was the only 'secret' he had – he didn't pick that terminology because it was 'clear' or 'natural' or 'simple', or in line with the categories of the pure understanding. He just lucked out. (1981: 193)

This view is highly reminiscent of Whorf, who raised the question:

> Are our concepts of 'time', 'space', and 'matter' given in substantially the same form by experience to all men, or are they in part conditioned by the structure of particular languages? (Whorf 1941a: 138)

Whorf suggested that when we find no similarity in our concepts of time, space and matter, it is wrong to lay the blame, as some have done, on the slowness of our intuitions; or to say, as some have said, that we are lacking in clarity of thought or in rationality. These explanations do not account for observed phenomena. He suggests that:

> The right answer is: Newtonian space, time and matter are no intuitions. They are receipts from culture. That is where Newton got them. (1941a: 153)

Whorf maintained:

> all observers are not led by the same physical evidence to the same picture of the universe, unless their linguistic backgrounds are similar or can in some way be calibrated. (1940: 214)

I would quibble with Whorf here only with regard to the phrase 'the same physical evidence'. If your view of reality is physicalistic, it opens the door to the ultimate goal of the discovery of this same physical universe. But as I shall argue later, physical universe, per se, is unknowable; only the socially constructed reality, has a chance of getting known. Nor is it helpful to attempt to salvage the situation, by postponing the attainment of Ultimate Reality to a distant future as Peirce (1960) seems to, when he says:

> Finally, as what anything really is, is what it may finally come to be known to be in the ideal state of complete information, so that reality depends on the ultimate decision of the community. (1960: 189)

I am no philosopher; but from the point of view of a layman, this could be interpreted in one of two ways. First, that when all members of a community believe a thing to be so, then that thing is 'the truth', 'the reality', for that community. In which case, it would seem, we are saying no more than what Whorf said when he talked about our being 'parties to an agreement' (Whorf 1941b). The second interpretation would be in line with the Cartesian argument that rationality will ultimately win; that since, as Peirce pointed out, 'our efforts are self-corrective' (Weiss 1952: 174), we would eventually end up seeing Nature as it wants to be seen. I have considerable difficulty with this interpretation, for it assumes not only that there will be a time when we shall know all that there is to know, but also that at the same time we shall know that we know all that there is to know. Such a hope, it seems to me, replaces the hope of that 'millennium' which the weakening of religious faith has taken away. As rigorous as the methods of science are said to be, the history of science even in that corner of the world whose ideology is now the most dominant, namely, the Western culture, does not appear to agree with this view. Newton was as certain of his facts as Einstein; and perhaps a future Einstein would be as certain of his facts as Newton or Einstein. I would agree with Rorty (1980) that to suggest that there can be an end of enquiry is a reactionary move, reminiscent of the role of the church in the matter of Galileo.

But once the notion of ultimate reality is taken away, what remains? What remains is not a void, but an affirmation that reality is relative – it is relative to time, to place and above all to people. The physical universe in which people live may be independent of its inhabitants, but the picture of it that communities operate with is as much an artefact as a work of fiction. To maintain effect, fiction demands a suspension of disbelief. My hypothesis is that to say that language is a shaper of reality is to say that language is instrumental in sustaining this suspension of disbelief.

Whenever the question of language in relation to reality has been raised, there have been cries of despair. To understand some of the causes of this despair, I would recommend Fishman's (1960) exegesis of the Whorfian hypothesis. I will add briefly that amongst the linguists of this century Whorf was perhaps the most resolute attacker of the ethnocentricity through which the findings of the western cultures could be presented as the only ultimate infallible truths. 'We do not know', he said, 'that civilization is synonymous with rationality' (1956a: 81). Since I consider Whorf one of the major thinkers on the subject of the relationship of language to reality, I will spend some time in the discussion of how Whorf's sayings have been interpreted. I hope that in the course of doing this, I shall also have pointed out some of the ways in which such a relationship should not be interpreted.

Whorf has often been understood as literally saying that language determines the perception of reality. It is quite likely that Whorf has actually used the phrase 'perception of reality'. But the spirit of Whorf's writing is quite opposed to the way in which the phrase has been interpreted by even such eminent scholars as Brown and Lenneberg (1954) or Lenneberg

(1967) who read it as a term synonymous with 'sense perception through the eye'. They proceed then to check whether or not the speakers of two distinct languages with differing colour terminologies would perceive colours differently. That this interpretation of the Whorfian phrase is not coherent with the structure of his argument does not appear to worry them. Lenneberg, moreover, comes to the conclusion that:

> Since the use of words is a creative process, the static reference relationships such as … are recorded in a dictionary are of no great consequence for the actual use of words. However, the differences between languages that impressed Whorf so much are entirely restricted to these static aspects. (1975: 554)

He goes on to add that:

> it is not appropriate to use the vocabulary meanings as the basis for an estimation of cognitive capacities. (1975: 555)

The irony here is that none of this has much to do with Whorf who would have agreed largely with Lenneberg on the question of vocabulary. Whorf warned that:

> the error made by most people who attempt to deal with … social questions of language (is that) they naively suppose that speech is nothing but a piling up of lexations, and that this is all one needs in order to do any and every kind of rational thinking; the far more important thought materials provided by structure and configurative rapport are beyond their horizons. (1956a: 83)

It was almost as if he anticipated the kind of misinterpretation to which he was to be subjected, for claiming that:

> Languages differ not only in how they build their sentences but also in how they break down nature to secure the elements to put in those sentences. (1941b: 240)

He went on to comment on the linguistic naiveté of logicians who:

> tend to pick out tables and chairs and apples on tables as test objects to demonstrate the object-like nature of reality and its one-to-one correspondence with logic. (1941b: 240)

It may be true that vocabulary from the domain of physical experience is easily manipulable for the type of laboratory experiments Lenneberg and Brown had designed, but it remains to be demonstrated that it was differences of this kind 'that impressed Whorf so much'. It is this mode of interpreting Whorf that Hoijer (1954) described as the 'vulgarization of the Whorfian hypothesis'.

What this discussion shows is that naive arguments about cultural pre-occupations on the basis of a handful of vocabulary relating to the domain of physical experience can neither confirm nor disprove the claim about language as a shaper of reality (Hasan 1975, 1978a). Moreover, it high-lights that conception of reality – and cognition – wherein physicalistic elements are imbued with a significance which is rarely, if ever, accorded to social phenomena. The physical reality of each one of my listeners is a fact that transcends language, but my view of you as an audience is a different matter altogether. This latter presupposes a certain kind of social practice, which without language could not easily have come about.

Cole and Scribner (1974), again, discounting 'Whorf's thesis' (which, of course, is not his thesis as I have just argued) deny that the 'absence or presence of a lexical distinction can be taken as an indicator of a corre-sponding perceptual or conceptual distinction'. Now Whorf was inevitably interested in the relation between thought and language: as Fawcett (1983) remarked, Whorf believed that semiotic systems were essential to thinking. Turning to Whorf's conception of the relationship of language to thinking, Cole and Scribner have this to say:

> The reasoning and thinking processes of different people in differ-ent cultures do not differ … just their values, beliefs, and ways of classifying differ. (Cole and Gay 1972; quoted in Cole and Scribner 1974: 25)

Their main thesis, then, is that thought processes are universal; 'the basic difference is in the material for thought' (1974: 26). But in expressing their position thus, they seem to me to act as an excellent example of precisely that quality of Western intellect which Whorf so brilliantly related to 'an aggregate of phenomena' in standard Average European languages. He argued that the overall design of these languages is admirably suited to the creation of an illusion (or a theoretical fiction, if you prefer) whereby it is possible to think of form without content, and content without form, thought process without thought material and thought material without thought process. It is indeed hard to imagine how 'thought process', as such, could ever be examined, without involving an examination of 'thought content' as well. Nor is it easy to see why the difference between values, beliefs and classification can be shrugged off into insignificance as 'just values, beliefs and ways of classifying', as if that is not as important as the process itself! Here is Whorf's own account of the assumptions about language and thought which underlie the approach exemplified by Cole and Scribner:

> According to natural logic, the fact that every person has talked fluently since infancy makes every man his own authority on the process by which he formulates and communicates. He has merely to consult a common substratum of logic which he and everyone else are supposed to possess. Natural logic says that talking is merely an incidental process concerned strictly with communication, not with formulation of ideas. Talking … is supposed only to 'express' what is essentially already formulated … Formulation is an independent process, called thought or thinking and is supposed to be largely indifferent to the nature of particular languages. Languages have grammars which are assumed to be merely norms of conventional and social correctness, but the use of language is supposed to be guided … by correct, rational or intelligent thinking.
>
> Thought, in this view, does not depend on grammar but on laws of logic and reason which are supposed to be the same for all observers of the universe – to represent a rationale in the universe that can be found independently by all intelligent observers (1940: 207–208)

Whorf continues his argument:

> Natural logic contains two fallacies. First, it does not see that the phenomena of language are to its own speakers largely of a background character and so are outside the critical consciousness and control of the speaker who is expounding natural logic. Hence, when anyone as a natural logician, is talking about reason, logic, and the laws of correct thinking, he is apt to be simply marching in step with purely grammatical facts that have somewhat of a background character in his own language … Second, natural logic confuses agreement about subject matter, attained through use of language, with knowledge of the linguistic process by which agreement is attained: i.e. with the province of the despised (…) grammarian. Two fluent speakers reach a point of assent … Because they thus understand each other … they think … that it is simply a matter of choosing words to express

thoughts ... The amazingly complex system of linguistic patterns and classifications ... is all background. (1940: 211) (But) ... the background phenomena ... are involved in all our foreground activities of talking and of reaching agreement, in all reasoning and arguing of cases, in all law, arbitration, conciliation, contracts, treaties, public opinion, weighing of scientific theories, formulation of scientific results. Whenever agreement or assent is arrived at in human affairs,

'THIS AGREEMENT IS REACHED BY LINGUISTIC PROCESSES, OR ELSE IT IS NOT REACHED.' (1940: 212, original emphasis)

I have quoted Whorf at enormous length for three reasons. First, he articulates an emphatic rejection of the notion that the lexicogrammatical categories of language are receptacles into which are poured intentions, meanings and values. As for Halliday, so for Whorf, the system of language is a meaning potential; it is not simply, to use Hjelmslev's terminology, the 'plane of expression', with the 'plane of content', as an external reality. Fawcett (1983) talks about the inadequacies of the Chomskian conception of language. There is not enough time to develop the theme that these inadequacies arise quite inevitably from pursuing the Cartesian notion of Rational Man, even if Aarsleff (1970) is right in claiming that Chomsky is guilty of the misinterpretation of Western intellectual history. When we take Reason as God-given, mirroring Nature, and think of language system – not just the ability to learn language but the system itself – as innate, inevitably, the categories of language appear to be just a formalism; the profundity of Man is seen as a function of his Natural Rationality, the language as simply its expression.

Second, and in sharp contrast to the latter position which I have just outlined, the extract denies the possibility of establishing forms of reasoning in the absence of language. Thus, if we ever came across a human organism (not a person, note, because persons are created through semiosis) lacking totally any form of language, it would not be possible for us to say anything about her/his forms of reasoning. Reasoning man is talking man; such a person is a being who has participated in semiosis. As Whorf said '"Talk" OUGHT TO BE a more dignified and noble term than "think"' (1940: 220). Third and last, this discussion has brought my argument full circle to the point where the claim is being reiterated that language is instrumental in *sustaining the suspension of disbelief with regard to the artefact of constructed reality*. It is perhaps obvious that these three points are closely related to one another. More specifically, I would argue that the first point about the system of language as meaning potential is a necessary postulate for arguing the relationship of language to forms of reasoning and for its ability to operate as an instrument in the suspension of disbelief. I will therefore look at the first point a little more closely.

In his *Philosophical Investigations*, Wittgenstein (1958) comments 'When we say: "Every word in language signifies something" we have so far said nothing whatever' (1958: 7e.13), for, this view of meaning can very easily be reduced to 'naming'. A natural language is not simply a naming-game. If it were, the idea that language simply expresses or names categories of content would be justified. In that case, categories of content would be established totally in independence from language, as the human body exists independent of its clothes. I am aware that even those scholars who reject the naming theory find the denial of the physical reality of existents worrisome. My own approach to this problem is to refuse to buy into it. To ask if we would or would not see a tree as a tree and a mountain as a mountain, even in the absence of language, is to raise what Rorty would describe as 'bad questions'; and we should avoid the temptation of giving bad answers. It is important to recognize that, in the nature of things, we can never answer such questions with any certainty; none of us knows a world without any language. It is doubtful if we shall ever find out how the world of physical reality appeared to the earliest group of *homo sapiens* as they struggled to create the various systems of semiosis.

Rather than speculate about the 'real' nature of physical reality as it must appear to a mind uninformed by semiosis and hence unevolved by culture, it seems far more helpful to say that confronted with the world, both the world outside and the one inside the organism, human beings proceeded to make sense of these phenomena; they developed means of communicating about these phenomena.

It is doubtful if to do this they only used the modality of language. Recent work in developmental linguistics points more and more to the continuities between the various semiotic systems (Halliday 1975; Shotter 1978; Newson 1978; Trevarthen and Hubley 1978; and many others). Nor can it be said that communication developed in independence from sense perception. But the acknowledgement that there exists sense perception does not necessarily lead to the view that language 'mirrors' this sensed reality. Let me develop this point, which is an important one.

Sense data, by its very nature, is private. Consider that the question: 'Is your pain as bad as mine?', in that form, is not susceptible to an answer, except with a 'well, I don't know how bad your pain is!', which amounts to saying that sensation is private. The various semiotic systems enable us to 'talk' about our experience of ourselves, our fellow beings and our environment. From this point of view, the expressions of language are not vocal replications of that which the senses experience. In fact we do not know what it would mean to say that the language sign replicates or presents an exact correspondence to the world, thus sensed. Instead all we can claim is that linguistic signs function as a necessary step to the creation of intersubjectivity.

With regard to intersubjectivity, I wish to raise two related points. One of these will take me directly to Saussure and Hjelmsdev, the other to Halliday. In the first place it is a necessary condition of any system capable of creating intersubjectivity that it should possess the attribute of what Berger and Luckman call 'detachability' (1967: 51). What I understand by this term as it would apply to language is that the linguistic sign does not name raw experience, irrespective of how we define that term. Any given sign is distanced from raw experience, to the extent that it must apply, and is so applied, by the members of the community, to distinct instances of a class of raw experiences, each of which is, in some sense, non-identical with the others. When we create the correspondence theory of meaning, we create a fiction that is essentially circular: all we can show is that the categories of language correspond to that which is created by language. It is for this reason that Saussure, and following him Hjelmslev, maintained that raw reality is unknowable. Hjelmslev, reasoning very closely, argued that language forms meanings; meanings are not to be found lying around, like apples on tables. Both the expression and the content of the signs in the system of language are already abstractions: they are not co-extensive with certain classes of humanly producible sounds or with what 'is in the world'. The notion of truth, in the sense of correspondence with raw reality, is alien to language. In fact, whatever aspect of raw reality has not been articulated semiotically remains unknown. This is the reason for suggesting that reality is not *found* but *shaped*, not *mirrored* but *constructed*. This construction is largely an artefact of the verbal sign system. Perhaps there are sayable things none of which is being said in any language anywhere; but, if so, there is no way in which we could come to talk about them except to the extent that the system of language itself may be a resource in enquiry. As F. P. Ramsey said in response to Wittgenstein: 'What we can't say, we can't say; and we can't whistle it either' (quoted in Skinner 1981). I would go one step further and say that one can't even know that one can't say it, because 'it' is not 'it' yet; in order to attain 'it-ness' it stands in need of linguistic articulation. The ability of language to function as a means to so many ends arises from the fact that, for the most part, it is used to deal only with what it, itself, has created.

This potential of language, to give satisfaction in all situations, is made possible, as Hjelmslev remarked, by the fact that language is not a collection of expressions, but a system of signs, such that each sign is related to others, and precisely by virtue of these relations – the configurations and the rapports – each sign is the union of expression and content. The fact must also be recognized that the sign system, as a system, possesses certain structural peculiarities, which permit:

> the unlimited possibility of forming signs and the very free rules for forming units of greater extension ... (This) makes it possible for a language to allow false, inconsistent, imprecise, ugly and unethical formulations as well as true, consistent, precise, beautiful and ethical formulations. The grammatical rules of language are free of any scale of values, logical, aesthetic or ethical; and, in general, language is independent of any specific purpose. (1961: 109–110)

Thus I am arguing that it is a gross misunderstanding of the nature of language to think of the sign simply as expression; the sign is a composite of meaning and expression.

The second point that arises from a consideration of intersubjectivity is what I would like to describe as the notion of 'validation'. Language grows not in isolation, not intra-organically, but inter-organically, to use Halliday's terms. This view entails the concept of validation. Shaped reality is validated reality; it is that which gets comprehended by the listeners and by doing so achieves validation. Whatever the nature of my experience – and it is bound to be in some respects unique to me – only that part of it is validated which is expressible and is, thus, seen as expressed. I believe that it is this idea of validation that G. H. Mead talks about (1910: 23) as follows:

> It is only through the response that consciousness of meaning appears, a response which involves the consciousness of another self as the presupposition or the meaning in one's own attitude.

Unless the formed meanings are thus validated through the practices of other members of the community, there would be no possibility for the creation of inter-subjectivity. For example, what passes as 'question' could not pass as 'question' unless its question-ness has been validated by the characteristic provision of answers; what passes as 'honesty' could not pass as 'honesty', unless it were recognized as 'honesty' by other members of the community. The selfsame pattern of behaviour could conceivably pass as 'stupidity' in another place, at another time, by another community; and, by the same token, by different subcommunities at the same time and the same place. The notion of validation is essential to the success of language in operating as an instrument for the suspension of disbelief. Beliefs are not personal in origin; they have to be socially legitimated. The precondition for this legitimation is the concept of validation. When I say: 'I am very tired', and my saying is validated by others in treating me as a person who is very tired, then my use of that statement to describe that condition is validated. When a community has validated, through its linguistic practices, the belief that the earth is flat, then for that community the earth is flat. They will go to enormous lengths to retain that belief, not because it is false and they are obstinate and stupid, but because, by their lights, it is the truth. This suspension of disbelief towards the linguistically shaped reality is capable of being disturbed only to the extent that within the language also lies the possibility of raising questions, of constructing arguments, of demanding proofs. For today's truth to turn into tomorrow's untruths, there has to be conversation. From the point of view of validation, the community is the central fact.

Once we have reached this point, we are forced to recognize the very fundamental role that the *use* of language plays in the creation, maintenance, and change of the *system* of language. No matter how anthropomorphically I may talk of the language system, the fact remains that neither could the system create itself, nor could it evolve intra-organically. On the one hand, the possibility of communication denies the possibility of such solipsistic origins for language; on the other hand, it demands both detachability and validation, without which communication could not take place. But the recognition of the latter two properties as central to the linguistic sign takes us back to the obvious answers with which I started. This is because there is no special *forum* for the creation and evolution of the system of language. It has got created – and has evolved over the period of human history – simply by the fact that it has been pressed into service in the interests of doing 'other things': things such as greeting, conversing, buying, interviewing, educating, and a host of others. It would be a tautology to say that as the use of language extends, so the domain of 'formed meanings' extends; for, from the point of view I have been presenting, the two expressions mean one and the same thing. It is in this manner that I interpret Halliday's saying that:

> The nature of language is closely related to the demands that we make on it, the functions it has to serve. (1970: 141)

Language is able to cope with our demands because it is in meeting these demands that its origin is rooted; it is able to give satisfaction in all situations because it is largely by and with language that these situations were created in the first place. We can see this principle at work clearly in the development of communication in children. Children don't first acquire language and then use it; there is a dialectic between the process, i.e., use, and the system whereby the successful acts of communication beget the potential for communicating. Somewhere in the early stage, which Trevarthen (1979) describes as 'primary intersubjectivity', the baby must recognize that interaction with the other is a possibility; and that this interaction can take specific forms, such as smiles, gurgles, eye contact, and bodily movements. It is hard to imagine that these specific forms of behaviour could be associated with communication by a baby in the absence of the care-giver's response. With the onset of 'secondary intersubjectivity' (Trevarthen and Hubley 1978) which coincides with the emergence of protolanguage, communication really takes off. But because of the internal structure of protolanguage which differs qualitatively from adult language (Halliday 1975), the child's meanings cannot be viewed as 'formed content'. That is why the care-giver's interpretation of the protolingual baby must rely on situational clues, a point to which Malinowski (1923), de Laguna (1927), Halliday (1975), Bruner (1978), and others have drawn attention. 'Formed content' – the kind of meaning that is specific to natural human languages – appears only with the emergence of adult language, since it is at that time that the structure of the system itself evolves to develop a means whereby 'formed content' becomes possible, namely through the emergence of the lexicogrammatical level. The systematic relations of the signs are essential to their status as signs.

Two remarks appear pertinent here. First, from the developmental point of view there is a continuity in communication as communication, especially if we see communication as meaningful behaviour. This meaningful behaviour must, in some sense, be related to the communicator's needs. In saying this, I am very conscious of the fact that 'need' is a term frowned upon in developmental linguistics, where it has been criticized vigorously by, for example, Lenneberg (1964). But if we take into account Lenneberg's assumptions about the nature of language, this would explain the basis of his criticism. To recognize needs as the mainspring of language and communication is to recognize that the system for communication has a teleological origin. If our basic postulate is that language is God-given and is innate, we cannot entertain the hypothesis that its emergence might arise simply as a response to human needs. I have argued, by contrast, for a conception of language as rooted in community and communication, a hypothesis which is a necessary step in accounting for the ubiquity of language. But if it is accepted that language is used as means to ends, it seems difficult to deny its teleological aspect. Thus my argument is that language could not develop as a means to the many varied ends unless its origins were rooted in the satisfaction of the user's needs. The continuity in the child's communication can be seen as a development and a refinement of the means whereby the child's needs can be attained. All we need is a wider, more socially viable concept of need than in Lenneberg (1964) where it gets restricted to a bottle of milk or a cookie. So, the first point I am making is that both purpose and a society where purposes get recognized are essential to the growth of language.

At the same time – and this is the second point – it is important to focus on the role of the adult in these early processes. This role can be seen as that of providing 'validation'. We have no definite way of knowing exactly what it is that the infant is attempting to communicate. It is just possible that there are certain bits of putative information, which are never validated by the care-giver. From this point of view the expansions that a care-giver returns to the immature expressions of the child could be as much a limiting of his universe as an enabling of the emergence of his social self. The word socialization is the learned name for the practices whereby a novice is brought to share the shaped reality; and for the most part it is reality shaped by the systematic operation of language. Minds are created by brain-washing. If the child grows up believing the beliefs of his speech community, this is not because such beliefs are transcendentally available to all of us as rational beings; it is because these beliefs are enshrined in the language of his community. So on the one hand I am arguing that language is purpose-free *qua* meaning potential (see above), while on the other hand I am suggesting that the development and attainment of a meaning potential for an individual can only come about through the continued and extended use of the resources already at that individual's command, which implies orientation to purpose.

It has become a commonplace of developmental linguistics to claim that by his fourth year, the child has acquired a mastery of his mother tongue. But if so, the phrase 'mastery of mother tongue' stands in need of close scrutiny. Let me share with you my own experience here. For the last few years I have run a course under the label of *Language and the Child*, where the students have the option of submitting a mini-research which calls for the examination of language data collected from children engaged in the performance of some naturalistic task. I have learnt much from the data collected by my students. A pertinent set of researches to mention here is one that requires the student to compare the seven-year old's 'mastery of mother tongue' in describing their participation in such events as a holiday or a visit to the zoo, or a trip into the city and the same child's description of the making of, say, a model, to someone who was not present at the time the model was made. The data from this set of researches is an eye-opener. The child who is voluble and almost unstoppable in describing the former produces language in the latter case that is halting: unfinished structures, even 'ungrammatical sentences' occur all over the place. The greatest differences are to be found in the manifestation of the textual function, ranging from awkward schematic structure to the disruption of cohesive ties. To my mind, there cannot be clearer evidence for the hypothesis that the growth of language in an individual is the function of that individual's engagement in a varied set of activities, calling for the use of language. You can only learn how to mean, by attempting to mean. There is a continued dialectic between the process: the use of the meaning potential, and the system: the community's or the individual's meaning potential, as such, at any given time.

This takes me to the final phase of my discourse. I claimed earlier that if the child grows up believing the beliefs of his speech community, this is because, as Whorf said, these beliefs are enshrined in the language of his community. To learn language is to learn to suspend disbelief with regard to these beliefs; to behave as if these beliefs have *sui generis* status. In the words of Douglas (1971):

> The forms of knowledge most taken for granted in any group come to be seen as absolute – as independent of the knowing minds, as out there. (1971: 27)

But what is the paradigm environment in which such knowledge and belief become the growing child's reality? Clearly not in a situation of direct debate on the matter. As Halliday points out:

> nobody teaches him [the child] the principles on which social groups are organized, or their systems of beliefs, nor would he understand it if they tried. It happens indirectly through the accumulated

experience of numerous small events, insignificant in themselves, in which his behaviour is guided and controlled and in the course of which he contracts and develops personal relationships of all kinds … The striking fact is that it is the most ordinary everyday uses of language, with parents, brothers and sisters, neighbourhood children, in the home, in the street and the park, in the shops and the trains, and the buses, that serve to transmit, to the child, the essential qualities of the society and the nature of social being. (1974a: 4)

It seems then that the paradigm environment both for learning language and for learning through language, for the child, is the environment of casual conversation. So I will now turn my attention to some cases of mother-child talk to provide some indication of how individuals' worlds are created, how reality is spun out of language, because that reality is already the domain of language.

First, consider the cases where the object of enquiry is the linguistic sign itself. I will present three cases. Each differs from the others in some respects, while each is alike in that the attention is focused on some linguistic sign.

Case 1 Kelly and mother are busy getting ready to cook corn bread. The incessant talk is about getting ingredients and utensils, and about measuring and mixing and chopping. Kelly is 3 years 7 months old.

> M. Now I'll cut up the onions and capsicums
> And I'll get you to grease the dish.
> K. What's grease?
> M. I'll put a little bit of oil in that dish.
> K. Mm.
> M. And then I want you to rub it around with your fingers …
> K. Mm.
> M. All over the dish …
> Only on the inside.
> That's right … Lovely.
> Yeah, that's right. With the tips of your fingers
> And do it all down the sides as well
> And get it all over there

This was a direct enquiry: what's grease? and was tied to a specific activity. The mother's explanation takes these facts into account. Unlike the *Oxford Learner's Dictionary* which states the following definition:

vt put or rub grease on or in (especially parts of a machine)

the mother ties her answer to the specific activity. Kelly has had her first 'go' at the validation of the sign 'grease' – she will need many more to arrive where her mother is.

Case 2 Carol, 3 years 6 months old, and mother are getting together their snack to take it outside in the garden. Annie, Carol's younger sister, is also included in the plan, but is too young to assist. The mother has announced and Carol has agreed tacitly that they are 'about to get morning tea and take it outside'.

> M. I'll put the grapes in a bowl and then everybody can share those.
> C. Mum will you share those?
> M. Yes I will …
> C. Mum will Annie share those?
> M. Hope so?
> C. Will I share them?
> M. Hope so …

It seems to me that the point of this interaction for Carol is to get the linguistic signs 'everybody' and 'share' straight. Just what is 'everybody'? But Carol's enquiry is indirect. Does sharing mean that everyone gets to have a go? Carol's enquiry is again indirect. But in asking these questions Carol displays a fairly mature understanding of the nature of meaning in language. Her hidden assumption is that the answers to her questions will provide a satisfactory account of the course of conduct that would arise if 'everybody' is 'everybody' and 'to share' is 'to share' as we understand these words. And note that she does not extend her enquiry about participants beyond the closed set that is pertinent to the planned sharing. And why should she? After all, she is not in the business of writing a paper on quantifiers!

Case 3 Nigel and mother are playing with Nigel's trains. Nigel is at this time 3 years 8 months old. The talk moves back and forth from the toy trains on the board to Reverend Audrey's engines. Reverend Audrey has written a series of stories about the railway in which each of the engines is a character perhaps larger than life, capable of jealousies, intrigues, enmities and friendships. Suddenly Nigel turns to mother with a serious expression:

> N: What's enemy, Mummy?
> M: (somewhat taken off guard) oh – um – enemy, well enemy is someone you think might hurt you. [A pause follows this response, and then Nigel pronounces with great conviction]
> N: But stone is not enemy.
> M: No stone is not enemy though it can hurt you.

This example is particularly interesting. It shows quite clearly a quality that Carol's questions had also contained, namely that to say that something is a linguistic sign is to grant it a set of implicational relations. In fact, this is part of what it means to say that language is a sign system: not a collection of words, 'not a piling up of lexation'. Nigel's comment to Mother's response shows an awareness acquired, almost on the spot, of the rapport between 'stone', 'enemy', and 'hurt'. You must guard against stones and enemies because both can hurt. Nonetheless enemies are different; they don't just happen to hurt you; they mean to hurt you; they are intentional beings like yourself. And yet this is not the view that the traditional Azande of Africa would necessarily share (Evans-Pritchard 1973). There, a stone doesn't just happen to hurt you, it means to hurt you. And if you want proof, that too can be supplied. After all, the stone was always there; if its being there was sufficient cause for its ability to hurt, why did it do it on one particular occasion and not on the others? The conclusion is arrived at almost inevitably: it is acting as an accomplice in the machinations of a malefactor.

This takes me to the larger example presented below.

224–5	C:	Mum do pussy cats die when people die? ...
226	M:	Do pussy cats what, love?
227	C:	Die when people die?
228–9	M:	Well pussy cats die when their time comes ...
230		Everything dies, one day.
231	C:	Do dogs do they one day?
232	M:	Do what?
233	C:	Do dogs die one way when ...

234   M: Yes dogs die, too …
235   C: Do fruit die?
236–7 M: Fruit dies, yes. In a different sort of way.
238   C: How?
239   M: Well, see how the fruit up there on the tree's green?
240   C: Mmm
241   M: See, how down here, it's gone all yellow and squashy and horrible?
242   C: Aa
243   M: That means it's died, it's …
244–5   Well, we don't call it, we don't say it's died, we say it's gone bad.
246   C: Mummy
247   M: Mmm …
248–50 C: Mum, see where the persimmons have dropped off the tree …
           cos um cos they're sick, and they've got germs.
251   M: Yes, that's right.
252–3 C: They're sick and they've got germs.
254   M: Mmm

I will leave it to you to decide whether this discussion between Carol and her mother is about language or about facts. Indeed, I find it difficult to draw a line between the two; the arguments that I have presented point to an inextricable mingling of the two. Let me set the scene for this larger example. It follows as a distant sequence of Case 2. Mother, Annie, and Carol are now in the garden eating their snack. Suddenly Carol notices a cat that has wandered into their garden:

185   C: Oh, a pussy cat!
186   M: It's up in the tree, isn't it?

There ensues a discussion on whether people mind pussy cats in their houses, whether cats are shy like birds or whether they are different. Mother and child turn to their snack when Carol notices that the cat has disappeared as silently as it had arrived. Some more discussion of cats' desirability follows. Carol says:

220–1   C: But sometimes when pussycat goes into people's gar-
                den, some people say 'Come back, pussycat! Come
                back!'
222–3   M: (is amused) Do they? Is that what they do?

They both laugh and there is a relaxed pause in the conversation, when
Carol begins again, and this is where the text starts

224–5   C: Mum do pussycats die when people die?

You might say that the mother's

226   M: Do pussycats what, love?

arises because of the form of Carol's question. Or you might say that she
is suitably impressed by the largeness of that enquiry. She wishes to be
quite certain that Carol has asked the question which she did ask. Carol
provides the essential answer (227). The mother handles that question very
seriously:

228–9   M: Well, pussycats die when their time comes.

As I listen to this reply, I am reminded of the song *There is a season turn,
turn ...* with the lines *There's a time to live, and a time to die*. The Mother
is voicing the same belief that the song voices; and the song is voicing a
belief from the most outstanding religious text for Christians. Do all communities in the world believe that you only die when 'your time has come'?
How well does this belief accord with our faith in medicine, our practices
in protecting ourselves from unnecessary risks? What is the 'right conduct', to use Peirce's phrase, that arises from a belief of this kind? The
Mother is not deflected by any of these considerations. She continued after
a small pause with a generalization:

230   M: Everything dies, one day.

Now Carol has to find out what that means.

231   C: Do dogs do they one day?

Note the Mother's response. She is not particularly hanging on every word
of Carol's. So far as she is concerned she has really dealt with Carol's

question: *Everything dies, one day*. But, nonetheless, she must attend to Carol; after all, they are engaged in a conversation. She asks for a repeat of the question:

232   M: Do what?

Carol specifies

233   C: Do dogs die one day when …

It appears that Carol is about to add either *when people die or when cats die* or even possibly *when their time comes* but she doesn't get there; the mother cuts in. That does leave open the question whether the notion of independent deaths – each organism dying when its time comes – has actually sunk in. The Mother's answer is affirmative:

234   M: Yes dogs die too ...

Note the pause. For Carol – as for most children in the Western world – cats and dogs must share some critical similarities. Still cats and dogs is not 'everything'. How can this part of the statement be tested? Obviously, by moving further away from the category to which cats and dog belong. Carol does just that:

235   C: Do fruit die?

Fruit is sufficiently different from the category into which cats and dogs can be subsumed. Does 'everything' include fruit? Carol is not disappointed; the Mother again takes that question seriously. But her answer supports an opinion which arises from her: *Everything dies, one day.* She appears to work with a general framework wherein death is only one form of mutability; other manifestations of mutability are death-like such as going bad; to the Mother dysfunction is death. For Carol, this is a far goal to reach; she is still groping towards this super-generalization, which permits the Mother to reply quite comfortably:

236–7   M: Fruit dies, yes. In a different sort of way.

This rider about manner is a more or less open invitation to further enquiry. It is not surprising that Carol should come back with a:

238   C: How?

This involves the Mother in an elaborated and staged explanation, each part of which is expressed as a question since, to make a demand is to demand attention. By employing this device the Mother secures the child's attention, waiting at each stage for the child's cues as an indication that her child is moving with her:

239   M: Well, see how the fruit up there on the tree's green?
240   C: Mmm.
241   M: See how down here, it's gone all yellow and squashy and horrible?
242   C: Aa.
243   M: That means it's died, it's ……
244–5   Well, we don't call it, we don't say it's died; we say it's gone bad.

Mutability is fearsome; death is not beautiful – every step that takes you closer to mutability represents an undesirable stage. W. B. Yeats' *Old Men Admiring Themselves* sit staring into the water as it flows by: their hands are like claws, their knees are twisted like old thorn-trees while they lament that everything that's beautiful drifts away. I am definitely not suggesting that the Mother is creating poetry; I am implying, though, that art too draws upon the same rich fund of knowledge which is the social possession of the community by courtesy of language. Contrast Yeats with a truly fatalistic culture, such as the Indian one. Here the poet has this to say:

The point of perfection, the acme of a drop of water is to 'die into' the ocean; when pain has passed the stage of endurance, it turns into its own cure.

I could not lay claim to a wide knowledge of Western literature but I suggest it would be difficult to find there such an expression of contentment (resignation yes, but contentment no) at the idea of mutability. This mother, with her 'yellow and squashy and horrible' certainly does not think of mutability as the point of perfection.

It is doubtful that Carol has grasped the finely finished notion of mutability which the Mother has presented to her. But that something in that direction has taken place is perhaps obvious from Carol's own essay into the area. As she picks up the Mother's theme and tries it out, we can almost see her groping to find her way:

    246   C: Mummy
    247   M: Mmm [a medium pause]
    248–50 C: Mum see where the persimmons have dropped off the
                tree ...
                cos umm cos they're sick and they've got germs.
    251   M: Yes, that's right.
    252–3   C: They're sick and they've got germs.
    254   M: Mmm

Note the child's covert connection between sickness and death; and the overt one between sickness and germs. No doubt she has had many goes at this latter connection; children are always catching germs and mothers are always talking about this experience. Its extension to the case in hand thus presents little problem for Carol; but it is doubtful if she has quite seen the connection between fruit going bad and animals dying. But there is no need to worry, for Carol will engage in other conversations and for the novice – such as the child – conversations are pregnant with facts about the world because language is the main fact-builder about the world.

I have done no more than scratch on the surface of this conversation. Much more could be said, specifically about the forms of reasoning that are learnt through conversations such as these. The examination of a statement, the structuring of argument, inferential relations amongst the sayings are also being learnt at the same time as language is being learnt. Holding the view that I do, I am able to agree with only half of what Rorty says about Sellars' view of what language means to social man:

> What is special about language is not that it 'changes the quality of our experience' or 'opens new vistas of consciousness' or 'systematizes a previously unconscious manifold' or produces any other sort of inner change. All that its acquisition does is to let us enter a community whose members exchange justifications of assertions, and other actions with one another. (Rorty 1979: 185)

It is meaningless to ask whether language changes the quality of our experience; for the experience that cannot be articulated is like the Einsteinian thesis from the point of view of Newton: it is not an impossibility *per se*, but to those located at a particular point, it is the unknowable, the unsuspected.

I may object to the flowery style of 'opens new vistas of consciousness' and the philosophical hang-ups underlying 'systematizes a previously unconscious manifold', but I have attempted in my own very sketchy analysis to show that language is instrumental in creating awareness, in articulating the similarities and the differences between whatever categories its speakers operate with. The trouble is that all of this becomes background phenomena. Philosophers behave as if they, and they alone, know anything worth knowing not only about our systems of knowledge but also about our language, although their work is not exactly distinguished either for linguistic expertise or the deep-going social orientation that is necessary to appreciate the role of language in the creation of social man and of his world.

I have not left myself any time to develop the implications of the hypothesis that language is a shaper of reality, that it is above all the instrument through which we maintain a suspension of disbelief against the precepts of our own culture. These implications are many but I would like to say a word about the one that appears more urgent to a multi-ethnic community such as ours. The search for an ultimate reality, for one right way of being, doing and saying, in a country such as ours is, in the last analysis, a power-game; the winners will be those who, in the colloquial phrase, are sitting pretty. One should not be misled by universalistic arguments which present the attractive hypothesis of finding Man's common factor through a set of reductionist techniques. To appreciate the bond of human brotherhood, the unity of the species – their alikeness – it is not necessary to reduce them to banality; to see our common heritage, it is not necessary to affirm 13 or 15 or 42 semantic universals. Rather, to honour human creativity, we should join Whorf in saying that:

> Linguistic knowledge entails understanding many different, beautiful systems of logical analysis. Through it, the world as seen from the diverse viewpoints of other social groups, that we have thought of as aliens, becomes intelligible in new terms. Alienness turns into a new, and often clarifying way of looking at things. (1942: 264)

And what is true across ethnic communities may be equally true of subcommunities within the same larger community. If these are characterized, among other things, by differing 'fashions of speaking', then the well-intentioned but misguided effort to show that underneath we are all alike does not help those whose fashions of speaking are the main factor in holding them back. It again helps only those who are already in an advantaged position. No one tells me that standard educated English is beautiful, so why do they need to convince me that Black English too is beautiful and logical? In tribute to Labov (1969), we would accept that *qua* system both are equal, in so far as they both possess the internal coherence and inter-relatedness which is characteristic of all human language. The reasons for which sub-standard varieties of language stand in need of championing lies ultimately in the social divisions, the hidden and ugly nature of which Basil Bernstein (1971) has explored. It is ugly precisely because while one can claim the two to be equal, while one can suggest that the fashions of speaking in the two polarized sub-communities are two legitimate fashions, the socio-economic institutions of the middle classes ensure that one and only one of these fashions of speaking, namely their own, affirm the values, the orientation to meaning, which are invariably associated with what counts as success in the macro-community. The argument that the lower socio-economic classes wish to stay where they are because of their spiritual values of friendship cuts about as much ice as the view that socio-economic frustration creates good poetry.

Language is a fearsome resource through which we not only do seemingly trivial things, such as greeting, gossiping, or buying a loaf of bread, but through it we can also have the power of doing enormously momentous things, such as monopolizing resources, putting others down, cutting them off from the road to personal fulfilment. We not only use language to shape reality, but we use it also to defend that reality against anyone whose alternative values might threaten ours. But, if language can be used to defend a reality, then by the same token, it can be used to examine the very reality created by it. Such examination is not to be found in habitual thinking and behaviour; it can only arise by the disturbance of daily habits and communal beliefs. The greatest justification for technical disciplines (e.g., for linguistics, for poetics, for chemistry, for physics, for the entire range of expert disciplines) is that they can disturb the suspension of disbelief which the everyday linguistic practices of a community perpetuate.

2 Directions from structuralism [1987]

The academic scene is fraught with mortality; the *-isms* of its trade have a way of dying a violent death. Take, for example, the -isms connected with the study of language: in this one field alone report of the demise of some -ism or other is always circulating. And yet, to speak thus is to give, perhaps, too decisive, too one-sided a picture. It may be that, like beauty, death too lies in the eye of the beholder. Perhaps the very phenomena some see as death violently perpetrated on an ageing conceptual system could be seen by others as simply a 'becoming' – an evolution, whose point of departure lay already within the system's earlier modes of being. But the latter view cuts out the drama, doing away with heroes; it denies the possibility of hero-worship. And, like death, hero-worship too is an essential ingredient of the academic scene: academics need to worship their heroes just as much as the religious need to worship their deities. So the cataclysmic view of change/becoming as violent death has a good deal to offer. Still if we are to make an announcement of death, then it is prudent that we should have at least some idea of the identity of the dying subject. One may exclaim: surely the identity of the dying subject in the study of language today is not so hidden that one would need to make this the central problematic of one's paper. Surely, it is a secret very well revealed that the dying subject is 'structuralism'. Does one need to say any more, once the name has been named?

I submit that one does, for at least two reasons. If structuralism is dying today, then this, its present death, is a 'second dying': could this second dying be just about as mythical as the 'second coming'? The question is at least worth exploring. Second, naming a name is not equal to saying what the name names: if what we are witness to now is 'post-structuralism', it is valid to ask what that structuralism is which this post-structuralism is 'post' to. Let me turn first to a regrettably potted history of the first death of structuralism, the first advent of post-structuralism, which was heralded by transformational-generativism. For there are a few ironic turns in this episode which somewhat discredit the dramaturgical account of how knowledge, if knowledge it is, progresses; the hero, the villain(s), the mortal combat to rescue the 'science of language' from the evils of structuralism – all, in this event, turned out to be figments of academic fantasy, which is not to say that nothing happened. But what happened was appreciably different from what either the *dramatis personae* or the not-impartial observers imagined was actually happening. The death-blow that Chomsky dealt against behaviourism (Chomsky 1959) was seen as annihilating the very basis of structuralism already said to be shaken to its roots by the advent of new 'trees' (Chomsky 1957). So it came about that the first dying of structuralism was proclaimed in the early 1960s; and as happens in many 'primitive' communities, including the academic one, the name of the dead subject became taboo: to be called a structuralist was to be counted as dead. The living were the transformational-generativists, emerging victoriously from the valley of death bearing the talisman of competence, of intuition, of infallible rules, and of innateness, for all of which, let the good god be thanked.

But if structuralism is dying now, then either it is taking a long time dying or it was something else that died in the 'Chomskian revolution'. It is to be noted that Chomsky displayed considerable indifference to the not inconsiderable differences between that aggregate of principles and practices that went under the name of structuralism in America, and that other such aggregate which went by the same name (same? in what sense 'same'?) in Europe (Greimas 1974; Halliday 1974b). Rather simplistically, the world of the study of language got divided into two neat halves – TG and the rest – pitted against each other. 'The rest' was, of course, defective: it was empiricist, data-oriented, behaviourist, incompetent to account for competence, for rule-governed creativity and much else, including the supreme gift of God to man in the shape of a universal grammar. For at least a decade, the Chomskian debate remained silent – or was it that it lacked all awareness? – about just those presuppositions regarding the nature of language which it shared with its adversary, the American structuralism. TG had arisen, not quite like some mythic race, out of divine fire, with no predecessors to its discredit, but from such distant ones that their voices could be heard down the corridor of time only by the chosen few. This too was necessary: Derrida (1974, 1978, 1982) has claimed that Western philosophy of language has been obsessed from time immemorial with the 'transcendental signified'; would it be equally valid to claim that

Western academia has been just as much obsessed by an élitist notion of 'originality' which runs counter to the interpretation of human history as 'becoming'?

I do not apologize for this partial account of the first death of structuralism, for its partialness is quite intentional; it is relevant here only in that I perceive certain commonalities between this episode of the past (?) and that which is said to be unfolding now. As in the past, so in the present, at issue is the identity of structuralism; as in the past, so in the present, the 'post-ness' of post-structuralism is but an affix to structuralism, almost as if the very structure of the word iconically announced the impossibility of a clear break. I perceive, then, two central issues there, which are inter-related: first, the identity of structuralism is far from clear and obvious; second, whatever that identity, the cataclysmic, dramatic 'break' is less a break than revived variations on some hitherto forgotten or ignored theme(s). By the same token, it is difficult to arrive at the identity of what is 'called "post-structuralism" (but not, perhaps, with sufficient embarrassment over how empty the term is)' (Schmidt 1985: 166). The situation is then one rather nicely tangled, providing linguists, philosophers and literary critics with an open, never-ending possibility of cross-talk – or 'writing' if you prefer. But it could not have been otherwise; and this would have been obvious if Derrida were taken seriously, if the grammatological precepts had been applied with the recommended rigour to the signifier? signified? sign? whose writing is *structuralism*. It too would have all the qualities of indeterminacy that would prevent the easy assumption of unity and self-identity, often ascribed to any *-ism*, as if '*-ism*-ness' were guarantee of definite 'content'. If, as a linguistic sign, *structuralism* were to be regarded as subject to the same indeterminacies, if there were no definite signified always attached/attachable to this signifier, as Derrida has so brilliantly argued for signs in general, then what would it mean to say '… the structuralist invasion …' (Derrida 1978: 3) or '… a structuralist reading, by its own activity, always presupposes …' (Derrida 1978: 24). Is Derrida suggesting there is some 'invariant' structuralism or is he talking about any structuralist reading? If the latter, is there an implication that Derrida knows the full possibilities of 'structuralist reading(s)'? If so, I submit that there is no evidence to encourage this view. What does it mean to say '… modern structuralism has grown …' (Derrida 1978: 27)? Is there an implication that there actually is a unified 'something' that could be called 'modern structuralism'? Even if we were to grant that Saussure is the first structuralist – a doubtful proposition on Derrida's own showing (1974); his voice echoes voices from the past – this does not preclude the possibility that in the manner of other, less momentous, sayings, Saussure's sayings too became at once same-and-different sayings in the discourse of others. *Structuralism* moved in so many directions, occurred in so many different textual environments, that it is no longer possible to talk about a structuralist reading, or modern structuralism.

The above comments are not meant to score a cute point: if anything they are offered as a sign of general puzzlement. Despite Rorty's stern warning about Derrida that 'he is not, to repeat, a philosopher of language' (Rorty 1982: 105), I have found Derrida's reflections on language fascinating – but this is not to say that the reading has not been mystifying. Part of the puzzlement arises from my perception that Salusinszky (1983) is not alone in believing 'that deconstruction, far from being structuralism's new ally, is that very movement which has undone structuralism'. Yet in many important respects, Derrida's positions appear to me to have been already voiced by precisely those scholars who would, by any definition, be regarded as structuralists – e.g. Saussure (1966), of course, but also Hjelmslev (1961), one of the few 'modern structuralists' to get some specific attention from Derrida. Take for example, the question of representation, a central concern of Derrida's from which arise critiques of the notions of signified, signifier, sign, concept, thought, etc. Derrida is concerned that in the Saussurean model 'not only do the signifier and signified seem to unite, but also in this confusion, the signifier seems to erase itself or to become transparent; in order to allow the concept to present itself as what it is, referring to nothing other than its presence' (Derrida 1981: 22).

True that the text attributed to Saussure contains such statements as 'it [i.e. sound] is only the instrument of thought; by itself it has no existence', but what kind of a theory of 'difference' is it that fails to see the working of 'difference' in actual practice? Derrida remarks about the *Course* that 'Saussure's text like any other is not homogeneous' (Derrida 1981: 52); and, it certainly is true that the use of concept, thought, signified is not invariant. Some of this non-homogeneity is indicative of the fact that Saussure, like all of us, was not operating in a vacuum; other voices had discoursed, were discoursing on language. Even though one might ambitiously undertake to rebuild all previous knowledge purely from within, ways of saying that one has participated in as sayer/listener become one's ways of being. So Saussure's voice is not simply his voice; it is also the voice of pre-Saussures. On this, hopefully, there is no disagreement. However, some non-homogeneity seems to have been deliberate, using as point of departure the ways of saying prevalent in the general community. This, in the context of *Course*, was important, for the audience here did not consist of philosophers. Passages such as the following do not quite fit in with the facile picture Derrida presents (see quote above) of Saussure's view of the relationship between signified and signifier:

> Without language, thought is a vague, uncharted nebula. There are no pre-existing ideas, and nothing is distinct before the appearance of language ... Phonic substance is neither more fixed nor more rigid than thought; it is not a mold into which thought must of necessity fit but a plastic substance divided in turn into distinct parts to furnish the signifiers needed by thought ... The characteristic role of language with respect to thought is not to create a material phonic means for expressing ideas but to serve as a link between thought and sound, under conditions that of necessity bring about the reciprocal delimitations of units ... Neither are thoughts given material form nor are sounds transformed into mental entities; the somewhat mysterious fact is rather that 'thought-sound' implies division, and that language works out its units while taking shape between two shapeless masses. (Saussure 1966: 112)

This and other such passages, easily found throughout the *Course*, do not sound very much like the celebration of the 'transcendental signified' or a dangerous tendency toward logocentrism. If 'thought', 'concept', etc. are used, they are used at this early, pre-theoretical stage precisely where the term 'signified' will be used later, and this context does alter the value of 'thought', 'concept' in the *Course*.

It is useful to note here that Hjelmslev commenting on the above passage from Saussure had some critical remarks to make:

> Saussure, in order to clarify the sign function, undertook the device of trying to consider expression and content each alone, without consideration of the sign function ... But this pedagogical Gedanken-experiment, however excellently carried out, is actually meaningless, and Saussure himself must have found it so. In a science that avoids unnecessary postulates there is no basis for the assumption that content-substance (thought) or expression-substance (sound-chain) precede language in time or hierarchical order, or vice versa. (Hjelmslev 1961: 49–50)

Structuralism, then, denies the 'metaphysics of presence', at least some of the time if not all the time. To select only those parts of the writing to which could be ascribed a hankering for the real thing out there shows a bias; and establishing the reasons for this bias could conceivably provide a good project for deconstruction! It seems to me that neither Saussure nor Hjelmslev affirms the ultimate phenomenality of the signified; in particular, Hjelmslev was quite explicit on this issue. Compare then Peirce's notion of the sign, which Derrida approves of, with some of Hjelmslev's sayings. First Peirce via Derrida:

> According to the 'phaneoroscopy' or 'phenomenology' of Peirce, *manifestation* itself does not reveal a presence, it makes a sign. One may read in the *Principles of Phenomenology* that 'the idea of manifestation is the idea of a sign'. There is thus no phenomenality reducing the sign or the representer so that the thing signified may be allowed to glow finally in the luminosity of its presence. The so-called 'thing-itself' is always already a *representamen* shielded from the simplicity of intuitive evidence. The *representamen* functions only by giving rise to an *interpretant* that itself becomes a sign and so on to infinity. (Derrida 1974: 49)

On the next page of this text, the approved definition of the sign is quoted:

> *Anything which determines something else (its interpretant) to refer to an object to which itself refers (its object) in the same way, this interpretant becoming in turn a sign, and so on ad infinitum* ... If the series of successive interpretants comes to an end, the sign is thereby rendered imperfect, at least. (italics as in Derrida 1974: 50)

Derrida goes on to comment, approvingly: 'From the moment that there is meaning there are nothing but signs. We *think only in signs*' (ibid.) ('*Think in*'? Surely not. *We think signs*.) How does all this compare with Hjelmsev's position? I neither have the time nor the ability to summarize Hjelmslev's already 'lean' statements. So a few quotations and comments will have to suffice.

Let us begin then with the fundamental Hjelmslevian point that in talking about signs, one is not talking about isolates/isolables, e.g. signifier *or* signified. 'The postulation of objects as something different from the terms of relationships is a superfluous axiom and consequently a metaphysical hypothesis from which linguistic sciences will have to be freed' (Hjelmslev 1961: 23). This general observation is pertinent to Hjelmslev's discussion of sign. Starting first with the 'vague conception bequeathed by tradition' according to which a sign 'is characterized first and foremost by being a sign for something else', Hjelmslev concludes from this popular notion that 'a "sign" is defined by a function. A "sign" functions, designates, denotes; a "sign" in contradistinction to a non-sign, is the bearer of a meaning' (Hjelmslev 1961: 43). Through an examination of what these meaning bearing entities are like (pp. 44–47), he proceeds to contrast the first view of the sign as 'an expression that points to a content outside the sign itself' with a second view in which 'the sign is an entity generated by the *connexion between an expression and a content*', attributing this latter view to 'in particular … Saussure, and following him … Weisgerber' (Hjelmslev 1961: 47; italics mine RH). This 'connexion' between 'expression' and 'content' is not one of apparent union, productive of confusion as Derrida would have us believe (see quote above). Rather, expression and content are functives productive of the sign function; Peirce's 'manifestation' or Halliday's 'realization' (Halliday 1979, 1987) are then precisely that 'connexion' between the functives which is constitutive of the sign function. To quote Hjelmslev, again:

> … a function [e.g. 'sign'] is inconceivable without its terminals [e.g. 'expression/signifier' and 'content/signified'], and the terminals are only end points for the function and are thus inconceivable without it … Thus there is … solidarity between the sign function and its two functives, expression and content. There will never be a sign function without the simultaneous presence of both these functives … The sign function is in itself a solidarity. Expression and content are solidary – they necessarily presuppose each other. An expression is expression only by virtue of being an expression of a content, and a content is content only by virtue of being a content of an expression. Therefore … *there can be no content without an expression, or expressionless content; neither can there be an expression without a content, or content-less expression.* (Hjelmslev 1961: 48–9; italics mine)

It seems to me that statements of this kind not only deny that the signified is 'always already' somewhere; they also deny that it makes any sense to say that the signifier is always already there (contra Easthope).[1] If I understand Hjelmslev right, in the domain of semiosis *nothing* is 'always already' there; the 'sensible' identity of the signifier is just as illusory as the 'intelligible' ideality or phenomenal presence of *the* signified. There is, in fact, no *the*-ness about any signifier except that which it acquires as a functive of the sign function; neither is there any *the*-ness about any signified, except in the same conditions as for signifier. The selection of nominal – signifier, signified – is perhaps a natural, i.e. non-innocent, use (for in semiosis the 'natural' is the 'non-innocent') of 'everyday language' which according to Derrida (1981: 19) 'is the language of Western metaphysics'. I personally prefer Whorf's formulation according to which, this is yet another example of 'objectification' (Whorf 1941/1956: 139), a characteristic of Standard Average European Languages – of their lexicogrammar; and Whorf would suggest that Western metaphysics arose out of the 'fashions of speaking' made possible by the structure of SAE. Curiously, to me this is more in keeping with Derrida's approach than Derrida's own comment, which assigns priority to metaphysics over language – or, shall we say, 'writing'? To return to Hjelmslev, because of his characterization of signifier, signified and sign, we could never attribute to him locutions such as 'the sign or the representer' (Derrida 1974: 49) which is to Hjelmslev 'a vague conception [of the sign RH] bequeathed by tradition' (Hjelmslev 1961: 43); we could also be quite certain that he does not allow 'the thing signified' 'to glow in the luminosity of its presence' (Derrida 1974: 49). Like Peirce, he too sees the sign function extending into infinity. To appreciate this point, one must look into Hjelmslev's notions of content-substance, content-form, and his connotative semiotic. And once these concepts are examined carefully, Hjelmslev too can be seen to extend the sign-function into infinity. Relevant as this is, I shall move on to other questions.

Let me reiterate that Hjelmslev saw his own discussion of sign as an elaboration of Saussure's approach; and I believe, the nonhomogeneity of Saussure's text notwithstanding, Hjelmslev's reading of Saussure is less biased, less partial than Derrida's. Even so, I would not suggest that there are no differences between Saussure and Hjelmslev. It is certainly true that most linguists – particularly European ones – 'borrow most of their concepts' from Saussure (Derrida 1981: 23) but no one knows better than Derrida – that originator of 'grafting' – that the borrowing of concepts is quite unlike my borrowing of someone's copy of *Grammatology*. The discourses within which such 'borrowed' signs are embedded, within whose linearity (within whose syntagms) they have their existence, thus hinting at what they contrast with, what their paradigmatic provenance is – it is within the process of these discourses that the borrowed signs announce their non-identity with the borrowed signs; thus borrowing a concept becomes 'a question rather of producing a new concept' (Derrida 1981: 26) – which is all a way of saying, for this 'new' concept is not to the 'old' concept, as a new pair of shoes is to the old. None of this should be news to anyone who has read in the Margins, played with 'differance', and wondered about 'trace'. The reason for talking about it is simply that it links, to my mind, once again with the question of the identity of *structuralism*. If Hjelmslev's structuralism is not the-same-as Saussure's, and yet also the-same-as Saussure's, how could one talk about structuralism as such? Given that we cannot equate structuralism with Saussureanism, post-structuralism ought not to be synonymous with post-Saussureanism; and if what one is talking about is post-Saussureanism, then perhaps a more careful explication of Saussure's text – homogeneous or not – is required than I believe has been offered in Derrida's writing. If on the other hand the debate is about structuralism, then we cannot stop simply with Saussure and Hjelmslev, Levi-Strauss and Jakobsen: the discourses of structuralism are vast indeed and include much, much more than the few names singled out by fame. The differences amongst these structuralists are as important as are the non-differences. Even to imply that the identities across the many who count themselves as structuralist, truly constitute the essence of the signified connected with the signifier *structuralism* is a simplification not very different from that practised during the hey-day of the Chomskian revolution.

Hjelmslev favoured the use of the word *sign* as 'the unit consisting of content-form and expression-form and established by the solidarity … called the sign function' (Hjelmslev 1961: 58). This does mean that every sign is constituted by the solidary 'connexion' between signifier/expression and signified/content; the fact that this connexion is not governed either by any inherent quality of expression or of content – i.e. the arbitrariness that Saussure spoke of – is not a barrier to this postulate. On the contrary, their status as the functives of the sign function requires this to be the case. Peirce's 'manifestation' or Halliday's 'realization' cannot be the same as 'iconicity' or 'indexicality'. From the perspective of Saussure, Hjelmslev or Halliday, it makes no sense whatever to say as Easthope (op. cit.) does 'that human beings are always already situated within the signifier, and then only secondarily come into a position where they are able to line up the signifier and the signified'. Nor is there any reason why the view of sign presented by Saussure and elaborated by Hjelmslev should prevent 'an effective account of how language changes diachronically' (Easthope, op. cit.). On the contrary, the arbitrary connexion between the functives – signifier and signified – of the sign function is absolutely criterial for the very recognition and occurrence of any variation – diachronic or synchronic. If there was a problem with regard to variation in the Saussurean model – and there was – the root of it lies not in Saussure's conception of the nature of sign; it lies elsewhere, as would become evident if one drew upon the work of yet another scholar, Vilém Mathesius, who would be regarded as much a structuralist as Hjelmslev. There is though a curious fact about Mathesius: a founding member of Prague Linguistic Circle, Mathesius was 'already' a structuralist before the appearance of the *Course*. In particular his paper *On the potentiality of the phenomena of language*, on which I draw here to show how 'post-structuralism' already existed before concepts relevant to structuralism could be even 'borrowed' from Saussure, was delivered in 1911 and was published that same year in Czech.

Mathesius (1911) questioned some of the most important concepts which were to become fundamental to the Saussurean model of linguistics. Saussure, as is well-known, saw '*langue*' and '*parôle*' as interdependent: *langue* was both the 'instrument' and the 'product' of *parôle*. He maintained, however, that this 'interdependence does not prevent their being two *absolutely* distinct things' (Saussure 1966: 18; my italics). Saussure has been greatly applauded for maintaining this sharp distinction (Culler 1975, 1976; Chomsky 1965, etc.), though there were those who doubted the validity as well as the usefulness of this distinction (Firth 1957a; Jakobson 1985, Halliday 1970, 1973, 1978; Hasan 1984a, 1985c, etc.). It is possible that the accolade grew with the mistaken interpretation of these terms as the rather pale precursors of the Chomskian distinction between 'competence' and 'performance'. Be it as it may, the sharpness of the boundary between *langue* and *parôle* is maintained while their interdependence is also recognized.

> what is language [*langue*]? It is not to be confused with human speech [*langage*], of which it is only a definite part though certainly an essential one. It is both a social product of the faculty of speech [*langage*] and a collection of necessary conventions that have been adopted by a social body to permit individuals to exercise that faculty ... speech [*langage*] is many-sided ... it belongs both to the individual and to society ... Language [*langue*], on the contrary, is a self-contained whole and a principle of classification. (Saussure 1966: 9)

Langue is a 'social fact'; it is 'not complete in any speaker; it exists perfectly within a collectivity'; it 'is not a function of the speaker; it is a product that is *passively* assimilated by the individual' (p. 14). And this is to be contrasted with *parôle*, which is the 'executive side' of *langage*. 'Execution is always individual, and the individual is always its master'

(p. 13). 'Speaking [*parôle*] … is an individual act. It is wilful and intellectual' (p. 14). In the 'confused mass of heterogeneous and unrelated things' 'straddling several areas simultaneously – physical, physiological, and psychological' (p. 9) *langue* is an island of sanity, of order, of even certainty which would 'provide a fulcrum that satisfies the mind' (p. 9).

> Language [*langue* RH], unlike speaking [*parôle* RH], is something we can study separately … We can dispense with the other elements of speech [*langage*]; indeed, the science of language [*langue*] is possible only if the other elements are excluded … Whereas speech [*langage*] is heterogeneous, language [*langue*] … is homogeneous. It is a system of signs in which the only essential thing is the union of meanings and sound-images, and in which both parts of the sign are psychological. (Saussure 1966: 15)

Although Saussure could not completely deny recognition to non-homogeneity in *langue*, the view of *langue* as a 'homogeneous' 'system of signs' was to dominate Saussure's thinking about the study of language. The study of variation in the Saussurean model poses a problem *not* because the sign is a function of its functives – signifier and signified; rather, the problem arises from Saussure's conception of the nature of that 'connexion' – its degree of determinacy. Although there are rare occasions when Saussure will recognize the possibility of indeterminacy as when he says: 'Among all the individuals that are linked together by speech [*langage*], some sort of average will be set up: all will reproduce – *not exactly, of course, but approximately* – the same signs united with the same concepts (p. 13; italics mine). However, in general, Saussure glossed over the possibility of this indeterminacy:

> Language exists in the form of a sum of impressions deposited in the brain of each member of a community, *almost like a dictionary of which identical copies have been distributed to each individual* (see p. 13). (Saussure 1966: 19; italics mine)

It is probably on the basis of two such passages, the one quoted from above and the other on p. 13 where 'storehouse' is used as a metaphor for *langue*, that Chomsky (1965, 1974, etc.) has criticized Saussure for thinking of language as an inventory of signs; Saussure's talk of 'identical copies' understandably did not perturb Chomsky since he too, as some scholar has remarked wryly, believes that each infant is born with a copy of the

Aspects of Syntax tucked away in the folds of its brain. Ironically, though, the problematic nature of Saussure's 'identical copies' is brought out all the more forcefully because the systematicity of *langue* is not only crucial to Saussure's concept of the sign, but also affirmed by him far more consistently than its 'inventory' aspect. About this, some more comments later. Here let me point out the conclusion that Saussure drew from the postulate of homogeneity: 'Taken as a whole, speech [*langage*] cannot be studied, *for it is not homogeneous* … We must choose two routes that cannot be followed simultaneously; they must be followed separately' (Saussure 1966: 19; italics mine). These two separate routes, Saussure dubbed 'internal linguistics' – linguistics concerned with the 'homogeneous' system of *langue* – and 'external linguistics' – linguistics concerned with the 'heterogeneous' 'individual and momentary' 'combinations that depend on the will of the speaker', in short *parôle* where the individual is always the 'master'. Rather grudgingly, Saussure allowed that 'one might *if really necessary* apply the term linguistics to each of the two disciplines and speak of a linguistics of speaking [*parôle* RH]. *But that science must not be confused with linguistics proper, whose sole object is language [langue]* (Saussure 1966: 19–20; italics mine).

The homogeneity of *langue* – that main attribute which makes 'internal linguistics' *the sole* object of linguistics – had far-reaching consequences; it bears a non-accidental relationship to such concepts as synchrony/diachrony, static/ evolutionary and infects the *état de langue* with the same simplification by which the homogeneity of *langue* itself got 'established':

> An absolute state is defined by the absence of changes, and since *language changes somewhat in spite of everything*, studying a language-state means in practice *disregarding changes of little importance* … a concept of language-state can only be approximate. In static linguistics, as in all sciences, no course of reasoning is possible without the usual simplification of data. (Saussure 1966: 102; italics mine)

Mathesius's 1911 article strikes against the assumption of homogeneity for the static, synchronic *état de langue*. 'By the term potentiality we mean … instability at the given period'; it is not the same as 'dynamic changeability … occurring in the course of time' (Mathesius 1964: 1). This 'instability at the given period' is sometimes called 'static oscillation', sometimes 'synchronic oscillation'. According to Mathesius, this phenomenon of 'static oscillation' concerns not only dialects but also 'language as the proper object of linguistic research' (p. l). According to Mathesius

> Language ... includes, *theoretically*, all the phenomena of language that occur in the concrete utterances of all individual speakers, belonging at the same time to the same broad language community ... *In reality*, of course, linguistics can never do justice to this fact, not only on account of the astonishing richness of language phenomena in general, but mainly in view of the fact that such a community ... witnesses the rise of new, even if transient, language phenomena day by day. For this reason ... linguistic analysis has almost invariably concentrated on [just RH] the main outlines of languages ... [since RH] such outlines usually prove to be more accessible to primitive methods of analysis. (Mathesius 1964: l)

But this concentration on 'the main outlines' using the available 'primitive methods' results in creating an illusion of 'simplicity', which is often naively regarded 'as an actual quality of the examined phenomena' (op. cit. p. 2) – i.e. language – rather than as the artefact of the artificial limitations 'almost invariably' imposed on the examination of language. Mathesius protests 'against mixing up the methodological simplification of language with its actual make-up' (p. 2), and recommends that linguists should examine more carefully the inherent instability – 'the potentiality of language phenomena' (p. 2) – to find out how this is 'actually manifested'. They should look into static/synchronic variation in the 'concrete' utterances of 'individual speakers within a community' as well as within the utterances of the same individual. The heterogeneity of *parôle* that Saussure was, perhaps just then in his lectures, setting aside as non-examinable constituted Mathesius' primary data. Here was 'post-structuralism' receiving ardent support from those who considered themselves 'structuralist' even before the arch-priest of structuralism, Ferdinand de Saussure, was recognized as 'the father' (Culler 1976) of modern structuralism. While Saussure was promising his audience that 'I shall deal only with linguistics of language [*langue*], and if I subsequently use materials belonging to speaking [*parôle*] to illustrate a point, I shall try never to erase the boundaries that separate the two domains' (Saussure 1966: 20), here was Mathesius claiming that an unnecessary simplification of language results by the simple affirmation *or* denial of absolute regularity: language is neither entirely homogeneous nor entirely heterogeneous; a recognition of both its systemic regularities *and* its variation is at once essential. Mathesius briefly reviews studies that indicate the presence of variation at the various levels of language: the phonic, the phonological, the lexicogrammatical and the semantic. The opinion although attributed to Kruszewski, I believe, would be shared by Mathesius that 'the basic feature of language' is 'the complexity and indefiniteness of its units' (Mathesius 1964: 27). It is in this inherent indeterminacy of language that the roots of its diachronic variation lie. 'The sentence, the word, the morphemic elements are indefinite as to their content. The sound, again, is indefinite physiologically …' (op. cit. p. 27). The acceptance of this inherent indeterminacy of the linguistic unit, however, does not seem to Mathesius any reason for suggesting, unlike Saussure, that in *parôle*, in his concrete utterances, the speaker is always the master. Mathesius, like Firth and Halliday later, would reject both the exaggerated regularity of a fictitiously homogeneous *langue* and the myth of complete 'free-will' for the individual speaker: human language is neither a prison-house nor utter freedom, with absolute autonomy and independence. Hence the term 'potentiality'; the units of language permit a potential, within which a great deal of variation – 'oscillation' – is possible. Writing approximately half a century before Labov (1968) and Weinreich, Labov and Herzog (1968), Mathesius suggested that the study of the potentiality of the phenomena of language in synchrony would provide the best basis for the study of diachronic variation (see Mathesius 1964, especially last para.). This pre-Saussurean(?) post-structuralist, thus, questioned the very edifice of 'internal linguistics', based on a fictitious homogeneity which prevented 'an effective account of how language changes diachronically' (Easthope, op. cit.).

What is most ironic here is the fact that Saussure's concept of sign – which is today blamed for everything – was fully compatible with Mathesius' notion of potentiality. Selecting without bias from Saussure's non-homogeneous text, I will attempt to show that Saussure denied the possibility of knowing a signifier/*a* signified in isolation. The signified is not a foot clad in an ill-fitting signifier-shoe, which slips (Eagleton 1983) to trip up the possibility of meaning. In the context of the Saussurean framework, it is mere obfuscation to talk of human beings as 'always already situated in the signifier' and 'only secondarily' coming to 'line up the signifier and the signified'. To me at least, such a formulation is tantamount to the claim that 'nothing' intervenes between the sensation of the hearing of some sound and the recognition of it as some signifier. Saussure's theory of sign neither affirms the presence of *a* signified nor of *a* signifier in isolation. If from the 'fictitious' point of view of an already given signifier, it is difficult to say how meanings get meant, the negation of the given-ness, in isolation, of either signifier or signified – and thus of the identity of the sign – does not make the question easier to answer. Nor do I believe that answers will be found simply by tracing the etymology of the sign *sign*. Carrying the sign *sign* back to Plato and beyond – as Derrida does – is an admirable proof of immersion in philosophical writing. Antiquity, however, is not a decisive court of appeal in disputes about the identity of a linguistic sign. There is no reason to assume identity of the sign *sign* across Plato and Saussure; and if there is any suggestion that Saussure's *sign* should have been the same as Plato's, what would such a suggestion be based on? Plato is not an obscure philosopher; if he had already solved the problem of the sign to Saussure's satisfaction, then Saussure would hardly be concerned with it, just as if Saussure had solved the problem of the sign to Derrida's satisfaction, Derrida would not have needed to write *Grammatologie*. Nor does the equation of Saussure's *signified* with *concept* in the sense of mental image appear justified to me. The image of image may conceivably be relevant where *signification* is the issue; however, Saussure's *signified* is not just *signification*; it concerns *value* as well: '… it is quite clear that initially the concept is nothing, that is only a value determined by its relations with other similar values, and that without them the signification would not exist …' (Saussure 1966: 117).

> to consider a term simply as the union of a certain sound with a certain concept is grossly misleading. To define it in this way would isolate the term from its system; it would mean assuming that one can start from the terms and construct the system by adding them together when, on the contrary, it is from the interdependent whole that one must start and through analysis obtain its elements. (Saussure 1966: 115)

Derrida's claim that Plato 'said basically the same thing' about sign though he had 'a more subtle, more critical and less complacent theory of image' (1974: 33) I note with interest, for it seems to me that whatever else Saussure's sign theory may be it certainly was not about 'image'. Saussure's *concept/idea* redefined as 'value determined by its relation to other similar values' certainly appears distant from Plato's 'ideal type'. The concept *concept* or *idea* undergoes a sea-change in Saussure's text, and it is in the light of this that I read the following:

> The linguistic entity exists only through the associating of the signifier with the signified … We constantly risk grasping only a part

> of the entity and thinking that we are embracing it in its totality
> … A succession of sounds is linguistic only if it supports an idea.
> Considered independently, it is material for a physiological study,
> and nothing more than that. The same is true of the signified as soon
> as it is separated from its signifier … Concepts … become linguistic
> entities only when associated with sound images; in language, a con-
> cept is a quality of its phonic substance just as a particular slice of
> sound is a quality of the concept. (Saussure 1966: 102–103)

Assertions of this kind throw into question the very basis of a concept such as *homonymy* e.g. in *bear* (a kind of animal) and *bear* (tolerate) as much as they raise questions about the *synonymy* of *bear* and *tolerate*. In the case of homonymy, are we hearing the same signifier? In the case of synonymy, are we faced with the same signified? Neither signifier nor signified indicates the identity of the sign: 'The idea or phonic substance that a sign contains is of less importance than the other signs that surround it' (Saussure 1966: 120). The identity of signifiers, signifieds, and so of signs, is their relationship to signifiers, signifieds and signs.

The relations that Saussure postulated are well known – and again interdependent: the associative, paradigmatic, *in absentia* ones, and the linear, syntagmatic, *in praesentia* ones. Like all Saussure's pairs, these two are interdependent: a paradigm is a paradigm by virtue of its potential disposition in a syntagm, while a syntagm is a syntagm by virtue of combining members of more than one paradigm. What is notable though is the fact that the contradictions, the hesitations and the simplifications which appeared in Saussure's discussion of *langue* and *parôle* are reflected almost exactly in his discussion of the syntagmatic relation. 'In discourse, … words acquire relations based on the linear nature of language because they are chained together' (Saussure 1966: 123). What is this *'because'*? Are linearity and chaining two different phenomena? If so, how? '… the notion of syntagm applies not only to words but to groups of words, to complex units of all lengths and types (compounds, derivatives, phrases, whole sentences)' (p. 124). But here another difficulty rears its head: we have already been told that one characterizing feature of *parôle* is 'the combinations by which the speaker uses the language code for expressing his own thought' (p. 14).

> The sentence is the ideal type of syntagm. But it belongs to speaking
> [*parôle*], not language [*langue*] … Does it not follow that syntagm
> belongs to speaking? I do not think so. Speaking is characterized by

freedom of combinations; one must therefore ask whether or not all syntagms are equally free.' (p. 124)

This line of enquiry leads Saussure to the conclusion that those syntagms are 'in' *langue* where improvisation, the exercise of free will by the speaker is impossible, as in 'fixed idiomatic expressions'; others where improvisation, exercise of free will is possible are 'in' *parôle*. '… But we must realize that in the syntagm there is no clear-cut boundary between the language [*langue*] fact, which is a sign of collective usage, and the fact that belongs to speaking [*parôle*] and depends on individual freedom' (p. 125). This last passage calls to mind those others in which *langue* is invariant 'not exactly, of course, but approximately' (p. 13) and where an *état de langue* too is declared invariant 'disregarding changes of little importance' (p. 102). Derrida has said a good deal about how the metaphysics of presence fouled up Saussurean thinking; and the validity of some of these comments I have questioned. My reading of Saussure's theory of sign does not agree with Derrida's. Saussure's concept/signified has no existence outside the system of relations; the notion of 'differance' is not ruled out by it – rather, it is implied by the centrality of the associative and syntagmatic relations to the identity of the sign. To me it seems that Saussure's problem arises from two dogmas that are hardly ever absent from academic thought in the West: the purity of categories, and the affirmation of the individual's free will since Adam. Given that the connection between signifier and signified is arbitrary, Saussure must accept the role of communal practice i.e. conventionality. Conventionality and some measure of regularity of behaviour are two sides of the same coin. A language can be used by various members of the community only if there is some element of stability/invariance in it. Thus something *langue-like* – a social, collective fact – is undeniable. However the principle of the purity of categories does not permit acceptance of both invariance and variance: the variant, as Plato argued, cannot be studied. Further, Saussure appears to subscribe to the notion of the individual's 'free will' which is accommodated by his conception of *parôle*. Ideologically, the regularity of *parôle* cannot be maintained; theoretically, the existence of some regularity cannot *but* be invoked; and, again, ideologically order and chaos – homogeneity and heterogeneity – cannot be the characterizing attributes of the very same phenomena.

All other problems in Saussure's framework are minor compared to this one. The purity of the categories of *langue* and *parôle* played havoc with Saussure's distinctions between associative and syntagmatic, between value and signification (Hasan 1985c), between signifier and signified, thus threatening the entire edifice of his theory, while rendering his notion of *langue* so simplistic that no one who ever wished to enquire into what people *do* do with their language could ever adopt the model in its original form. But those who wished to find out what people *do* with their language, and how, were mostly those who got described as 'data-oriented'. And this is yet another structuralism. In pointing out directions from structuralism, I propose to conclude my contribution with an account of this 'data-oriented', 'behaviourist', 'taxonomist' structuralism. There is nothing like giving an academic a name and the rest follows. For lack of space, I shall refer only briefly to just two linguists: Firth and Halliday.

Firth rejected Saussure's *langue/parôle* dichotomy as well as his 'internal linguistics':

> we study language as part of the social process, and ... the systematics of phonetics and phonology, of grammatical categories or of semantics are ordered schematic constructs, ... a sort of scaffolding for the handling of events. The study of the social process and of single human beings is simultaneous and of equal validity. (Firth 1957a: 181)

The elements of the schematic construct 'have no ontological status ... being or existence. They are neither immanent nor transcendent, but just language turned back upon itself' (p. 181). The study of language as part of the social process meant looking at what Mathesius called 'concrete utterance'; thus, Firth's reputation in the Chomskian revolution as data-oriented. Firth also objected to any account of meaning as a relation in the mind between 'facts:, 'things' and words: 'As we know so little about mind and as our study is essentially social I shall cease to respect the duality of mind and body, thought and word, and be satisfied with the whole man, thinking and acting as a whole, in association with his fellows' (Firth 1957a: 19). For Firth meaning is not 'relations in a hidden mental process'; it is seen chiefly as

> situational relations in a context of situation and in that kind of language which disturbs the air and other people's ears, as modes of behaviour in relation to the other elements in the context of situation ... Meaning ... is to be regarded as a complex of contextual relations, and phonetics, grammar, lexicography and semantics each handles its own components of the complex in its appropriate context. (p. 19)

To remarks such as these can be attributed his fame as 'anti-mentalist', 'behaviourist', – a corrupting influence indeed in the age of the creativity of the innate rule-governed grammar. For Firth, the object of linguistics was to make statements of meaning. However, 'the statement of meaning cannot be achieved by one analysis, at one level, in one fell swoop' (p. 183), Human languages have *minor and major modes of meaning*: according to Firth phonetics and phonology are tools for making statements of meaning, just as much as the schematic construct called context of situation is a tool for the same purpose. The theory of context of situation, which Firth 'borrowed' from Malinowski (1923, 1935), was designed to describe 'language as part of the social process'. On the one hand Firth maintained that 'every time you speak, you create anew' (p. 142), on the other, he definitely did not allow Saussure's individual the same freedom, the same absolute mastery that the speaker enjoyed in the Saussurean framework, 'Once someone speaks to you, you are in a relatively determined context and you are not free to just say what you please' (p. 28). I should add that the notion of context with which Austin (1962), Searle (1969) or Derrida (1977) operate is somewhat different from that of Firth who thought of the term 'context of situation' as a technical term 'a suitable schematic construct to apply to language events … a group of related categories at a different level from grammatical categories but rather of the same abstract nature' (p. 182). Just as with the notion of language Firth would accept both systemic regularity and the existence of variation, so also Firth's context of situation is concerned both with what is typical of various social processes as well as what is relevant to some specific instance of a given type of social process. It was the notion of language as system, the denial of any need to grant physical presence to the referent, the idea that human language could be described as relations of relations that unites Saussure, Hjelmslev and Firth. The idea of the homogeneity of *langue* so dear to Saussure was quite foreign to Firth who maintained that 'unity is the last concept that should be applied to language. Unity of language is the most fugitive of all unities whether it be historical, geographical, national or personal' (Firth 1957a: 29). Denying 'unity', Firth, unlike Saussure, could also see language as systematic,

Halliday's framework, known now as the Systemic-Functional model, embraces the idea of system. For Halliday language is a 'resource for meaning' – it is a potential, not a constraining reproductive mechanism. The systemic quality of language does not imply reproducing the same linguistic units with the same sounds and the same meanings. The system is a resource for process. Anti-languages (Halliday 1976a) show quite clearly that there are varieties in which speakers will not 'reproduce' even 'approximately', the same signifier united with the same signified. Despite this, Anti-languages stand in a systematic relation to the systems of non-antilanguages. Departure from system is as much a 'regard' to system as conformity with system; the unusual is unusual only by reference to the usual. When Halliday refuses to participate in the current dramatic lamentations about failures of communication, it may be useful to see this in its perspective. For Halliday, language has always been associated with the idea of the possibility of variation. But this variation is nonrandom in important respects: variations across social class, across generations, across professions – in short, across ideologies. Like Whorf, Wittgenstein (1958) and Bernstein (1981), Halliday believes that consciousness – and so ideology – is an artefact of processes of meaning. Ways of speaking are ways of meaning; and ways of meaning are ways of being, behaving and saying (Hasan 1984b; 1985c; 1986a). Failures of communication across ideologies do not have to be documented as a *notable* happening: 'contact' (cf. Pratt 1987) is not necessarily 'convergence' – communication across ideologies, no doubt, takes place in the sense that some meanings do get exchanged but precisely because of the systemic variation – ideological-linguistic – it is very much open to question how the 'saying' and the 'hearing' calibrate. To accept the possibility of systematic variations of this kind is to be aware of the possibility of 'failures of communication' – a term used all too glibly, whose explication might throw the entire notion of the slipping signifier, 'the always already there' signifier into a vortex, The shock of the realization of the possibility of the failure of communication is thus not a spectre that arises unexpected in such frameworks as it does where the predominant belief had been in *'une langue, une'* or in 'idealized' 'competence'. Variation is non-identity of meaning and wording; language is inherently variable. From this perspective, it is the successes in communication that need to be marvelled at, rather than failures (Halliday 1987: 136); failures ought to occur more often!

The recognition of variation in Halliday's framework proceeds hand in hand with the affirmation of invariance. Using Malinowski (1923, 1935) and Firth, as his point of departure, Halliday has argued that the structure of language and its functionality are in a dialectic relation. Experience from the point of view of the sensing subject may be 'raw sensation', but experience of the world both outside us and inside us, if it is to be shared must be constructed through semiosis. As a mode of semiosis, human language 'performs' an *ideational* function: it permits the construction of sharable experience. In the structure of human language, we would find a specific part of the lexicogrammar which *realizes/constructs* the ideational function. Sharing implies some social relation: the *social relations* too are *created/altered/maintained* through language. This is the *interpersonal* function of language realized as a specific aspect of the organization of the lexicogrammar. All sharing is situated – it is situated in the contexts of that community and is recognizable as some kind of social process within the terms of reference set by the community's culture. Discourse, talk, writing – managing its continuities and discontinuities is the *textual* function of language. This function of language too is *realized/constructed* by a particular aspect of the lexicogrammar of a language. The structure of language and the function of language are two sides of the same coin. These metafunctions of language are non-accidentally related to the 'schematic construct' called context of situation. If, arriving in the middle of an ongoing dialogue, we are, more often than not, able to say what is going on, how the interactants see each other, what social activity is at issue, this is not because there exists a mysterious telepathic bond between members of a community: it is because language constructs our world for us. The context is as much in language as it is outside language.

What such a theory says is that *speaking is wilful*: but the will that exercises control is not some divine freedom, not some self-enclosed intentionality, not the breath of God; it is the breath of others who matter in the life of the speaker. *Speaking is purposeful*: but the purpose is not autistic – it is fashioned by the community of purposes of those who surround us, whom we exploit or defend, whom we fight or protect. *Speaking is always a potential* – open and unlimited in its potentiality: but the actuality of speaking – and hearing – is always limited by who we are, how others see us, what rights we enjoy, what obligations we carry. If meanings get meant, if the potentiality of the sign is translated into 'an' actuality, this is because we are always already situated within a social context – a social context that we ourselves have brought about by our own sayings, our own interpretations. 'Language is the best show man puts on' (Whorf): it is freedom certainly, but let that freedom not blind us to the fact that it is also the most powerful weapon for social reproduction. And it is this potentiality of language that we can never ignore, for whilst we ignore it, it inexorably surrounds us. With a linguistics of this kind we do not need 'contact linguistics' (cf. Pratt 1987); we only need to understand the meaning of 'contact' as a sign.

I have tried to show in this paper the variation, the potentiality, the synchronic oscillation, of the sign *structuralism*. I have not been able to always explicitly relate today's post-structuralist dictums, often dramatically displayed, with the approaches of others, but, hopefully, the reader can make such connections. If Schmidt (1985: 166) is right that *post-structuralism* is a term embarrassingly empty of content, it may be because there is too much content in the *structuralism* that it claims to supersede.

Note

1   Editor's note: Antony Easthope raised a number of issues after M. A. K. Halliday's paper (1987), particularly as these concerned what he termed 'the alternative tradition' in linguistics represented by the work of Bakhtin (Voloshinov) and Michael Pecheux. He suggested that communication models of language (citing those presented by Leech) presuppose 'that the signifier and signified are always already united in the sign'. He argued that the communication model should be challenged by an alternative argument: that human beings as speaking subjects are always already situated within the signifier and then only secondarily come into a position where they are able to 'line up' signifier and signified. Easthope further proposed that language change would be better explained by the latter model ('the signifier acquires new signifieds: within every discourse it is acquiring a new signified') than by the communication model with its insistence on the already completed sign. This position is more fully developed by Antony Easthope in *Poetry as Discourse*, London, 1983.

3 Linguistic sign and the science of linguistics:[1] the foundations of applicability [2014]

> … we boldly submit that discussion is in vain unless you know what you are discussing …
>
> [Ferdinand de Saussure 2006: 166]

3.1 Introduction

Systemic functional linguistics, especially the variety associated with the name of Halliday,[2] has been perhaps unique in explicitly and defiantly celebrating the inherent relations of theory and practice from its earliest stages (e.g., Halliday 1960). The actual range of purposes for which SFL has been used is indeed remarkable (Appendix A; Hasan, Matthiessen, and Webster 2005, 2007; Halliday 1985: xxix–xxx, 2008: 190ff). But my aim here is not to join in praise or denigration; I wish instead to raise a basic question: *what enables a linguistic theory to become appliable*? Why do some theories such as SFL or Prague School linguistics become widely appliable?[3] Why do other models, some with claims of elevated intellectual pedigree, remain above or below human use?

It occurs to me after some reflection that the property of appliability in a linguistic theory is simply a by-product: the features that facilitate applications are not found there *because* someone remembered to insert them specially as additional elements. Rather, the power of appliability in a linguistic theory has its origins in ideas about language, which is what gives the theory its identity.

3.1.1   The essence of language

The acknowledged complexity of language has led to much debate about the nature of linguistics. The founder of modern linguistics, Ferdinand de Saussure, clearly identified what *he* thought to be central to linguistics: it is clear from both the earlier *Course* (1966) and the more recent *Writings in General Linguistics* (2006; henceforth *Writings*), that the first step in finding the 'truth in linguistics' is to successfully identify the nature of the linguistic sign: thereafter its exploration will lead the theory to everything that is important to understanding language. The impact of Saussure's theory of the linguistic sign has been such that modern linguists and their theories have since been positioned by reference to him: they are known as pre-Saussurean, Saussurean, anti-Saussurean, post-Saussurean, or non-Saussurean (c.f. Firth 1957a: 179). SFL is post-Saussurean: its point of departure is Saussurean; it accepts his concept of sign and agrees with much he has to say about the linguistic sign system, but goes beyond Saussure in developing his position and elaborating many of his theoretical concepts (section 3.4.3, below). This leads me to hypothesize that *the primary foundation for the appliability of a linguistic theory resides in a faithful description of the nature of sign and what follows from that description*: Halliday's SFL is such a theory.

3.1.2   Theorizing the concept of language as langue

I will begin this chapter by assuming with Saussure that the prime object of study for linguistics is the 'interplay of signs, called LANGUE (Saussure 2006: 21), that 'language is a system of signs that express ideas' and as a theory of signs, 'linguistics is only a branch of the science of semiology'[4] (Saussure 1966: 16). This means establishing Saussure's views about the nature of sign and its attributes (section 3.2); in section 3.3, the linguistic sign will be compared with other, non-linguistic sign types, in order to examine the validity of Saussure's claim. This will form the foundation for drawing attention, in section 3.4, to relevant implications of adopting the Saussurean positions. I will indicate, this time with an eye to the theory as developed in SFL, some characteristics of language, which although deemed external to langue by Saussure, *have to be* considered essential to a theoretically valid description of the linguistic sign system. I will argue that, judged by standards of inferential thinking set by Saussure himself, the working of langue as the nub of the semiotic system can neither be validated nor represented explicitly without close attention to these so-called 'langue-external' issues chief amongst which is PAROLE. If the aim of linguistics is to *account for all those phenomena concerning langue which Saussure takes to be central for discovering the truth of language*, then the object of enquiry for linguistics has to be SFL's elaborated conception of language: from this wider perspective, Saussure's 'langue' would be simply one aspect of the object of enquiry for an explanatory linguistics (Hasan 2013). Granted, langue is central to viable linguistics: it captures the basic semiotic properties which 'enable' the language system to work the way it does in the community; but, without the extensions and elaborations undertaken by SFL, the concept of langue itself will remain *jejune*. Attention to the systemic nature of language use, i.e., PAROLE, is essential if linguistics is to explain the working of langue in the community's social life.

3.2   Sign: The basic unit of language

In the *Course* (1966), Saussure's discourse on linguistics commences with the linguistic sign and concludes with the possibility of the science of semiology. The clarification of the complex relations of SIGNIFIED and SIGNIFIER deeply occupied Saussure's attention in the earlier chapters of the book. Beginning with a rather simplified account where he said that 'the linguistic sign unites not a thing and a name, but a concept and a sound image' (1966: 66), Saussure moved to the complexities of these terms. The sign, Janus-like, presents two faces in one unit: the signifier refers to the sign's material expressive aspect and the signified to its abstract semantic VALUE on which SIGNIFICATION, the act of referring to the extra-linguistic world, depends. Saussure was at pains to show that, in isolation from each other, neither face of the linguistic sign could be recognized as a 'signing' entity. In and of themselves, neither had any semiotic status, and in this sense their materiality as well as their abstractness are less noteworthy than their sign-constituting function (2006). Today with the added evidence of his *Writings* (2006: 15ff) it is obvious that Saussure was caught between the need both to affirm the sign as one unit and to confirm that the sign's material manifestation and its 'psychological' import are phenomena of distinct orders: in unity alone can they present both the meaning-evoking and the evoked meaning aspects of the sign.

The sign's make-up is the primary theoretical axiom for Saussure's linguistics of langue: thinking inferentially from this axiom, he came to a number of rich concepts that pertain to the linguistics of langue, such as the sign's SYSTEMICITY, its VALUE and IDENTITY; ASSOCIATIVE and SYNTAGMATIC relations, STRUCTURE as a 'template' as opposed to the material continuity of sign, which forms the outer face of parole. Saussure (1966: 67) assigned 'two primordial characteristics' to the linguistic sign: (i) ARBITRARINESS; and (ii) LINEARITY.

3.2.1 Characteristics of the linguistic sign: (i) arbitrariness

The term 'arbitrary' applies to only one relation in Saussurean linguistics, namely, that which unites the signifier and the signified: everything in his linguistics flows *logically* from the sign's nature. He carefully spelt out the meaning of this term: 'The word 'arbitrary' … should not imply that the choice of the signifier is left entirely to the speaker; … I mean that it [i.e., the choice of the signifier] is unmotivated, i.e., *arbitrary in that it actually has no natural connection with the signified'*. (1966: 68–69; *emphasis added*). Saussure points out that even though speakers of English will normally take a given phonic form such as /sistə/ as evoking the meaning 'sister', no reason exists for seeing this association except the *communal conventions of a language* whereby this 'acoustic image' becomes associated with that particular value/meaning (1966: 73; *original emphasis*):

> Even if people were more conscious of language than they are, they would still not know how to discuss it. The reason is simply that any subject in order to be discussed must have a reasonable basis. It is possible for instance to discuss whether the monogamous form of marriage is more reasonable than the polygamous form and to advance arguments to support either side. …; but language is a system of arbitrary signs and lacks the necessary basis, the solid ground for discussion …

As Halliday (1999; 2005) says the sign's substance belongs to the material realm while its meaning, created by 'the interplay of signs called langue' (Saussure 2006: 21), belongs to the semiotic realm. So the secret of the acceptance of a particular signifier evoking a particular meaning has its foundation not in a nature relation but in social convention, i.e., in the regular practice of using *that* 'sound image' with *that* 'sign value'.

3.2.2   Characteristics of the linguistic sign: (ii) linearity

The second attribute, linearity, inheres in the material nature of the sign's 'form', i.e., the signifier: whether encountered as speech or as writing, language use can only run along the single dimension of space-time. By default, the elements 'form a chain' (1966: 70). To those not familiar with the language in question, the chain of speech does not offer any obvious principles for identifying the boundaries of individual signs as the phones/ graphs occur one after the other in parole: the identity of a particular signifier or signified is not 'within' a particular sign. Speakers of a language easily 'locate' individual signs and make sense of them due to the robust communal conventions whereby they have grown up hearing and later speaking the language of their speech community. However, it is not in social conventions that the identity and the value of signs have their foundations: as Saussure points out 'a' particular sign works because 'all' signs in a language work together (e.g., 2006: 153):

> The ultimate law of language is … that nothing can ever be said to exist in *one* term (since quite simply linguistic symbols have no link with what they are meant to refer to), *a* cannot refer to anything without the help of *b*, and the same goes about this term without the help of *a*; either both are validated by their reciprocal *differences*, or neither is valid, …

3.2.3   Characteristics of the linguistic sign: (iii) systemicity

Both arbitrariness and linearity arise from the internal make-up of the linguistic sign, while the systemic nature of the sign may be seen as rooted in the sign's arbitrariness. A linguistic sign in itself can have neither an identity nor a value: the signified has no 'logical' link with what it actually refers to, and the signifier has no natural reason for being associated with a particular signified; 'man' is as good a sign for referring to a 'human adult male' as the Urdu sign /admI/ or the French 'homme'.

This negative character of the linguistic sign is counteracted in two ways: first, members of a speech community use linguistic signs in their parole, thus reinforcing the association of the signified and signifier of a particular sign. But more importantly, underlying this 'typically reinforced association' is 'the 'interplay of signs', i.e., the mutual relationship of signs, which fixes their value and identity. The relationships are of two kinds: (a) SYNTAGMATIC and (b) ASSOCIATIVE; Saussure characterized them as '*in praesentia*' and '*in absentia*', respectively. These relations are analogous to the axes of CHAIN and CHOICE in SFL (Halliday 1963).

The axis of chain i.e., syntagm is a property of language use, i.e. parole. Their spatio-temporal patterns of contiguity become indicative of 'syntagmatic relations', contributing to the 'determination' of mutual values, as evident from examples 1–3:

1. On Saturday the bank closes at 1 o'clock.
2. The bank is being shored up to contain the huge overflow of water.
3. Every page of that article contained at least one figure or a table.

As exemplified by the above, on the syntagmatic axis all the interacting signs are present on 'the scene', i.e., they are '*in praesentia*'. Firth's COLLOCATION would most probably have been regarded as an '*in praesentia*' relationship, though Saussure's own examples fit better his concept of COLLIGATION.

The associative relation differs in this respect; here interaction between signs occurs through remembered relations though the signs themselves are absent from 'the scene', i.e., they are 'in absentia'. The associative axis is concerned with choice from a range of inter-related signs such that only one sign will be present from among all those that 'qualify' as members of the same 'associative range' (i.e. PARADIGM); the bond is there by virtue of the speaking person's familiarity with the paradigm: it depends on a mental recognition of the paradigm. Thus when the syntagm justifies seeing the sign /beə/ (written as 'bear') as in associative relation with 'tolerate' or 'reject', it will have a different value from that /beə/ ('bear') which is in associative relation with 'bearing, bore, born, birth'; each of these /beə/ differs in value from /beə/ ('bare') that is in the same paradigm as 'bares', 'bared', 'naked', 'clothed', 'dress'; and all the foregoing differ from /beə/ as in 'polar bear', 'grisly bear'; and so on. Because each sign in a syntagm carries both its syntagmatic '*in praesentia*' relations and also the penumbra of its associative '*in absentia*' relations, the acculturated brain familiar with the speech conventions of the community readily identifies a given sign as a particular sign, different from all the others, and yet similar in behaviour to some of them. These two relations represent the major modes of the sign's interplay.

It is not the shape/form of the 'acoustic image' that 'produces' the sign's meaning: the meaning (the signified) is 'in' the morphology, i.e., created by the relations of all the signifieds in a given language. This account of producing linguistic meaning indicates the independent status of linguistic meaning, which is not constrained by the 'real' world of objects or the 'mental' world of thoughts and ideas: according to Saussure (1966: 112): 'There are no pre-existing ideas, and nothing is distinct before the appearance of language.'

3.3   The semiological nature of signs: Some implications

In this section, using insights from Firth, Halliday and, to a lesser extent from Hjelmslev, I will attempt to elaborate some details pertaining to the concept of semiology/semiotic as introduced in section 3.2.

3.3.1   The linguistic sign in the context of other sign types

Saussure set great store by assigning the status of sign to the basic unit of language. The *raison d'être* of a sign is that it brings meaning into being. Thus every category of sign may be said to 'have' a signified/meaning which is 'brought to notice' by something that is experienced bodily, i.e., every sign 'has' a part analogous to a signifier. The signifier is *always* fashioned 'materially'; and as such, in terms of Russell, it is SENS-IBLE. By contrast, the signified is purely 'INTELLIG-IBLE': its interpretation depends on the acculturated brain, i.e., 'the mind'. This is one *crucial* respect in which all signs are alike, although the terms as applied to the linguistic sign are remarkably different from the others as the brief comparison of the sign types would show.

Figure 3.1: The world of signs: A tentative account

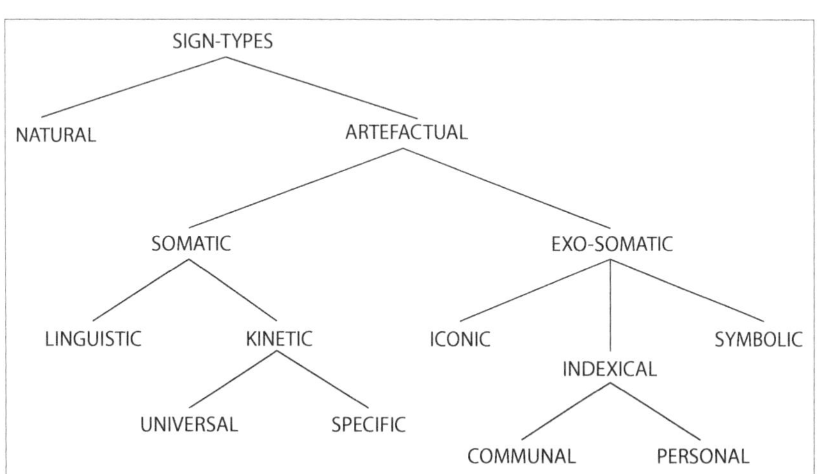

Table 3.1: Sign types and their properties

s-type	s-maker	s-medium	user-volition	sd/sr-relation	systemic	example
natural	nature	natural force	none	physical logic	no	dark clouds → rain
artefactual	human	material	–	–	–	[general category; various]
somatic	”	user body	–	–	–	[” ” ”]
kinetic	”	”	uncertain	uncertain	not inherent	[” ” ”]
universal	”	”	”	”	”	Smile happy
specific	”	”	”	”	”	[culturally variable gesture]
linguistic	”	”	yes	arbitrary	inherent	'go away!' → order to leave
exo-somatic	”	matter	”	–	no	[general category; various]
indexical	”	”	”	arbitrary	”	[see next two entries]
communal	”	”	”	”	”	school bell → play time
personal	”	”	”	”	”	front door bell → visitor
iconic	”	”	”	similarity	”	✂ 'cut here'
symbolic	”	”	”	similarity+	”	scales → justice

The nature of sign types has been much discussed for many decades; nonetheless, the accounts are neither exhaustive nor is there terminological consistency across different approaches. The sketch of the world of signs shown in Figure 3.1 has benefited from the work of many other scholars including Aarsleff (1982); Saussure (1966, 2006); Wittgenstein (1953); Peirce (1955); Firth (1957a); Halliday (1992, 1993, 1999); the final responsibility is mine. The various signing phenomena usually discussed as MULTIMODALITY in SFL have been ignored for lack of space.

For the same reason the sign types and their properties are not discussed but presented briefly in a table (Figure 3.1). Some of the properties of the non-linguistic signs will be mentioned to highlight how they contrast with the linguistic ones.

3.3.2   The linguistic sign viewed as a sign amongst signs

It will be useful to position Saussure's conception of the linguistic sign *vis-à-vis* the non-linguistic ones by revisiting its characteristics in terms of the features by which other sign types have been identified in Figure 3.1. In doing so, I will also highlight some implications of Saussure's claims.

Like most of the other signs, the linguistic sign too is ARTEFACTUAL, which implies that users are able to control the production and use of the sign; they can consciously decide whether to speak, what to say, and how to say it. Yet one must question Saussure's claim that, in parole, the speaker is 'the master': speaking *is* using the semiotic system of language, but the reason for using language is not inside the semiotic system: the process is socially 'regulated', and regulation extends beyond the instance to the system through its role in the genesis of linguistic variation (section 3.4.2 below). An important implication is that the degree of conscious management of parole varies according to what the social context requires (Hasan 1989). Later I will argue that sign morphology *à la* Saussure is impossible without consulting the systemic patterns of parole, which is also central for providing an explanatory account of the SEMOGENIC processes of language (Halliday and Matthiessen 1999).

3.3.2.1   The sign's value, reality and reference

Like the kinetic sign types, the linguistic sign is SOMATIC, so its production and use require nothing else than the user's body and an acculturated brain; but unlike the universal kinetic sign, the 'signifier-signified' pairing of *particular linguistic signs is never universal, although the sign's basic design and attributes including its systemicity are universal*. Due to the 'wholly arbitrary' relation of the signifier and signified, the felicitous use of this sign type depends on acculturation. The internal logic of language makes even onomatopoeia sound 'unfamiliar': in Urdu the rooster goes /kʊkRũkũ/; in English /kɔkədudldu/, in French /kokoriko/, and so on. Saussure doubted that intuition or common sense would help one understand the nature of language as a sign system; in fact intuition could be quite misleading by encouraging the belief that a sign's meaning 'is' actually a particular concrete object in the world. For example, it might appear justified to an English speaker to imagine that the referent of the word 'sun' 'is' actually that shining orb in the sky. To counteract this, Saussure reminds the reader of languages 'in which' one 'cannot sit *in* the sun'. Urdu, happens to be one such: as a speaker of that language what I see shining in the sky is called /surədz/ but I cannot sit *in* /surədz/; what I sit in is /dhup/, the bright warmth shed by /surədz/. Common sense, supported by sensuous experience, might lead the Urdu speaker to believe that the 'division' of the referential domain in his language is really real, that the English sign 'sun' is 'lacking in specificity'; it neither refers to the orb up there in the sky, nor to the warm light shed by it on the earth; it simply 'confuses' the two. Common sense would be mistaken in both cases: the simple fact is that ordinary speakers of any language are unable to 'see through' the linguistic system without a painstaking 'scientific' analysis. What this discussion highlights is the *fundamental independence of the linguistic sign from the so-called 'real world'*: languages place different grids on the world of reality, thus shaping 'the real' in human experience.

3.3.2.2 *The inherent systemicity of the linguistic sign*

The INHERENTLY SYSTEMIC nature of the linguistic sign compensates for its 'wholly arbitrary' quality. This too has some serious implications as evident from closer examination of the discussion of 'sun' v. /surədz/, /dhup/. As Saussure pointed out repeatedly, no linguistic sign, in itself, can be said to 'have' a meaning or even an expression form that is *its own*; the identity and value of the linguistic sign inheres in its relation with other signs: simplifying, if Urdu had only one sign to refer to that domain, no matter whether /surədz/ or /dhup/, the difference between that sign and 'sun' would not be noticeable. By comparison with all other sign types, the linguistic signs are quite different in the intensity of their mutual relationships; the non-linguistic signs typically represent a collection of individuals, so the life of one sign bears no consequence for that of any other. The *unequivocally robust individual systems* of the linguistic signs can be easily integrated into larger system networks following principles that inhere in the nature of the language (Hasan 2013). As Firth (1957a) suggested, language is a system of systems.

The 'wholly arbitrary' and systemic nature of the linguistic sign as described here frees the signified from being bound by any pre-existing phenomena: the fact that the object sun exists and is sensed by all human beings as a shining orb in the sky is not a binding fact for the linguistic sign; it creates a parallel universe in a complex relation to objects, and their specific qualities, or space-time location in the sensuous world. This is part of the secret of the SEMIOTIC POWER of language: instead of signs being modelled on pre-existing things or events whether in nature or in culture (e.g., saturated clouds bringing rain, the scissors indicating 'cut here', or the evenly balanced scales symbolic of justice), language sets its own parameters for the referents of its signs. It can create what has never been, what cannot be sensed, and what exists only virtually: it is this quality of the linguistic sign that enables it to 'create' frameworks of concepts which may correspond to invisible existents, to work out their interactions which may not be sens-ible, and thus 'build' theoretical structures, the proof of whose existence lies in their efficacy in action rather than in being visible. The valued human social institutions such as those producing knowledge and technology, law and medicine, religions and aesthetic artefacts, owe their existence largely to this source of the sign's semiotic power. This, in turn, implies that a linguistic theory able to tap into the semiotic power of language would have a better likelihood of being appliable.

3.3.2.3 *Speech and writing: Two ways of accessing language*

A characteristic of the linguistic sign that Figure 3.1 fails to show is the emergence of an additional 'mode of discourse': the primary mode for the expression of the linguistic sign had been exclusively ORAL-AURAL. However, with the arrival of writing, language acquired a secondary mode, GRAPHIC-VISUAL. In the world of signs represented in Figure 3.1, this 'bi-modality' is unique to language: the first technology to engage with language, writing became another mode of communication. What is notable is the non-random division of labour between the use of spoken and written modes: the choice became a resource opening up a path for the evolution of language into distinct varieties. Whatever the virtue of an oral culture, it is unquestionable that writing is a cultural resource (Goody 1977, 1978; Hasan 2016).

3.3.3 The place of linguistics in the science of semiology

Now that we have a fair idea of how the various sign types in Figure 3.1 are positioned in relation to each other, we may ask: is linguistics *a branch of semiology,* 'a science that studies the life of signs within society'?

First, if semiology is a science that studies the life of signs within society, it would need to use language for the purpose because no other sign system is capable of performing this activity: they do not have the affordance. Second, it is far from clear that sign types other than the linguistic ones are capable of being *scientifically* studied, if the term means more than simply describing the empirically observed phenomena objectively: an observationally correct account of an arbitrary inventory of signs such as the exo-somatic ones is feasible, including information about how they operate in society and the history of their evolution. But how would this measure up to the *science of the linguistics of langue* such as Saussure envisaged? None of the non-linguistic sign types have so far got to what Saussure called 'the first principles' in linguistic research: their description is presented largely as an inventory of 'isolated individuals'. Is the point of departure for their discussion amenable to scientific study? Strange as it may sound, Saussure would share the doubts expressed here: commenting on the significance of the 'wholly arbitrary' nature of the linguistic sign, he had concluded (Saussure 1966: 68; *emphasis introduced*):

> Signs that are wholly arbitrary realize better than the others the ideal of the semiological process; that is why language, the most complex and universal of all systems of expression, is also the most characteristic; *in this sense linguistics can become the master-pattern for all branches* of semiology although language is only one particular semiological system.

As emphasized throughout this chapter, the consequences of the sign's primordial attributes are incalculable: 'arbitrariness' is a case in point. All sign types, including the linguistic ones, are encountered by individuals as social conventions; few are created anew.[5] In this sense they are all conventional; but while the massive materiality of other sign types modifies their conventionality (scissors are used for cutting; so a scissor ready to cut 'says' *cut here*), the behaviour of the 'wholly arbitrary' linguistic sign is intensely systemic; without its systemic relations the linguistic sign would not be a sign of anything.

3.4   Language use in community and the linguistic system

While accepting Saussure's impressive ideas on the linguistic sign, this section will follow the directions implicit in that description, thus elaborating the likely shape of a more developed Saussurean linguistics. The heart of Saussure's projected linguistic theory consists of the study of the 'interplay of signs called langue'; to achieve this Saussure identified certain aspects of language which he deemed either as *external* or *internal* to that linguistics. This led to certain contradictions, which were perceived as 'Saussurean paradoxes'. I will argue that SFL's development of theoretical concepts since the early 1960s are compatible with Saussure's view of sign and that they have made it possible to re-evaluate most of the so-called Saussurean paradoxes. In following faithfully where the nature of Saussure's view of the sign leads, SFL goes BEYOND Saussure's professed notions. The justification for these departures and modifications is very simple: they are necessary because *without these departures* neither the nature of the sign nor its impressive systemicity as evident in the 'interplay of signs' can be fully investigated; in short, *Saussure's linguistics of langue cannot be achieved*. Phenomena that Saussure had considered *the heart of the study of langue* cannot proceed beyond an abstract principle without extensions and modifications. To my mind this is justification enough.

The move outlined above is relevant to the validation of the claim (section 3.1.1 above) that *the primary foundation for the appliability of linguistics resides in a faithful description of the nature of sign and the pursuit of what follows from that description*: if SFL is such a linguistic theory, and SFL is also recognized as appliable, there is a *prima facie* case for maintaining that appliability is a by-product of the linguist's conceptualization of language.

3.4.1   The linguistic sign: implications of its essential duality

The first Saussurean paradox lies in the *essential duality of the sign* as discussed earlier. Common sense would reject the Saussurean view as self-contradictory, but a semiological theory of language must agree that Saussure is right on both counts.

However, problems have arisen in the presentation of the sign's essential duality. One way of resolving such problems is to theorize, as SFL does, the relations of signified-signifier by using the concept of STRATIFICATION *à la* Hjelmslev (1961): something stratified can be viewed analytically

Figure 3.2: The dual essence of language: An elaboration

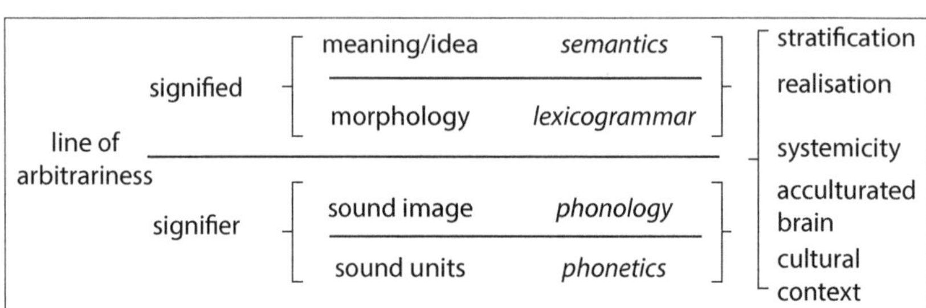

as two (or more) separate orders of abstraction, with the unity of the stratified object implicit in the metaphor of stratification: this solidary relation inheres in the stratified object. To refer to that particular kind of solidary relation whereby two distinct orders of abstraction are related to each other, SFL has borrowed Hjelmslev's term (1961: 40) REALIZATION.[6] Figure 3.2 shows this stratification of the sign, identifying strata within each part.

In Figure 3.2, the line of arbitrariness runs between signified and signifier forming the primary strata. Saussure's terminology for further stratification of the strata is shown in ordinary script, the current SFL terms which 'translate' them are in italics. The big open brace lists the main implications of viewing the linguistic sign through the mediation of these concepts, some of which have been adumbrated in sections 3.2 and 3.3. Instead of methodically following this listed order of implications, the sections below discuss them under two general headings: both relate ultimately to Saussure's conception of sign, and both demonstrate, though in different ways, why following the sign faithfully where its nature leads is a critical factor in creating an appliable linguistic theory.

- (a) the sign, its user and the users' community (3.4.2 and subsections)
- (b) the sign, its morphology, and templates (3.4.3 and subsections)

The central feature of Saussurean linguistics is its commitment to the systemic aspects of language; it ignores the accidental as irrelevant to linguistics. So, the systemic nature of the linguistic phenomena will be emphasized below, especially where SFL has been led to depart from, add to or modify Saussure's ideas.

3.4.2 The life of the linguistic sign in society: Context, sign and sign users

Saussure often refers to 'community', locating therein the origin of language. He appeals to it in connection with conventionality; further, a recognition of the community's linguistic behaviour is treated as relevant to the genesis of diachronic change. It should be obvious that a particular configuration of features define the boundaries of *états de langue*, a concept essential to the SYNCHRONIC LINGUISTICS of langue, whose origin is said to lie in parole. Despite the centrality of 'community' to such important issues 'culture' remains untheorized in Saussure, and this has infected other concepts including the relation of 'parole' to *langue* and of linguistic variation to synchronic linguistics, which is in effect the linguistics of langue. As pointed out, Saussure (2006) rejects the ability of common sense to scientifically analyse the sign; I suggest the same applies to the analysis of social context seen in relation to language as system and process: it needs to be theorized to provide a valid account of the relations of language and culture.

To SFL, oriented to discourse analysis (Halliday 1964) for decades, context and language variation have been familiar concepts; SFL has used context as a device for placing grids on language use, thereby introducing system into parole. Language use occurs overwhelmingly with reference to some social activity: the environments for social practices are culturally specific, which is what SFL refers to as context of SITUATION. It follows that situation must be 'aware' of CULTURE: just as behind parole lies the language system, so also culture is instantiated as situation. As linguists, our interest in culture and situation is from the perspective of language SYSTEM (*langue*) and language USE (*parole*), with the implication that the theorization of their relations should offer a valid account of the relations of these four categories. Figure 3.3 is adapted from Halliday's graphic representation (1999) of just such an account where the principal concepts and their relations are specified.

This figure should be seen as an extension of Halliday's theoretical concepts relating to register variation. According to it, the linguistic system is REALIZATIONALLY related to the context of culture, just as the use of language, i.e. text, is to the context of situation.[7] Contexts of situation hosting social activities INSTANTIATE the system of culture, just as the process of language i.e., parole, in the shape of text(s), instantiates the system of language.[8] The relations in Figure 3.3 help locate the precise relations of categories such as language system, language use, culture, situation, linguistic varieties, and change: it is here that conventionality and innovation find their measure.

Figure 3.3: Two Systems and their relationships: Realization and instantiation

<table>
<tr><td></td><td></td><td colspan="2" align="center">instantiation</td><td></td></tr>
<tr><td></td><td>SYSTEM</td><td colspan="2">────────────────</td><td>INSTANCE</td></tr>
<tr><td>CONTEXT</td><td>context of
culture</td><td colspan="2">────────────────</td><td>context of
situation</td></tr>
<tr><td rowspan="3">realization</td><td></td><td>(cultural
domain)</td><td>(situation
type)</td><td></td></tr>
<tr><td></td><td>(register)</td><td>(text type)</td><td></td></tr>
<tr><td>LANGUAGE</td><td>language
as system</td><td colspan="2">────────────────</td><td>language
as text</td></tr>
</table>

Note: Culture instantiated in situation, as system instantiated in text.
Culture realized in/construed by language; same relation as that holding between linguistic strata (semantics: lexicogrammar: phonology: phonetics).
Cultural domain and register are 'sub-systems': likeness viewed from 'system' end.
Situation type and text type are 'instance types': likeness viewed from 'instance' end.

3.4.2.1 Linguistic sign, context and social activity

The sign's signing function relies for its efficacy on the contexts of social activity: its status as a functional sign is confirmed only if it is active in some recognizable context. Thus, attention is paid to a road sign only if it is encountered in the proper context of driving; the same board showing the same 'sign' is not treated as 'a sign proper' *if found lying by the roadside*. A toddler, playing by his parents, ignores all linguistic signs passing between them; but as soon as the talk turns to, say, a visit to the zoo or the toyshop, the child will prick up his ears and attend to the linguistic signs more closely. So activities are central to sign use. Not all kinds of social activity are equally relevant to every member of the community: a selective sense of relevance develops in members of the community as they continue engaging in the range of social activities relevant to their patterns of life; people develop the ability to recognize the identity of types of social activity and the meanings appropriate to them simply by participating in acts of semiosis with other members of their speech fellowship (Bernstein 1990; Firth 1957a).

Reflection on the last comment points to an exotic property of systems whose origin lies in communal life: 'would be' system users learn the systems only by using them with other members of the community. Consider, for example, the learning of the mother tongue: infants learn to speak by 'speaking' and 'being spoken to' by caregivers who know their mother tongue; their language develops by languaging even as the community's system of language evolves by being used. The linguistic sign system whose origin Saussure always located in the community is an extreme case of this kind. Above we discussed the inherent systemicity of linguistic sign: (sections 3.2 and 3.3 above) if the meaning of a particular linguistic sign lies in its relation to other signs, the same is true for the meaning of these *other* signs, and so on *ad infinitum*. This, in ordinary logic, implies that to 'know' *a* particular sign's meaning one must already know the *other* signs' meanings. If 'learning the mother tongue is learning how to mean' (Halliday 1975), it should pose serious problems to the infant because of the hermetically sealed circle created by the inherently systemic nature of the linguistic sign system (Hasan 1985a). How does the child break into this circle?

3.4.2.2   Learning the social semiotic of mother tongue in context

It was Malinowski (1923, 1935) who pointed to an answer: the key for entering the closed circle of meaning lies in the context of early child–adult interactions. Notably infants interact far less frequently with other infants than with their caregivers who are, by definition, acculturated adults: they use the language of the speech fellowship; they know its ways of being, saying and doing, i.e., its culture (Halliday 1975, 2004b; Hasan 2005a, 2009a). The interactions occur most frequently in the material situational settings of everyday life; so the exchanges relate to the here and now; the sens-ible is foregrounded. In such contexts, the sign's SIGNIFICATION helps the child by referring directly to the world outside, thus opening the door to how the community means: *the context of interaction becomes the primary calibrator of meanings*.

The meanings the child learns thus are not the same as the adult's: they lack the power of systemic sign values. But parole is overwhelmingly systemic with reference *to* context; in everyday contexts of living, the meanings and the elements of everyday social activities are calibrated (Halliday 1964; Hasan 1999; 2016; Butt and Wegener 2007). In this way, the sign-meaning introduced initially to the child through signification begins to turn systemic (Halliday 1975, 2004b; Painter 1984; Torr 1997).

3.4.2.3   *From context to meaning to consciousness*

Fascinating as the topic of mother tongue learning is, my concern here is with the general significance of that process: in Halliday's words (1980) it includes 'learning language, learning through language, learning about language'. For the child, learning the mother tongue is the way into internalizing his social universe: ways of being, doing and saying become routinized: nurture becomes 'second nature'. Now, *nurturing is a semiotic activity*; *it can only be achieved by using signs*: in the material world of 'real things', signs are the only 'meaningful things' capable of interpreting the world; and due to its *semiotic power*, language signs enter most areas of the internalized universe.[9] In and by this process, the physical brain is transformed into 'a personalized brain' (Greenfield 2000; Edelman and Tononi 2000; Damasio 2010): *acculturated individual minds* with personalized forms of consciousness are created by semiosis in the community's cultural contexts; so nine-tenths of what is called 'cognition' is, in fact, the gift of parole. This is SFL theory's response to the so-called *Saussurean paradox of locating a psychological sign system in a social community*: to reiterate, in a community, an acculturated brain is not isolated; it is united by the means of intellection, developed communally in 'acts of meaning' (Halliday 1993).

3.4.2.4   *'Saussurean paradoxes' seen in context*

Babies are not the only ones to interact in context. The adult contexts of talk vary more widely, each situation type hosting social practices regulated by the speakers' SOCIAL POSITIONING (Bernstein 1990). Generalizing, speaking with reference to context is done systemically (Hasan 1999), so that the semiotically developing child's language turns into the adult's 'ways of saying'.

Language active in social context implies a conjunction of doers (TENOR), doing (FIELD), and means of calibrating doer and doing (MODE). The specific features of these contextual parameters *vary systemically*, so in field, the sphere of social action may be *'quotidian'* or *'specialized'*; the tenor may be *'friendly'* or *'reserved'*; the mode may be *'spoken'* or *'written'*. Varying syndromes of such systemically valid contextual features constitute CONTEXTUAL CONFIGURATIONS (CC) which underlie specific varieties of REGISTERS and TEXT TYPES: on the one hand CC is relevant to the Generalized Structure Potential of a register, and on the other, variation in the CC forms the basis of LINGUISTIC VARIATION ACCORDING TO USE. The second kind of variety is LINGUISTIC VARIATION ACCORDING TO USER; its distinguishing patterns are realized largely by features of the sign's signifier: in these varieties, known as ACCENT and SOCIAL DIALECT, the same meanings are exchanged but with distinct varieties of expression devices.[10] The distinctive contextual features correlating with these LECTAL VARIETIES pertain only to the tenor underlying the texts: they relate to certain user characteristics e.g., sex, age, age relation, and social and/or geographical location. The parole of socially highly significant groupings of users, in particular that according to social class, displays the linguistic variation known as SEMANTIC VARIATION (Hasan 2009a; Cloran 1994; Williams 1995): it is characterized by variation in SEMANTIC ORIENTATION.

The types of linguistic variation described here are common to *all états de langue*, which implies they inhere in language; to the extent that these inherent variation types are systemic, they would be 'in the langue' as studied in Saussure's synchronic linguistics. Ignoring variation would be acceptable only if it contributes nothing to the morphology of the sign system; this however is not the case (section 3.4.3.2 below). Further diachronic linguistic change is logically impossible without the simultaneous presence of innovation and large scale stability in chronolects. Establishing the systemicity of variation is SFL's response to the *Saussurean paradox of recognizing* états de langue *while treating linguistic variation as external to the linguistics of langue.*

The SFL theoretical framework has introduced a systematic account of TEXTURE and STRUCTURE in individual texts and text types, identifying the contextually regulated semantic structuring of texts in the three kinds of linguistic varieties mentioned above (Hasan 1984c, 1985b; Halliday 1977a). Frames have been produced for analysis demonstrating the systemic regularities of parole in everyday discourse (e.g., Hasan 2009a; Cloran 1994; Williams 1995; Eggins and Slade 1997) as well as in specialist interactions in official pedagogy (e.g., Halliday and Martin 1993; Williams 1995; Martin and Veel 1998; Christie and Martin 2007; Christie and Maton 2011). This theorization of the social context supports the claim that *parole is systemic;* it helps also in identifying linguistic varieties as a site for the evolution of sign meanings: *social context is not only integral to the growth of the mind but also to the growth and circulation of 'the interplay of signs'* (section 3.4.3, below).

Halliday (1973, 1979) suggests that the three parameters of the contexts of social practice leave their traces on the FUNCTIONAL-FORMAL ORGANIZATION of sign morphology: language is adaptively related to the classification of meanings by social parameters of activities, and so to the lexicogrammar due to the 'natural' relations of meaning and wording: this makes language

METAFUNCTIONAL. If these claims are true, then obviously context cannot be ignored in the analysis of sign morphology.

The non-randomness of *parole* is evident from this account. The systemicity of context and semantics may differ from that of syntax and phonology; but to say that in parole the speaker is 'the master' is not only to underplay the power of cultural contexts, it is in fact to undermine the possibility of establishing a *conventional* relation between the signified and the signifier. Conventionality, an important concept in Saussure, requires regularity, and the measure of regularity is in the signs' systemic relation to contexts of talk. Without such regularities 'phonic shapes' such as 'appropriate' and 'relevant' would go begging for their meaning. With such a theorized context, when we claim that engagement in the use of linguistic signs is voluntary, it is with the understanding that the speaker, in all the uniqueness of his individuality, still works with a brain personalized by cultural experience; so this brain is as 'au fait' with language as it is with the contexts of social activities: the speaker would know when not/speaking is a viable option (Hasan 1989). *Speaking is not simply a semiotic act*; it is also *social*: Saussure saw language system as a *semiotic* object, but to work in the community's life, the system *has* to be a *social-semiotic*.

3.4.3   The interplay of signs: Developing descriptive categories

Turning to the second major issue, according to my reading, for Saussure meaning is the essence of the linguistic sign: systemicity counteracts the arbitrary relation of the signified and signifier; it generates 'value' and identity, while templates in language clearly depend on systemicity. So the concern will be with identifying the internal resources in language for establishing the signs' values. But before exploring this, a warning about the meaning of terminology is needed: some of the linguistic terms in use today are signalled by the same 'vocal forms' as used in Saussure's time but with significantly different meanings. For example, Saussure's (1966, 2006) term 'psychological' does not mean 'innate' or 'hard-wired', but 'internalized' and/or 'intellig-ible'. Similarly, the word 'form' does not refer to syntactic form as today, but to a *bona-fide* 'signifier'; his 'morphology of sign meaning' is pretty much the same as 'the lexicogrammatical realization of meaning' in SFL. And some time his usage may be inconsistent (section 3.4.3.2, below). This may be due to translation problems or because one is reading notes Saussure made only for himself. Sometimes confusions occur because Saussure 'has no words' for referring to some category or relation: in other words, theorization of some category or relation may not have been completed.

3.4.3.1 Morphology: The interplay of signs that is langue

For Saussure 'morphology' was concerned with explaining the mechanisms for realizing the sign's meaning; thus 'The real name of morphology should be: the theory of signs and not forms' (2006: 123); 'form' here equals 'the sign's expression'. The aim of his projected linguistics was to explain both the sign's meaning and its systemicity by the concept of morphology (2006: 15; emphasis original):

> The study of language as a system, in other words of its morphology, comes down either to the study of *use of forms*, or the study of *representation of ideas*. It is wrong to believe that there may be *forms* (existing in themselves, independently of their *use*) or *ideas* (existing in themselves, independently of their *representation*).
>
> A form without a use is a *vocal figure*: a physiological, acoustic notion. Moreover this gives rise to an immediate contradiction, since there are many *forms* that are identical in terms of sound, though no one would dream of associating them. That is the best proof of the complete absurdity of an entity *form* divorced from its use.

So if there is a vocal figure that is not associated with some meaning it is simply a 'phonic' event, not a 'form'; and since it is not a sign, it cannot be treated as internal to the linguistics of langue.

Saussure offers the syntagmatic and associative relations of signs as the means of establishing the identity and value of particular signs (sections 3.2.2–3.2.3 for discussion). He accepted that there are systematic aspects of the syntagm which always display regularity (i.e., we know these as 'syntactic structure' today): they owe much to the sign's inherent systemicity. But he went on to suggest also that syntagms carry other regularities than just that of syntax: thus (1966: 123, footnote 5; emphasis introduced, RH) 'It is scarcely necessary to point out that the study of syntagms is not to be confused with syntax. *Syntax is only one part of the study of syntagms.*' In other words, there is more to syntagm than syntax; other forms of syntagmatic continuity exist. What Halliday and Hasan (1976) referred to as the texture and structure of text types leading to the patterns of cohesive harmony and GSP (Hasan 1985b) are two attested examples of such regular patterns of continuity in the syntagm; other strong candidates are RST (e.g., Mann, Matthiessen, and Thompson 1992) and rhetorical units (e.g.,

Cloran 1994), and phasal analysis (Gregory 2002). Saussure had reservations against the popular definitions of such terms as syntax, morphology, lexicology as used among his contemporaries, which are still maintained in formalistic linguistics. Discussing the various 'sub-disciplines' recognized in his contemporary linguistics, he commented (1966: 135):

> the distinctions were illusory. ... Form and function are interdependent, and it is difficult, if not impossible, to separate them. Linguistically, morphology has no real, autonomous object. It (i.e., 'morphology as the study of declensions' RH) cannot form a distinct discipline from syntax. ... it is not logical to exclude lexicology from grammar. ... we notice at once that innumerable relations may be expressed as efficiently by words (i.e., lexeme/lexical item. RH) as by grammar.

These Saussurean views on the 'science of linguistics' would perhaps be just as unpopular today in linguistics as they were in his times. SFL is perhaps the only exception: on theoretical grounds it rejected the separation of lexicon and syntax (Halliday 1961), reconceptualizing the two in the unity of 'lexicogrammar'. SFL is in fact quite close to Saussure's ideas about the essentials of how meaning and lexicogrammar should be studied in his linguistics. So in discussing the second issue the concern is more with the elaboration of his ideas, not so much with departures or extensions, except in the introduction of concepts that assist the study of sign morphology.

3.4.3.2 On realization across linguistic strata

The arbitrary relation in the sign is crucial to its make-up and so to the description of *langue* as a whole; thus, SFL views stratification in multiple steps (Figure 3.2; section 3.4.1 above), the primary being the line of arbitrariness stratifying the signified and the signifier. The secondary step applies to each of these primary strata: the signified is stratified as (a) 'idea/meaning' (in SFL 'semantics'); and (b) 'meaning morphology' (in SFL 'lexicogrammar'), the signifier as (a) sound image (SFL 'phonology'); and (b) sound (SFL 'phonetics'). These four strata are viewed as the *language internal* strata, each stratum representing a distinct order of abstraction, each with a unique concern and function, compared to the others. Together these two pairs of strata on either side of the line of arbitrariness provide the necessary and sufficient resources for the description of language as a semiotic system: *in principle, the sign system is analysable in its entirety*, and this is clearly necessary for the model's appliability.

Figure 3.4: Language as a social semiotic system [Hasan 2012: 255]

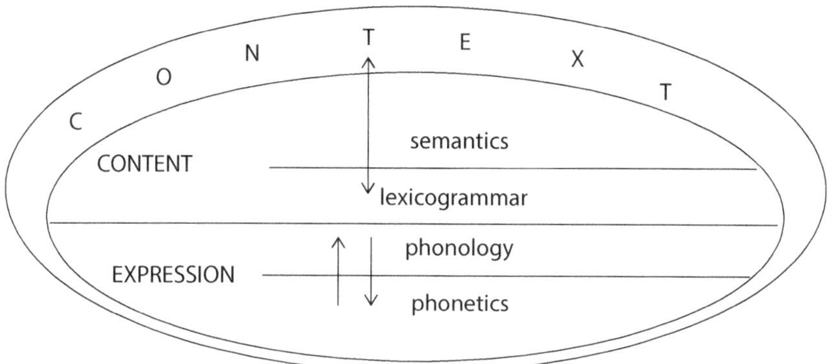

As argued above (sections 3.4.2.1–3.4.2.4), a viable explanatory theory of the sign system must recognize the context of culture and situation; on this ground, with a third step in stratification, context forms the fifth stratum in the SFL theory, which, unlike the other four, is language-external: it acts as the environment for the language-internal strata and brings the linguistic system into relation with the community of its users. Figure 3.4 represents these relations.

SFL treats the five strata in Figure 3.4 as realizationally related: context of situation is realized as the largest semantic unit, text, which is realized as some lexicogrammatical unit(s), which is realized as some phonological unit(s), which is realized as some phonetic unit(s). In the normal course, a sign, no matter how big or small, is produced only with all strata working together; and, conversely, an analysis of the internal make-up of the sign functioning in community should present the same five strata as necessary and sufficient to the description of language. An exhaustive analysis of this kind is a highly ambitious goal, to my knowledge, so far not achieved by any model.

3.4.3.3   *The lexicogrammatical realization of meaning: Construing value*

In Saussure's work, the nearest we come to a representation of the interplay of signs is in the discussions of specific examples of items, i.e., instances of the category word/morpheme, as for example, in offering the associative bonds of 'enseignement' in Figure 3.5.

The English version retains the same four Saussurean distinctions. Saussure's comment (1966: 126) on his own diagram was: 'a particular

Figure 3.5: Associative bonds (adapted from Saussure 1966: 126)

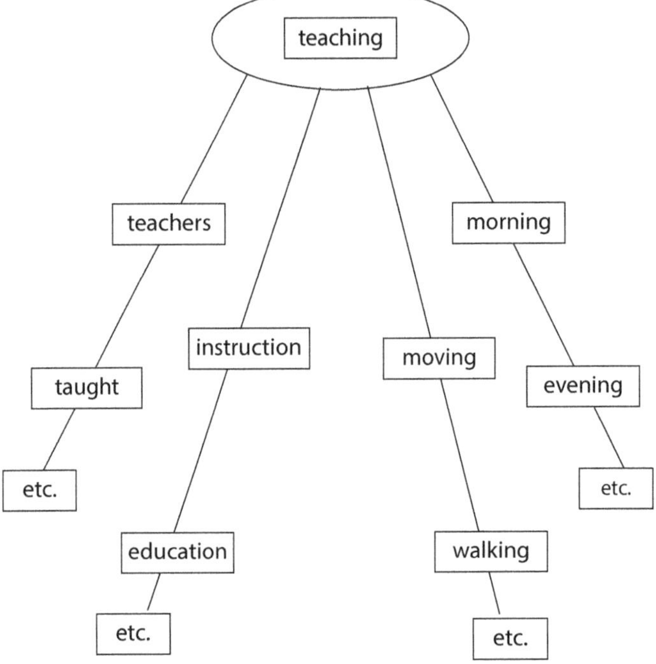

teaching

teachers

morning

instruction

moving

taught

evening

etc.

education

walking

etc.

etc.

etc.

word is like the centre of a constellation; it is the point of convergence of an indefinite number of co-ordinated terms.'

By contrast with Figure 3.5, SFL follows a more abstract route: it does not offer the description of single isolated signs, but begins its descriptive work from the concept of UNIT. Each unit at any language-internal stratum may function as the POINT OF ORIGIN for a SYSTEM NETWORK of FEATURES; the realization of these calibrated CHOICES provide a series of descriptions. The systemic description of every single sign of the language, in theory, demands a visit to every stratum in Figure 3.4. The system at issue pertains to some category not to an instance: thus there is no system network of 'eat' or 'love'; but there is a system network of the unit VERB which acts as process in the clause and belongs to the VERBAL GROUP at the lexicogrammatical stratum. What these descriptions identify are templates for specific 'unit-types'. Many actual examples of system networks and detailed discussions of concepts pertaining to systemic representations will be found in the SFL literature (e.g. Halliday 2009; Halliday and Webster 2009; Halliday and Matthiessen 2004; Hasan 2009a; Matthiessen 2007, and many others).

The description of the sign is thus dispersed into system networks across the entire linguistic system. Using this information each 'line of description' in Figure 3.5 can be located more precisely: thus, moving from left to right, for (a) in Figure 3.5, assume *teaching* is semantically a process, so time is relevant, the latter is lexicogrammatically realized as some tense, whose phonological realization is conditioned by (i) tense choice, and (ii) the choice of number in the noun at Subject *if* primary tense is simple present; for (b) assume, *teaching* is semantically an activity; lexicogrammatically realized as nominalization functioning as Thing/Head in nominal group, whose phonological realization takes the form 'verb'+tion; for (c) assume, *teaching* is semantically again an activity, realized lexicogrammatically as nominalization functioning as Thing/Head in nominal group, the phonological realization taking the form 'verb'+ing; (implying –tion and –ing belong to the same class of lexicogrammatical unit, members of which occur under distinct conditions); and finally for (d) by-pass semantic, grammatical description; assume all signs ending in the phonological form '–'+ing related by 'rhyming'.

Saussure sometimes highlights the 'difference' between signs as most important to their identity/value, and sometimes it is the similarities that are said to bring them together, as in Figure 3.5. SFL descriptions based on systemic choices simultaneously track the differences and similarities in a sign's relation to other signs in the language: linguistic description based on systemically related choices is a description of language as a meaning potential; its focus is on the *possible* rather than the *actual*. Such descriptions do vary in delicacy: the least delicate description is in terms of constituency; the most delicate grammatical system network is capable of describing units of lexis (Hasan 1987; Tucker 1998), which comes closest to 'item'.

SFL descriptions of this kind for a substantial part of a language have not been produced, but (a) in theory the potential of such description is present in SFL: the sign in its entirety can be analysed; and (b) the analyses of actual uses of language carried out up to certain degrees of delicacy have supported the belief that such descriptions are helpful in revealing the meanings of the texts (Halliday and Matthiessen 1999; Hasan 1985c, 2009a).

3.4.3.4 *Morphology, templates and parole*

Saussure made modern linguistics aware of the peculiar logic whereby the linguistic sign maintains itself in the communicative act by defying the logic of the logicians. He insists on 'the morphology of meaning' as *the* most essential component of the linguistics of *langue*. It is, therefore, mystifying to find him at the same time treating parole as external to that discipline. In the absence of attention to what happens by way of parole, the morphology of meaning could only make one simple statement: the meaning of a sign is produced by the sign's relation to other signs. But no evidence of any relations such as shown in his associative bonds could ever be produced except through the study of parole. In other words the only site for the interplay of signs is in parole: the linguistics of *langue* would be impossible and/or highly reductive unless parole is treated an essential part of the science of linguistics.

Then, consider also the regularities in syntagm other than those attributable to syntax/structure: In SFL, the structure is 'built up' on the basis of realizational statements of systemic features: there is no descriptive value to a claim that at the stratum of semantics there is a type of question, characterized by the presence of the features

demand;information:confirm:verify:reassure

unless the claim can be backed up by stating: (a) what unit at the lexicogrammatical stratum is the point of origin for the system whose features realize these semantic features; (b) what part of the lexicogrammar of that unit is relevant to realizational features; and (c) how the selected features are realized as a structure. Without going into details (Hasan 2009a), the unit clause is the point of origin for the network whose features would realize the above selection expression; the relevant part in the lexicogrammar of the clause will be in MOOD; the realizing features of the clause (Hasan 2013 table 7):

declarative:tagged:reversed:negative

and the actual elements of the MOOD structure of the clause critical to its realization may be stated as follows:

Subject^Finite; polarity positive ^Predicator...Finite; polarity negative ^Subject

An instance of this clause type would be: *you like dad, **don't you**?* where the elements critical to realization are highlighted in bold. What is at issue here is the concept of the 'template', not items e.g., 'like' or 'dad'.

Selection expressions from a given system network specify a structure that Saussure would have called templates: they are not the structure of just one unit but apply to a class of units.

3.5 Conclusion: Appliable linguistic theory and the description of the sign

I began with the hypothesis that a valid conceptualization of the sign is 'the first principle' on which an appliable linguistics can be built by taking the sign's description to its logical end. SFL has adopted Saussure's widely accepted view of the sign, and in developing the sign's theorized description it has needed to widen the scope beyond Saussure's concept of the linguistics of langue. The most important moves in further theorizing some Saussurean concepts and relations are:

- Stratification as the relation between signified/signifier; extended to language as whole, entailing recognition of realizational relation across strata;
- Revealing the systemicity of parole, by theorizing relations of community and *langue*, leading to identification of the basis of linguistic varieties;
- Relating systemic description to categories rather than to instances, leading to a systemic description potentially capable of identifying 'everything that is systemic in language'.

The strength of parole lies in its relation to the life of speakers doing ordinary things in ordinary ways. Much of sections 3.3 and 3.4 has insisted that the principles of its regularities argue for the recognition of parole. The mastery of syntax and lexicon is a necessary condition for speaking, but relevant speaking is impossible without the knowledge gained from using language in the day to day contexts of communal life.

Linguistic meanings intercede at every point in the living of life, but meanings in relation to each other are only encountered in parole, and best described by reference to the regularities of language use. Descriptions yielded by the use of scientific linguistics need to be validated: the reliability of the categories of the theory of linguistics needs to be established. In the absence of this, claims about the scientific status of linguistics is without basis. To accomplish this validation of the model the linguists' descriptions have to be matched with the patterns of the community's behaviour: there has to be a renewal of connection between the abstract principles and the real instances. The theorization of register and the description of the instances of the many registers, including the analysis of the text's texture and structure, can certainly be validated by reference to communal semiotic practices.

The development of linguistics to the point where it can produce linguistic descriptions of registerial categories, as SFL has done, would play an important role both in establishing the validity of the analysis and in increasing the resources of an appliable linguistic model. It is social practices of different kinds that act as the environment for the application of linguistics: this expertise will be in demand only if it can offer viable ways of describing 'how language works' (Halliday 1964), for this is what opens the door to solving problems with their origin in linguistic semiosis. When a model is able to describe to a substantial degree of delicacy the language used in many different classes of social activities, then it has become appliable: appliable linguistics is not dedicated to some particular problem; it should be capable of being used to help solve any problem that implicates language in any social activity.

I hope I have given some evidence of this ability which arises from the pursuit of a viable conception of the sign such as Saussure's to its logical end. I am suggesting this is the secret of the appliability of linguistic theories such as SFL.

Notes

1   This chapter is a distant relative of a plenary at the 10th Chinese National Conference of Functional Linguistics at Xiangxi Normal University, 2007. My thanks are due to Halliday for his comments on an earlier draft.

2   Two other declared varieties of SFL are (a) Martin's (e.g., 1992) genre based modelling of language; and (b) Fawcett's (e.g., 2000) theory of systemic functional syntax. Both rely in many important aspects on Halliday's SFL, but diverge at some points, critical enough to the debate here. In this chapter read SFL as Halliday's SFL.

3   Prague School Linguistics has been applied, among other things, to the study of linguistic variation, translation, functionalism, and stylistics.

4   'Semiology' has lost its currency today; it is now replaced by 'semiotics' following the philosopher, Peirce (e.g., 1955).

5   During the transition from proto-language to mother-tongue, Nigel invented as do other small children, some 'linguistic signs', such as 'quoise' for a particular shape, 'go-getti-go' for the shape of a Rugby ball; but hardly any such signs get transported into the mother tongue: they lack the communal support i.e., conventionality.

6   The term realization was used by Hjelmslev (1961: 40), who mentions other solidary relations, only some of which may be treated as realizational. The use of the term in SFL while at first in keeping with Hjelmslev's definition, has now been further elaborated (Hasan 2009a, 2010) which distances it from Hjelmslev's term.

7   Cultures are realized multi-semiotically; language is only one semiotic systems amongst the others. However, the semiotic power of language means it is the most pervasive.

8   For a discussion see Hasan 2009, 2012. For further discussion of langue/ parole Halliday 2008, 2009; Matthiessen 2007 for realization and instantiation as theoretical concepts; for context, register and text Hasan 1999, 2016; Butt 2005; Butt and Wegener 2007.

9   This is not to deny the efficacy of non-linguistic experience in the development of 'mind'; however the externalization of experience does imply the mediation of language (Hasan 2011).

10   Social dialects differ in accent as well as certain variant lexicogrammatical features e.g., the in/famous use of 'not' and concord (c.f., copula deletion). Neither variety makes any difference to the meaning they 'give'; they however 'give off meaning' due to the association of the expression with a particular user groups. This latter is closest to Labov's sense of 'social meaning.

4　A view of pragmatics in a social semiotic perspective [2012]

4.1　Introduction

The aim of this paper is to present a view of pragmatics in a social semiotic perspective; but a view of which pragmatics? This is not an easy question to answer specially for a non-practitioner: like beauty, the identity of pragmatics too seems to lie in the eye of the beholder. This is not surprising for a discipline Bernstein (2000: 155–174) would have described as instantiating a 'horizontal knowledge structure': different conceptions of the same field and different 'languages' for its description, have long been typical of the human/social sciences: pragmatics is no exception, and a visit to some of the literature dealing with pragmatics (e.g., Leech 1983; Levinson 1983; Davis 1991; Blakemore 1992; Mey 1993, 1998; Verscheuren *et al.* 1995; Green 1996; Huang 2007) illustrates the situation admirably. It seems better, then, to adopt a view with the widest scope such as for example Mey's (1993: 5) 'pragmatics is the science of language as seen in relation to its users'. As an identification of that field of human experience which forms the concerns of the science of pragmatics (whatever the word science might mean in this collocation), Mey's characterization at first glance seems like a catch-all phrase wide enough to cover the full range of issues pragmaticians tend to discourse on; but precisely because it displays such remarkable inclusiveness, this definition may prove more effective than narrower ones, such as Levinson's (1983: 9) 'pragmatics is the study of those relations between language and context that are grammaticalized, or encoded in the structure of a language'.

My preference for Mey's definition and its implied rationale are perhaps supported by his comment (Mey 1998: XXVI) that 'the user perspective on language … opens all aspects of a potentially infinite window on all human activities'. But by the same token, this 'infinite window' cannot be closed simply by fiat, as in Mey (1993: 5) which appears to shut out 'the science of language as seen in relation to' its formal potential for construing meanings and for manifesting them in ways that contribute to users' access to those meanings, and therefore to their interpretations. I am not saying that the interpretations of what is said are entirely based on linguistic form, simply that the linguistic form always makes some contribution to the listener's interpretation; so its hasty dismissal from pragmatics might prove problematic. Besides, in the end, what is in and what out of pragmatics can only be decided in view of its definition as presented (Mey 1993: 5), which as I interpret it does not appear to license such exclusion; quite the contrary.

The important issue raised by Mey's definition is not so much about what topics belong to pragmatics: one may anticipate that the identity of users, the range of uses, the nature of context and sources of variation in the processes of meaning and interpreting, and even discussions of methodologies for achieving viable descriptions of these phenomena, would be relevant to the field; however, these are all at the level of description. Assuming that some theoretical position, whether consciously recognized or not, underlies the practice of description, it is necessary to identify what positions, if any, are implied by Mey's view of pragmatics. I suggest that a probing of the definition will reveal that the central issue is theoretical; and it is concerned with the conceptualization of language. In support of that interpretation, note that underlying Mey's definition is the belief that language can be seen in relation to its users. It seems reasonable to ask: what would that view reveal about the nature and origin of language? Linguists who have witnessed the intellectual climate of dominant linguistics mid-1950s–mid-1970s would probably agree that the question is not frivolous: the decades long discourse on the status[1] of pragmatics and the failure to find an integrating principle for the selection and treatment of topics whose descriptions count as 'doing pragmatics', seen together, present an implicit account of what was meant at that stage by 'doing linguistics proper', especially if this referred, as it did, only to the dominant model of that period. If that 'linguistics proper' presented itself, as it did, as a variety of linguistics, it must have had some conception of language,[2] but this must have been a conception that could not have agreed with the view of language when seen in relation to its users.

Taking my question to be valid, I will attempt to answer it below. Having identified in Section 4.2 the attributes that must be assigned to language when seen in relation to its users, in Section 4.3 I will explore their implications in greater detail. Section 4.4 of the paper will show that the exploration of these attributes leads to a conceptualization of language as a social semiotic: this, I suggest in section 4.5, is the approach logically predicated for pragmatics in view of Mey's definition if it is taken seriously. The paper closes with brief remarks on certain aspects of pragmatics as it is currently practised.

4.2   Seeing language in relation to its users

To see language in relation to its users, we need to have some recognition criteria for the referent of the word 'language'. This should not be seen as a prelude to some deep philosophical debate. Rather my interest is in establishing the users' view of the referent of the word language; so what is needed is a simple statement about what typically gets seen as 'language' by those who use it. With this in mind, as a first observation, language may be identified as a specific type of bodily action, not just any bodily action but a particular set which always results in the production of certain patterned noises and/or marks on some surface (henceforth, I refer to this product as sounds/graphs). Such actions taken together are universally described by speakers of any language as 'speaking'; whether to initiate a similar action in an 'other' or to respond to it. The products of such action, i.e., sounds/graphs, are overwhelmingly referred to as (instances of) 'language'. Recognized in this way, language possesses the property of materiality: it is an object with internal patterns of regularities whose manifestations are accessed by human senses;[3] whether in producing or in attending to sounds/graphs, language will embark on its journey in the life of its users by first impinging on their bodies.

I have deliberately used this highly attenuated recognition criterion, in order to better indicate what if any features[4] of language become apparent when it is seen as in relation to its users. With apologies[5] to Russell (1962: 9), 'when our enquiry is finished, we shall have arrived at [some]thing radically different from this unphilosophical position ... we shall have come to see a complicated picture where we thought everything was simple'.

4.2.1   Language: A versatile resource

The use of the word 'users' in the co-text of Mey's definition already implies a view of language as something that is useable/useful: this feature of language is obvious from its massive and continued use in a large variety of social practices all over the world. It seems reasonable to suggest that language proved so effective in the performance of human practices not because it presents itself as sounds or graphs. Rather, to prove effective, it must have possessed the property of being meaningful: its elements must have been capable of relating to the experiences of the users. Accordingly, in all major cultures of the world there has been a tradition of treating[6] language as a system of signs (the calibrations of) which function as the means of expressing meaning. Saussure's seminal text (1966: 65–70) elaborated on this long accepted tradition by describing the sign as a union of content and expression, i.e., signified and signifier. He went on to show that the *valeur* and identity of both the signified and the signifier are established by the dense associative and syntagmatic relations each contracts with the other signifieds and signifiers in the same language (Saussure 1966: 102–127). In Saussure's framework, it is the *valeur* of the sign which is critical to the signification[7] of the sign. And since the associative[8] and syntagmatic relations constitute the form of language, they can justifiably be described as the linguistic resource for meaning. In this way, Saussure theorized the term *meaning* distancing it from the pre-theoretical notion of naming, which is what underlies the truth functional theory of meaning. Meaning in the Saussurean perspective, interfaces the speakers' experienced universe and the semiotic system of language.

An intricate set of implications follow from the acceptance of this position. First, besides the property of materiality in language, now its semantic[9] potentiality must also be recognized as essential to the sign system. It is notable that the European tradition of Saussurean linguistics attaches equal importance to both meaning and materiality: this is manifested in the acceptance of the content-expression cycle, treated as inherent to the internal structure of language (Firth 1957b; Hjelmslev 1969; Halliday 2003a: 1–29). But since linguistic meanings are 'un-meanable' without linguistic form, and inaccessible without its materiality, language has to be conceptualized not as a binary system of 'content-expression' but a multiple coding system, as displayed in Figure 4.1. The figure presents context as a stratum in the theory of language because to use language is to mean and to mean is to be positioned in social context; the strata of semantics[10] and lexico-grammar have a closer relation to context than those of phonology and phonetics. The acceptance of meaning logically allocates a central place to context (discussion section 4.3): it cannot be seen as a disambiguator, or accidental helper in interpretation, as it often is in formalistic models. Whenever speakers speak, some meaning is construed on the basis of what is said, irrespective of whether what is understood by the addressee is the so called 'speaker's (intended) meaning' or not. When someone recognizes that the speaker's intended meaning has failed to come across to the hearer this clearly implies that there is some other meaning on the floor, which happens not to match the speaker's intention,[11] and that the hearer must perform some implicature analysis, perhaps as recommended by a pragmatician aware of the importance of context. However, this implicature analysis too must clearly be responsive to the speaker's wording; not any implicature analysis will do with any wording. The fact remains: words never fail to mean, and language users seem to have a close relationship to worded meanings: the majority of language users will recall the meanings construed by the wordings in context overwhelmingly more often and more faithfully than they will the form of language, including its syntax, the shape of which is seldom retained in memory.

So in view of the above discussion, seeing language in relation to its users is to see it as an intermediary in some interactive event; and by definition interaction is an exchange of meaning. Meaning itself is an interface between the users' context of use and their language's formal resources: in fact, the idea that there could be meaning without wording, or that wordings exist without meaning functions makes no sense in Saussurean linguistics (discussion below, section 4.3). Assuming that the development both of linguistic form and of linguistic meaning is rooted in language use, it is remarkable that in most frameworks for the study of language the full importance of language use has been quite invisible. Behind that invisibility lie conceptions of language in decades of linguistics concerned solely with its formal aspects, whether in order to prescribe or to proscribe.

Figure 4.1: Strata in a theory for the description of language as social semiotic

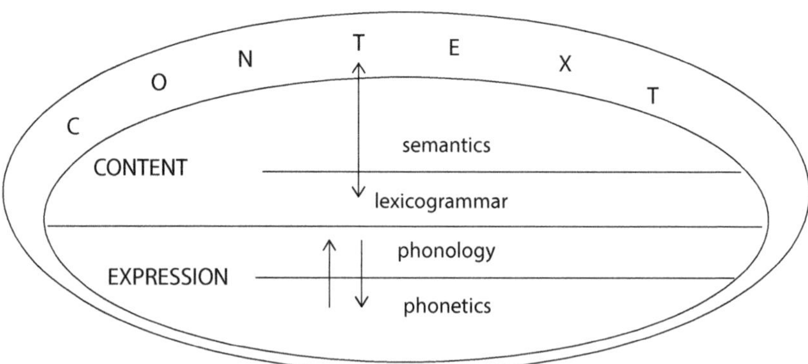

Thanks to ideas about the innateness of language which flourished in the dominant formalistic model current in the 1960s and the early 1970s,[12] language use, also known as performance, has been considered a surface phenomenon, and as such banished from the most privileged and privileging form of linguistics; this was said to be the study of the native speaker's competence, a mental record of the system of rules whereby judgements on issues of grammaticality could be made by native speakers endowed with sound minds. In the excitement over this mental language, the majority of linguists failed to notice the astonishing ability of language in use to meet the needs of its speakers in different types of social practice which varied synchronically and diachronically within and across cultures. Not many linguists asked: what kind of resource is language-in-use (Hasan 1984a, 2009b: 8–24) that it is able to maintain its efficacy despite the changing needs and differing activities of its users?

4.2.2   Diachronic language change and the users of language

Had the question been raised, one universally accepted fact might well have been cited as the explanation: that language is subject to change; it changes with speakers' changing needs and changing social practices. I return to this explanation below; here let me just point out that it is only language that is active in its users' experiences, in the words of Firth (1957b: 187) an 'experienced language' that is subject to change. To repeat the obvious: languages without living users are dead languages; they do not change. So users must play some active role in the process of change, albeit not deliberately. From this perspective, to see language as Mey desires is to see it as a dynamic phenomenon, actively developing and open to change.

With reference to diachronic change, a quick comment about the early models of 'formalistic linguistics': i.e., linguistics whose primary object of enquiry is the syntax of innate mental 'language': so far as predictions about change in the mentally coded syntactic rules/principles are concerned, there is less than compelling evidence of their viability (e.g., Fischer and Leek 1987: 79–113; Lass 1987; McMahon 1994: 107–137); and looking at the model's rule based descriptions of already completed change raises a question of principle. Clearly, such change becomes visible thanks only to the data of experienced language, i.e., to performance. What exactly is the relationship between competence and performance, and why should changes displayed in the data of performance have any relevance to a theory of competence without granting that performance and competence are germane to each other in some specific way? What is that relation? Lass (1987: 154) points out in connection with diachronic descriptions that 'a consideration of specimens of historical linguistic work widely judged to be substantive and lasting shows *that whatever linguists may think privately about the ontological import of what they do, they proceed in practice as if it were irrelevant*' (italics added). To avoid this charge, it is necessary to explain how the 'I[nternal] language' (Van Valin and LaPolla 1997: 9) reveals itself without appearing as perceived feature(s) of the 'E[xternal] language'?

4.2.3   Attributes of language seen in relation to the user

Quite a few unexplored openings can be found in subsections 4.2.1 and 4.2.2. Before turning to elaborate on these in section 4.3, I will list them here, both to give some idea of the density of 'meaning' in the expression 'users of language', and to anticipate critical features of the concept of language in a social semiotic perspective:

(a) language has users in the plural; its typical use is in interaction: i.e., there must be some exchange of meaning to which wording as a rule must bear some relation;

(b) language has the property of materiality; the material aspect of language, its expression-substance is, in terms of Russell, sensible: i.e., using language is using the body;

(c) language must relate to speakers' and listeners' contexts of living, which is to say it has the property of meaning; meanings being abstract must be accessed by the intellect; in terms of Russell, meaning is intelligible: i.e., using language is using the mind;

(d) language is used in the performance of concerted human activities by the user: the social contexts of human life, especially aspects which concern Action, Relation and Contact (Hasan 2001), are central to using language;

(e) language meets varied demands from its users in the performance of these social activities across time and culture: it varies diachronically and synchronically with reference to the contexts of its users and their uses;

(f) language use continues over time which implies it gives satisfaction despite changing circumstances; to manage this, language must be semantically sensitive to changing context: this changing language must underlie change and development as observed in language.

4.3   Fundamental issues: Language in society in language

This section will further explore the view of language as seen in relation to its users. On the basis of what has been said so far, it seems highly likely that the exercise will lead us to a view of language in a social semiotic perspective. It is a perspective where language is viewed as a semiotic system that is responsive to the system of culture. To say that language is a semiotic system is to maintain it is made up of signs. Following Saussure, I would define a sign[13] as a union of dissimilars, without any logical relation between the two except a semiotic one of one 'thing' signifying another. To say that the relation between the two dissimilars is 'not logical'; is to say that, the union does not result from either the materiality of the signifier or the properties of the phenomena to which the signified refers; instead, as displayed in Figure 4.1, signs are typically conventional – or to use the term much misread in linguistics, 'arbitrary'. The linguistic sign system is perhaps the most arbitrary of any. However, this arbitrariness is severely constrained in language: the value and identity of both members of the pair (a specific signifier and its signified) is established entirely by reference to the total set of relationships they enter into. As Saussure put it, language seemingly allows its speakers a free choice, but at the same time by this requirement in what could count as some specific linguistic sign it constrains the possibility of what might be seen as a sign element of a particular language. The value and identity of a sign of any size or shape determine its potential for signification (section 4.2.1) with the obvious implication that there can be no 'true synonyms' in any language. The linguistic sign bestows a licence of freedom from material, sensible reality based in the here and now, with the result that it may be used to construe contexts of the past (as in biographies, histories), or those imagined in parallel to experienced contexts (as in fictive narratives, such as *Pride and Prejudice*), or a mélange of these two (e.g., historical fiction, say, Salman Rushdie's *Shame*); or those imagined which run counter to at least some experienced contexts (such as Kafka's *Metamorphosis*), or those imagined on the basis of certain accepted or postulated logical relations (hypotheses and theories). In short, the significative power of language is held in check only by the limits of human imagination.

This seeming independence of language from actually surrounding contextual elements, such as ongoing processes, existing objects, persons and so on, is possible only because: (a) the relations at the levels of linguistic form have already created a meaning potential which is independent of the referent's material presence; and (b) the inherent resources for construing this meaning already exist, to be exploited in the construal of extrapolated meanings as enabled by the current state of the language. This gives language a free hand to participate in any kind of social activity, seemingly anywhere, anytime. But although the formal mechanisms which enable the construal of meaning are inherent to language by virtue of its being a semiotic system, the actual semantic reservoir of a language, i.e., its communal semantic potential which is in principle available to every speaker of the language,[14] is in fact responsive to the speech community's uses of language in the contexts of their social life. The responsiveness of the semantic to the social develops in language only in the course of its continued use, with the members of the community 'doing things with words'. Language use in context is the site where the semiotic and the material come together; whenever language is used, meaning interfaces the speakers' world of experience and of semiosis. As Halliday has commented (2005: 59): 'Both matter and meaning are involved in all the regions of our experience. Meaning relies on matter to make it accessible to a receiver; and matter relies on meaning to organize it.' It is this principle that gives intersubjective objectivity to the interpretation of acts of linguistic semiosis, i.e., of referring by words, phrases and sentences to phenomena concrete and abstract. The interpretation of signification is thus grounded in experienced contexts, real and imaginable (Malinowski 1935; Hasan 1985a).

The make-up of the users' social world is in a reciprocal relation to the users' semiotic systems. For an individual, language, especially one's mother tongue, is not a matter of choice. The infants' mother tongue develops in interaction with their immediate meaning group; the trajectory of this development is responsive to the family's social positioning, which reveals itself in the maturing individuals' use of language in society favouring one set of social practices rather than another. Many attributes of language said to be inherent to it are so, only thanks to the fact that language develops, changes, is maintained in a community: it is able either to flourish or else dwindle in keeping with the life of the speech community. The exchange between the two is ongoing: while language plays a critical part in the development of social institutions, participating in the developing society's material and intellectual capital, society in its turn penetrates the language, acting on its formal resources and its semantic potential (Hasan 2009b). Douglas once remarked (1975: 87): 'if we ask of any form of communication the simple question, What is being communicated?, the answer is: information from the social system. The exchanges that are being communicated constitute the social system.' This has implications for the study of both linguistics and sociology: the orientation of a theory underlying their description must be exotropic (Hasan 2005b: 48–67, 2005d: 4–17), leaving windows open to permit an adequate description of how this inter-penetration occurs, and what contribution it makes to the nature and development of both.

4.3.1 The language-society connection as revealed by linguistic change

One serious problem in explaining linguistic change as a reflection of change in society or vice versa is the implied temporal linearity whereby change in one has to be temporally prior so as to cause change in the other. This picture does not agree with our experience of the world, thus as I have argued (Hasan 2009b: 21–23) everywhere, at every stage of human history, preachers and politicians have persuaded, and are persuading, their listeners purely through discourse to support some line of action which is designed to bring change to society. Obviously such preaching has to precede the social action and its outcome (Hasan 2009b: 22). At the same time, we can easily cite examples demonstrating the priority of social need for some class of linguistic change: one familiar example is that of brand names for artefacts, which get integrated into the mainstream of language, such as Hoover and Xerox in English.

Change, whether in society or in language, is a complex phenomenon, which we do not yet understand fully enough to be able to offer viable explanations, or reliable predictions. What we do know with certainty is that change is endemic to both, and apparently one factor that is indispensable for change in either language or society is 'real, live people' (Mey 1993: 5) interacting semiotically and materially. The instinct for establishing and maintaining contact with an 'other' comes natural to many animal species including *homo sapiens*: it is the pressure of this instinct in human beings that underlies the evolution both of society and of the different modalities of semiosis, including language. This is not a new insight; it needs reiterating only because we have been too preoccupied with I[nternal] language to try and understand the E[xternal] one which in fact changes the quality of human life – either for better or for worse depending on who you are. There appears to be no convincing evidence at all that language began with rules of syntax or even with sentences, grammatical or ungrammatical, any more than that society began with templates of institutions or conventions for social practice. Neither the hypothesis of language as mental organ nor the causal way of viewing the connection between language and society does justice to their relationship. Rather, in view of the history of their evolution, it seems more likely that, from the very beginning, their evolution has been governed by a co-genetic logic. Recent research in archaeological anthropology (Noble and Davidson 1996; Marwick 2005; Davidson 2007) which examines both somatic and social changes in the early hominid supports this view: these researchers would agree with Whorf (1956b: 156) that 'In the main they [i.e., language and culture] have grown up together, constantly influencing each other', and with Halliday (2003b: 380) that 'Language neither drives nor is driven by it [i.e., culture]; the old question about which drives which can be put aside as irrelevant, because the relation is not one of cause and effect'. There exists no causality, simply a reciprocity.

4.3.2 The language-society connection: Mother tongues and minds of individuals

Studies concerning the ontogenesis of communication (e.g., Trevarthen 1979) which chart the infant's journey in semiosis in terms of 'moving and meaning' (e.g. Halliday 1975, 2003e, 2004a; Painter 1989; Torr 1997; Matthiessen 2004) highlight the fundamental part that the interpenetration of the social and the semiotic plays in the development of infants and very young children who are learning how to mean by means of language. The infant's facial expressions and bodily movements are validated (Hasan 1984a; Painter 1989) as semiotic acts having some specific meaning, which is validated by consulting their material situational settings (Hasan 1973); as the children move to vocal actions, using their child tongue, i.e., proto-language in Halliday's sense of the word, those patterns of noise are also interpreted by caregivers as 'acts of meaning' whose significance is initially arrived at by the adult by reference to the immediate context. It then takes a certain degree of familiarity with the semiotic mechanisms of the mother tongue for the child-speaker to construe relevant contexts by the use of worded meanings. Throughout this development we note two equal partnerships: one between social context and acts of semiosis, and the other between the apprentice child and the acculturated adult.

Just as without the benefit of recent anthropological research, Whorf had already arrived at the co-genetic relation between culture and language, so also, without the benefit of a large body of empirical research in this area, scholars such as Vygotsky, George Herbert Mead and Gregory Bateson had already pointed out that the development of specifically human mental functions is, in terms of Vygotsky, socio-genetic: human mental functions develop in human social environments in interaction with other human beings (Vygotsky 1978). Their claims are now supported by the findings of neuroscientists (Deacon 1997; Edelman and Tononi 2000). One conclusion derived from such research is particularly relevant to the present discourse: that the human mind is essentially a personalized brain (Greenfield 1997); it is brain 'turned into' mind by the internalization of the experience of living. According to recent research, there seems to exist no evidence for innate principles which would help the child decide which grammar is to be paired with which actual language of the world, much less of any ready-made rules of syntax appropriate to all such languages. In view of the phylogenetic evolution of language and its ontogenetic development in children, it seems much more likely that the infant is born with the ability to grasp the essential nature of something being a sign – that the appearance of something does not determine its meaning/significance. The ability to see something as indexical of another is not teachable: what is teachable is what is indexical of what, and that significative association of the semiotic with something being sensuously experienced is a function of language in use, i.e., performance.

There is no need to elaborate what it means to grow up in a 'meaning group' (Halliday 2003e: 218), its central role for one's language – the accent, the formal patterns, the semantic reach for doing things with words – and what these imply for the formation of beliefs, intentions, attitudes and the quality of mental functions (Hasan 2009d: 309–351). The literature on these topics is well documented, and today more than ever before it seems imperative to pay attention to the part that our sociality plays in our ability to participate actively in the future of this planet. Behind all enterprises, big and small, lies the triad: socio-cultural experience, semiotic and material action, and mental orientations. This does not imply that any one of the disciplines, be it language, or society, or mind must be explained wholly in terms of the other(s). Each has its own history and its own specific qualities; nonetheless their histories have converged and will continue to do so. It is therefore necessary to understand how the affairs of this world have been shaped by these convergences.

4.3.3 Contexts, community and individual: Variation according to use

Linguistic variation, which is a feature of language-in-use as highlighted by the exploration of Mey's definition in section 4.2, can be seen from two perspectives: languages have 'varieties according to user' and 'varieties according to use' (Halliday 1964: 77). We begin with the 'use' perspective below.

Users use their language in social contexts. But it would be misleading to talk as if context preceded social practice, since it is out of social practices that contexts are constituted. Context does not vary randomly from instance to instance; nor is it wholly material. Its internal order may be viewed from two perspectives: (a) visible patterns of instances of social interaction consisting of features that users are typically aware of; and (b) invisible, systemic principles, acting as the constitutive basis for social practice while being grounded in those same social practices. As the human child learns language by languaging, so also the principles of human social institutions emerge in and by social practices. Most users suffer from a miscognition of the invisible principles (Bourdieu 1990), considering themselves autonomous actors in relation to most visible features of social context.

The tradition of context studies to be sketched here is derived from Malinowski (1923, 1935), which was developed by Firth (1957b: 177–189, 1964: 93–118), Halliday (1964: 75–94, 1977a: 176–225, 1999: 1–24), Mitchell (1975) and their colleagues. With primary focus on visible context, the importance of invisible contextual phenomena[15] is increasingly being recognized as this condensed account shows. In Halliday's systemic functional linguistics context is a stratum in the theory of language (Figure 4.1, section 4.2.1), and is conceptualized as a conjunction of three situational dimensions: (a) field of discourse; (b) tenor of discourse; and (c) mode of discourse: social context is no more raw situation than phonetics is raw bodily noise, both being seen in relation to the nature of language.

Field of discourse concerns the use of language in carrying out some social activity. The action may be primarily verbal, where only language is involved, as in lecturing, writing a story or a report, or chatting casually with a friend: such language use is constitutive of the activity. Or an action may be primarily material. If so, the linguist's interest arises only if there is some use of language relating to the action: such associated verbal action is called ancillary. Social activities are the visible expression of some social institution(s): behind the action of buying an avocado ultimately lie various commercial enterprises which enter into a network of relations ranging from the internal revenue system of the country right down to the member of the family who adores avocados and hates turnips! These connections stretch from the communal to the individual, and increasingly, the communal is becoming global. Consider buying a car of foreign make in Australia: this buying will differ significantly not only from buying avocados, but also from buying the same car in Pakistan. The term buying refers to numerous activities in which perhaps the only thing in common is that there is some exchange of goods and services. Field is also classified by reference to the sphere of action: is it quotidian, as chatting is? or specialized as teaching language or talking to a client is? and if specialized, what domain of specialization (Hasan 1999) does the activity pertain to? In correlation with these and other such distinctions, the worded meanings exchanged in the on-going interaction will also differ notably, not only in what they refer to but also in the shape of the entire interactional protocol. It is generally assumed that activities are intentional, purposive, goal driven, but these notions are quite complex: they apply to some action types more readily than to others; and they need to be better understood, before predictions become easy to make. Where the contextual description will focus in this vast domain depends on the motive for description. Accumulating descriptions can lead to deeper conceptualization of context only if they probe for principles underlying instances. Pulling out contextual features to explain imaginary problems of interpretation in imaginary instances as if contextual features were visible and transparent does not contribute much to the understanding of the context.

Tenor of discourse concerns the enacting of human relationships in language: who is interacting with whom? The focus is not on specific individuals but on features that establish their positioning in society (Bernstein 1990), e.g., mother-child, teacher-pupil, colleagues, neighbours, and so on. Even in the most equitable societies, interactants are socially located *vis-à-vis* each other by reference to their material, cultural and intellectual capital. For the acculturated, labels for social relations act as a condensed handbook outlining ways of doing, being and saying with respect to the label holder. The ways of behaving are not engraved in stone; they are negotiable to varying degrees, depending on certain contextual features, e.g., the interactants' ethnicity, skin colour, gender, accent, appearance and the quality of social distance (Hasan 1973: 271–279) between them. The critical factor in establishing the quality of social distance is their shared interactive biography: the greater the sharing the lesser the distance; the lesser the social distance, the more negotiable their 'treatment' of each other. Underlying the social expectations regarding who will say what, to whom, and how, are these and many other such contextual features: there is no such thing as one set of conversational maxims that fits all conversations (Hasan 1984b: 105–162, 2009d). This is obvious if one analyses a substantial quantity of naturally occurring interactions, conversational or otherwise, with 'real, live people' as interactants. Navel-gazing, whatever its uses in internal linguistics, is not much use in describing 'experienced language'.

Mode of discourse concerns the organization of the material and relational aspects of the activity: how do features of material contact between interactants impact on their ways of saying? Are the interactants materially present, talking face to face, or on the phone, or interacting by writing? If the latter, is the addressee known personally to the 'speaker' or is it a prototype such as 'the young child' or 'the sophomore'? Also, the channel of communication makes a difference to the interaction. Users do not write when they can speak to each other; and they use language differently in the different modes of contact. It is possible, of course, to write as if one were speaking face to face, as in conversations between the characters of a novel, and one can read the written as if producing extempore speech as in staging plays on the radio, or 'speaking' a written up 'talk'; but such instances precisely establish the point.

Why are just these three dimensions selected as relevant to language in use? The three dimensions represent aspects of relevant context which can be re-construed by the worded meanings, representing, say, a displaced text (Hasan 1979: 369–390): the language of the text will provide information about who was doing what (field) with whom (tenor), and how (mode). Each situational dimension is a variable, which is instantiated by particular values. The values of each variable are systemically related contextual features (Hasan 1999: 274–314). On each occasion of use, a specific configuration of some of these features from amongst the vast number of systemic possibilities will be chosen[16] as the instantiation of that variable. The term contextual configuration refers to the total set of systemic features pertaining to some specific occasion of language use: these are the features 'encapsulated' in the wording of the text, and it is the linguistic realizations of these features that the acculturated reader uses to 'place' a 'displaced text' in its original context of situation.

4.3.4 Contexts, community and individual: On language use and linguistic functionality

A text is a representation of the worded meanings exchanged by the users in some specific social context. A corpus of a large number of such representations is capable of offering a faithful picture of the users' language in use: it is information that intuition can never achieve, since intuition is considerably limited in its scope, no matter how prodigious one's memory.

When a large corpus of texts is interrogated it reveals general regularities, and regular variations. With respect to the former, although each text is 'unique' each embodies the three variables of field, tenor and mode. When the worded meanings relevant to the realization of each variable are examined, another point of similarity emerges: each variable displays a particular mode of meaning and lexicogrammatical construal (Halliday 1970: 140–165, 1979: 57–79; Butt and Wegener 2007: 590–618; Matthiessen 2007b: 70–84; Hasan 2009b: 17–20). The implication is that there exists a realizational dialectic (Hasan 2010) such that typically each contextual variable is realized as a specific kind of meaning and each of these in turn as a specific kind of lexicogrammar. Simplifying enormously, field-construing meanings are primarily a classification of events, of event incumbents and of some of their material properties, which in a paradigmatic grammatics such as systemic functional linguistics will be construed by choices in transitivity systems, e.g., relations of process, participant, circumstance; in entity systems and certain modification systems; and in recursive systems such as expansion and projection. The syntagmatic structures manifesting such phenomena tend to be particulate. It is the ideational metafunction of language that underlies the entire realizationally related assemblage of the features of field, and the specialized features of semantics and of lexicogrammar: the functionality of language resonates through context to the higher strata of the linguistic system. Tenor-construing meanings are primarily rhetorically oriented, and concerned with degrees of discretion and evaluation; they are enacted lexicogrammatically as systems of choices in mood and modality, certain systems of attribute and attitude (Hood and Martin 2007: 739–764). This affordance of language is referred to as the interpersonal metafunction. Mode-construing meanings concern features of contextual contact management e.g., options in monologue/dialogue, in message pairing, and in identity and similarity relations; these are lexicogrammatically created by grammatical systems setting up the flow of information and systems of cohesive devices, e.g. phoricity (Martin 1992), ellipsis and substitution, cohesive chains and other aspects contributing to coherence (Hasan 1984c). Halliday referred to this function of language as the textual metafunction.

Metafunctions are a higher order abstraction than the notion of 'function' as in Bühler (1990), or as used in speech act theory with terms such as promise or command (Searle 1969). Metafunctions are universal to human language, not because they are innate but because sign systems are put to similar uses all over the world; if there is anything innate it consists in belonging to the same species inhabiting the same planet. To survive, speakers need to act; actions implicate others, are manipulative of the environment including the persons in it, and semiotic systems have limited modes of access. These are the phenomena in the language users' social context that are active in the development of these metafunctions; which in turn get elaborated in different ways in different languages depending on their speakers' conditions of material and social existence.

4.3.5   Contexts, community and individual: Variation according to user

Subsections 4.3.3 and 4.3.4 discussed varieties according to use: speakers are able to speak different varieties according to use and choose one according to what they are doing (field), with whom (tenor), and how (mode). Access to registers is a social phenomenon, not a natural one; in the words of Bernstein (1990) some registers are privileged and privileging: access to them is a weapon in the hegemonic control of communal resources. This is amply illustrated by comparing the register reservoir of the languages of under-developed nations as opposed to those of the affluent regions of the world.

With varieties according to users, each user has one primary variety; it is this variety that is spoken irrespective of the use for which it is employed. Varieties according to users correlate with variations in speakers' intimate circumstances, of which the outstanding is the speaker's location, whether in physical time and space or in the social system; cutting across these are such features as ethnicity, age, gender or education. These varieties are known as dialects. Dialects can potentially vary at any stratum of language, though both in old dialectology and in dominant sociolinguistics, the primary focus has been on variation at the level of phonology (Labov 1972). But if Saussure's *état de langue* (i.e., chronolect) is treated as a dialect correlating with some temporal stage of a language, then these dialects would vary significantly both phonologically and lexicogrammatically as well as semantically as Old English and modern English do. In studies of language use around Sydney, Hasan (2009a) provided strong indication of semantic variation in sociolects correlating with the social location of the speakers.

Apart from the chronolectal varieties of a language, which have never been subjected to communal evaluation perhaps because most members of a community never come across them, both geographical and social dialects have undergone such evaluation. In all speech communities, there are some that are assigned a high value; semiotic features such as differentiation by accent and other highly visible features of speakers such as skin colour and physiognomic features, are also particularly susceptible to such evaluation, as mainstream sociolinguistics has well demonstrated. The damning of the dialects is by association: if the speakers occupy comparatively underprivileged social location, then the dialects they speak are quaint', ugly', ignorant' and the like; these attitudes are often unwittingly allowed to continue unchecked due to the sentimental refusal of scholars to unmask the nature of this prejudice seemingly with the best motives in the world (for discussion, Hasan 2009c).

4.4   Language in a social semiotic perspective

It should be noted that throughout this paper, the term language in use has been used pretty much as if it were a novel expression, never heard before – as if invented expressly for defining the science of pragmatics. In fact, nothing could be further from the truth. Modern linguistics beginning with Saussure (1966) has used his much misinterpreted pair *langue* and *parôle*, revised by Hjelmslev (1969) as system and process, and some time known also as code and behaviour: here *parôle*, process and (language as) behaviour are pretty close to language-in-use. Interestingly, Saussure's basic reasons for recognizing *parôle* are also in agreement with what the exploration of Mey's definition tells us about language in use. Mey would appear to shun the study of the second member of the pair, namely *langue*, but Saussure, whose *langue* and *parôle* have been often mistakenly (Hasan 2005c: 286–287) equated with Chomsky's competence and performance, was quite clear on the significance of their relationship:

> language [i.e., *langue*] is necessary if speaking [i.e., *parôle*] is to be intelligible and produce all its effects; but speaking is necessary for the establishment of language, and historically its actuality comes first … speaking is what causes the language (*langue*) to evolve … Language and speaking are then interdependent; the former is both the instrument and the product of the latter. But their interdependence does not prevent their being two absolutely different things. (Saussure 1966: 18–19)

If *parôle* made these important contributions to *langue*, why did Saussure select *langue* as the primary object of study in linguistics, treating *parôle* as peripheral? An adequate response to this question would require a paper to itself, but the decisive issue in any principled study is to focus on the essential attribute(s) of the primary object of study so as to capture faithfully the nature of the phenomenon. Unlike competence, Saussure's *langue* was communal; it could not be confused with the language uses or the variety repertoire of any one individual. Its essence resided in the syntagmatic and associative (i.e. *in praesentia* and *in absentia*) bonds underlying all the signs (Thibault 1977: 1–13) current in the community. What could be a more appropriate goal for linguistics than the study of *langue* defined as the totality of the relations of the signs that make up the language system as common to the community, especially when circumscribed by the limits of one *état de langue*?[17] It clearly focused on 'the essential' and avoided what was 'accessory' or 'more or less accidental' (Saussure 1966: 14): thus, it did not matter whether a content, say, 'father' was expressed as *dad* or *papa, abba, abbu,* or *baba, pidar, pitaa ji* or *baapu* … ; it is the sign relations that would identify the sign's signification; sound-expression is '"accidental"\', it is 'accessory' to the sign accessed in actual use. In language study, *langue* was central, *parôle* peripheral.

As Halliday points out (2003b: 376), this strong classification of *langue* and *parôle* by Saussure has haunted our late twentieth-century linguistics, which has oscillated wildly between system and instance. While appreciating Saussure's deep insight into the nature of language, Halliday presents a case for rejecting Saussure's strong boundary between *langue* and *parôle*:

> Saussure problematized the nature of the linguistic fact; but he confused the issue of instantiation by setting up *langue* and *parôle* as if they had been two distinct classes of phenomena. But they are not. There is only one set of phenomena here, not two; *langue* (the linguistic system) differs from *parôle* (the linguistic instance) only in the position taken up by the observer. *Langue* is *parôle* seen from a distance and hence on the way to being theorized about. (Halliday 1996: 30)

Figure 4.2 (Halliday 1999: 8) presents his social semiotic interpretation of the relations between language system and context of culture, as well as between language system and language use. Preserving Saussure's pretheoretical observations about their relations of interdependence, Halliday theorizes them. *Langue* and *parôle* are not two different things: *parôle* instantiates *langue*; and the communal nature of *langue* is theorized by postulating the solidary link of realization between language system and context of culture on the one hand, and context of situation and language use on the other. The introduction of these concepts forestalls the issue of

Figure 4.2: Language and context: Realization and instantiation (Halliday 1999: 8)

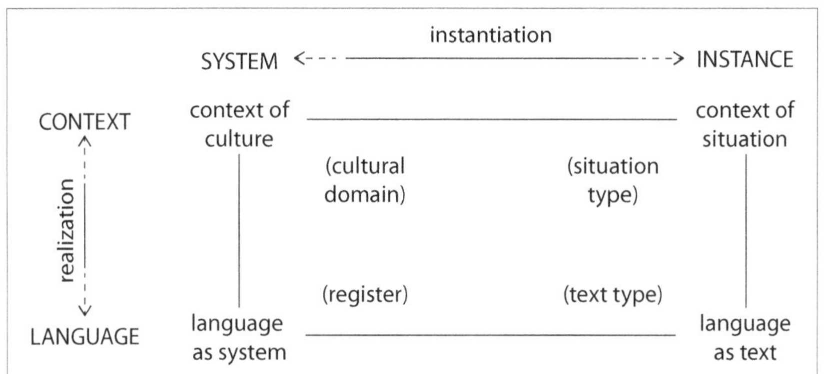

Note: Culture instantiated in situation, as system instantiated in text.
Culture realized in/construed by language; same relation holds across linguistic strata
(semantics: lexicogrammar: phonology: phonetics).
Cultural domain and register are 'sub-systems': likeness viewed from system end.
Situation type and text type are 'instance types': likeness viewed from instance end.

causal linearity: the question 'which came first?' becomes redundant since
neither instantiation nor realization imply a causal link (Hasan 2009b:
10–14).

Let me present a brief discussion of these relations, beginning with realization, which has already been mentioned (Section 4.3). In Figure 4.2,
the vertical axis of realization links language as system and context of culture. The realizational relation is quintessentially semiotic – it describes
the make-up of the sign system. Realization is a relation whereby different
orders of abstraction 're-present' the 'same information': it is this 'translation' whereby the sense of the concrete referent moves by steps from
an abstract 'intelligible' meaning of a certain linguistic sign to the bodily
accessible level of the expression-substance. Language depends on the
resources of brain-body; it is active only in a live human organism. The
'intellect' grasps the import of the semantic units which realize the material and abstract phenomena in the context of culture. The term, context of
culture, refers to a frame for addressing communal issues such as social
institutions, conventions and ideologies. Ideologies underlie conventions
as well as the classification and evaluation of social practices. The ideologies current in a context of culture range over the entire communal belief
systems, including both those which originate with concern for the human
and those which focus on the superhuman – both supporting the material

body and also creating sustenance for soul/spirit/inner being, i.e. systems of faith and religious beliefs. The ideologies of complex cultural systems are polysystemic, tolerating ambiguity and contradictions which exist, for example, between faith-based ideologies and knowledge systems, between ethical and moral systems and aesthetic systems. The context of culture is thus relevant to a vast area of human existence; only the non-interactive somatic actions and the body's sensing apparatus seem relatively independent of the influence of cultural systems.

But what is the relation between language system (*langue*) and langue use (*parôle*)? I referred to this relation as instantiation above. In Figure 4.2, instantiation links language system and language use on the one hand, and on the other, it relates context of culture to context of situation. Instantiation is a relation between the potential and the actual – it simply links two points of existence of the 'same' phenomenon to each other. Describing instantiation in terms of the relation between the observed phenomena, Halliday (2003d: 121) elucidates the situation by analogy to the relation between climate and weather:

> just as, when I listen to the weather report every morning, and I hear something like 'last night's minimum was six degrees, that's three degrees below the average', I know that the instance has itself become part of, and so has altered, the probability of the minimum temperature for that particular night in the year – so every instance of a primary tense in English discourse alters the probabilities of the terms that make up the primary tense system. (Halliday, 2003d: 121)

Viewed in this way, *langue* and *parôle* are not two different things but two states in the natural life of linguistic elements, one of having become (part of a system), and the other on the way to becoming (part of a system); the latter is analogous to *parôle*, the former to *langue*. Features of language that are today elements of the language system began as occurrences in language use – something that diachronic linguistics foregrounds so well. It is at this point that we find out how language in use is able to meet the changing needs of its speakers. The system of language acts as a resource for language in use: the grid formed by the patterns of the system is an active force in the interpretation of whatever is said or written. Innovations, analogies, metaphors, similes, and sound play can be enlisted in the construal of new meanings because the system offers ways of viewing them. It is not a template for replication; it is a resource to be exploited in ways that suit the user's communicative purposes.

4.1   Saussure and linguistics in a social semiotic perspective

Living in the Durkheimian era, Saussure was sensitive to the social, and it goes without saying that his deconstruction of the linguistic sign system as a semiotic entity has stood the test of time: notwithstanding the contradictions in the seminal text attributed to him, he viewed *langue* and *parôle* in a social semiotic perspective. Note that Halliday's account maintains the important element of the relationship between *langue* and *parôle* as introduced by Saussure, but Halliday's language system does not refer to just any one specific *état de langue*. In the end, *état de langue* is simply one kind of idealization. Without idealization, the system would encompass all the text types and all the dialectal varieties that have ever existed during any historical stages of a language. In practice, no linguist has ever managed to exhaustively describe even the syntax of just one variety of a system, and work on syntax is where most of the effort has been directed in the last five decades; so language as system is simply a theoretical construct, in theory available to any one for analysis but in practice defying exhaustive description by any single available strategy. Thus the system of language, seen in relation to the other three categories embedded in Figure 4.2, represents the thickest modelling of the nature of language so far encountered in linguistics: the language to be described begins with the first hominids struggling to communicate and evolves with their interactions into the languages of *homo sapiens*. The realization relations between language and context in Figure 4.2 create a vast canvas. Through the relation of signification, which is just one form of realization, the canvas allows language its full play, not attempting to constrain its limits arbitrarily; by the same token, there has to be some method of navigation in this terrain so as to enable the analyst to recognize where his/her own personal interests and concerns are located. Systemic functional linguistics as an instance of a social semiotic perspective on language, provides the theoretical concept of strata and realization (Figure 4.1): on the one hand, realization represents an important, orderly connection between the strata of linguistic theory, and on the other, it keeps the strata separate, effecting a division of labour in their description.

Delimiting the reference of a linguistic sign, obviously, depends on the experience of the sign in social context, but the identity of a contextual phenomenon is not materially given: the linguistic sign is not a tag to be attached to contextual elements since their pre-identification is problematic (cf., Saussure's discussion of sign, section 4.3). Like the level of lexico-grammar, the units at the semantic level are also metafunctionally organized. The theory recognizes meanings that are experiential (i.e., referential, what the formalistic linguist calls truth functional), logical (which construe relations of inclusion, exclusion, sequencing of events, properties and relations of entities, inherent or not, and other such relations), interpersonal (meanings which enact relations between persons) and textual (which make the semiotic phenomena coherent, rendering them suitable for mental action). Below this semantic level and activated (Hasan 2010) by it is the formal level of wording metafunctionally organized (Halliday and Matthiessen 2004; Matthiessen 2007a, 2007b). Below the level of lexicogrammar lie the levels of sound. Given the description of the identity and value of signifier, phonology and phonetics in Saussurean linguistics need to be treated as levels with formal properties: the units at the phonetic level are not 'raw' sound; they are linguistically specific, formed to express the elements of a specific language, or else there would be no problem of accent variation. They are realized via bodily articulation, perceived as noise of a very special kind – i.e., semiotic noise, relatable also to purely physical phenomena but not explained by them.

There is no problem in homing in on any point in this terrain to describe the phenomena that interest the analyst: what is worthy of analysis is not a hierarchy from most to least essential in the examined phenomena of language, because language is not a knowable object unless all the strata presented in Figure 4.1 are working together. If knowledge of language depends on all, then every stratum is essential to knowing language. To decide what must be analysed, the question is simply who is analysing and why. We thus get back to syntax and the consumer (Halliday 2003c: 36–49). No analysis is ever going to be a complete analysis of language.

In my view, in contemporary linguistics, the model that best respects the nature of language as a social semiotic phenomenon is Halliday's systemic functional linguistics, which explains my repeated references to its theoretical categories (Hasan *et al.* 2005, 2007; Matthiessen 2007a, 2007b; Halliday and Webster 2009). This theory appears to be an exception to the rule enunciated by Lass (1987: 154) that 'whatever linguists may think privately about the ontological import of what they do, **they proceed in practice as if it were irrelevant**' (emphasis added; discussion above in section 4.2.2). Lass's comment was with specific reference to diachronic linguistics, but it is applicable to other areas of language description as well. The outstanding exception to Lass's generalization is systemic functional linguistics; it is true to its conceptualization of the nature of language. Elsewhere I have described it as an exotropic theory (Hasan 2005b, 2005d), in that it attempts to see its object of enquiry not as an island, accidentally appearing into the sea of human life, but as a system that maintains

and is itself maintained by systems other than itself, all impinging significantly on the activities of human life.

4.5   A view of pragmatics in a social semiotic perspective

So what about pragmatics? Is it really a science of language as seen in relation to its users? In this paper I have used Mey's definition as my point of
departure; throughout, I have tried to show how language will need to be
seen if, in keeping with that definition, users are foregrounded. Pragmatics
cannot ignore these attributes of language if the chosen definition is taken
seriously. Listing the attributes once again: language in use acts as a versatile resource in social contexts, is a potential for meaning, is able to meet its
users' changing needs, displays variation, contributes to the development
of the language, is the site for changes at the levels of meaning, wording
and sound, and is able to provide evidence of these changes in the records
of language used across time; it therefore appears as a dynamic force in the
life of its users. The relevant question to ask of a science that would study
language of the kind just described is: how should this language be theorized so as to describe these phenomena? For surely, it would be only such
theorization that can function adequately at the centre of pragmatics as
defined by Mey. Looking through the literature on pragmatics, it does not
seem that the question has been raised, much less that a valid conception
has been enunciated.

To me, it seems that that question is far more important than worrying
about the status of pragmatics: is it a component? The answer is: it depends
on how the object of enquiry at its centre is seen. If it is seen as described
above (section 4.4), then pragmatics is certainly a component, because it
does not appear to have much to say in a systematic manner about the formal organization of language or about its diachronic stages or its varieties
– one could continue the enumeration: so from the point of view of the
architecture (Halliday 2003a; Matthiessen 2007a) of language as seen in
relation to its users, pragmatics certainly does not represent the entire field
of linguistics. But how is that any different from, say, doing simply phonology, because that is what concerns the analyst? From the social semiotic
perspective, being a component is not a problem: linguistics is concerned
with the study of language as defined in relation to its users; the canvas as
I showed is vast, and there is no hierarchy of privileged positions in this
terrain.

It is valid to ask: why do pragmaticians choose to do the things that count as doing pragmatics? What makes them part of the same general story? Whatever the history of its genesis, pragmatics seems to have been co-opted to act as a series of supplements 'for the many lacks' created by the theory whose conception of language it has chosen to work with for reasons which remain unexplained. The dominant linguistics of the 1960s and 1970s presented itself as the science of linguistic competence; accepting the validity of competence as universal syntax, pragmatics attempts to supplement this by creating the science of performance. It seems doubtful, however, that as a science, pragmatics could ignore systemic features of the phenomena it seeks to describe even if as process/performance. Process and system are two faces of the same coin. If pragmatics really dreams of being the science of language as seen in relation to its users, it might ask itself: how does the notion of competence or I[nternal] language serve any purpose in turning that dream into reality?

Notes

1   See especially Verscheuren *et al.* (1995) for one such discussion.
2   Lass (1987: 155) quotes Chomsky (1980: 90): 'Language is a derivative and perhaps not a very interesting concept.' Van Valin and LaPolla (1997: 9) refer to Chomsky (1986) which 'has further distinguished "E[xternal] language" and "I[nternal] language", where E-language corresponds roughly to the pre-theoretical idea of what a language is and I-language is a speaker's internal grammar'. The early Chomsky (e.g., 1965) left some room for doubt; consider, for example, the ambiguities of competence (Hasan 2005d: 286–287). Nonetheless mental language was very much at the centre of Chomsky's 1950s–1960s linguistics, which is what is relevant because pragmatics was a reaction to those early Chomskyan inspirations.
3   I mean no disrespect to readers' pets, but the access of pets to 'linguistic sounds and graphs' does perhaps require a more objective approach than it has received.
4   The fact that a feature becomes apparent in some circumstance does not necessarily imply a causal relation between the feature and the circumstance, though assuming that language is an adaptive system, its adaptation to changing environment may be part of the story of its evolution.
5   The original words used by Russell (1962: 9) were 'It is not to be supposed that when our enquiry is finished, we shall have arrived at anything radically different from this unphilosphical position. What will have happened will be that we shall have come to see a complicated picture where we thought everything was simple'

6   For those particularly relevant to modern linguistics, see Aarsleff (1982) and
    Eco and Marmo (1989).

7   There is a good deal in common to signification, naming and correspondence,
    the latter two appear pre-theoretical in comparison with signification, which is
    well theorized by Saussure.

8   Saussure's term 'associative' was later replaced by the term paradigmatic,
    though it could be argued that 'paradigmatic relations' as conceptualized
    by Hjelmslev are in fact not identical to those covered under the rubric of
    Saussure's term, (compare Hjelmslev's examples (e.g., 1961: 35–37) with
    Saussure's (1966: 126).

9   Note this use of semantic is 'inclusive'; since Saussure was freeing sign from
    naming, truth conditions would have been of little interest to him.

10 The term semantic is used here as in the Saussurean tradition, to refer to all
    meanings irrespective of whether they are truth functional (correspondence
    based) or not. The rationale for this lies in the concept of linguistic form and its
    metafunctional nature (section 4.3.3; also Halliday 1970, 1979; Matthiessen
    2007a).

11 An interesting question here is: who is the arbiter for the speaker's intention.
    One is reminded here of Wittgenstein's pregnant remark (1958: 108e; 337):
    'An intention is embedded in its situation, in human customs and institutions.'

12 The continuing revision of what might be innate necessitates a careful spec-
    ification of the stage of the hypothesis one is referring to. Much of what was
    believed in the 1960s concerning the structure and functioning of the human
    brain is now questioned by neuroscientists. Green's cautious claim (1996: 5,
    footnote 4) already substantially different from views about LADs and innate-
    ness current in the mid-1960s, suggests that what must be innate is 'the prin-
    ciples (emphasis added, RH) constraining … the *so called rules of universal
    grammar*'. But even this seems unlikely in view of current research in neuro-
    science according to which nothing as specific as 'principles governing rules
    of universal grammar' could be innate; of course, the terms of this formulation
    by Green too could be diluted in time losing reference to any form of concep-
    tual organization.

13 This is a simplified description of the sign, just sufficient for the purposes of
    this paper.

14 Though it needs to be immediately acknowledged that this access is not free;
    and thereby hangs the persistent story of social hierarchy.

15 A more detailed bibliography of studies on context in this tradition is available
    in Hasan (1999: 219–328). The study of the invisible aspects of context in
    systemic functional linguistics (e.g. Hasan 2001: 1–46) is based on the work
    of sociologists such as Bernstein and Bourdieu.

16 It is not possible to discuss the notion of choice in the limited scope of this
    paper, except to register my disappointment with Verscheuren (1995: 13–16).

17 It must be remembered that the technology for collecting and using large scale
    corpora was then absent.

5 Choice, system, realization: Describing language as meaning potential [2013]

> … in linguistics language is turned back upon itself. We have to use language about language, words about words, letters about letters.
>
> (Firth 1957a: 121)

5.1 Introduction

'Choice' is a 'common word' borrowed to function as a technical term in Halliday's Systemic Functional Linguistics (SFL).[1] However, the continued use of common words in the realm of theory alters their semantic identity: they put away things non-theoretical, and their meanings are largely governed by the co-ordinates of the theory, with the word's value and signification becoming equally virtual. The 'things and relations' they refer to represent 'constructs' that 'have no ontological status … They are neither immanent nor transcendent but just language turned back on itself' (Firth 1957a: 181; also Halliday 1988). Ideally then, technical terms should perform some precise functions demonstrably essential to the theory's working: in fact, their validity can be judged only by the work they do in construing a model of language (Halliday 1996; Butt 2005; Butt and Wegener 2007).

But the reverse is just as true: a theoretical term is only as valid as the 'ideas about language' modelled by the theory (Halliday 1976b, 1977b): I have argued (Hasan 2012, 2014) that the SFL modelling of language has reached considerable success, which is not to claim that the *theoretical* profile of language has become simpler; simply that the processes of the system as identified by the theory agree with the users' experience of it as a

MEANING POTENTIAL: a successful theory must allow the renewal of connection with the data of experience current in the community.

These remarks suggest that the exploration of theoretical terms such as, say, 'choice' in SFL or 'string' in String Theory ranges over a wide area of concerns. It is one thing to say how a term is used in a theory and quite another to judge whether as a technical term it functions efficiently, or whether the theory's conceptualization of language is competent. Clearly some serious topics of research await attention in a serious exploration of choice. But for lack of space and time, like others I too will regrettably skirt most of them. The present chapter will be concerned with one claim, namely that *choice in SFL is theoretically motivated as a fine-tuned activator of the systemic paths and their realization, which together represent language as meaning potential, a property that inheres in SFL's conception of language as a 'social semiotic'* (Halliday 1978).

5.2   Is language a social semiotic?

How would one justify the conceptualization of language as a social semiotic? Why attach such fundamental importance to it? There is a general problem in answering these questions: given that theories of language are usually partial to the theorist's concept of language, what *reasonable* grounds can be suggested for judging this concept valid? Linguists have often been preoccupied with the defining properties of a 'good' theory, but they have seldom questioned if what a linguistic theory is describing can be taken as a valid conceptualization of 'language', leave aside identifying bases for judging the validity of the response. Meanwhile different conceptions of language have always been around, and often they have excited what Peirce (1955) would call a 'doxic belief'. It is reasonable to ask: Which conceptions should be accepted and why? Are they mutually incompatible? If not, what does this imply about the nature of linguistics as a science of language? Such questions spell the *real* issues for determining the value and signification of the expression 'linguistic theory', and without viable answers claims about the 'true' nature of language will remain a gleam in the theorist's eye.

5.2.1 Language as a 'pure' semiotic

Faced with this dilemma, I turn to an exceptional scholar, Ferdinand de Saussure, who did offer some justifications for *his* conception of the object of enquiry for linguistics by naming a single inherent property of language and deriving most of his categories of language description as a set of corollaries arrived at logically by probing that axiomatic property. According to Saussure (2006: 21) 'language is a system of signs that express ideas', and linguistics, the science that studies it, 'is only a branch of the science of semiology' (Saussure 1959: 16). The robustness of this property of language is universally affirmed in human experiences of the exchange of meaning, while the sign's function in the exchange of meaning points to it as the basic unit of language. Saussure has left an outline of a theory based on those properties of the sign that enable the sign system of language to work as it does in the daily exchanges of meaning.

This approach is a reason for interest in his conceptualization of language, but there is another, more relevant reason for mentioning the topic here. I have argued (Hasan 2014) that Saussure provides a remarkably impressive basis for an explicit and coherent description of *langue* as a sign system, i.e. as a SEMIOTIC; but his linguistics of LANGUE is unable to achieve its aims precisely because it attempts to describe language simply by reference to just one aspect of a semiotic, namely its SYSTEMICITY which characterizes *langue*, ignoring the PROCESS of semiosis, i.e. PAROLE. I say this not because *parole* is important as the only evidence for *langue*, the system, but much more primarily because the research project he outlines just cannot be carried out without investigating the regularities in *parole*. Saussure's descriptive categories are derived exclusively from the sign and the sign's regular, systematic relations. Nothing would be admitted into his linguistics that is not derivable from *langue*, or not guided by TEMPLATES, i.e. regular underlying patterns whose instances were subjected to unprincipled variation in the syntagms of *parole* on which the study of syntax is based. The reason he excluded *parole* from the linguistics of *langue*: *parole* is not subject to systemization; it displays no regularities. He certainly would not have accepted the existence of any 'morphology of folklore'. This creates a paradox whereby the sign becomes a 'sign in itself' independent of the users' sense of its value and signification, and yet by necessity, the value must depend on the relations revealed by regularities in *parole*.

5.2.2 Language as a social semiotic

As a post-Saussurean linguistic theory, SFL adopts Saussure's postulates about the linguistic sign, but in developing the logical implications that follow from probing that characterization, it rejects Saussure's exclusion of *parole* as external to a linguistics whose declared aim is to offer a *full* logical description of the sign and its value (Hasan 2014). There are three reasons for this: (1) SFL offers proof that *parole* is systemizable, citing conditions that presuppose regularities; (2) without the inclusion of *parole*, the Saussurean linguistic theory is bound to fail: in excluding *parole* it will lose all evidence of the 'MORPHOLOGY of meaning' or 'the interplay of signs called *langue*' (Saussure 2006:21); there will be no ground for suggesting that the value of a sign resides in its relation to other signs; and finally (3) Saussure's theory as it stands is riven with paradoxes; SFL demonstrates that the paradoxes and lacunae are created by the exclusion of *parole*; they disappear when the semiotic process is theorized as internal to the structuring of language as a semiotic system. Saussure (2006) maintains that a sign is known by its meaning, the scientific description of which is the primary aim of the linguistics of *langue*. What he does provide in his seminal writings (1966, 2006) is an incomplete, albeit brilliant, account of language as a purely semiotic system: what SFL has done is to develop it with a potentially exhaustive and explanatory theory of language as a social semiotic. I am not claiming that SFL consciously undertook this as a mission: the simple fact is that it began with language as a communicative system operative in social life and it pursued those ideas about language by following the same kind of inferential logic as Saussure had used some decades ago. SFL had developed an extensive technical vocabulary which was shaped by a theory which is remarkably congruent with the Saussurean directions except for one outstanding difference: SFL rejected Saussure's exclusion of *parole*, and in so doing it resolved most of the Saussurean paradoxes (Hasan 2014). For lack of space, I simply enumerate the major features of the theory which enabled SFL to achieve this accomplishment:

- SFL theorizing Saussure's views on the 'essential duality' of sign as evident in the arbitrary relation of signified and signifier; although Saussure's distinction between sign-meaning and the sign's morphology as well as the distinction between sound image and sound units was not so obvious until recently (2006), SFL had theorized these relations as the STRATIFICATION of the sign system of language as SEMANTICS (= Saussure's sign-meaning), LEXICOGRAMMAR (= morphology of meaning), PHONOLOGY (= sound image) and PHONETICS (= sound units). The unity of the stratified system experienced in *parole* as a single seamless stream is explained in SFL by the REAL-IZATION relation (see the discussion of stratification and realization in, e.g., Matthiessen 2007a; Halliday 1992, 2009; Hasan 1995,

Figure 5.1: The inner stratification of language: Saussure and SFL

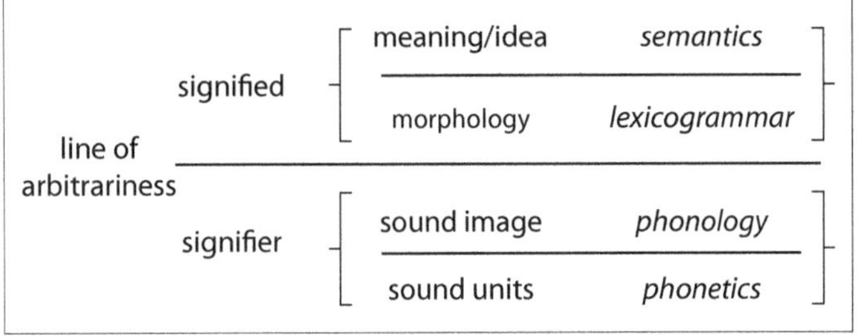

2014). Figure 5.1 presents the congruence between Saussure's and SFL's views of the inner structure of language.

- Theorizing the relations of *langue* and *parole*: for SFL, *parole* is not simply a sequence of signs along the spatio-temporal axis; it also participates in social activities which occur in some context of situation; these situations instantiate the community's cultural context. SFL theorizes the relation of *parole* to context of culture as well as to the system of language, demonstrating that the choice of linguistic signs is not random in *parole*: it correlates with the activity types; the cultural regularities in social practice are construed in language, which implies patterns of regularity in language use. These relations are displayed in Figure 5.2 (from Halliday 1999; for some discussion, see Halliday 1999, 2009; Matthiessen 2007; Hasan 2009b, 2012).

- Using categories of units as the focus of systemic description rather than instances: Saussure's associative relations (e.g. 1959: 126, on *enseignement*) are replaced in SFL by a paradigmatic description in terms of systemically calibrated choices focusing not on items but on categories of stratal units. The realization of these are TEMPLATES for Saussure; SFL, using terms such as SYSTEMIC PATHS, SELECTION EXPRESSIONS and REALIZATION has refined this concept: the realization of a systemic path is a template (i.e. STRUCTURE). Not all syntagms are syntactic: some may be derived from regular patterns of occurrences in *parole*, such as COHESIVE HARMONY (Hasan 1984c), GSP (Generic Structure Potential; Hasan 1978b, 1985c), PHASAL ANALYSIS (Gregory 1985), RST (Rhetorical Structure Theory; Mann *et al.* 1992) and RHETORICAL UNIT (Cloran 1994).

Figure 5.2: System and instance: Language and culture, text and situation

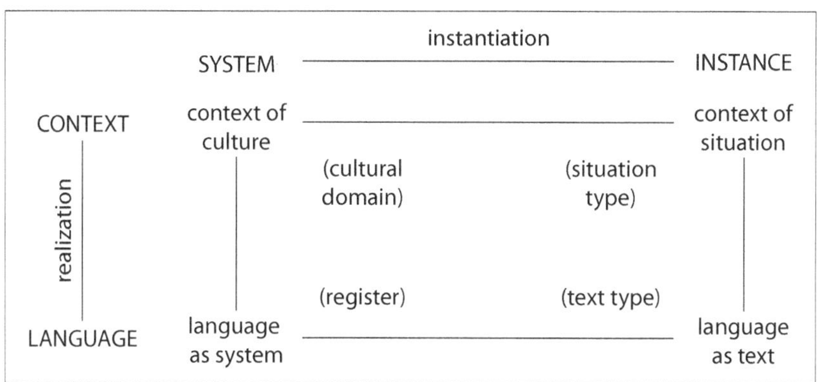

Note: Culture instantiated in situation, as system instantiated in text.
Culture realized in/construed by language; same relation as that holding between linguistic strata (semantics: lexicogrammar: phonology: phonetics).
Cultural domain and register are 'sub-systems': likeness viewed from 'system' end.
Situation type and text type are 'instance types': likeness viewed from 'instance' end.

5.2.3   The reciprocities of the social and the semiotic

What makes SFL a *social* semiotic is its insistence on the reciprocal relations of language and society: language as a sign system enables meaning exchange in the performance of social practices, but it is the systemic aspects of culture that legitimize the choice of meanings that can be meant appropriately in the context of that social practice. The interplay of the social and the semiotic systems is equally important to the shaping of culture and to the meaning potential of language. Halliday (1970: 141) has observed that '[t]he nature of language is closely related to the demands that we make on it, the functions it has to serve'. Deriving his concept of METAFUNCTIONS from this observation, Halliday (1973: 101) indicates its basis in register variation, i.e. in the common practice of 'Speaking with Reference to Context' (Hasan 1999). The details of the specific meanings of signs are metafunctionally shaped at the strata of both semantics and lexicogrammar: there is no other way for the production of meaning by speaking except through what Saussure (2006) called 'the morphology of meaning', and this morphology presents itself only with signs in use: when *parole* is excluded from linguistics, as in Saussure, the theory loses not only this resource but also the important concept of linguistic variation. The reciprocal relations of language and culture inform not only register

Figure 5.3: The sign system of language embedded in context of culture

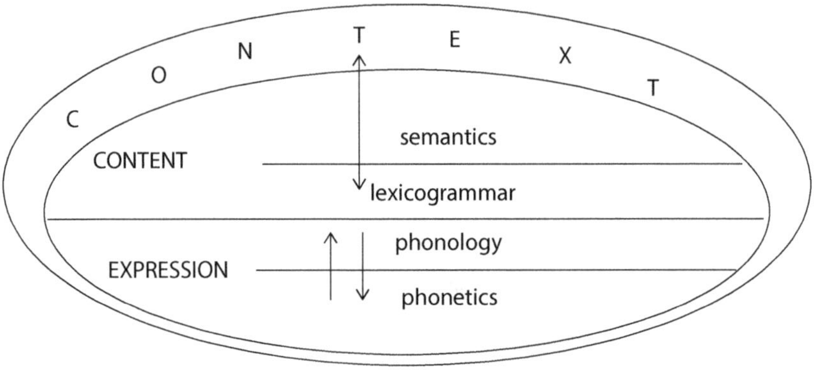

variation, but other forms of SYNCHRONIC LINGUISTIC VARIATION; and scholars (e.g. Labov 1972) suggest synchronic variation as a precursor of DIA-
CHRONIC CHANGE. SFL has cogent reasons for recognizing the CONTEXT (of
culture and situation) as a stratum in linguistic theory.

Figure 5.3 represents the SFL view of language as a social semiotic,
where surrounding the four language-internal strata is a fifth and necessary stratum in the theory, called 'context of culture and situation', typically abbreviated as CONTEXT. This language-external stratum represents
the theory's concept of social environment, essential for *parole* and for the
creation, maintenance and development of language (for discussion, see
e.g. Halliday 2009; Hasan 2009b, 2009e, 2010, 2012). If the sign system
of language is essential to the exchange of meanings, then the exchange
of meanings also needs a cultural other to exchange the meanings with:
language and culture work on co-genetic logic. Cultures as we know them
with all their benefits and constraints could not have come about without language; and language without human associations could not have
evolved as it has. Saussure showed that the conjunction of the signified
and signifier sets in motion each sign's dependence on other signs for its
identity. Accepting that Saussurean insight, SFL has also taken seriously
the fact that to remain alive and to develop, language systems must work
in societies where each member's individuality is defined by that of the
others: the systemic aspects of culture are engendered in accommodation,
aggression and assistance. Language as an inventory of fixed patterns,
be they sentences, syntactic patterns, words or morphemes, cannot cope
with such a complex situation: as an adaptive signing system it must be

an open-ended, ever-changing and accommodating potential for making meaning. It is this argument and its pursuit that make SFL a social semiotic. The theory must model this always changing, always stable system of signs: in CHOICE, SYSTEM and REALIZATION, it has developed a method of description that represents language as a meaning potential (see Section 5.4). There is no claim that all avenues and aspects have been turned into actualities, simply that the theory opens the door to the study of all phenomena relevant to understanding language (Hasan 2009b, 2014).

5.3   The semantics of stratification

Section 5.1 claimed that technical terms are accountable to the theory's modelling of language. In Sections 5.3.1 to 5.3.5, I draw attention to three concepts explicitly represented in Figure 5.3: (a) stratification; (b) realization; and (c) context. I will also introduce the terms UNIT and SYSTEM, although Figure 5.3 does not show them: for reasons discussed above, these concepts are just as relevant to SFL's view of language as social semiotic as they are to the operation of 'choice' in the description of language as a resource for meaning in the living of life.

5.3.1   Stratification in language as a sign system

Each stratum in Figure 5.3 represents a distinct order of abstraction: the nature and function of patterns at each stratum is different, and requires separate descriptive categories. This is the basis of stratification, and as indicated (in Section 5.2.2) it was implicit in Saussure's concept of sign as an entity made up of two logically unrelated parts, whose union is nevertheless essential to the recognition of the entity as a unit capable of signing. The *primary step in stratification* consists in theorizing signified and signifier as stratified; it was taken *explicitly* not by Saussure but by Hjelmslev (1969), as CONTENT and EXPRESSION PLANES, respectively. Unknown to Hjelmslev, Saussure (2006) provides justifications for recognizing a *secondary step* by abstractions within both signified and signifier, with each further divided into two (cf. Figure 5.2). These are approximately the same abstractions Hjelmslev recognized as CONTENT SUBSTANCE (= meaning) and CONTENT FORM (= morphology) on the content plane and as EXPRESSION FORM (sound image) and EXPRESSION SUBSTANCE (sound unit) on the expression plane. As is obvious from the European linguistic literature, the four inner strata of language (Figure 5.3) had been widely recognized, albeit by different names, by the time SFL first appeared on the scene (in 1961; see Halliday 1961 [2002]). Today we can confidently claim that language is universally multistratal: there is no adult language with less than four strata.

Anyone interested in enquiring into the usefulness of theoretical terminology (sometimes called 'jargon') need only compare Saussure's vocabulary with that of Hjelmslev's or Halliday's, say, with reference to the term *signified*. Saussure (1959, 2006) would refer to the signified as 'meaning' or 'idea' or occasionally 'concept'. And he would use precisely the same set of words in referring to 'the meaning created by the interplay of signs' (*content substance* for Hjelmslev, and *semantics* for Halliday), as opposed to the 'interplay of signs that produces sign-meaning' (*content form*, for Hjelmslev, and *lexicogrammar* for Halliday). Clearly the words *meaning*, *idea* and *concept* do not mean the same thing in the two different environments. Saussure recognized the distinctions at each point, as do Hjelmslev and Halliday; but unlike the latter two he did not theorize them: to do that, he would have needed to seek the common denominators across these distinctions. For example, Halliday treats each stratum as distinct from the others but also points to something in common with them: each stratum represents a different kind of abstraction, which implies that the descriptive categories pertaining to one cannot be applied to those of the other(s); at the same time the strata are alike in that each of them is equally essential to achieving the total description of the language as a sign system, and the organization at each stratum is both similar and different.

5.3.2   Strata and unit scale

One example of this latter quality is the concept of UNIT SCALE (known also as RANK SCALE). At every language-internal stratum there will be an array of units which vary in size from the biggest/highest to the smallest/lowest; the relation between them will be that of CONSTITUENCY. Just as the number of strata across the languages of the world can vary so long as it is not less than four, so also the number of units at each stratum can vary so long as it is not less than two. Figure 5.4 presents the units on the rank scales of English semantics and lexicogrammar.

Each stratum presented here carries four units on its rank scales; the 'higher' unit in each case 'is made up of' one or more than one units 'next below'. Thus in Figure 5.4, at the semantic stratum the unit TEXT is made

Figure 5.4: Unit scale at semantic and lexicogrammatical strata in English

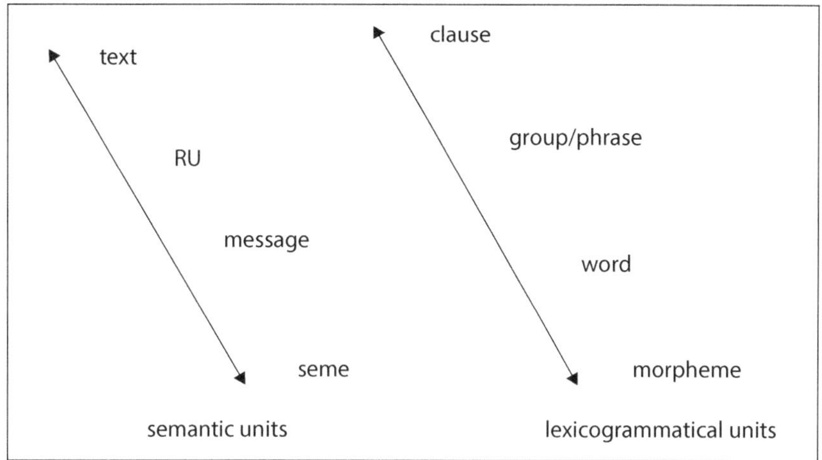

up of one (or more) RHETORICAL UNIT (= RU), each RU is made up of one (or more) '*message*' which is made up of one (or more) '*seme*'. Similarly, with lexicogrammar, the highest unit, CLAUSE, is made up of one GROUP/PHRASE (or more), a group/phrase is made up of one word (or more), which is made up of one MORPHEME (or more).

5.3.3 Realization: The essential unity across distinct strata

Saussure argued that the duality in the unity of the linguistic sign was essential for its signing function: to act as sign, the sign-parts need to be both distinct and united as one.[2] The concept of stratification foregrounds the distinct nature of the two parts, while the unity of the strata is announced by the relation of REALIZATION (Matthiessen 2007a; Halliday 1992, 2009; Hasan 1995, 2009b, 2010; Butt 2008).

The realization relation re-presents the phenomena of one plane in a different guise on another. Simplifying somewhat, the signified is patently *not* the signifier, but it is presented to the senses as a signifier, a re-presentation of meaning as sound: in other words, *there is a realization relation between the signifier and the signified*. Realization is, thus, a relation that eventually bridges the distance between the intellig-ible and sens-ible faces of language. Acting bi-directionally in SFL, realization enables the process of meaning exchange across the stratal hierarchy: from the speaker's perspective, a semantic construct is realized as a lexicogrammatical one realized as a phonological one realized as a phonetic one. From the perspective of the listener, the phonetic patterns realize the phonological ones realize the lexicogrammatical ones realize the semantic ones. The vertical arrows linking all the strata in Figure 5.3 represent this situation (further discussion in section 5.3.4).

However, all analogies are imperfect: talking of realization as translation/transmutation/re-presentation may suggest a one-to-one correspondence, as may happen sometimes in re-presentation between the original and its copy. But realization is quite unlike re-presentation in this respect: the units of strata are never in a one-to-one relation *across the board*; instead, a substantial proportion are related by variable degrees of 'regularity of coupling'. For languages to work as they do in communal life, this regularity must be above the level of chance. But if the strength of probability turned into certainty across the board, the setting up of distinct strata would become an extravagance: every phenomenon on one stratum would become explicable by its counterpart on the other stratum. This led Hjelmslev (1969: 112) to suggest that 'the two planes must not be conformal'. Had the strata been conformal, the term 'choice', if it were still applicable, would refer to qualitatively different relations.

Returning to the unit scale in Figure 5.4, the realization of meaning as a lexicogrammatical category is not subject to a mechanical rule whereby meaning A always and only corresponds to wording A_1; it is quite common to find one-to-many and many-to-one correspondences. This does not imply 'anything goes' in language; a delicate and complex calibration of meaning and wording comes through probabilities of their occurrence in specifiable environments, which suggests that there are default couplings as well as conditioned ones (Hasan 2011).

5.3.4 Context and the exchange of meaning

The context of culture and situation is equally relevant to the system and process of language as a signing system (see Figure 5.2). As Firth said, we never encounter language as system: what we do encounter as available to the senses is the system in use; insights into the nature of the system is provided by its instantiation in *parole*; hence Hjelmslev's (1969) observation that process determines system. How does context come into this determination?

I introduced the primary and secondary steps in stratification in section 5.3.1. The recognition of context, as a language-external stratum in the theory, is *the third and final step* in stratification; it brings the four inner strata of the linguistic semiotic system in relation to the social/cultural system. Figure 5.3 indicates the primary step in stratification by a line dividing the inner ellipse in two halves; this separation indicates the arbitrary relation between signified and signifier, which remains applicable to the two halves of the ellipse as they are further divided by a secondary step in stratification. SFL treats the relations of the two strata of semantics and lexicogrammar as 'natural' in the sense that the default condition of a semantic category is to be 'construed' by some particular lexicogrammatical one: in the last analysis, there is no linguistic meaning without linguistic form, nor is there a meaningless lexicogrammatical form.

These observations are relevant to the concept of realization: I have suggested (Hasan 2009b, 2010) that the three strata in the upper half of Figure 5.3, context, semantics and LEXICOGRAMMAR, are related by a REALIZATIONAL DIALECTIC whereby the higher stratum ACTIVATES the lower and the lower CONSTRUES the higher. Speakers do not happen to mean serendipitously in a meaning exchange: the meanings they mean are those called for by the CONTEXTUAL CONFIGURATIONS (henceforth CC), i.e. by the interactants' sense of what is relevant to that social activity at that given point. CC is that abstraction from the context of situation which activates linguistic meanings, activating lexicogrammar. From the addressee's point of view, the lexicogrammar is what construes meanings, and meanings construe the CC, so that a picture of the relevant goings-on is built for the interactants by the relations between the linguistic meanings and relevant elements of the context of situation (Hasan 1999). This *dialectic* holds context, meaning and wording together (the upper half of the ellipse): stopping at the line of arbitrariness, it does not cross to the lower half of the ellipse.

More pervasive a relation than construal, the relation of activation extends beyond the lexicogrammar to the strata in the lower half of the ellipse in Figure 5.3: in other words, lexicogrammar activates phonology and phonology activates phonetic choices. In this way phonology and phonetics, acting together, realize the lexicogrammatical patterns; *they become the voice of lexicogrammar making the realizations physiologically accessible to the listener*. And while it is true that phonetic units construe the phonological units, in my view, it might be an error to suggest that phonology, especially segmental phonology, with or without phonetics, could *construe* a lexicogrammatical unit in the sense of providing clues to its identity as an instance of a particular category. Theoretically, this would be an anomaly; and speaking objectively, it is not phonology that helps the addressee recognize whether a lexicogrammatical pattern such as *walks* in some actual syntagm realizes plural common noun or a main verb with simple present tense. *It is not the phonological shape of the signifier, but the lexicogrammatical relations accompanying* walks *that unobtrusively provide the criteria for deciding whether a given occurrence of* walks *is the instance of an entity or a process*. This is implicit in the arbitrary relationship of the signifier and the signified; the phonological unit has no affordance for providing recognition criteria for any aspect of the signified: it simply SIGNALS the presence of some associated signified on the basis of conventional practice. The identity and value of the signified is created by the syntagmatic and paradigmatic relations of the concerned units across the strata in the upper half of Figure 5.3. A somewhat different case may be made, perhaps, for prosodic phonology: for example, the options in the system network of KEY are realized as patterns of intonation, and they do make a difference to meaning: but significantly, the locations where the occurrence of a specific intonation can construe a particular meaning has to be specified by reference to the lexicogrammatical environment (Halliday and Greaves 2008); in other words, they themselves cannot construe the value of the signs in question.

5.3.5   Systems for describing linguistic units

The idea of system in SFL has evolved from Firth (e.g. 1957a: 7–33, 1968), who used that term (in one of its senses) to refer explicitly to the range of instances capable of functioning as a 'substitution counter' at some element in some linguistic structure.[3] The larger structure in Firth's systemic description would be viewed as a 'context' within which a set of choices were possible, only one of which could occur in an actual case: each choice made a difference to the value of its context.[4] SFL has been refining this concept over the decades: today, working intimately with choice and realization, system has become a powerful device for the description of language as a meaning potential (Halliday and Matthiessen 2004; Halliday 1995).

All descriptions in SFL are focused on stratal units. Every stratal unit can be either a 'simplex' or a 'complex' of units from the stratum below, implying a range of possibilities for the configuration of constituents in the unit, only one of which can actually occur as an instantiation of the unit at any specific point in a meaning exchange. In a theory that models language as social semiotic, which in turn characterizes language as a meaning potential, the problem the description faces is not: Given the range of possible constituents, how many different unique ways of combining them can be calculated? Rather, the question is: How do the resources of this unit work to produce a range of patterns, each playing a part in the construal of some distinct meaning? The answer to this will depend on which metafunctional perspective is under investigation. Patterns pertaining to a unit, especially at the strata in the upper half of Figure 5.3, are multifunctional, which implies that the choices accessible to the same unit would differ according to metafunctional orientation. From this point of view the choices are not made in terms of the range of the possible concatenations of constituents available to the unit in question. Rather, each unit is a resource for meaning-making in terms of a METAFUNCTIONALLY REGULATED range of features, such that the choice of a feature makes some difference through its realization to the configuration of a unit's patterning; as I will attempt to demonstrate in section 5.4, each set of the selected features together with their realization will represent a valid pattern of the unit, differing from all the others in terms of both meaning and form.

The possibilities of the choice of features are systematically calibrated, being continually redefined on the basis of the choices being made and the relations contracted with other features, i.e. they form a SYSTEM. *A system is, thus, a metafunctionally regulated grouping of calibrated features, capable of specifying the variant values and shapes of a specific unit through the systemic path of the choices and their realizational statements.* Thus, together with the range of choices and the principles underlying their calibration, a system functions as a device for specifying the meaning-making resources of a unit: the description of language is both systemic and functional; its aim is to describe language as a MEANING POTENTIAL rather than as a set of actual structures.

Taking a unit as the POINT OF ORIGIN, each metafunctionally regulated system describes that unit in terms of its meaning potential; the choices in the system are neither items nor structures, but simply a systemized set of opposing features which relate to each other systemically and whose reactance is made manifest in the syntagms created by the realization statements (discussion in section 5.4). The following section will attempt to demonstrate how choice, system and realization work together to describe language as meaning potential.

5.4   How choice works in SFL

In sections 5.3.2 and 5.3.3, I have attempted to build a case for the validity of conceptualizing language as a social semiotic system by first tracing the roots of the conception to certain inherent properties of the sign which in turn indicate what an explanatory and explicit description of language as a sign system demands. To describe explicitly the means whereby the signified 'acquires' its meaning potential, it became necessary to take into account 'the interplay of signs', i.e. the 'morphology of meaning' (Saussure 2006): this, in terms of SFL, is lexicogrammatical relations. There is a very close relationship between lexicogrammar and language use: reciting a column of the dictionary gets one nowhere in a meaning exchange, and the grammatical structures as configurations of elements are unknowable without lexical flesh.[5] No explanatory and systemic account of language use can be provided without taking into account the regulation of *parole* by the context of culture and situation where the origins of metafunctions lie and where speakers find themselves under pressure to 'voice their meanings', one crucial constitutive step of which is to use the systems of wording (Halliday and Hasan 1985). With the introduction of the stratum of context into the theory, Sections 5.2 and 5.3 have jointly constructed an outline of some aspects of the theoretical infrastructure – stratification, unit, realization, system – which supports the description of language as a resource for meaning exchange.

Choice, a theoretically motivated category in SFL, is essential to the systemic description of language as a meaning potential (Section 5.3.5): in this environment it functions as a fine-tuned activator of systemic paths and their realizations. Choosing a feature, here, is equal to identifying how the selection of one feature makes a difference to the meaning-making resources of the unit under description; at the same time it enables an explicit indication of the paradigm of the structural shapes potentially available to that unit, foregrounding in this process the details of the relationships among the members of the paradigm. I believe the best way of demonstrating these achievements is to model the working of choice in the description of some specific unit by presenting a case study. The unit of language I want to use for the purpose is MESSAGE at the semantic stratum (see Figure 5.4), and the specific subclass of *message* under description will be QUESTION, not to be confused with INTERROGATIVE: the default lexicogrammatical realization of a *question* may be as interrogative but, as will be seen, neither are all *questions* interrogative, nor are all interrogatives *questions*.[6]

5.4.1 Leading up to questions: a systemic description of message

Speakers normally act as if meanings are 'natural'; one 'instinctively' knows what to mean. But the SF linguist must ask, with Labov (1972): *Why does anyone say anything?* One simple answer is: *mostly because the speaker believes the occasion of talk demands it.* This, in keeping with the claims in section 5.3, ascribes the responsibility of the activation of *parole* to the context of situation, and by the same token it is no longer a semiotic choice; it becomes a cultural one, 'prompted' by what is going on in the social context. This need not necessarily stop the choice from being systemic, but I will not offer an account of its activation in terms of the 'systemic features of context': system networks of context do exist but they are in a nascent stage, despite efforts by some scholars (e.g. Hasan 1999, 2009e; Bowcher 2007; Butt 2004a; Matthiessen 2012).[7] So I will just assume that the asking of a question is taken by the interactants as a contextually relevant act.

Figure 5.5: Message as point of origin for a primary and simple semantic system

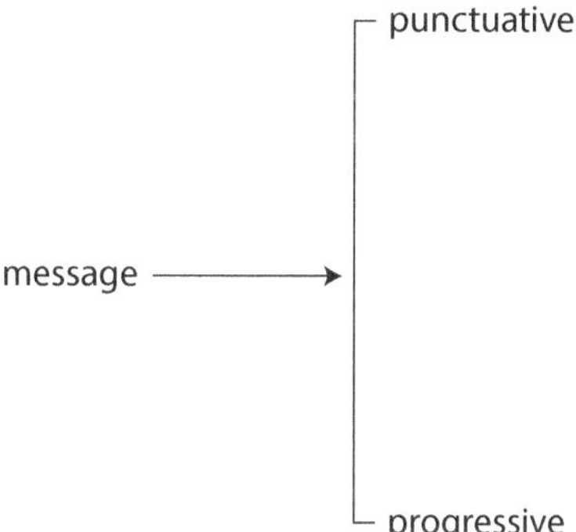

5.4.2 The first step in describing how units enact relations

With that assumption I will begin from the earliest point in the history of the semantic unit *question*. It is a subclass of the unit *message*. So *message* is the point of origin for the first systemic choice (see Figure 5.5). As the first system following the point of origin, it is by definition a PRIMARY SYSTEM. It also happens to be SIMPLE: its features bear the single relation of mutual exclusion. Speaking technically, system is primary, simple and DEPENDENT; it should be read as: **IF** the given environment is *message* **THEN EITHER** the choice of the feature PUNCTUATIVE **OR** of PROGRESSIVE applies.

Dependency is an inherent condition of every system: the existence of the system is predicated by choice being made available under some *condition*: nothing can be a system unless the features that form the system are mutually exclusive; no matter how many features there may be, each will bear the either/or relation to the others. It is graphically indicated as a right-facing open square bracket (see Figure 5.5).

The feature *punctuative* is a resource for a message enabling the 'management of ongoing interaction', e.g. 'hullo', 'goodbye', 'sorry!', 'pardon', 'you know what?', 'wow!', 'how d'you do?', 'hey, you there!', and so on. Normally occurring in the spoken mode, it is typically realized as a minor clause: the crucial requirement is that grammatically the clause is non-productive; it does not form structural paradigms. By contrast, the default realization of the feature *progressive* is a major clause: essential for continued interaction, it participates in the performance of every kind of social practice that is not performed by the *punctuative message*. Example (1) (from Hasan 2009a) presents an extract from a naturally occurring dialogue between three-year-old Karen and her mother.

KAREN : (25) how did you get that? …
MOTHER : (26) mm?
KAREN: (27) how did you get that? (28) you didn't get out of [?]
MOTHER : (29) I walked over (30) and got it (31) didn't you see me?
KAREN : (32) nup
MOTHER : (33) you must be blind

Here only message (26) is *punctuative* (a variety of 'sorry/pardon'). The remainder are all *progressive*.

5.4.3 From system to system network: Increasing descriptive delicacy

A system represents an analyst's hypothesis about the properties of the unit under description. To be valid, the hypothesized description requires the 'renewal of connection' with actual instances of the unit: it must meet the requirements of the realization statements attached to the choices along all the systemic paths in the system. A system may be maximally valid without being descriptively efficient. A trivial example of this is the primary system in Figure 5.5: implicit in it is the eminently verifiable hypothesis that every English *message* is either *punctuative* or *progressive*. But because the sub-categories of messages are defined only in terms of one single relation in a primary system, its descriptive efficiency is low: it will fail to indicate most of the unit's resources for meaning. Even if there had been a bigger range of choices in the dependent primary system, for obvious reasons the description could not improve in efficiency. What is needed is both the density of choices as well as the validity of hypotheses to ensure descriptive efficiency: the greater the depth of the valid systemization of choice, the more detailed the analysis of the unit.

It is this fact that provides the impetus for developing an individual system into a SYSTEM NETWORK (sometimes called simply 'system' or 'network') together with testable realization statements. After the primary system, the formation of a system network depends on a systemic choice itself 'turning into' an ENTRY CONDITION, that is to say, a choice becomes the environment for further systemically related feature(s) to choose from: simplifying, a choice made may act as the gateway to choice(s) to be made. Technically known as SECONDARY SYSTEM(s) each of these systems provides more distinctive details about the unit under description, thus adding to the depth of the unit's description. The set of choices related to each other in this way is known as a SYSTEMIC PATH, and the set of choices made along that path is called a SELECTION EXPRESSION. Each selection expression provides a systemic description of a subclass of the unit under description. System networks can thus be measured for their depth of detail, the technical term for which is DELICACY. The simple primary system yields the 'least delicate' description; the 'most delicate' point of description is reached at the last choice of a systemic path, when the description cannot proceed any further.[8]

5.4.4 Choice as entry condition to simultaneous systems

As noted above (section 5.4.1), access to a dependent system means that one and only one choice must be made from that system. Sometimes the same choice allows entry simultaneously into more than one system. Such systems, however many there may be, are known as SIMULTANEOUS (or CONCURRENT) SYSTEMS. This happens in Figure 5.6, where, using the feature *progressive* as a simple entry condition, the beginnings of a polysystemic description of *progressive message* is presented. Through the discussion of Figure 5.6, I hope to introduce other types of systemic relations while drawing closer to the category of *message* called *question*.

The biggest left-facing open brace in Figure 5.6 indicates the simultaneity of the four vectors which identify the metafunctional regulation

Figure 5.6: Choice as entry condition: simultaneous system

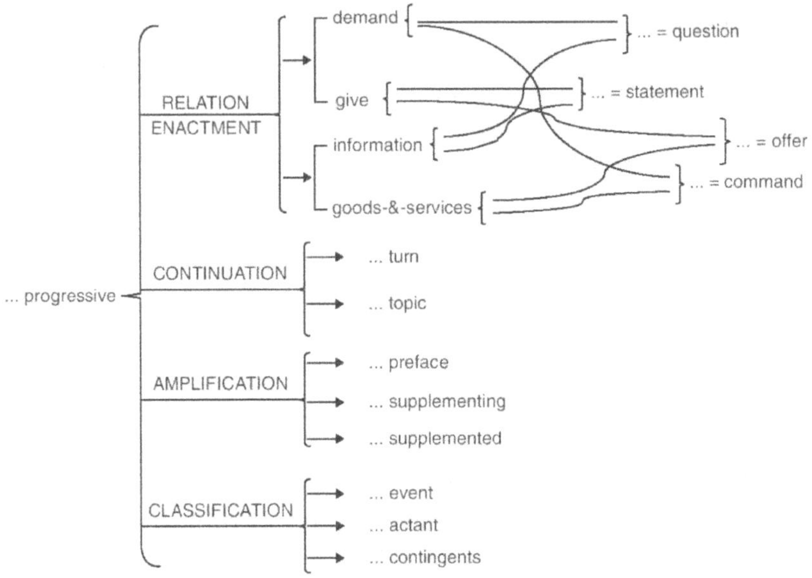

RELATION ENACTMENT

- demand { ... = question
- give { ... = statement
- information { ... = offer
- goods-&-services { ... = command

CONTINUATION

- ... turn
- ... topic

... progressive

AMPLIFICATION

- ... preface
- ... supplementing
- ... supplemented

CLASSIFICATION

- ... event
- ... actant
- ... contingents

of the systems, with the implication that choices from each vector will apply simultaneously to any *message* with the feature *progressive*. The first, RELATION ENACTMENT, indicates interpersonal regulation;[9] the second, CONTINUATION, textual; the third, AMPLIFICATION, logical; and the last, CLASSIFICATION, experiential. The number of systems in each vector is not identical, but each leads to simultaneous systems, which is to say that the choice *progressive* has allowed access to all four vectors and to the simultaneous systems pertaining to each. The network will develop by choosing from these systems.

The simultaneous systems are a collection of distinct dependent systems, all made available by the same entry. So when it comes to making choices from those individual systems, the same principle applies: one feature may be chosen in each such system; but because there are two or more such systems simultaneously dependent on the same choice, this logically results in a principle for accessing choices known as a **BOTH–AND** choice: **BOTH** one choice from this system **AND** one from the other simultaneous one(s). To illustrate, in Figure 5.6 the choice *progressive* allows access **both** into the system with the features *give*-or-*demand*, **and** into the system *information*-or-*goods-&- services*. It is possible, though not required, that each feature of the first system is co-selected with each feature of the next one(s) – in fact this is what happens in Figure 5.6) – this multiplies the number of features that become part of the descriptive detail. It follows that two or more simultaneous systems, even if each is simple, consisting of only two choices, will potentially provide more descriptive detail together than a single dependent system could have. So entry to simultaneous systems can be viewed as another way of adding to the degree of delicacy in description. In general terms, it may be concluded that relations which a choice enters into make some significant difference to the description of the unit, whether this is due to choices functioning as some kind of entry condition or to requiring a particular pattern of choice access. For this reason it will be important to look into the meaning of these relations as much as into the realizational implications of the choice of particular features.

Simultaneous systems typically form part of a system network; and, in fact, each vector shown in Figure 5.6 has been developed into a system network (Hasan 1983), though in this chapter, interest is limited to the two simultaneous systems introduced by the relation enactment vector because it is here that the category of message called *question* is located; besides, it can be used to illustrate three different kinds of complex entry condition.

5.4.5 Complex entry conditions: Conjunct entry

The most frequent entry type is a SIMPLE ENTRY CONDITION. In this kind of entry the *choice of just one single feature* functions as the condition for entry into either one single dependent system or into some simultaneous systems. Thus in Figure 5.6, a single feature *progressive* allows access to all four metafunctionally regulated vectors and therefore to the systems governed by each vector. In a COMPLEX ENTRY CONDITION, *more than one choice* stands in some specific relation in order to enter (a) subsequent system(s) whether single or simultaneous. The development of the *relation enactment* systems in Figure 5.6 helps illustrate one particular type of complex entry condition.

Note that in Figure 5.6, each choice in one system combines with each choice from the other so that in each case two distinct choices from two distinct systems combine validly (see section 5.4.4): this conjunction is a condition for access to some choice(s) from a subsequent system. When two or more choices from two or more systems combine to create the environment to access subsequent systemic choice(s), this is called a CONJUNCT ENTRY CONDITION. For obvious reasons this complex entry condition is available only in the environment of simultaneous systems. The combination of two choices is by far the most common but in principle any number of choices can combine to function as a conjunct entry condition. As Figure 5.6 shows, small braces play an important part in signalling these types of entry: the left-facing small open braces show a conjunction of lines which connect with the two (or more) features forming the conjunct entry condition; conversely, where the same feature enters into two distinct entries, this multiplicity is indicated by the lines in the right-facing small open braces which are placed close to the feature in question. So *demand* combines with *information* to form one conjunct entry condition that gives access to the system of choices for asking *questions*; and *demand* also combines with *goods-&-services* to form another conjunct entry condition which gives access to the system of choices relevant to issuing *commands*.

Altogether four conjunct entry conditions have been created by the combination of choices in the simultaneous systems in *relation enactment*, each providing entry to a more delicate system for some category of *message*, as the label for each shows. The meaning of these labels may not necessarily correspond with their common usage. For example, an *offer* in terms of analysis includes 'promise', which in terms of the description is simply a *distant offer*, as opposed to *invite*, which is *immediate*, as opposed to *urge* which is *insistent*:[10] the entire system network will be predicated on the conjunction of the feature *give* and *goods-&-services*, which is the point of any kind of *offer*. Table 5.1 presents each of the categories identified in Figure 5.6 as they occurred naturally in a dialogue between a mother and her daughter.

The systemic paths pertaining to each of the utterances in Table 5.1 are stated in the first column of the table: they await entry into the more delicate system networks (e.g. that shown in Figure 5.7). Each category of these *messages* will be realized as a major clause; their DEFAULT and CONDITIONED realizations can be stated by reference to the lexicogrammatical

Table 5.1: Default function of conjunct choices: Relation enactment

E1 choice; E2 choice	*Function of message*	*Examples of functions*
demand; information	Question	(i) What's the matter Kristy?
give; information	Statement	(ii) I can't get this on
demand; goods/services	Command	(iii) OK bring it over here
give; goods/services	Offer	(iv) and I'll help you

choices from the system of MOOD, which, like *relation enactment*, is an interpersonally regulated system.[11]

Before leaving this discussion, it is clear that systemic descriptions demand space and time. The graphic representation serves the purpose of placing the analyst's hypotheses about the unit's description up front; the realization statements are condensed indicators of what needs to be said about the function and form (i.e. shape) of the signs under description: they do not constitute description in detail. Chapters of the present kind can hardly accommodate a delicate description of even one familiar category such as *question*. So while the system networks I present (though far from being exhaustive) hint at the resources of English for meaning exchange, not much detail of these resources can be provided here. Often the presence of systems can only be indicated by dots. For example in Figures 5.6 and 5.7, the dots indicate the locations where some system networks and/or their details have remained undisplayed.

Figure 5.7: Choice in asking questions: A simplified system network

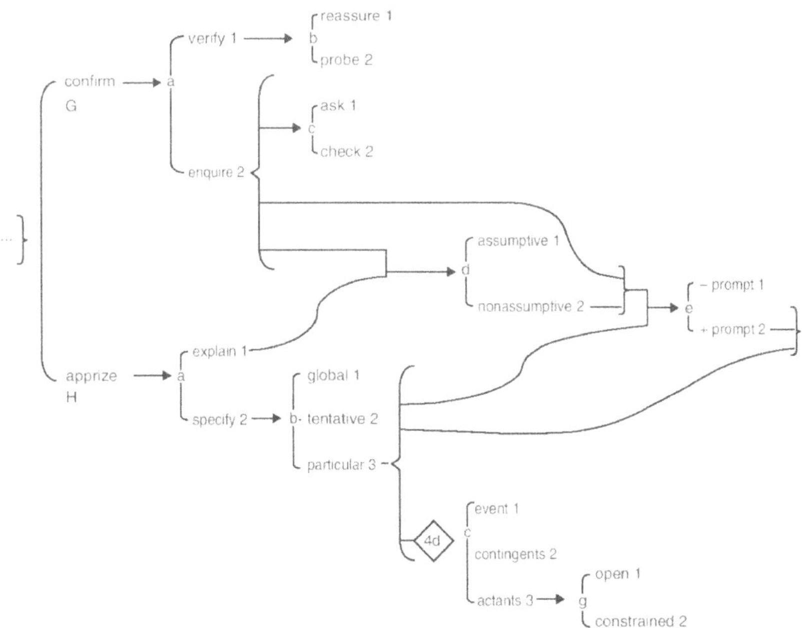

5.4.6 Systemic choices for asking questions with complex entries

Access to the system network in Figure 5.7 is provided by the conjunction of **both** *demand* **and** *information*. As pointed out above this figure represents the semantic choices designed to describe the sub-category of message *question* up to a certain degree of delicacy.[12]

The first system accessed here is a single and simple dependent system with the options CONFIRM and APPRIZE. For ease of reference, the latter have been labelled as G and H, respectively: these letters refer to two choices which form the foundation of the entire remaining set of subsequent systemic choices in the question system network; ultimately everything in this network depends on **either** *confirm* **or** *apprize*. The system and choices in each part, G-systems or H-systems, have been identified by numbers starting at 1 for each individual system in each part. Lower-case letters starting with a̱ in each part identify the individual system to which those numbers pertain. Thus in G-systems, the letter a̱ on the first arrow following the feature *confirm* and the numbers in the system dependent on it must be read as: 'the feature *confirm* is the entry condition for the individual dependent system a̱ consisting of a choice between feature a̱1 *verify* and feature a̱2 *enquire*'. This address of systemic choices has proved unambiguous; thus Ga2:c1 says 'in G-systems the features *enquire: ask*'.

Table 5.2: The common systemic history of G-/H-systems

Semantic feature	↘ LG feature	↘ LG structure
message	↘ go-to clause	↘ constituents group/phrase
progressive	↘ major	↘ insert Predicator → Pred
demand; information	↘ go-to MOOD	↘ insert Mood → Mood• Pred
G – confirm	↘ indicative	↘ expand Mood → S • F • Pred
H – apprize	↘ interrogative:	↘ insert interrogative marker
	non-polar	preselect wh-/ S • F • Pred

LEGEND:
↘ = realization statement
→ = resulting structural description
• = order in sequence not specified
/ = conflate per instruction
LG = lexicogrammatical

The presence of the left-facing small open brace initiating Figure 5.7 indicates that the systemic path for *confirm* and *apprize* is identical until the selection of these features: when those features are selected the systemic paths of the two are set on different courses. Column 1 (Table 5.1) showed their common history. Table 5.2 offers brief realization statements attached to each feature in the systemic path up to the point where their common history diverges, i.e. at *confirm* vs. *apprize*.

To say that at *confirm* vs. *apprize* systems diverge is to say that up to this point they had a common systemic path (as shown in column 1 of Table 5.1); from this point onwards the actual features in their selection expressions will differ from each other. Even if they come together at points, their realizational statements will never be the same after a divergence. The discriminatory function of either/or ensures this. The pre-entry systemic history, i.e. selection of features and their realizational statements, becomes part of the history of the newly chosen feature, but each subsequent choice will change that history. If I understand correctly this is what Mann (1985) was referring to when he introduced the concept of REALIZATIONAL INHERITANCE (RI); these are choices associated with a systemic path up to some particular point identified by reference to 'choosing points'. Nothing in it can be deleted, contradicted or altered (except in degrees of delicacy) at the integration of the new choices joining that systemic path. The principle is clearly necessary to ensure the validity of description.

By these devices, a series of what Saussure (2006) called 'templates' would be created where each member of the paradigm would differ from the others, often in terms of one single systemic choice. But if so, Saussure's 'template' cannot be equated with an 'orderly ordered syntactic structure'.[13] He appears to have differentiated rigorously between templates and structures as they occur in the syntagm of some instance of *parole*. Templates have a direct relation to the 'morphology of meaning', and they seem to be built on a stable relation between meaning and its realizational devices. A template thus has greater stability in the bond between meaning and wording. To my mind it is very much like a feature in a semantic system network and its realization in terms of lower strata, particularly lexicogrammar.

If I am correct, then what Saussure is asking linguistics is to provide reliable information about the entire set of templates pertaining to some linguistic sign system whose instantiations are encountered in *parole*, where they occur with some combinations and variations as the range of actual structures. As pointed out, SFL accords equal status to every metafunction: the implication is that the description of units cannot be deemed complete unless the contribution of each metafunction to the meaning-making resources of a unit has been sufficiently described. Halliday's arguments (e.g. 1979) suggest that templates must be metafunctionally distinct; and they must be calibrated to show how language enacts relations, construes experience, maintains relevance, and observes semiotic logic, all of this simultaneously in the same utterance(s). This is what the volumes of *Introduction to Functional Grammar* (e.g. Halliday 1994) have been attempting to model. With these general remarks, I turn to some choices for asking questions in English.

5.4.7   Systemic choices for asking questions, and their realizations

The G-systems describe the sub-category popularly known as 'yes/no questions' while the H-systems describe 'wh-questions'. This is already an indication of the distinct paths to be followed by the systems dependent on *confirm* as opposed to *apprize*. Table 5.2 does not provide specific structural shapes for any choice: although *confirm* or *apprize* as sub-categories are clearly more delicate than *progressive* or *punctuative*, their description is still at an initial stage; and the ordering of structure at an early point could pose problems when that degree of delicacy is reached where 'Who did that?' and 'What were you eating?' are differentiated. They are both wh-questions, but only the structure of the second allows the canonical 'interrogative' ordering of elements; but for the presence of *who* as Subject, the structure of the message 'Who did that?' resembles a declarative order. Note that both sub-categories of question (G-systems or H-systems) carry information about their QUERY POINT; this provides a measure for recognizing an 'adequate answer'.

The choice of the feature *confirm* (Figure 5.7) acts as a simple entry condition to a single dependent system with the choice VERIFY or ENQUIRE. The realizational inheritance of the choice *verify* will include everything up to the point of origin: this follows from the discussion of RI and the information supplied in Table 5.2. The realization of the choice *verify* would add the following details to that realizational inheritance: the clause realizing this choice would select the lexicogrammatical choice [DECLARATIVE : TAGGED]; and the instruction to order elements S • F • Pred (Table 5.2) as S^F^Pred … ^F^S. The choice of *verify* gives access to the dependent system of options, either REASSURE or PROBE. The realization statements of these choices will specify more delicate information about the realizing clause: the choice *reassure* is an instruction to select the feature [REVERSED polarity] in Tag, whereas for *probe* the lexicogrammatical feature [CONSTANT polarity] must be selected in Tag. The polarity of a 'reversed tag' reverses the polarity in the clause: if the clause is positive, the tag must be negative and vice versa. With 'constant tag', the polarity of the tag is the same as that in the clause. The difference between these two categories of question is fairly delicate: a message with the choice *reassure* seeks reassurance that the speaker's voiced understanding of some event is shared by the addressee: the unmarked expectation is that the polarity in the answering clause would agree with the polarity of the realizing clause. By contrast, a message with the choice *probe* seeks to find out whether something is the case or not: the unmarked expectation is that the polarity of the answer would agree with that in the tag.[14]

The choice *enquire*, which contrasts with *verify*, is relevant to three systemic entries: two of these systems are simultaneous. System c̲ offers a choice of either ASK or CHECK: the choice *ask* is realized as [INTERROGATIVE: POLAR], e.g. 'Are you leaving?' or 'Has he arrived?', with obvious consequences for instructions about the formation of their lexicogrammatical structure. The choice of *check* is realized as [declarative: NONTAGGED], on Tone 2: the former are 'straightforward yes/no questions', whereas the latter are 'yes/no questions with an attitude'. For example, saying 'You are leaving?' on Tone 2 would normally be interpreted as asking for a 'yes/no' response while showing surprise, concern or some other reaction (e.g. 'Let me get your coat for you!'). The other simultaneous system to which *enquire* gives access consists in the choice of either ASSUMPTIVE or NONASSUMPTIVE. Here the latter choice is clearly implicated in a complex entry, as indicated by the lines and brackets in its environment. This is discussed in Section 5.4.8 together with another complex entry. First, a word about H-systems, which are implicated in both cases of complex entries.

The choice of the feature *apprize* allows choice from the system: either EXPLAIN or SPECIFY. The realization of both these features will be through the selection of the lexicogrammatical features [interrogative: non-polar].[15] With *explain*, it also carries the instruction 'wh-conflates with Adjunct, realized as a causal adverb': the most frequent item to actualize this instruction would be 'why', less likely 'what for', and very much less likely 'for what reason'. Two examples: 'Why does Nana like that chair?' and 'Why does it fall down?'. The choice *specify* questions some details of event structure: so the more delicate choices it enables access to are GLOBAL, TENTATIVE, PARTICULAR. The choice *global* enquires about the overall goings-on, as in 'What's going on?' or 'What happened?'; the *tentative* leaves the state of affairs unclear, naming just one component of it, as, for example 'What about cat?'; and with the choice *particular* the message raises the question about some particular aspect of the state of affairs. Hence the set of choices in c̱ EVENTS or CONTINGENTS or ACTANTS. One might ask, for example, 'What were they doing?' or 'What happened then?' (c̱1 *event*); or 'Where do you do your shopping?' or 'When did you see him last?' (c̱2 *contingents*); or 'Who told you that?', 'What were you reading?' (c̱3 *actants*). As is obvious from the examples, the realization of all these choices will call for the lexicogrammatical features [interrogative: non-polar], and their transmutation into syntagms will call for preselections and conflation of specific classes of groups with the wh-. As Figure 5.7 shows, *particular* is the entry condition to two other choices. These will be discussed below with the complex entry conditions.

5.4.8   Do divergent systemic paths rejoin? On disjunct entries

Complex entries always implicate more than one choice, each pertaining to two distinct systems. Thus in a conjunct entry condition, two or more choices, each from distinct simultaneous systems, together form the environment for access to a more delicate system of choices (see Section 5.4.5). There is, however, a complex entry condition where: (a) two or more choices function as the entry point to a more delicate system; and (b) both access the same system, but; (c) unlike choices forming a conjunct entry, they do not combine to achieve this end; they access the more delicate choice separately; and (d) the choices so selected become part of separate systemic paths. This kind of separate access to the same system by two or more options from distinct systems is called DISJUNCT ENTRY CONDITION. It is illustrated in Figure 5.7, and the choices implicated in that entry are *enquire* in G and *explain* in H. The system to which both get access is *assumptive* or *nonassumptive* (see Section 5.4.7). It is as if, their paths having diverged, they are brought back into contact through their participation in accessing the same system. However, due to the previous divergence they cannot combine, each gaining access to the same system of choices *mutually exclusively*. The latter system thus represents choices that the two systemic paths have in common despite belonging to different subcategories of *question*. Here are the details of this entry.

As the left-facing open brace in G-systems (Figure 5.7) shows, the choice *enquire* allows entry into two simultaneous systems: c̱ *ask* vs. *check* and ḏ *assumptive* vs. *nonassumptive*. The former has already been described (see Section 5.4.6 and Table 5.3). With the choice *assumptive* the realizing major clause must have negative polarity, as in 'Didn't you see me?'

{= *ask; assumptive*} or 'You didn't see me?' {= *check; assumptive*}; asking such questions implies that the speaker assumes the addressee should in all reason respond 'Yes, I saw you' (Hasan 2009a). By contrast, the feature *nonassumptive* is realized as a major clause with positive polarity, as in 'Did you see me?' or 'You saw me?' This description of *assumptive* vs. *nonassumptive* stands also when the system is accessed by the choice *explain*, as evident from a comparison of 'Why don't you love Rosemary?' with 'Why do you love Rosemary?' It is part of the same story that, due to their distinct RIs, the realizing clause for *enquire* will interrogate with *ask* and declarative +Tone 2 with *check*, while for *explain*, it will be a non-polar interrogative preselecting *why* as detailed above (see Section 5.4.7). However, their systemic paths remain distinct, as evident from Table 5.4.

There are other ways of graphically representing these disjunct choices: the system of choice *assumptive/nonassumptive* could have been inserted twice, once as part of G-systems, allowed entry by the choice *continue*, and then again as a dependent system entered by *explain* in H-systems. In that case the G-/H- systems would never have been shown to be in contact, and in practical terms there would have been fewer lines in the network: the formal information would be easy to read. However, the point of the

Table 5.3: Selection expressions and realization of some choices

Assume for every systemic path as given message: progressive: demand; information
↘ clause: major → S • F • Pred

Selection expressions	LG features	LG structures	Examples
G:			
confirm: verify: reassure	declarative: tagged: reversed	S^F pos^P...F neg^S OR	You like sugar, don't you?
		S^F neg^P...F pos^S	You don't like sugar, do you?
confirm: verify: probe	declarative: tagged: constant	S^F pos^P...F pos^S	You like sugar, do you?
		S^F neg^P...F neg^S	You don't like sugar, don't you?
confirm: enquire: ask	interrogative: polar	F^S^P	Do you like sugar?
confirm: enquire: check	declarative: untagged Tone 2	S^F^P	You like sugar?
H:			
apprize: explain	interrogative: non-polar	Wh-/Adj^F^S^P (wh- preselects why as Adj)	Why do you like sugar?
apprize: specify: particular...event	interrogative: non-polar	Wh-/C^F^S^P (wh- preselects what as C)	What did you cook for dinner?
apprize: specify: partic...contingnt	interrogative: non-polar	Wh-/Adj^F^S^P (wh- preselects where as Ad)	Where did he go?
apprize: specify: partic...actants	interrogative: non-polar	Wh-/S^F^P (wh- preselects who as S)	Who was calling?

* When two systematically differing realizations are possible, as here, there is a strong case for further research on what principle underlies this regularity; it is likely that there is a systemic meaning distinction which can be made.

** This is normal usage in some varieties of Australian English.

information would have been lost, namely that two major sub-categories of *question* differ from each other but they are also similar by sharing the same semantic options despite belonging to distinct systemic paths. This 'coming into contact' of G-/H-systems is not accidental: their early history is the same, and they come into contact again via a second disjunct entry condition, accessed either by the choice of {enquire; nonassumptive} in G-system or by {specify: particular} in H-system; the system of choices they enter separately is e̲, –prompt or +prompt. But a price has to be paid for the insistence on maintaining both formal and functional information: this explains the complexity in access to either *–prompt* or *+prompt*.

Basically two facts are important here: (a) the choice of *–prompt* or *+prompt* may be accessed either from the feature *nonassumptive* in G-system or from *particular* in H-system; (b) Table 5.4 shows clearly that *nonassumptive* enters into three distinct systemic paths: two pertain to G-systems {*enquire: ask; nonassumptive*} or {*enquire: check; nonassumptive*}; the third pertains to H-systems {*explain: nonassumptive*}. The question now is whether the choice of either *–prompt* or *+prompt* is available to all three paths. It turns out the answer is negative: the path with {*explain: nonassumptive*} cannot enter the choice of either *–prompt* or *+prompt*. The conjunction of *enquire* and *nonassumptive* in G-systems represents these facts: it says '**if** the path has {enquire: nonassumptive} **then** it has access to either the choice *–prompt* or *+prompt*. But the entry into the latter system is disjunct: the other path of entry is from *particular*, which, as is the case with disjunct entry conditions, separately chooses either *–prompt* or

Table 5.4: Disjunct entries to the same system by choices in distinct systems

Assume as given for every systemic path message: progressive: information ↘ clause major → S • F • Pred

Selection expressions	LG features	LG structures	Examples
confirm: enquire: ask; assumptive	interrogative: negative	F neg^S^P	Didn't you see me?
confirm: enquire: check; assumptive	declarative: negative: +Tone 2	S^F neg^P	You didn't see me?
confirm: enquire: ask; nonassumptive	interrogative: positive	F pos^S^P	Did you see me?
confirm: enquire: check; nonassumptive	declarative: positive: +Tone 2	S^F pos^P	You saw me?
apprize: explain: assumptive	wh-/ interrogative: neg	wh-/Adj^F neg^S^P preselects *why*	Why didn't you call?
apprize: explain: nonassumptive	wh-/ interrogative: pos	wh-/Adj^F pos^S^P preselects *why*	Why did you call?

+prompt. Thus the system notations explicitly indicate the exclusion of {*explain: nonassumptive*} from the latter choice.

What choices are these, and what difference do they make to a *question*? Table 5.5 shows the paths of choice and their lexicogrammatical realizations. An example of a G message with *+prompt* would be 'Did granny say that or daddy?' As a message with the choice *verify* in its systemic history, it ought to be answerable as yes/no, but quite clearly this is not likely with a *+prompt question*: the choice +prompt calls for a response which to be adequate needs to provide a specific piece of information: either granny said that or daddy did. The same applies, *mutatis mutandis*, to the H message. An example would be 'What are you eating, an apple?': here the *adequate* answer is 'yes/no'. The H systemic path has an additional systemic choice: it may have a *simple* or *alternative* prompt as in 'Who's cooking dinner, you or me?' Here, unlike the last example, yes/no would not be an *adequate* answer; it will have to be either 'you' or 'me'. Now, it is worth noting here that there do not appear to be any English *messages* such as: 'Why did he stay home, because ill?' In other words, the exclusion of {*explain: nonassumptive*} from access to choice from *–prompt* or *+prompt* appears to be validated. Of course, in all these cases other kinds of responses are possible, but they carry their own 'semantics', which is not part of the present story. Table 5.5 displays the relevant parts of the systemic paths and their lexicogrammatical realizations.

5.5 Conclusion

In this chapter I set out to establish that choice is a theoretically motivated term in SFL. To this end, I substantiated SFL's concept of language as a social semiotic functioning as a resource for meaning. Choice with system and realization is the main instrument in achieving the SFL objective of describing language as a meaning potential. My claim is not that such a description of the language has been fully accomplished, simply that the theoretical machinery to achieve this goal is in place. Modern linguistics has in general accepted that a linguistic sign is known by its value, and that value is the artefact of the relations in which signs participate. The 'interplay of signs' is, thus, one of the most important areas to explore in understanding language as a meaning potential: this is basically what I hope choice, system and realization have demonstrated in Section 5.4 by working with the features pertaining to the unit of *message*. But message is not unique; each unit on the inner strata of language, especially on the

Table 5.5: A disjunct entry condition with a difference

Relevant selection expressions	Realizing features	Examples
confirm: enquire: ask; nonassumptive: –prompt	interrogative: positive	Did granny say that?
confirm: enquire: check; nonassumptive: –prompt	declarative: positive + Tone 2	Granny said that?
confirm: enquire: ask; nonassumptive: +prompt	clause complex: 1 \interrogative: positive +2 \ elliptical except for 1 element	Did granny say that or daddy?
confirm: enquire: check; nonassumptive: +prompt	clause complex as above but 1\ declarative +Tone 2	Granny said that or Mum?
. . . specify: particular: –prompt . . .	wh-/interrogative	What's she doing?
. . . specify: particular: +prompt: simple; event	clause complex: 1\wh-preselects *what*: interrogative +2 "elliptical except for Pro (main verb)	What's she doing, singing?
. . . specify: particular: +prompt: simple; contingent		When's Dad coming, tonight?
. . . specify: particular: +prompt: simple; actant	clause comp: 1\wh-preselects *where/when*: interrogative +2 "elliptical except for Adjunct (phrase)	What're you eating, an apple?
. . . specify: particular: +prompt: alternative; event	clause comp: 1 \ wh-preselects *who/what*: interrogative +2 "elliptical except for S/C (nominal)	What's she doing, sleeping or reading?
. . . specify: particular: +prompt: alternative; contingent	clause complex: 1 \ wh-preselects *what*: interrogative +2 "elliptical except for Pro (verbl grp complex)	When's Dad back, tonight or tomorrow?
. . . specify: particular: +prompt: alternative; actant	clause complex: 1 \ wh-preselects *where*: interrogative +2 "elliptical except for Adjunct (phrase complex)	Who's cooking dinner, you or me
	clause comp: 1 \ wh-preselects *who/what*: interrogative +2 "elliptical except for S or C (nom complex)	

* The total number of choices and the order of choice selection in the systemic paths of G-/H-systems can be easily calculated by putting Tables 5.2–5.5 together; for lack of space the realizational statements are regrettably highly condensed.

** The choice *particular* gives access to choices in system c̲ in H: thus every systemic path with the feature *particular* must be followed up by **either** *event* **or** *contingent* **or** *actant*, as well as **either** *–prompt* **or** *+prompt* is chosen in the systemic path, this must be followed by **either** *simple* **or** *alternative*; the entire range of systemic paths has not been presented here for *–prompt* in H.

higher two strata, is expected to reveal a similar organization. The features combine, diverge, and are affected by their environment: their capacity to create delicate meaning distinctions appears almost infinite. Choice is active in shaping the system by specifying the relations of features; and the validation of the working of both through realization depends on the description's renewal of connection with the speaker's experience of meaning in action.

These theoretical metaphors enable the analyst to enter into an explicit discourse on how language as a semiotic system becomes a powerful resource for the exchange of meanings in social contexts. Each choice of a systemic feature identifies one element of difference/similarity across classes of units by the systemic relations that the feature contracts with other features of the same unit; this interplay of features rather than of items is 'translated' into the unit's value. The unit's value identification is not completed in one step by examining one unit at one stratum: it demands also the realizational journey up and down the strata, across the scale of units at each stratum, until the description comes face to face with 'substance' in the shape of phonological entities, made sens-ible either as sound or graph; ideally, that is when the identification of meaning in language is achieved. Real language is highly complex: to locate it simply in the brain, or simply in a culture, simply in the template or in the syntagms, cannot do justice to it. Nothing shows this more clearly than the working of systemic choices grounded in realization.

Choice as in choice of meaning is not the same thing as choice when used to describe the construal of meaning in language. Systemic choice as used in the description of *any language-internal unit* has no concern with individuality, freedom, will or all those other qualities that dictionaries assign to the act of choice. It is simply a metaphor for linking one feature with other relevant ones whose patterning underlies the linguistic pattern, making explicit how it comes to have the value it has. Choice, system and realization together represent one critical aspect of the semiotic mechanism whereby the linguistic sign comes to have some conventionally shared meaning in speech fellowships. Individuals may and do choose whatever meaning they want to; they may or may not act relevantly, appropriately, conformingly; this may be intentional or not. None of this has anything to do with the inner workings of language. The inner workings of language through choice, system and realization act only in respect to the creation of that conventionally accepted meaning which Saussure called signified, expressed by its signifier.

Notes

1 'SFL' refers here to my interpretation of the systemic functional linguistic theory associated with Halliday's name. There is no assumption that Halliday or colleagues will necessarily be in agreement.

2 In fact stratification is a condition of something being a sign: all signs 'point to content'; all content implies 'content expression'. Unlike some other signs (Hasan 2014) language is a system, and the system has multiple coding, typically displaying four strata.

3 The graphological form 'system' signifies different meanings in SFL; it refers to the system of language as a whole; to the individual choices dependent on a choice, e.g. imperative system; it is used also to refer to a system network, or any component of it. One feature applies to all its uses: it always implicates choice.

4 'Context' is a useful word for showing connections between things; but in SFL it is typically used as an abbreviated form of reference to 'context of culture/ situation'. So it may be helpful to use its near synonym 'environment' in other environments.

5 This is not all that language use does for lexicogrammar. The secret of the evolution of grammar lies in how it is used in the living of life, i.e. the cultural contexts which it helps in bringing about and which in their turn help grammar to grow. This is well captured in Halliday's description of grammar as 'the theory of human experience'.

6 Italics are used for terms at the semantics stratum.

7 It is not clear if Matthiessen's account of context is a systemized description; the visual representation differs, and more importantly, there are no systemic realizational statements invoking categories of meaning associated with specific elements of context.

8 This happens regularly in the description of 'fully grammatical classes of word', e.g. those functioning as DEICTIC in a nominal group. It is also feasible to reach this completion point in describing 'content words', i.e. LEXEMES, but this has rarely been attempted in practice (Hasan 1985b, 1987; Tucker 1998).

9 I have recently adopted 'relation enactment' as the most inclusive term. This term replaces 'rhetorical stance', which had replaced 'role allocation'.

10 Of course many other choices are relevant as well to each such distinction.

11 For some discussion of default and conditioned meaning – wording relations see Hasan (2011: 355ff.).

12 The system of choices presented here is the most recently revised form of earlier versions, some of which have appeared in Hasan (2009a).

13 I am attempting to use this term as in Saussure (2006); and the comments I make at this point are based on my understanding of this fragmented writing.

14   When these semantic networks were first designed (Hasan 1983) the relevance
     of the key system (Halliday and Greaves 2008) to the interpersonal meaning
     of clauses was not as obvious to me. Today, by bringing in this information,
     the meanings of the choices would certainly be increased a good deal.

15   As Table 5.2 shows, it is assumed that the realization of [interrogative: non-
     polar] does not always imply the order F^S.

II
LEXICOGRAMMATICAL DESCRIPTIONS

6 The grammarian's dream: Lexis as most delicate grammar [1987]

1 The lexicogrammatical stratum

It was over two decades ago that Halliday remarked: 'The grammarian's dream is … to turn the whole of linguistic form into grammar, hoping to show that lexis can be defined as "most delicate grammar" ' (Halliday 1961: 267). This chapter briefly explores the reality of that dream by examining two questions: (1) is the project feasible? and (2) what would be the 'implications of 'turning the whole of linguistic form into grammar'? This formulation, by implication, rejects the views that: (a) lexis is not form; and (b) that its relation to semantics is unique.

Drawing upon Halliday (1977) I shall make the following assumptions:

1. Language consists of three strata: semantics, lexicogrammar and phonology.
2. These strata are related by 'realization': meanings are coded as wordings, wordings are coded as sound patterns.
3. Each stratum is describable as a network of options; the description is, therefore, paradigmatic, with environments for options also being defined paradigmatically.
4. The semantic stratum is organized into four meta-functional components: experiential, logical, interpersonal and textual.
5. Each meta-function specifies a particular (set of) option network(s) as its output at the lexicogrammatical stratum.
6. Each act of choice – the selection of each option – contributes to the formation of a structure.
7. A unified structure in its totality is the output of selections from four distinct (sets of) lexicogrammatical networks, specified by the four meta-functions.

8. 'It is the function of the lexicogrammatical stratum to map these structures one on to another so as to form a single integrated structure that represents [the output of] all [meta-functional] components simultaneously' (Halliday 1977).

Assumption (6) is immediately relevant. Grammars have traditionally been concerned with describing the formation of syntagms, using the syntagm itself as the starting point for explaining the syntagm-formation phenomena. The Systemic Functional model has abandoned this approach in favour of one foreshadowed by Saussure (1916), Hjelmslev (1961) and Firth (1951b), where the grammar of a language is viewed as a network of paradigmatic relations. If 'systemic options contribute to the formation of structure', and if the description of structure-formation is what characterizes grammar, then such system networks ARE the grammar. The question of feasibility can, then, be paraphrased as: 'Is it possible to extend a lexicogrammatical network in delicacy so as to turn it into a device for the description and generation of units of form called "lexical item"?' If so, then we shall have shown that lexis is delicate grammar.

This argument shifts attention to mechanisms whereby the paradigm and the syntagm – the option network and the structure – are brought into relation. (Henceforth the 'options' and 'networks' referred to are lexicogrammatical ones, unless otherwise stated.) An option can be viewed as instruction(s) to operate in a certain way; a specific structure is the outcome of following these operations. The technical term for such instructions is 'realization statement'. So realization statement is a mechanism mediating between networks and structures.

Six categories of realization statement will be used here:

1. *insert* structural function x;
2. *conflate* two/more functions into one element;
3. *order* elements a and b (and ... n) *vis-à-vis* each other;
4. *sub-categorize* some function or feature;
5. *pre-select* some feature as a concomitant of some insertion/ subcategorization;
6. *outclassify* some function/feature as incompatible with some insertion/sub-categorization

This view implies that options have consequences: they are justified by what they 'do'. And, since the doing takes cognizance of relations within the language, an option's justification is intra-linguistic. Simplifying greatly, the options for the description and generation of *enquire* and *ask*

Figure 6.1: The entry condition for transitivity

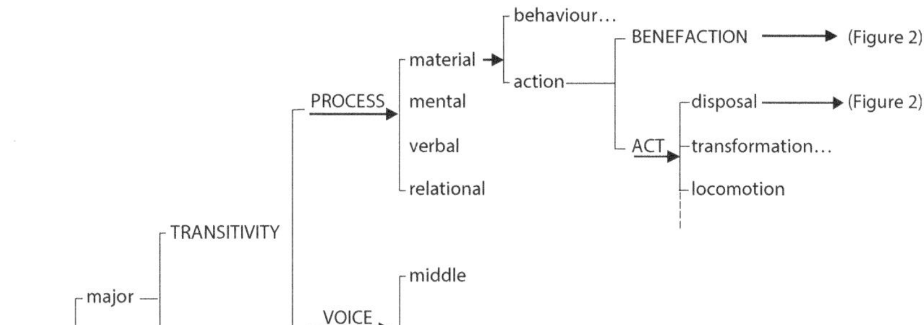

might differ in some respects; if so, the justification would not arise from the two activities differing physically, psychologically or socially, but from the differential lexicogrammatical patternings of the two lexical verbs. So ultimately, a delicate network is an enquiry into what Whorf (1956b) called 'reactance'.

The network examined here is a minute part of the experiential metafunction's output, known as TRANSITIVITY, whose entry condition is [major] clause. (The technical terms in what follows are used as in Halliday (1985); features are shown in square brackets except in the networks themselves.) Figure 6.1 places TRANSITIVITY in relation to other systems applicable to [major] clause. Systems concurrent with TRANSITIVITY, e.g. MOOD, THEME, etc., will be ignored. Within TRANSITIVITY itself, VOICE options will be constantly assumed as [effective:active]. The portion of the network discussed belongs to PROCESS, and it has [disposal] as its entry condition. It is part of the lexico-grammar which constructs the semantic area that can be informally described as 'activities whose completion results in gain/loss of access to things'.

6.2   The lexicogrammar of acquisition: Gather, collect, accumulate

[disposal] entails the options [material:action], which are built into its history, with the implication that the contribution they have made to the formation of the structure, remains a constant wherever [disposal] itself is selected. No part of this contribution can be negated by any instruction attached to [disposal] or options dependent upon it. This principle operates across the system, irrespective of the degree of delicacy. Part of the contribution made by [effective:active] VOICE in conjunction with [material:action] PROCESS is:

A: 1. the functions Process, Medium and Agent are inserted
    2. Process pre-selects Event
    3. Medium and Agent each pre-select Thing
    4. Event is sub-categorized as /material action/

By virtue of having to follow a particular systemic path, the selection of [disposal] inherits the bundle specified in Al–4. This I shall call PI, for 'systematic path inheritance', to keep it distinct from SI (semantic inheritance) (Brachman 1979; Collins and Quillian 1972) and 'conceptual dependency' (Schank 1972, 1975; Schank and Abelson 1977) in the AI literature. PI differs from both, in that it is not item-centred and is more rigorously defined. To see how PI works, imagine a network with options 1 through 7 as in Figure 6.1a. If (a, b) are the contribution of [1], (c, d) of [2], and (e, f) of [3], then the PI for [2] and [3] is (a, b); for [4] and [5], (a, b, c, d), and for [6] and [7] it is (a, b, e, f). Each progressive step in the network specifies both identity and uniqueness between classes of structures. When the network reaches a point where further uniqueness cannot be postulated, this is the logical endpoint; and the total selection expression – i.e. path specification – will, among other things, specify some formal structure(s) known as 'lexical item(s)'. The uniqueness of each lexical item is widely recognized (Berry 1977; Fawcett 1980; Fillmore 1977; Leech 1974; Lyons 1977). In this chapter I begin by concentrating on the identities of, for example, *give, share, collect, lose,* etc., and work toward their uniqueness.

Figure 6.1a: A simple system network

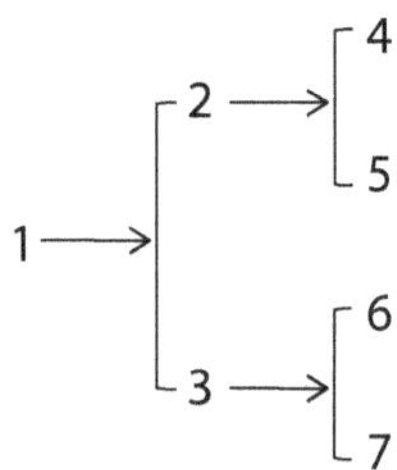

The realization statements attached to [disposal] are:

B: 1. sub-categorize Event as /(material action) of disposal involving change in location of Medium/
   2. sub-categorize Medium Thing as /alienable object/
   3. sub-categorize Agent Thing as /human, person(s) or institutions/

For lack of precise formal information, sub-categorization is expressed informally. It should not be confused with Chomsky's selection restriction rules (1965): the latter operate on items; possess directionality, e.g. assign 'features of the Subject and Object to the Verb'; (1965: 92); and their non-observance leads to linguistic malaise. None of these is necessarily true of sub-categorization. However, if B1–3 are not followed, the semantics of the resultant clause would be distinct from that of a clause whose underlying selection expression contains [disposal]. Consider:

(1a) Susan collected a lot of leaves.
(1b) The roof collected a lot of leaves.
(1c) She collected her thoughts.

(1a) is in keeping with B1–3; most speakers will 'read' it as Susan gaining access to a lot of leaves when the collecting is done; Susan is the 'doer', and the leaves are 'done-to'. In (1b), instruction B3 is not followed; the Agent is not human. Note that the roof is no longer 'doer', but 'location'. (1b) contains a grammatical metaphor (Halliday 1985), whose congruent pair would be *A lot of leaves collected on the roof.* The non-following of B3 will not always produce the semantic value of 'location' for the Agent (compare *These pipes distribute steam into the system* or *Her room carries the most amazing trash*); it will, however, produce a metaphorical effect. In (1c), B2 is not followed: the Medium is not an object, but rather a concept/abstraction. The clause is a good example of Whorf's 'objectification' (1956b), where something itself not an object is treated as such. In English, a standard objectifying device is to use an abstract noun as the Medium of a Process, which normally requires a concrete noun as Medium. But this Medium-like thing, e.g. *her thoughts* in (1c), is not the Medium, as it would fail most of the heuristic tests applicable to that function. (Consider *What is she doing to her thoughts? – Collecting them* and *It is your thoughts you need to collect.*) (1c) is an instance of a complex metaphor, where the entire expression *collect+ … thoughts* must be seen as a unit, since in another

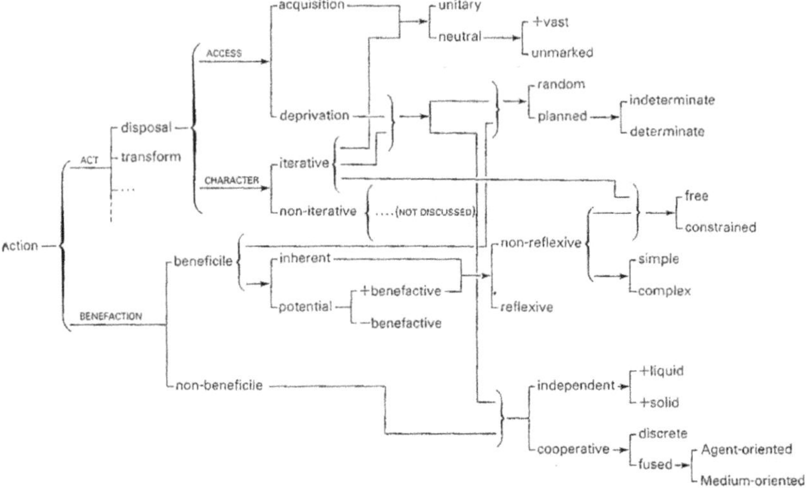

Figure 6.2: The process type [disposal:iterative]

such occurrence *collect* may bear little or no resemblance to *collect* in (1c). (Consider *She collected a good deal of kudos from that*.) This discussion, incidentally, justifies the validity of B1–3.

The system of BENEFACTION applies concurrently with that of ACT and is developed in Figure 6.2, where the systems dependent on [disposal] are also presented. This device will ensure that all systemic options relevant to [disposal] can be seen at one glance. The selection of [disposal] will demand the selection of one path from each of the three systems developed in Figure 6.2; while the systems of ACCESS and CHARACTER are directly dependent on [disposal], that of BENEFACTION is entailed by virtue of the dependence of [disposal] on [action].

ACCESS options are concerned with the result of the activity. The selection of [acquisition] implies the Agent's gain of access to the Medium, unless otherwise indicated. [deprivation] implies the reverse – the Agent loses access to the Medium. Indicating PI within brackets as before, the instructions for these options are:

C: 1. [acquisition]
       a. sub-categorize Event as /(material action of disposal involving change in location of Medium) leading to Agent's gain of access to Medium/

   2. [deprivation]
      a. sub-categorize Event as /(material action of disposal involving change in location of Medium) leading to Agent's loss of access to Medium/

CHARACTER options are concerned with the nature of the activity. The selection of [iterative] implies an inherently repetitive activity, in which the Agent-Medium configuration inherently remains identical; [non-iterative] implies an activity that is not inherently repetitive. The instructions are:

D: 1. [iterative]
      a. sub-categorize Event as /(material action of disposal involving change in location of Medium) inherently repetitive/
      b. sub-categorize Medium Thing as /(alienable object) divisible
   2. [non-iterative]
      a. sub-categorize Event as /(material action of disposal involving change in location) NOT inherently repetitive/

BENEFACTION options are concerned with specifying the benefit of the activity. [beneficile] implies that the activity is capable of permitting the indication of some benefiting party; [non-beneficile] implies that the activity is not capable of permitting such indication. On [beneficile] depend the options [inherent] or [potential]. [inherent] implies that the benefiting party MUST be specified; [potential] that the benefiting party MAY be specified: the resource is there; it may or may not be taken up. [+benefactive] implies that the resource is to be positively deployed, and a benefiting party is to be specified. [–benefactive] implies that the resource has been passed up, and so no benefiting party is to be specified. When the benefiting party is specified – as entailed by the selection of either [inherent] or [+benefactive] – the option between [reflexive] and [non-reflexive] operates. It is concerned with the specification of the benefiting party's identity. [reflexive] implies that the Agent and the benefiting party are one and the same; [non-reflexive], that they are not the same. The selection of the latter permits the selection between [simple] and [complex] – both being concerned with providing further details about the benefiting party. [simple] implies that only one benefiting party is to be specified; [complex], that two discrete benefiting parties are to be specified. The remaining two options – [free] and [constrained] – will be discussed later. Here I provide the instructions attached to the BENEFACTION options presented so far:

E: 1. [non-beneficile]
        a. sub-categorize Event as /(material action) INCAPABLE of requiring function Benefiter/
        b. outclassify function Benefiter

    2. [beneficile]
        a. sub-categorize Event as /(material action) CAPABLE of requiring function Benefiter(s)/

    3. [inherent]
        a. insert function Benefiter-1
        b. sub-categorize Benefiter-1 as Recipient
        c. Benefiter pre-selects nominal group with Thing animate
        d. sub-categorize Event as /(material action) NECESSARILY requiring Benefiter/

    4. [potential]
        a. sub-categorize Event as /(material action) NOT NECESSARILY requiring Benefiter/

    5. [+benefactive]
        a. sub-categorize Event as /(material action) requiring Benefiter/
        b. insert function Benefiter-1
        c. sub-categorize Benefiter-1 as Client
        d. Benefiter pre-selects nominal group with Thing animate

    6. [–benefactive]
        a. sub-categorize Events as /(material action) not needing Benefiter/

    7. [reflexive]
        a. Benefiter pre-selects (nominal group with Thing animate) and co referential with Agent

    8. [non-reflexive]
        a. Benefiter pre-selects (nominal group with Thing animate) NOT co referential with Agent

    9. [simple]
        a. outclassify Benefiter-2

    10. [complex]
        a. insert Benefiter-2
        b. Benefiter-2 pre-selects (nominal group with Thing animate not co referential with Agent)
        c. sub-categorize Benefiter-2 as Ultimate Client

    d. Ultimate Client pre-selects prepositional group with preposition *for*
    e. conflate functions Ultimate Client and Prepositional Complement
    f. order Prepositional Complement to follow *for*

The notion 'benefiting party' or Benefiter is not self-evident. As Halliday (1985: 135) points out, the Benefiter does not necessarily benefit in the everyday sense of the word as shown by *Jocasta gave Claudius a dose of poison*. Again, in *John drove to the office*, from a common-sense point of view, John could be said to benefit from his driving. So it is important to point out that not only is the function Benefiter at the 'receiving end', but also it is recognized only if there is a dissociation between it and the Agent. The limiting case of the Benefiter is with the option [reflexive], where the benefiting party is coreferential with the Agent (see E7a above). But even here the meaning of Agent^Process^Medium is not the same as Agent^Process^Benefiter^ Medium. Consider:

(2a) Susan bought a dress   (Agent^Process^Medium)
(2b) Susan bought herself a dress (Agent^Process^Benefiter^Medium)

Although in the absence of Good Reason, (2a) would be interpreted as Susan buying the dress for herself, the possibility is always open that this may not be the case; with (2b) this indeterminacy does not exist. Compare:

(3) Susan couldn't find a better present for Pam,
    (a) so she bought a dress.
    (b) so she bought herself a dress.

Because Susan's buying a dress does not have to be interpreted as Susan buying it for herself, so (3a) in this context can be 'read' as 'she bought a dress as a present for Pam'. (3b) does not permit this reading and will remain odd unless further appropriate speech work is done. The impossibility of conflating the Agent and Benefiter roles is important, as we shall see later.

The differences between [beneficile:inherent] and [beneficile:potential:+benefactive] are also important. Consider:

(4) I gave John a book. [beneficile:inherent]
(5) I bought John a book. [beneficile:potential:+benefactive]

In (4), the function Benefiter is entailed (E3a and d); in (5) it is simply permitted. *I gave a book* implies an implicit Benefiter (Hasan 1984b, for implied vs. implicit); *I bought a book* does not. This aspect of the meaning of *buy* is captured by assuming that the BENEFACTION options underlying this item are [beneficile:potential]. Note the difference in the Benefiter roles inserted in response to [inherent] (E3b) and [+benefactive] (E5c) respectively. When combined with the option [simple], the Benefiter role for the former is more specifically Recipient, for the latter, Client. If the selection expression contains both the option [non-iterative] and [simple], then under certain specifiable conditions, the Recipient and Client-roles can be mapped on to Circumstance. If so, Circumstance will pre-select a prepositional group, which in the former case will pre-select the preposition *to* and, in the latter, *for*, with the Benefiter nominal group as its Complement. The result in the case of (4) and (5) would be:

(4a) I gave a book to John.　　[non-iterative; … :inherent:simple …]
(5a) I bought a book for John. [non-iterative; … :+benefactive:simple …]

The difference between [inherent] and [+benefactive] is displayed even more sharply if, instead of [simple], the option [complex] is selected. This option inserts the function Ultimate Client (E10c), which can only pre-select a prepositional group, initiated by *for*, with the Benefiter nominal group as Complement. (4) and (5) would then be:

(4b) I gave John a book for Iona.　　[non-iterative; …
　　　　　　　　　　　　　　　　　　inherent:complex]
(5b) I bought John a book for Iona. [non-iterative; …
　　　　　　　　　　　　　　　　　　+benefactive:complex]

Again, under certain specifiable conditions (4b) – but not (5b) – can take the following forms:

(4c) I gave a book to John for Iona.
(4d) I gave a book for Iona to John.

Parallel to the above we do not have:

(5c) I bought a book to/for John for Iona.
(5d) I bought a book for Iona to/for John.

A related observation is that while underlying (4e) would be [complex] (with Recipient implied and implicit), (5e) can only be read as [simple]:

(4e) I gave a book for Iona.
(5e) I bought a book for Iona.

The distinction between Recipient and Client as well as that between Client and Ultimate Client appears motivated. Note that when Ultimate Client is inserted, this creates a point of identity in the semantic value of Recipient and Client: both are a means whereby the Medium is passed to the Client. Many interesting questions arising from these details must be shelved, as this much will suffice for the discussion of the [iterative] processes, which is the main focus here. But two generalizations appear appropriate: first, a function inserted by two distinct options – e.g. Benefiter-1 inserted by [inherent] or by [+benefactive] – is not identical in ALL respects; and second, the semantic value of an option – the meanings that it constructs – depends on the environment of that option.

Returning to systems of ACCESS and CHARACTER, the combination of [iterative] and [acquisition] is the entry condition for choice between [unitary] and [neutral]. The combined PI of [iterative;acquisition] is the conjunction of C1 and D1a–b. The instructions for the [unitary] and [neutral] are:

F: 1. [unitary]
     a. Medium pre-selects nominal group with Thing/(alienable, divisible) and plural/

    2. [neutral]
     a. Medium pre-selects nominal group with Thing/(alienable, divisible) and plural OR non-count/

Ignoring BENEFACTION, the selection expressions of PROCESS up to this point are:

(i)   [material:action:disposal:acquisition;iterative:unitary]
(ii) [material:action:disposal:acquisition;iterative:neutral]

Note that [unitary] is the endpoint of one path in Figure 6.2. Does it specify any unit of form that may be a recognizable lexical item? I claim that the linguistic unit capable of realizing the Event in selection expression (i) must refer to an activity which is concrete, involves change in the location of the Medium, is inherently repetitive, leads to the Agent's gain of access to the Medium, and is such that the Medium is constrained to be 'plural'. In English the only linguistic form that can meet all these requirements is *gather*. The formulation of the realization statement (Cl;D1a–b;F1a), while permitting (6c), throws light on the source of the oddity of (6a–b):

(6a) Leonie gathered the water/meat in the bowl.
(6b) Leonie gathered one book from her shelf.
(6c) Leonie gathered some roses from the garden.

Selection expression (ii) does not represent the endpoint of a path; dependent upon [neutral] are the options [+vast] and [unmarked]. Nonetheless, taking the selection expression as it stands, it can be said confidently that a form capable of functioning as Event here must differ from *gather* at least in one respect: it should be capable of 'taking' a Medium in which the Thing may be either [plural] or [non-count]. Ignoring the archaic *amass* altogether, in English there appear to be only two lexical items suiting these requirements: *collect* and *accumulate*.

I believe we need to recognize that the orthographic word *collect* is the expression for two distinct – even if related – lexical items: *collect-1*, which is an antonym of *deposit*, and *collect-2*, which is an antonym of *scatter/strew*. Only the latter *collect* is [iterative] and thus subject to the requirement D1b. You can deposit one book or collect it from the library, but you cannot scatter/strew one book or collect it in the sense of *collect-2*. Again, *collect-1* appears to be [non-beneficile]; this is not true of *collect-2* (compare *I collected Iona her son from the school*, which is odd, with *I collected Iona some flowers*, which is quite unremarkable). Given F2, the following are perfectly ordinary English clauses:

(7a) Susan collected the water in the bowl.
(7b) Susan collected some leaves from the garden.

But what about *accumulate*? It is at this point that the final option between [+vast] and [unmarked] is needed. Compare:

(8a) Susan collected some solution.
(8b) Susan accumulated some solution.
(8c) Susan accumulated gallons of solution.
(9a) Leonie collected two dollars.
(9b) Leonie accumulated two dollars.
(9c) Leonie accumulated thousands of dollars.

Of these triplets, only the member (b) appears odd, and traditionally it would be described as 'stylistically infelicitous'. But style is not independent of grammar; a delicate grammar can point to the source of stylistic infelicity, as in this case. The instructions for [+vast] and [unmarked] are:

G: 1.   [+vast]
     a.   Medium pre-selects nominal group with Thing /(alienable, divisible, plural or non-count) NECESSARILY indicating high degree of extent/

     2.   [unmarked]
     a.   Medium pre-selects nominal group with Thing /(alienable, divisible, plural or non-count) indicating any degree of vastness/

These instructions provide a basis for explaining why, side by side with (8a), (8c) and (9a), (9c), we may also have:

(8d) Susan collected gallons of the solution.
(9d) Leonie collected thousands of dollars.

and why of (8a–d) and (9a–d) only the (b) member appears stylistically infelicitous. Note also that of the three lexical items yielded by the network so far, *collect* is the most 'versatile', by virtue of the options [neutral:unmarked] (see F2a/G2a). I would suggest that of the three [acquisition;iterative] processes, *collect* would be the most frequently used and *accumulate* the least. If this hypothesis is empirically substantiated, this would imply that a delicate grammar can point to a non-random relationship between the frequency of a particular linguistic unit and its selection expression.

[disposal] options are concurrent with the BENEFACTION ones. Thus although the unique identity of three lexical items has been already established, more can and must be said about them. In the environment of [disposal] BENEFACTION options carry implications for ACCESS. The combination of [acquisition] and [beneficile] implies that the Agent's gain of access to the Medium can be passed over to some Benefiter(s). Interestingly, [acquisition] combines most frequently with [beneficile:potential], though some exceptions can be found, e.g. *snatch*, *grab* or *inherit*. The combination of [deprivation] and [beneficile] implies that the Agent's loss of access to the Medium is some Benefiter's gain of access to that Medium. [deprivation] combines readily either with [beneficile:inherent] or with [non-beneficile]; it is rare for it to combine with [beneficile:potential], though, again, exceptions can be found, e.g. *scatter* or *throw*.

Assuming that the systemic paths originating at the conjunction of [acquisition;iterative] lead to the selection of Event which can only be expressed as *gather*, *collect* or *accumulate* as shown above, we may claim that the conjunction of options [acquisition;iterative] carries an instruction:

C1a–D1a: [acquisition;iterative]
a. Process pre-selects options [beneficile:potential]

This is tantamount to claiming that there is no process in English whose selection expression contains [acquisition;iterative], but not [beneficile:potential]. If this is true, then *gather*, *collect* and *accumulate* should each be capable of 'taking' the function Benefiter; and this is indeed the case. In the examples of these lexical items above, the BENEFACTION selection has been [beneficile:potential:–benefactive]; but the selection [beneficile:potential:+benefactive] is also possible. But at this point some delicate distinctions between *accumulate* and the other two lexical items come to light. Consider:

(10a) I gathered Jenny some flowers.
(10b) I gathered some flowers for Jenny.
(11a) I collected the kids some water in the bowl.
(11b) I collected some water in the bowl for the kids.
(12a) ? Leonie accumulated John great wealth.
(12b) Leonie accumulated great wealth for John.

To use traditional terminology, of the three items, *accumulate* alone cannot 'take a direct beneficiary'. There are at least three possible ways of interpreting this difference: First, underlying *accumulate* is the option [nonbeneficile] instead of [beneficile: potential]. If so, we imply that *for John* (12b) has a radically different function from *for Jenny* (10b) and *for the kids* (11b), but this is dubious. Second, *for John* is the Ultimate Client because this Benefiter function is always realized only prepositionally (see E10c–d) where the prepositional group takes the form *for + Benefiter*. Against this solution, I would draw attention to (4e)–(5e), and the fact that according to E10c, Ultimate Client is a more specific label for Benefiter-2. Unlike *gather* and *collect*, *accumulate* cannot take a Benefiter-2:

(10c) I gathered Jenny some flowers for her mother.
(11c) I collected the kids some water in a bowl for their dog.
(12c) ? Leonie accumulated John great wealth for his children.

To treat *for John* as an Ultimate Client in (12b) would contradict the generalization that this function is inserted only if the function Recipient/Client is systemically 'present' as in (4b) and (5b). Third, in the final interpretation, *for John* (12b) is a Client, implying that its function is similar to *for Jenny* (10b) or *for the kids* (11b). Each has the role Benefiter-1 (=Client); however, to (10) and (11) apply certain systemic options from INFORMATION, to which (12) is not susceptible. If the option [beneficile:potential: +benefactive] combines with [(acquisition;iterative):neutral:+vast], then the item capable of acting as Event – i.e. *accumulate* – cannot take a direct Benefiter; it is constrained to take a Benefactive Circumstance, as in (12b) but not in (10) or (11). In this respect, then, *for John* (12b) differs from *for Jenny* (10b) and *for the kids* (11b). I take the last solution as the most acceptable, largely because cases comparable to (12b) will be found at least in the environment of the option [iterative].

This insight is built into the network by indicating that, concurrent with the option [simple] vs. [complex], another systematic choice operates open to any clause whose selection expression contains both [iterative] and [... nonreflexive]. The terms are [free] and [constrained]. The instructions for [constrained] are:

H. 1. [constrained]
    a. Client pre-selects prepositional group with preposition *for*
    b. Recipient pre-selects prepositional group with preposition *to*/*between*/*amongst*
    c. conflate Benefiter-1 with Prepositional Complement
    d. order Prepositional complement to follow preposition

Option [constrained], then, acts upon function Benefiter-1 alone, irrespective of whether it combines with [simple] or [complex]. The two important aspects of the option are (a) that Client/Recipient are constrained as specified above (H1a–d), and (b) that certain specific INFORMATION options do not apply to it. In passing, note that characteristic (b), but not (a), is common also to clauses whose selection expression contains [potential:+benefactive:non-reflexive:complex]; but if characteristic (a) is lacking, they would not be said to contain option [constrained]. The point of similarity between the [constrained] and [potential:+benefactive:non-reflexive:complex:free], as exemplified by (5b), (10c) and (11c), can be indicated by a realization statement which would demand pre-selection of some specific INFORMATION option(s).

To summarize the discussion so far, the following array of selection expressions will require that the Event be expressed either by *gather* or *collect* or *accumulate*. Common to each member of the array are the following options:

[material:action:disposal:acquisition;iterative;beneficile:potential]

These options are not repeated but assumed present in each member of the array below:

I: [:unitary;–benefactive]
Event = *gather* e.g. (6c)

II: [:unitary;+benefactive:non-reflexive:simple;free]
Event = *gather* e.g. (10a-b)

III: [:unitary;+benefactive:non-reflexive:complex;free]
Event = *gather* e.g. (10c)

IV: [:neutral:+vast;–benefactive]
Event = *accumulate* e.g. [8c, 9c)

V: [:neutral:+vast;+benefactive:non-reflexive:simple;constrained]
Event = *accumulate* e.g. (12b)

VI: [:neutral:unmarked;–benefactive]
Event = *collect* e.g. (7a, 7b)

VII: [:neutral:unmarked;+benefactive:non-reflexive:simple;free]
Event = *collect* e.g. (11a, 11b)

VIII: [:neutral:unmarked;+benefactive:non-reflexive:complex;free]
Event = *collect* e.g. (11c)

6.3 The lexicogrammar of deprivation 1: Scatter, divide, distribute

Turning now to the options permitted by the combination of [deprivation] and [iterative], the BENEFACTION options have to be taken into account from the very start. This implies that the basis of distinction between the various [deprivation] processes lies not only in whether they are [iterative] or not but also whether they are [beneficile] or not. When [deprivation;iterative;beneficile] combine, this presents a complex entry condition for a choice between [random] vs. [planned]. The former implies that there is no particular design to the disposition of the Medium, while the latter implies an activity in which the disposition of the Medium follows a more or less equitable design. Note the PI for these options is a combination of C2,D1a-b,E2a; and the instructions attached to them are:

J: 1.   [random]
         a.   (co-select option [potential]
         b.   sub-categorize Medium Thing as /(alienable, divisible)
              plural or non-count, solid/
     2.   [planned]
         a.   co-select option [inherent]
         b.   sub-categorize Benefiter-1 as /(animate) non-singular/

As [random] represents the endpoint of one systemic path, the selection
expression containing the option can be stated as follows:

(iii)   [material:action:disposal:deprivation;iterative;beneficile:
        potential]

In English, the only lexical item capable of functioning as the Event in a
clause with the above selection expression is *scatter*. Although the item
strew resembles it in certain respects, it will not suit the requirements of
[beneficile:potential], for this implies that a clause of this kind can 'take'
the function *Benefiter*. With *strew* this possibility is not open (consider *she
strewed the pigeons some breadcrumbs*).
    Given J1a–b, (13a–b) are normal clauses of English; (13c) is not:

(13a) she scattered her clothes all over the place.
(13b) she scattered the toys on the floor.
(13c) she scattered juice on the table.

Given the presence of [potential] in (iii), the option between [–benefactive]
and [+benefactive] applies. (13a–b) present examples of the former option,
while underlying (14) is the option [+benefactive]:

(14) she scattered the pigeons some breadcrumbs.

The selection of [+benefactive] has a somewhat interesting by-product:
it creates an impression of intentionality, which is absent from (13a–b).
This may not be just an accidental feature of this particular lexical item;
so compare *she broke a stick* vs. *she broke them a stick* and *she found a
sixpence* vs. *she found them a sixpence*.
    When the options [random] and [+benefactive] combine, this seems to
bear a consequence for the nominal group pre-selected by the Benefiter:
not only does the Thing have to be animate, but there is a very strong probability of it being non-human. Compare (14) with (15):

(15) she scattered the children some bread.

(15) conjures up a picture of a nasty female – perhaps the traditional step-mother in a fairy-tale. Again, [+benefactive:non-reflexive] allows either the selection of [simple] or of [complex], though with [random] the probability of the selection of [simple] is much higher than that of [complex]. We would rarely find clauses such as (16):

(16) She scattered the pigeons breadcrumbs for their chicks.

Although (15) and (16) may be less frequent than (13a) or (14), neither is odd, unlike (13c). So while (13c) would be attributed to a mistake, (15) will be seen as playing upon that part of the meaning of *scatter*, constructed by [random], while the rarity of (16) might arise from a combination of [random] and [+benefactive:non-reflexive:complex]. The former implies that the Medium is being disposed of without any particular design, whereas the selection of the option [+benefactive] raises the possibility of the Agent having a particular design for the disposal of the Medium. Specifically, the selection of the Ultimate Client (which is inserted in response to [complex]; see E10a–f) goes against the lack of a particular design for the disposal of the Medium. So it would appear that all these important facts about *scatter* can be stated without adding any more options to the network in Figure 6.2. The array of selection expressions which would require that the Event be expressed as *scatter* are now described.

Common to each member of the array are the following options, which will be assumed present in IX–XI:

[material:action:disposal:deprivation;iterative;beneficile:potential]
IX: [:random;–benefactive]
                    Event = *scatter* e.g. (13a, 13b)
X: [:random;+benefactive:non-reflexive:complex:free]
                    Event = *scatter* e.g. (16)
XI: [:random;+benefactive:non-reflexive:simple:free
                    Event = *scatter* e.g. (14)

There may be one problem with the description of *scatter* presented here. I have implied that if option [free] is present, then with the selection of certain options from the INFORMATION system, the function Client would be realized as a Benefactive Circumstance. More specifically, the prepositional group would take the form *for*+Benefiter-1 nominal group. The proportion between (14) and (14a) is the same as that between (10a) and (10b):

(14a) she scattered some breadcrumbs for the pigeons.

But is (14b) also an equally normal clause?

(14b) she scattered some breadcrumbs to the pigeons.

If so, then *scatter* would appear to allow a Benefactive Circumstance, which is allowed to occur only if the Benefiter-1 role is sub-categorized as Recipient; and I have argued that this role only occurs if the option [inherent] is selected (see e.g. 4b–4e). If *scatter* is neutral as between taking Recipient or Client, then the instruction J1a is incorrect; and the network is misleading. However, while I am certain that (14a) is a perfectly normal clause, I am not certain about the status of (14b). So I shall leave the discussion of *scatter* with this query.

[planned] permits a choice between [indeterminate] and [determinate]. The instructions are as follows:

K: 1. [indeterminate]
  a. sub-categorize Medium Thing as /(alienable, divisible) singular, plural or non-count/
  b. co-select options [inherent] and [constrained]
 2. [determinate]
  a. sub-categorize Medium Thing as /(alienable, divisible) plural or non-count (i.e. outclassify singular)
  b. co-select options [inherent] and [free]

The implication is that if the option [indeterminate] is selected, then any item capable of acting as the Event can take a singular/plural/non-count noun as Thing in the Medium; the activity must imply a Recipient (as for *give*, cf. e.g. (4a–4e)); and the Recipient can only take the form of a Benefactive Circumstance, where the prepositional group begins with *to/ between/among*. The only lexical item in English capable of meeting these requirements is *divide*. Like *collect*, *divide* expresses two distinct lexical items: *divide-1* which is roughly synonymous with *cut*, and is an antonym of *join*; the closest in meaning to *divide-2* is the item *distribute*, or the archaic *apportion*; its closest antonym is the iterative *collect*, and possibly *hoard*. I am concerned only with *divide-2* here. Together with the PI of [indeterminate], K1a–b explicitly allow for the following:

(17a) she divided the apple between John and Jenny.
(17b) she divided the sweets amongst the children.
(17c) the Head of School divided the money between the two research directors for their assistants.

Note how (17a) differs from (18a-b):

(18a) she divided John and Jenny an apple.
(18b) she divided an apple for John and Jenny.

The *divide* in (18a–b) is *divide-1*, not a material action of disposal but of transformation. This *divide* does not have [inherent] BENEFACTION; so it is also possible to say (18c) without implying a Benefiter role:

(18c) she divided an apple (in half).

How right Whorf was in maintaining that 'we are all mistaken in our belief that any word has an "exact meaning" … the reference of the words is at the mercy of the sentences and the grammatical patterns in which they occur' (Whorf 1956b: 258–259). It is only by constructing delicate grammars that we can show which grammatical patterns determine what reference for some linguistic form. The description of *divide* as of *collect* perhaps shows clearly that it is more important to devise ways of making explicit 'reactances' between units of linguistic form than to concentrate on ways of segmenting given strings, and reordering and labelling the products of the segmentation.

The combination of [deprivation;iterative;beneficile:inherent] has another consequence, captured in J2b: the nominal group pre-selected by the Benefiter must have the feature plural. Note the difference between (17a) and (18d–e):

(18d) she divided John an apple.
(18e) she divided an apple for John.

The [iterative] *divide* is said to have the option [constrained] precisely because Benefiter-1 can never occur as a direct beneficiary. The option [inherent] is said to be pre-selected because Benefiter-1 will always be interpreted as a Recipient (as with *give, sell, lend*). These features, together with the option [planned], might explain why the Benefactive circumstance can be realized only by a prepositional group with *between* or *amongst*. But I believe that another aspect of [planned] processes is important here.

Just as the selection of [+benefactive] with [random] (*scatter*) creates the impression of intentionality, so also the combination of [inherent] and [planned] is capable of creating an impression of 'exhaustivity' (17b), for example, creates the impression that after the dividing is done 'the sweets' are exhausted, though this impression can be overridden by indicating otherwise (e.g. *she divided some of the sweets amongst the children*). Note, however, the difference between:

(19a) she distributed some medicine to the refugees.
(19b) she distributed some medicine amongst the refugees.

I feel that only (19b) creates the impression that 'some medicine' was exhausted after the distributing was done. If this is so, this may provide a better explanation for the selection of *between/amongst* with *divide*, which may be said to carry the connotation of exhaustivity, unless otherwise indicated. Note that further detail will be needed to differentiate between the selection of *between* and *amongst*, but perhaps the lines along which this may be done are clear enough not to need discussion.

The array of selection expressions requiring that the Event be expressed as *divide* are entered below (XII–XIII). Common to each are the following selections, which are not repeated in the individual arrays:

[material:action:disposal:deprivation;iterative;beneficile:inherent:
nonreflexive]
XII: [:indeterminate;simple;constrained]
                    Event = *divide* e.g. (17a, 17b)
XIII: [:indeterminate;complex;free]
                    Event = *divide* e.g. (17c)

If the option [determinate] applies, the implication is that any item capable of acting as the Event cannot take a singular noun as Thing in the Medium; the activity must imply a Recipient (this is, of course, in addition to all the characteristics inherited through the PI up to this point). The lexical item that will meet all of the requirements is *distribute*. Compare (17a) and (20a):

(20a) she distributed an apple to the children.

Again, if we have *they distributed some medicine*, a Recipient is implied in the same way as it is in *I'm giving a book (as a present)*. I am treating *distribute* as having the option [free] (see K2b). This implies that it can take a direct Benefiter-1, as in:

(20b) the government distributed the peasants a new high-yielding variety of wheat seeds.

The option between [simple] and [complex] also applies:

(20c) to celebrate the event, they distributed everyone bags of sweets.
(20d) on Mother's Day, we distributed the children presents for their mums.

Note that the non-singularity of the Benefiter can be indicated in different ways, and it is likely that the sub-categorization statements in Kla–2a will need to be formulated more carefully. Consider:

(21a) she distributed pamphlets to the students.
(21b) she distributed a pamphlet to each student.
(21c) ? she distributed pamphlets/a pamphlet to a student.

The array of selection expressions requiring that the event be expressed as *distribute* are entered below (XIV–XV). Common to each are the same selections, shown above for XII–XIII, and these are not repeated:

XIV: [:determinate;simple;free]
>   Event = *distribute* e.g. (20a, 20b, 20c)
XV: [:determinate;complex;free]
>   Event = *distribute* e.g. (20d)

6.4   The lexicogrammar of deprivation 2: Strew, spill, share

The above section concludes the description of processes which combine [deprivation; iterative;beneficile]. When [deprivation;iterative] combine with [non-beneficile], this acts as a multiple entry condition for the options [independent] vs. [cooperative]. The option [cooperative] implies that the activity cannot be carried out without a 'co-doer'. So that just as a Recipient is always 'present' in a clause with the option [inherent], so a function I shall call Cooperant is always 'present' in a clause with [cooperative] as in (*Eric is so sweet*) *he always shares his toys*. When the option is [independent], the function Cooperant is not permitted; in this sense, then, I am making a distinction between 'joint' doing as in *Eric and Jim played with the toys*, and cooperancy as in *Eric shared his toys with Jim*. The instructions for the two are:

L: 1. [independent]
    a. sub-categorize Event as/(material action inherently repetitive, leading to Agent's loss of access to Medium, incapable of requiring Benefiter) and NOT INHERENTLY REQUIRING a co-doer/

    2. [cooperative]
    a. sub-categorize Event as /(material action inherently repetitive, leading to Agent's loss of access to Medium, incapable of requiring Benefiter) and INHERENTLY REQUIR-ING function Cooperant/

[independent] is the entry condition to two options, which are so obvious they do not need much discussion. They lead to the sub-categorization of the Medium as follows:

M. 1. [+solid]
    a. sub-categorize Medium Thing as (alienable, divisible) plural or count, solid/

    2. [+liquid]
    a. sub-categorize Medium Thing as (alienable divisible) liquid

The options [independent:+solid] require that the Event be realized by *strew*, while the options [independent:+liquid] require that it be realized by *spill*. It may be argued that *scatter* is a possibility for the former; but note that *scatter* has also the options [beneficile:potential]. When this combines with [...:–benefactive], there would appear to be some inter-changeability between *strew* and *scatter*. So we can have:

(22a) she had scattered everything on the floor.
(22b) she had strewn everything on the floor.

But, as lexical items, *scatter* and *strew* cannot be said to be exactly alike. There are no such clauses as:

(23a) she strewed the pigeons some breadcrumbs.
(23b) she strewed some breadcrumbs for the pigeons.

Another question may be raised: why should option [independent] be recognized in the case of *strew* but not in that of *scatter*? This is because it is only in the environment of [deprivation;iterative;non-beneficile] that the contrast carries any significance, since all other [disposal] processes are uniformly like *strew* in not being able to require the function Cooperant. As a lexical item, *strew* appears far less frequently than *scatter*; and this may be because *scatter* can do everything that *strew* can and also some more things which *strew* cannot do, e.g. take a Benefiter.

Spill differs from *strew* only in that its Medium must 'be' liquid. Note the metaphoric nature of *spill the beans* and *spill his guts*. Here is an example of *spill* comparable to (22b):

(22c) the waiter spilt soup on her dress.

Turning to the option [cooperative], it is best first to develop the notion of the function Cooperant. A Cooperant differs both from a Benefiter and from the informal notion 'joint doer'. A Benefiter, I have argued above, is not only always at the receiving end but must also be dissociated from an Agent. This is not true of Cooperant. Consider:

(24)   they shared the sweets.

This clause would be interpreted as *they shared the sweets between/amongst themselves*. But if so, this is because the functions Agent and Cooperant are both systemically present and realized by *they*. Compare (24) with:

(24a) he shared the sweets.

Here the Cooperant is both implied and implicit; notwithstanding the absence of explicit mention of a Cooperant, the assumption is that the function is essential, since in the absence of the Cooperant the activity of sharing cannot be undertaken. So, unlike a Benefiter, a Cooperant is neither at the receiving end nor does it necessarily have to be disassociated from the Agent, though it can be as in:

(24b) John shared the sweets with Jenny.

In (24b) the function Cooperant is realized by *with Jenny*, that of the Agent by *John*.

Cooperant is also different from 'joint doer'. In

(25a) they walked together to the station.
(25b) Eric walked to the station with Jim.

there is no cooperant function. In the first place, the activity of walking can be carried out without two or more persons' involvement; second, no matter how many persons function as the Agent, each is responsible for his/her own action. Not so with *share*. Sharing cannot be done without involvement of at least two persons; and the action of one is a condition for that of the other. There are certain non-disposal-type processes that resemble *share* in this respect, e.g. *marry, fight, meet, agree*. But of the disposal processes *share* alone has this characteristic. And although *sell, lend* might appear to be like *share*, there is an important difference. In

(26) John sold/lent Melanie a car

although John and Melanie are involved in the same exchange, their roles *vis-à-vis* the Event are not the same. If John shared sweets with Jenny, then it follows that Jenny shared sweets with John; but if John sold Melanie a car, it does not follow that Melanie sold John a car.

But if the relationship of the Cooperant and the Agent to the activity is the same, then why should two separate functions of Agent and Cooperant be recognized? The simple answer is because the functions can be separated from each other. We would not need to dissociate the functions Subject and Actor and Theme, if, under certain specifiable conditions, each could not be realized by a different constituent of the clause. Moreover, there is a meaningful distinction between (24b) and (24c):

(24c) John and Jenny shared the sweets.

In (24b), John is likely to be seen as the one who had prior access to the sweets; (24c) is neutral about the prior ownership of the sweets. Moreover, (24b) leaves no room for indeterminacy; (24c) does, as comparison with (24d) shows:

(24d) John and Jenny shared the sweets with Benny.

It is important, then, to recognize a distinction between [discrete] and [fused] – the two options shown to depend on [cooperation]. The option [discrete] would carry the following instructions:

N: 1. [discrete]
    a. insert function Cooperant
    b. Cooperant pre-selects prepositional group with preposition *with*
    c. conflate Cooperant with Prepositional Complement
    d. Prepositional Complement pre-selects nominal group animate not co-referential with Agent
    e. order Prepositional Complement to follow preposition *with*

Underlying (24b) then would be the options [:cooperative:discrete], while underlying (24c) would be [:cooperative:fused]. The only instructions for [fused] are:

N. 2. [fused]
    a. insert function Cooperant
    b. Cooperant pre-selects nominal group animate

This option is the entry condition for a further systemic choice between [Agent-oriented] and [Medium-oriented]. (24c) exemplifies the former; an example of the latter would be:

(24e) John shared Jenny's sweets.

I suggest that in the absence of a Good Reason, (24e) would be interpreted as 'John and Jenny shared the sweets and the sweets were Jenny's'. This is one reason why it is possible to clinch the matter by saying:

(24f) John shared Jenny's sweets with her.

The instructions for the last pair of options are as follows:

P: 1. [Agent-oriented]
    a. pre-select nominal group complex
    b. pre-select additive complexing conjunction *and*

    c.   order Agent to precede *and*

    d.   order Cooperant to follow *and*

2.   [Medium-oriented]

    a.   Cooperant pre-selects possessive - *'s*

    b.   conflate Cooperant with Possessive Modifier in Medium

The difference between (24d) and (24f) is important. In the former, *with Benny* is Cooperant, while John and Jenny are (joint) Agent. In (24f), the function of *with her* is different; it is a kind of 'marking' and I am assuming that the option(s) that govern its appearance do not belong to TRANSITIVITY, but to options from some other system network which is the output of the textual meta-function. Such marking can also occur with [Agent-oriented] as in:

(24g) John and Jenny shared the sweets with each other.

Note that the prepositional groups here are constrained to be co-referential with the Cooperant; thus if (24f) had been *John shared Ben's sweets*, then the prepositional group would have been *with him*. I shall not pursue this any further here, but conclude with the comment that the only lexical item capable of acting as the Event in a clause with options [deprivation;iterative;non-beneficile;cooperative] is *share*.

The array of selection expressions requiring that the Event be expressed as *strew* or *spill* or *share* is presented below (XVI–XX). The selections common to each and so not repeated are:

[material:action:disposal;iterative;non-beneficile]
XVI: [:independent:+solid]
                       Event = *strew* e.g. (22b)
XVII: [:independent:+liquid]
                       Event = *spill* e.g. (22c)
XVIII: [:cooperative:discrete]
                       Event = *share* e.g. (24b, 24d)
XIX: [:cooperative:fused:Agent-oriented]
                       Event = *share* e.g. (24c, 24g)
XX: [:cooperative:fused:Medium-oriented]
                       Event = *share* e.g. (24e, 24f)

6.5   The continuity of grammar and lexis

The above discussion has, hopefully, established nine distinct lexical items:

gather	scatter	strew
collect	divide	spill
accumulate	distribute	share

Common to these lexical verbs is the characteristic that they can function as the Event in clauses whose selection expression contains the options [disposal] and [iterative]. There appear to be some seventy-odd [non-iterative] [disposal] processes. It has not been possible to discuss any of these for reasons of space; this is a natural concomitant of attempting to write a delicate grammar. However, I hope that the description will permit the claim that the project of turning the whole of linguistic form into grammar is feasible. In fact I believe that I have demonstrated not only that 'lexis' equals 'delicate grammar' but also that there is [grammar beyond lexis]. So far as *gather*, *collect* and *accumulate* are concerned, their unique identity *vis-à-vis* each other can be established by virtue of the options [unitary], [neutral], [+vast] and [unmarked]. To show the combination of these with BENEFACTION options is to do grammar after lexis, which has hopefully led to a better understanding of the identities and differences between members of the paradigm.

It needs to be made quite clear that the description presented here of the nine items is not complete. This follows from assumption (7) in section 6.1. The account is simply the output of one meta-function – the experiential. In the description of larger linguistic units, e.g. the clause, the validity of assumption (7) has been demonstrated by Martin (1985), Fawcett (1980), Halliday (1969a, 1970, 1977, 1985), Mann and Matthiessen (1983), Young (1980) and others. It remains to be seen whether the postulate of concurrent multiple structures extends right down the rank scale to the smaller units, e.g. the lexical item. *A priori* there seems no reason to rule out this possibility; rather there is some favourable suggestive evidence. For example, synonymy is a well-recognized concept, though a troublesome one (Leech 1974; Lyons 1977). If pairs such as *ask/enquire*, *buy/purchase*, *smile/grin*, *cry/bawl* are examined closely, we are likely to find that while their experientially motivated grammatical structure is the same, their interpersonally motivated structure differs. A similar phenomenon is evident in *day*, *today* and *two*, *both*: both members of each pair are likely to have the same experientially motivated structure, though they most probably differ in their textually motivated structure. Unlike larger structures, the lexical item is unsegmentable; but if we accept that, in principle, different functions can be conflated on to the same segment, there would appear to be no reason for denying that a lexical item could be the expression of two or more conflated grammatical functions. These remarks are speculative, and are intended as an invitation to closer examination.

One may ask: What exactly is the basis of these options? Where do they come from? And isn't there some circularity? Is one simply pretending to start from the network as if it were *sui generis*, while in fact the options appear to be postulated precisely because certain lexical items are known to exist? I would answer this by saying that no matter what aspect of the lexicogrammar we describe, we are in the last analysis describing the possibilities of only that which is known to us, and this knowledge is based upon our experience of language. The options of the networks are not 'universals', 'primitives' or godgiven truths: they are schematic pointers to manmade meanings which can be expressed verbally. The options are presented in certain relations to each other because this is how I understand English ways of meaning; they are not there because the making of any other kind of relation is impossible. For example, in Urdu, while there seems to be a close parallel to the options [unitary] vs. [neutral] (cf. tʃunnə and dʒʌmə kʌrnə), the distinction I needed to recognize by [+vast] vs. [unmarked] does not appear necessary. The networks REPRESENT a language; they do not INVENT it. Moreover, I doubt that any grammar can invent a language, though it can make an effort to distort other people's meanings to make them appear as replicas of, say, English meanings (cf. Hasan 1984b).

Lack of space does not permit a detailed discussion of the implications of turning the whole of linguistic form into grammar, but if the account of the nine lexical items presented above has appeared valid, then it certainly upholds the systemic functional view of an uninterrupted continuity between grammar and lexis. It rejects the approach wherein the bricks of lexis are joined together by the mortar of grammar. The notion of the lexicon as an inventory of items, each having its own meaning in itself, stands refuted, and the insights of Saussure (1916), Firth (1935), Hjelmslev (1961), Whorf (1956b) and Halliday (1961) are confirmed. The complex relation between the signification and value of a linguistic sign is also highlighted.

The concept of reference has been a problematical one in semantics (Lyons 1977). The interpretation of the term 'reference' as an onomastic relation to existents is a limiting one, which arbitrarily cuts the sign system into two distinct areas: there are signs such as *tree* 'referring' to TREE, a concrete object, a member of a class 'out there'; and there are signs such as *gather*, *collect* which lack referents. This leaves the question unanswered: how is it that such signs make any contact with the world of action/state, which is the only reason for their existence? Why is it that where it will do to say *the book is in that bag*, it will not do to say *the book is on that bag*?

The description offered here implies that the ways in which the reference of *book* or *bag* is achieved is essentially the same as that for *is*, *in*, *on*, *that* and *the*. Saussure created an unnecessary enigma in his account of value and signification. In part this was due to the cleavage between *langue* and *parole*. Any viable account of reference will have to take *parole* into account, and this not just so that we know that the name *John* and *the man in blue jeans* may point to the same person. But *parole* dissociated from contexts of human living is an anomaly. The reason Malinowski (1923, 1935) was able to turn Saussure's relation of value and signification upside down (Hasan 1985) was that ways of saying – *parole* within contexts – is creative of the *langue*. This is how I understand Hjelmslev's comment that process determines system; a phenomenon cannot achieve the status of a process without systematicity. Value and signification are indeed two sides of the same coin. Looked at from the point of view of the system – the *langue* – we may claim that signification depends on value; looked at from the point of view of process – the *parole* – our claim would be that value depends upon what the speakers have consistently signified by sign – how it has meshed in with their structures of action and thought. Looking for meaning in use (Wittgenstein 1958) implies looking at both kinds of use – how a sign combines or contrasts with other signs in a string or a paradigm and how (some part of) the string applies to the world.

This line of argument needs further exploration. In most linguistic writing today, there is an uneasy amalgamation of two irreconcilable views: language as the representation of meanings that exist *sui generis*, and language as the construction of meanings, whose existence is beholden to the existence of that network of relations which, for short, we call 'language'. From the latter point of view, what is called 'world knowledge' or 'knowledge structure' is largely constructed by language itself; from the former, it is divorced from language, so that 'knowledge of the world' and 'knowledge of language' are seen as two distinct concepts. Such a view can be criticized at least on two counts: in practice it presents the advanced Western peoples' knowledge of the world as THE knowledge of the world; if to them the shape of that world appears eminently reasonable, it is only because they are not at the receiving end of being brainwashed into someone else's ideology. Second, current postulates of world knowledge fail to address the fascinating question of how the information constructed by the various semiotic systems is integrated into some kind of working whole. When interest in this question arises, a delicate grammar of the type presented here would be an essential prerequisite to the enquiry. The notion of PI explicitly points out that the implicational shadows of signs are very long indeed. Such grammar has the potential of making explicit the concepts of 'semantic inheritance' (Brachman 1979) and 'conceptual dependency' (Schank 1975). At the same time, it seems likely that it will be of considerable use in explaining much of what Wilkes's preferential semantics is based on Wilkes (1978).

The Systemic Functional model has always rejected the absurd postulate that transformations are meaning preserving – a view that can be upheld only if semantics equals the experiential meta-function and certain parts of the interpersonal meta-function selected on an *ad hoc* basis. It has also rejected the view that the only valid form a grammar can take is to trace the genealogical relationship between transformationally related strings. Once these two presuppositions are removed, transformations are transformed into the relation of agnation; and the rationale for the existence of certain transformational possibilities can be made explicit on the basis of a grammar of the type presented here (Hasan 1971).

When the grammarian's dream comes true, it will in all likelihood enable us to throw better light on the notions of synonymy, antonymy and hyponymy. It will force us to make more explicit the basis of the distinction between 'grammatical item' and 'lexical item'. Also, I believe, it will help in making more precise Firth's view of collocation (Firth 1951a). Meanwhile, in order to translate the dream into reality much work is needed. The beginning made here represents no more than an iota of the total potential of English language for constructing meanings.

Note

1.   Compare the discussion of marking in section 1.3 of Martin (1987).

7 Lending and borrowing: from grammar to lexis [1985]

Sometimes we are asked: 'What does this word mean?'; and often we are able to respond by offering a synonym, a paraphrase, or some sort of description – otherwise, there is always the Macquarie Dictionary! Since, in everyday life, we are able to provide the meaning of lexical items in this manner, it is not surprising that when we turn to the description of lexis in linguistics, we attempt something along the same lines, taking each lexical item in isolation, and 'decomposing' it into the smallest necessary elements of its meaning. This creates the questionable illusion that the identity of a lexical item is given, that its meanings are largely independent of the grammar of the language, and that the fact of its being used thus and thus can be explained in terms of its having this or that meaning. We are even tempted to ask 'whether there is … a correlation between the meaning of a lexeme and its syntactic properties' (Lyons 1977), as if the lexical meaning could be prior to and/or independent of the overall systemic relations within a language.

It is, however, possible to take a radically different view, wherein a lexical item does not have a mysterious, *sui generis* existence, and where the task of grammar *vis-à-vis* lexis is not simply to determine the syntactic classification of items; rather, according to this view, grammar is what constructs the very meaning of a lexical item, giving it its identity as a sign in the system of language. This view would negate the traditionally cherished sharp boundary between syntax and lexicon, recognizing instead, an integrally inter-related level of form – a lexicogrammar (Halliday 1985). Such a lexicogrammar would consist of, among other things, networks of options, which, *in toto*, serve to express a language's semantic potential. If, for example, clause as a meaningful unit is one of the outputs of such a grammar, then so would be the lexical item. The difference lies in how detailed the grammar has to be before one comes face to face with the two types of formal units. And this difference, in its turn, is closely linked to the syntagmatic nature of the clause, as opposed to the synergetic nature of the lexical item (Hasan 1971). A lexical item as a formal unit will be the output of 'the most delicate grammar' (Halliday 1961). But if what one is doing is grammar, then it follows that, even at the greatest degree of delicacy, statements are generalizations (or 'rules', if that term pleases better!) about categories, rather than single items. It is a hyperbolic claim that in describing the lexicon, 'one has to record as many individual facts as there are lexical items' (Chao 1968) But is there any indication that the view of lexis as most delicate grammar is a viable one? To answer this question, I propose to look at *lend* and *borrow*, whose meaning is so well known that the following description holds few, if any, surprises. The aim is simply to see if the entire configuration of the meanings of these items can be captured through increase in the delicacy of grammar.

First, however, some basic assumptions must be stated. The grammar of a language is an inter-related set of networks of systemic options, whose relevant characteristics for the present are as follows: (a) Systemic options display dependency; e.g. the systemic option #male# v. #female# depends on the option #animate#. So one option acts as the context for some other systemic options; logically the description is complete, when no further dependent options can be postulated. (b) A single option may furnish the context for the operation of two (or more) simultaneous systemic options; e.g. the systemic option #male# v. #female# is simultaneous with #human# v. #nonhuman#; both depend on the option #animate#, but the selection of terms from the two systems is entirely independent. (c) Two (or more) options may conjointly act as the context for some systemic option(s); e.g. the options underlying items such as *uncle, brother* … ultimately depend on #male# AND #human#. (d) Two (or more) options can act disjunctly as the context for some systemic option(s); e.g. a valid context for the systemic option #+tag# v. #–tag# is EITHER #declarative# OR #imperative#; for example, we say *he sings, doesn't he* and *do sing, won't you* but not *did he sing, did he* – at least not in Standard British: this caveat is necessary as the last construction appears not infrequently in some Australian varieties. (e) Systemic options have consequence in the determination of syntagms: they may specify: (i) some permitted and/or entailed functions; e.g. the option #major# entails the function Process, so every English clause with the option #major# 'has' a segment whose role in the clause structure is Process; (ii) the order in which two (or more) functions may combine in a syntagm; e.g. #active# entails the conflation of functions Subject and Agent, so an English clause with this option has a segment which carries the dual role of Subject and Agent; for example, in *Mary had baked a cake*, *Mary* has the role of both Subject and Agent; (iii) the crucial properties of a (sub-)class, capable of instantiating some function; e.g. #passive# requires the selection of a sub-class of verbal group, viz. 'passive'. All systemic options appeal to the form of language as the constructor of the language's semantic potential; ideally, no option is semantically empty, and no semantic facts exist except those validated by the lexicogrammar.

To approach the description of *lend* and *borrow*, I begin with the clausal function Process, e.g. *to forgive* in *to forgive an error, being* in *being late*, or *sneezed* in *he sneezed loudly*. To specify the range of other clausal functions – entailed and/or permitted – the systemic options applicable to Process (among other things) must be explored, since obviously nothing can sneeze anyone anything, just as nothing can be loudly. I shall limit myself to an exploration of systemic contrasts mostly in PROCESS and some options in BENEFACTION, while assuming a set of options as constants. The paradigm case of assumed constants is exemplified by *Mary had baked a cake*, where the VOICE is #effective: active# (*Mary* has the dual role of Subject and Agent); the MOOD is #declarative# (Subject precedes Finite – *Mary had* … not *had Mary* …); Theme is #unmarked# (*Mary* is both Subject and Theme, in contrast to *yesterday Mary had baked a cake*, where Theme is *yesterday* and Subject *Mary*).

So far as PROCESS is concerned, the most primary options underlying *lend* and *borrow* are #material:action#. With the above assumptions, the clause would contain functions Agent Process Medium, in that order; but #material:action# would underlie both *Mary had baked a cake* and *Mary had borrowed a book*. However, *bake* and *borrow* are distinct types of processes, with distinct privileges with regard to what other functions may be selected in that clause. We thus need to examine options dependent upon #action#; these are #disposal# v. #creation# v. #transformation# (v, some others which need not concern us here). The option underlying *bake* is #creation#, that underlying *lend* and *borrow* is #disposal#. The latter option specifies that: (a) Medium 'is' – i.e. is instantiated by a nominal category, whose element Thing is – 'alienable goods' e.g. *a book*; (b) Agent is 'animate'; (c) completion of activity implies change in the relationship of Medium and Agent. These requirements apply to all lexical items to which option #disposal# pertains, e.g. *give, take, accumulate, send, distribute, scatter...* Two concurrent systems of options depend on #disposal#, viz. #acquisition# v. #deprivation# and #iterative# v. #non-iterative#, #acquisition# implies gain of access to Medium on Agent's part at completion of activity. Note the unilateral implicational relation between *Mary has borrowed my pen* and *Mary has (got) my pen (now)*. #deprivation# implies loss of access to Medium on Agent's part at completion of action. Compare the last two examples with *I returned his book yesterday* and *I don't have his book* (*any more*). From the point of view of these two options, *distribute, scatter, lend, sell, give, send* ... are alike: #deprivation# underlies each item of this class, which contrasts with *accumulate, borrow, buy, receive, take, find* ... as underlying the latter class is the option #acquisition#.

Cross-cutting the above systemic contrast is that between #iterative# v. #non-iterative#. The former implies that process is inherently repetitive, as in *accumulate, distribute, scatter* ... It requires that Medium be 'divisible'. Consider *Sheila scattered a book*. As this option does not underlie *lend* and *borrow* and has been discussed elsewhere (Hasan 1987/1996), it will be ignored here except for comparison. #non-iterative# implies activity is not inherently repetitive; note that Medium is not required to be 'divisible' – cf. *she borrowed a book/four books*. This option underlies items e.g. *take, find, lose, borrow, sell, buy, give, send, deliver, receive* ... So *lend* and *borrow* are at once alike and different; both are #non-iterative#, but while *lend* is #deprivation#, *borrow* is #acquisition#.

The options discussed so far can be presented in system network as shown in Figure 7.1.

Simplifying somewhat, look at two systems dependent on #non-iterative#. These are #reciprocal# v. #non-reciprocal# and #time-free# v. #time-bound#, #reciprocal# entails an additional function. If it co-occurs with #deprivation#, this conjunction entails an additional function Recipient. Thus *Mary* is Recipient in *I lent Mary a pen*. The claim is that whenever the options #reciprocal# and #deprivation# underlie an item, the item will display the grammatical property traditionally known as 'inherent benefaction'. This can be expressed technically as: 'the conjunction of

Figure 7.1: PROCESS system: Options dependent on #disposal#

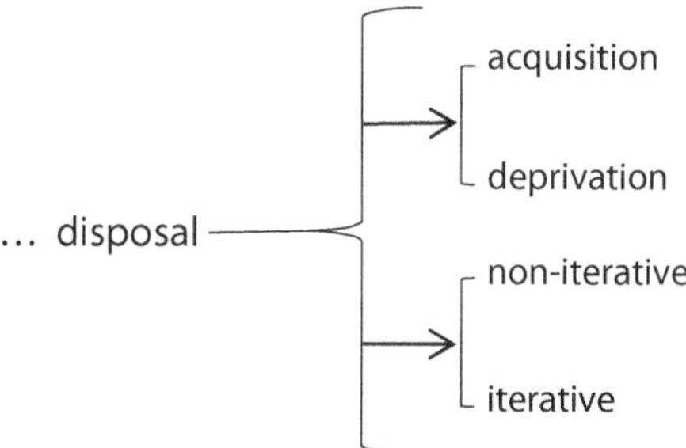

#deprivation#' and #reciprocal# requires pre-selection of options #benefi-cile:inherent# from BENEFACTION system'. When #reciprocal# occurs with #acquisition#, this conjunction entails an additional function, which I shall call Agentive Source. *From me* is an example of Agentive Source in *Mary borrowed a pen from me*. The function thus accounts for the converse relationship between *I lent Mary a pen* and *Mary borrowed a pen from me*.

Option #reciprocal# underlies such items as *give, receive, send, deliver, lend, borrow, buy, sell, bequeath, inherit* ... The conjunction of #recip-rocal# and #acquisition# requires the preselection of options #benefi-cile:potential# from BENEFACTION system. This means that the possibility of selecting the function Beneficiary is open; but if Beneficiary is selected this must be done explicitly. Note the difference between *I have lent my pen* and *I have borrowed Jim's pen.* In the former case, *(to) someone* is implied; this is because the function Beneficiary is entailed with options #depriva-tion# and #reciprocal#. In the second example there is no implication of a Beneficiary (on the question of treating *I* as the carrier of the roles Agent and Beneficiary, see Hasan 1987/1996). However, it is possible to say *I have borrowed you Jim's pen*, where *you* carries the role of Beneficiary. Note that the nature of this function, when it is selected as a consequence of the options #beneficile:potential: +benefactive# is not identical with that of function Beneficiary selected as a consequence of the options #benefi-cile:inherent#. In the former case, Beneficiary is more delicately describ-able as Client; so *I have borrowed you Jim's pen* corresponds to *I have borrowed Jim's pen FOR you*, while in the latter case – i.e. with inherent benefaction – Beneficiary is more delicately describable as Recipient. So *I have lent Mary my pen* corresponds to *I have lent my pen TO Mary.*

The selection of option #non-reciprocal# does not entail the functions Recipient or Agentive Source; this option underlies such items as *lose, find, pick up, discard* ... It needs to be pointed out that items with option #non-reciprocal# may or may not be also #beneficile#. So while we have *I found Mary a clean piece of paper* we do not have *I discarded Mary a clean piece of paper*. Additionally, if the option #beneficile# is selected together with #non-reciprocal#, there is a pre-selection of the option #potential#. In other words, items with the option #non-reciprocal# are never 'inherent benefactive'; consequently the function Recipient cannot be selected with such processes.

The options in BENEFACTION system are presented in a network in Figure 7.2.

Figure 7.2: Some BENEFACTION options

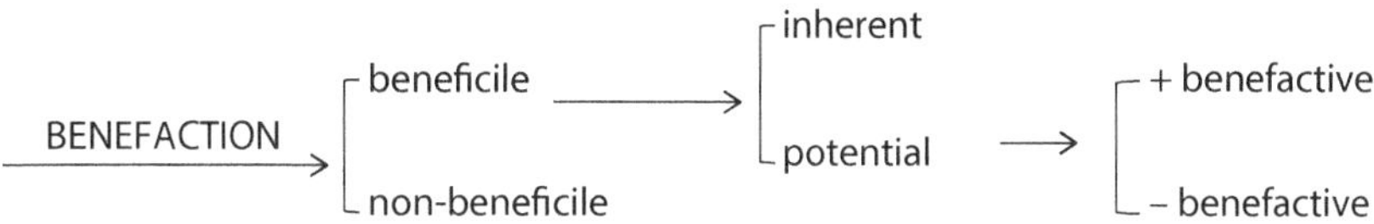

This network displays only the options that have been discussed here. Figure 7.3 presents the options dependent on #non-iterative#.

Figure 7.3: Options dependent on #non-iterative#

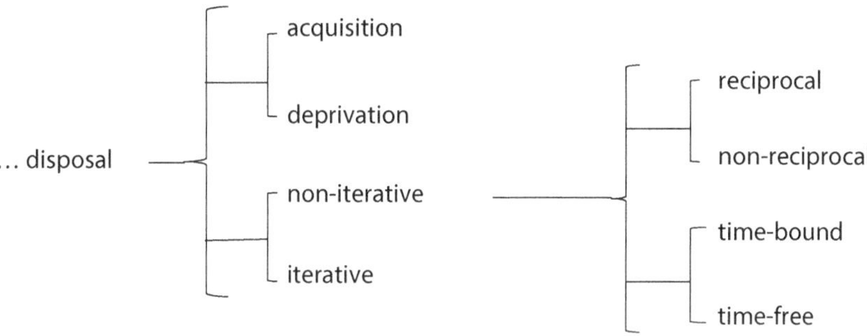

Let us turn now to the systemic option #time-bound# v. #timefree#. The option #time-bound#: implies that the process has an inherent time-condition. Instances of this sub-class are *buy, sell, lend, borrow, pawn, let, hire, rent* and *lease*. #time-free# implies that process type does not have an inherent time condition. This sub-class is instantiated by such items as *give, deliver, send, take.* The former option places restrictions on Circumstance of Temporal Extent. Dependent upon #time-bound# are the options #temporary# v. #permanent#. The option #temporary# entails Circumstance of Temporal Extent, where Extent must be a portion of time-span, and duration-indicating prepositions *till/for/until* must be selected. So, while we say *I will lend you this book till Thursday/for a few days* we do not say *I will lend you this book for ever* much less ... *not for ever*. The option #permanent# prohibits Circumstance of Temporal Extent unless Medium is a 'kind', not a member. Note the difference between *we have been selling our house for the last six months* and *we have been selling this model for the last six months*. The infelicity of *I sold my car for ever*, and *I lent my car but not for ever* is comparable to the infelicity of *my male brother*. The option #permanent# underlies such items as *buy, sell, inherit,*

bequeath, donate..., while #temporary# underlies such items as *borrow, lend, pawn, rent ...*

The option #reciprocal# provides the context for the systemic options #economic# v. #personal#. The former option entails a Circumstance of Equivalence. *For fifty dollars* is an example of this function in *I sold granny's chair for fifty dollars*. Note, then, that if #economic# is selected, then both #acquisition# and #deprivation# are 'tempered': while it is true that gain or loss of access to Medium follows the generalization made earlier, the presence of #economic# implies gain of equivalent value for Medium on Agent's part if the process is #deprivation#, and its loss, if the process is #acquisition#. *John sold his car* means, in the true sense of meaning, that John lost access to his car but that he gained access to its equivalent value. This is why there is no lack of cohesion in *I sold my car finally and gave the money to my mother*, where both *the* and *money* are fully interpretable due to the lexicogrammar of *sell*. The option #economic# underlies items *buy, sell, borrow, lend, pawn, let, rent ...* The option #personal# prohibits the Circumstance of Equivalence. This option underlies a large number of #reciprocal# processes, e.g. *give, receive, send, bequeath, donate, bestow* ... Note that an exchange of some kind can be indicated with items of this class e.g. in *she gave him some money in return for his help*, but I feel it would be misleading to think of *in return for his help* as a Circumstance of Equivalence.

When both #economic# and #temporary# co-occur, their conjunction is a context for another systemic option, viz. #cyclical# v. #noncyclical#. The former implies that the Circumstance of Equivalence is recurrent, and entails the selection of Circumstance of Temporal Cycle. So in *we are renting this flat for 150 dollars per week*, the phrase *per week* instantiates the function Circumstance of Temporal Cycle. This option underlies *lend, borrow, rent, lease, let, hire ...* The presence of #non-cyclical# prohibits the selection of Circumstance of Temporal Cycle. The only item in English with the options #... economic:temporary:non-cyclical# is *pawn*, and we do not say *I pawned my watch for five dollars per week*.

Dependent on #cyclical# is the systemic option between #goods# and #meta-goods#. These options sub-categorize Medium, the latter requiring that Medium belong to a class 'sum of money' – i.e. meta-goods, which can be used for procuring goods. The former option requires that Medium be 'property other than cash', and it underlies the items *let, rent, lease, hire*. The option #meta-goods# underlies the items *lend* and *borrow*. These options are presented in network form in Figure 7.4.

Figure 7.4: Options dependent on #economic:temporary#

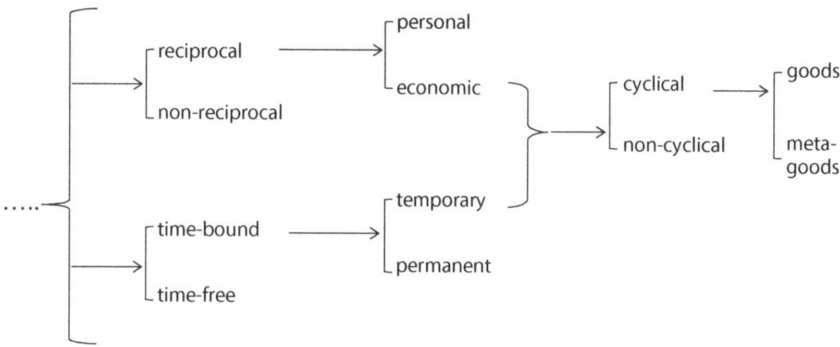

According to the description presented here, there are only two respects in which these two items differ from each other: *lend* has the option #deprivation#, *borrow* #acquisition#; and while the options #beneficile:inherent# underlie *lend*, the options #beneficile:potential# underlie *borrow* i.e. it is free to 'take' a Beneficiary, but unlike *lend* is not forced to. Minimal differences of 'meaning' have often been cited as a characteristic of anonymous pairs; the account presented here makes the degree and nature of that difference explicit. It is perhaps also obvious that as the delicacy of description increases, we come close to the basis of the 'intuitively' recognized collocational relation between *lend/borrow* and the lexical set *money*. Collocation thus proves to be a formal relation with its basis in the lexicogrammar of the language.

The full description of *lend* and *borrow* in terms of the options discussed above can be presented as follows:

lend:	#material:action:disposal:deprivation; non-iterative: reciprocal:economic; time-bound:temporary:cyclical: meta-goods; beneficile:inherent#
example:	*the bank lent us $15,000 at 13% per annum.*
borrow:	#material:action:disposal:acquisition; non-iterative: reciprocal:economic; time-bound:temporary:cyclical: meta-goods; beneficile:potential#
example:	*we have already borrowed $15,000 at 13% a year from our bank.*

Note that each of the options in the above description applies to more than one lexical item; and equally importantly, the consequences of the (configuration of) options selected remain constant. So, for example, the consequence of the option #economic# or #reciprocal# does not change whether it underlies *sell* or *lend*. In the description of the lexis we are naturally moving towards unique member classes, but this does not necessarily imply that the generalizations being made on the way will apply to one item at a time. Hopefully, the generalizations made here are such that they can be subjected to scrutiny.

Although *rent, let, lease* and *hire* present a fascinating study, particularly because of a certain degree of indeterminacy and overlap, I shall not pursue their description here. It is perhaps worth commenting, though, that between *lending* and, say, *renting* there is virtually no difference except what it is that could be lent as opposed to rented; we do not lend a house for a sum, as we do not rent money for a sum. It perhaps goes without saying that the system of options dependent on #reciprocal# – particularly #economic# and its dependents – would be absent from the language of communities where cash economy is not developed. For example, I doubt if any of the options pertaining to *hire, rent, buy, sell* would be present in any of the Australian Aboriginal languages, or in Malinowski's Kiriwinian, especially before contact with money-oriented civilizations. There is no reason to believe that the options relevant to one language are necessarily relevant to another.

Lend and *borrow* are interesting. Their description presented above pertains mainly to one specific register – that of financial dealings. It is only in this environment, that the option #economic# is applicable. In everyday dealings – the lending and borrowing of books, paper, even cars and items of personal use to friends and relatives – the option #economic# does not apply. So while the bank lends me money at some interest rate, my son or friend may lend me something – even small sums of money – without any gain to himself. Thus in these environments, the option #personal# is operative. This case is somewhat different from Putnam's 'division of linguistic labour' with regard to the reference of gold (Putnam 1975), since here most adult speakers of English appear to be fully aware of both references of *lend* and *borrow*. There seems to be no reason for suggesting that one of these references is more accurate, or even historically prior, as the descriptions of these items in the OED will show. So the question may be raised whether we have the same lexical items in these two cases – whether it is a case of homonymy, polysemy or simply another example of the inherent indeterminacy of language. Any answer we give must be consistent, at least in principle, with what we would wish to claim about such uses as *lend me a hand, why are words borrowed?*, *do not sell your soul to the devil*, and *this is just a tactic for buying the Union's co-operation,* etc.

One possible approach to such locutions is to say that they are ungrammatical. An advance on this position is to recognize that only the uninterpretable is ungrammatical, and there is no doubt that locutions such as the above are interpreted successfully every day. This line of argument would suggest that human language possesses the means for metaphorical coinage. The readiness to accept this, does not, however, absolve us from asking: how are new metaphors interpreted? What is there in the make-up of a metaphor that permits us to get our meanings across? I would suggest that even metaphorical coinage relies on certain kinds of lexicogrammatical consistency. After all, why do languages *borrow* words? Why don't they *buy* them? Why don't we *lend* our soul to the devil, instead of *selling* it? I suggest that a systemic description of the type presented here can provide a framework for certain hypotheses.

In talking about the evolution of a language's lexis, the item *borrow* – and its morphological scatter – is used quite frequently. I would suggest that it is not irrelevant that in everyday dealings, the options underlying this item are #...; acquisition; non-iterative:...personal#. The paradigm instance of #acquisition# is *get/acquire*; its implication is *have*. The option #personal# permits the process to unfold without the postulate of exchange equivalent. The interpretation of *borrow* in the context of the description of a language's history, depends precisely upon these options, which are interestingly at the less delicate end of the system network. I would suggest tentatively that a productive mechanism for metaphor coinage is precisely that an item is used so as to retain its primary options, while ignoring the more delicate ones. This is one reason why the interpretation of new metaphors is not perceived as a problem. Another reason which is equally important is the pervasiveness of metaphors in almost any kind of language use. So it is not just *borrow* that is used metaphorically; *lend* too is used – as well as *loan*. And again we find that the paradigm instance of #deprivation# i.e. *give* and *provide* are used interchangeably with *lend*, just as *borrow* is used interchangeably with *get, have, appropriate, acquire,* etc. *A History of English* by Barbara Strang (1970) will furnish many examples. So ... *we borrowed mammoth and astrakhan, but steppe came to us through French* ... (p. 126) ... *Norwegian gave us lemming, which it had got from Lapp* (p. 126); *Turkish provided dolman, coffee..., as well as jackall, which it had borrowed from Persian* (p. 127); ... *monsoon, which Dutch had borrowed from Portuguese, which had it from Arabic, and springbok, the only noteworthy loan as this early date from South African Dutch* (p. 124). And while 'borrowed' words are never returned, their potentially temporary character is, perhaps, not entirely unacknowledged in constructions such as *English has discard a number of items picked up* (p. 129).

It seems obvious that *lend* (*loan*) and *borrow* (*borrowing*) are naturally – i.e. by the nature of their place in the system of English – well suited as metaphors to describe the phenomena in question, the metaphorical use of these items carries a good part of the meaning of the options that underlie their literal use. In this context of discourse such a claim could not be made for such items as *buy, sell, rent, hire,* etc. So one may claim that the seed of the metaphorical extension of a lexical item lies within the lexicogrammatical disposition of that item. Equally important, so far as the interpretation of the metaphor is concerned, the position is not qualitatively different from discourse comprehension in general. The interpretation of a lexical item is naturally dependent upon its environment, as the above description of *lend* and *borrow* and *sell* and *buy* has attempted to show: they mean what they mean because of the way they are used – because of the constructions in which they appear. In their metaphorical use, this principle is not abandoned; here, too, the environment of the item plays a primary role – as the examples from Strang show it is not simply that *borrow* and *lend* are used figuratively, but throughout the discourse we find indicative support for the correct interpretation of these items in that context.

III
ON THE RELATIONS OF FORM AND MEANING

8 Syntax and semantics [1971]

An obvious statement regarding language is that it is a symbolic system serving the purposes of communication. Of course there are other symbolic systems, some of which, it may be argued, are better adapted to certain types of communication. Nevertheless, language remains the most popular system for it is the most encompassing and the most widely effective of all. These statements are obvious to the point of being cliches; their only interest lies here in their relevance to the notion of semantics. In a linguistic model, the recognition of the level of semantics is called forth precisely because language is a system – or to use Vinogradov's formulation (quoted in Vachek 1966: 28) 'a system of systems' – and because its use, *par excellence*, is for communication. The systemic nature of language argues for the recognition of a set of consistent relations governing the value(s) of various elements of the system. Such consistency of relations, which is essential to the very definition of the elements of a system, cannot be accidental; it must arise from some characteristic fundamental to the system as a whole. In a language system such consistency can be traced back ultimately to its communicative function. This same function also implies that a point of contact between language and the extra-linguistic universe must be postulated since it is essential to most language communication. Whatever the areas of disagreement amongst linguists – and these tend to be numerous – it is generally accepted that in a linguistic model it is the semantic level which provides such a contact. Thus 'naming' and 'reference', two of the concepts from the semantic level, simply result from attempts to define the nature of this contact. It would seem therefore that two problems central to any discussion of semantics are: one, how is the semantic level related to other levels of a linguistic model, and two, what is the nature of its contact with extra-linguistic reality? I am concerned here only with some aspects of the first of these problems, concentrating in particular on the relationship of the semantic level to the formal levels of grammar and lexis.

Following Lamb (1964), I see this relationship as a hierarchic one: for encoding, the semantic level dominates the levels of grammar and lexis. The latter two levels stand in a representation relation to it; that is to say, in the production of a message, a certain concatenation of semantic components is selected, which in its turn dictates the selection of the grammatical and lexical categories suitable for encoding the semantic components. Semantics is thus a dynamic linguistic level: its categories are the input, whose ultimate output – a string of meaningful noise – is mediated through the categories of grammar and lexis. This view of semantics puts meaning before the actual selection of the set of meaning-encoding categories, structures or symbols; at the same time it claims by implication that the only linguistic level capable of handling the notion of meaning in language is that of semantics. Like most simplified statements, the view that in some sense the apprehension of the meaning-to-be-encoded must precede – however infinitesimally – the actual encoding of it, is open to misunderstanding in various ways. Let it be added at once that this view does not entail that linguistic meanings are immanent or independent of language (see section 8.3 for a fuller discussion). Nor do I mean to claim by this statement that we have all reached that state of cool rationality in which we always think before we speak, if the word *think* is used in its most frequent sense. I intend to claim only that some apprehension of the meaning structure of the message must be available, at whatever level of consciousness, before it can be encoded in the formal categories of language. That, in the present state of our knowledge, we do not know what specific form such an apprehension takes is not sufficient argument against holding the view; it has at least the merit of agreeing with the speaker's intuition. The reference here is to such indirect expressions of the speaker's intuition as conveyed by a statement such as 'I wanted to say something but didn't know what to say', which does not mean 'Unfortunately, I ran out of deep structures'. If anything, it must mean 'I didn't apprehend the meaning appropriate to the occasion; hence I did not use my language mechanism'. Again when we have the unmistakable feeling that the way we are saying something does not really mean what we mean to mean (!!), it is perhaps an indication that some component of the meaning structure of the message has not been adequately mapped on to the language categories and that meaning is a stage distinct from and prior to that of its encoding. In listening to natural speech, one is struck by the fact that most speakers are not aware of having produced ambiguous sentences – though perhaps an exception should be made with regard to linguists, who seem to be almost pathologically obsessed with ambiguity! When the ambiguity of a sentence just uttered is pointed out to a speaker, his reactions indicate that he was far from being aware of even the potentiality of ambiguity; in producing his sentence the speaker is concerned primarily with the meaning. So far as he is concerned, the encoding categories are identified by their relation to these components of meaning. Naturally, then, they remain unambiguous for him, unless some extraordinary circumstance arises to shift his focus to the encoding categories. As Lashley has shown (Lashley 1951; quoted from Sol Saporta 1961: 193), 'elements of the sentence are readied or partially activated before the order is imposed upon them in expression'; it is not fanciful to suggest that this partial activation of the elements of sentences takes place due to the prior apprehension of meaning.

8.1   Relevance and creativity in competence

The notion of competence (Chomsky 1965: 4) is a commonplace of linguistics today; the ideal speaker of a language has an internalized knowledge of the entire set of rules governing the grammatical, lexical and phonological patterns of his language. Theoretically, therefore, he has the ability of producing any pattern at any time. If we consider the production of speech under normal circumstances, which appears to be qualitatively different from the recall of material learnt for specific purposes, an interesting question presents itself: what is the device that regulates a speaker's choice of a particular sub-set of patterns at a particular time, in exclusion to the rest? It would seem that the speaker matches sense with situation, producing just that set of sentences which is relevant, judged by some standard of relevancy. Asked *Where are you going?* no ideal speaker replies *I ate fish and chips for dinner last night*. This ability to produce relevant sentences is no less central to linguistic competence than the ability to produce grammatical sentences. After all, we would not consider a person's knowledge of a foreign language complete if he were in the habit of producing irrelevant sentences, even if these sentences happened to be always grammatically correct. This aspect of a speaker's competence should be reflected somewhere in a linguistic model, also because it permits novelty and creativity in language use in a non-trivial sense. Linguists have recently been fascinated by the discovery that a competent speaker can produce and understand an infinity of novel sentences, and that in theory a sentence can be infinitely long, which they have equated with creativity in language. However, a much more fascinating fact is that the majority of the so-called novel sentences are novel neither in their grammar nor in their lexis or phonology. Their novelty lies most often in a novel concatenation of non-novel meaning components. This is quite obviously the case since otherwise both encoding and decoding would be impossible. We tend also to ignore a rather important aspect of creativity in language; it is in general not recognized that many sentences which are non-novel can be integrated in a speech interaction which is radically different from that in which they might have been said or heard before. It seems to me that the novelty of *the king of Patna loved the princess of Ruritania* is trivial even though it is quite certain that this sentence has never been heard. By comparison, it is an interesting fact that a non-novel sentence such as *little girls love dolls*, which is not even ambiguous, has a variety of possibilities of being integrated in a number of radically different speech interactions, this integration in each case creating a novelty. I believe I am right in claiming that this is a characteristic specific to human language alone.

To return to the discussion, the postulate regarding relevancy presupposes that the speaker knows what the sentence not yet articulated is about. Now, the only linguistic level that can handle the notion of what a sentence is about is the level of semantics. It would therefore seem reasonable to suggest that the semantic level functions as the regulative device in natural speech production. The speaker's apprehension of the meaning to be encoded guides his selection of appropriate encoding categories from the formal levels of language. Consequently, where the meaning to be encoded so demands, speakers of a language will produce complex patterns with an ease which suggests that our notion of complexity in linguistic patterns stands in need of some serious revision. Given the appropriate occasion, sentences with double negatives are no less easily produced than those with a simple positive. Of course, one may maintain that the apprehension of meaning has nothing whatever to do with language, *per se*, and that it somehow comes about through a cognitive structure, largely independent of language. If so, we need to explain how such a cognitive structure can be acquired. Is the cognitive structure of a congenitally deaf person the same as that of a normal speaker's? If this is not the case (see section 8.3), then could this difference not be attributed to the nonavailability of language? At the same time it should be noted that once the semantic level is denied the capacity of specifying what a sentence is about, the notion of depth for grammatical or lexical categories will be rendered meaningless, since their depth is the function of their interaction with the semantic level. In the last resort, sentences lend themselves to certain transformations or not depending on whether they encode certain semantic components or not. So *the boy frightened the dog* and *the boy admired the girl* lend themselves to different sets of transformations in as much as the deep syntactic functions assigned to *the dog* and *the girl* differ from each other.

8.2   The semantic level represents the meaning structure of language

8.2.1   What are semantic components?

If the semantic level has the capacity of specifying what a sentence is about, then it must also represent the meaning structure of a language. It is important here to emphasize that the meaning structure of language is not co-extensive with the total meaning structure with which a normal human being must operate. Not every abstraction, symbol or object to which the epithet 'meaningful' is applied is necessarily a part of the semantic level of language; the possibility should be granted that something may be meaningful without being a semantic component. A smile, a scowl or a clap are culturally meaningful, but these gestures themselves are not semantic components. The components of the semantic level may be characterized as that sub-set of meaningful abstractions and relations whose meaningfulness can be determined language-internally. This is how the term 'semantic component' is used throughout this paper. Thus the lexical item *smile*, a symbol of the code English language, realizes a set of semantic components, which are themselves language-determined abstractions referring to the extra-linguistic gesture of smile. They are not replications of an extra-linguistic process, object, or state, etc. but have to be seen as theoretical constructs, with no concrete existence. Thus a fragment of the semantic components realized by the lexical item *smile* could be represented as follows:

SMILE: **[process of reaction; ascribed to animate partici-pant;[1] limited to the ascribed participant; attitudinal modification; . . .]**

All of these components are abstractions and none may be pointed out individually in the real world of our experience. The actual layout of the information is here not central to our discussion; other, and perhaps better, modes of presenting the same information may be found. However, there are certain points I would like to make regarding the substance of the information.

The set of semantic components realized by any one item or category is partially ordered; that is to say, the presence of some component(s) may argue for that of some other(s). For example, wherever, in a set, we find the component **process**, this implies that somewhere within the set will be the components specifying **participant** and **modification**, as in the above case. The two last mentioned components are, however, not ordered with respect to each other. Thus the components of a given set may be seen as a kind of dependency structure involving relations of hierarchy (e.g. **process** *vis-à-vis* **participant** and **modification** here) and of simultaneity (e.g. **participant** *vis-à-vis* **modification** here). One may raise the question whether attitudinal modification can be regarded as a component of the semantics of *smile*; after all there can be messages without any modification of the process such as *the baby smiled*. I would suggest that such sentences notwithstanding, **attitudinal modification** is part of the semantic description of *smile*. In our example *the baby smiled*, this part of the meaning of the item is latent. Should the concatenation of meanings to be encoded in the sentence so require, an item will be selected to realize the circumstance explicitly. In making **attitudinal modification** a part of the semantics of *smile*, it is being claimed that there is a fundamental difference between *the baby smiled happily* and *the baby smiled in his sleep*, which can be expressed in a bracketing thus: (*the baby*) (*smiled happily*) and (*the baby smiled*) (*in his sleep*). The circumstance *happily* is integral to the process, while *in his sleep* is not. Further, it enables us to show why *tremendous* in a *tremendous smile* is interpreted differently from *tremendous* in *a tremendous fright*. It follows from this discussion that all the semantic components constituting the description of any one item or category need not be manifest in any one given string in which the item appears; however, the semantic components that remain latent still function as a restrictive as much as if they were manifest.

Attached to each component of such a description, I visualize a (set of) realizational statement(s). In the linguistic model, such statements bridge the gap between the semantic and the formal levels, much as the realizational statements attached to the categories of deep grammar bridge the gap between deep grammar and surface string.[2] For example, take the first semantic component in our analysis of 'smile', **process of reaction**, whose realizational statement would allow any of the three following possibilities:

1. select verb as predicator[3] of a clause as in *smile* in *the baby smiled*; or
2. select noun as head of a nominal group as in *smile* in a *happy smile*; or
3. select deverbal adjective as epithet modifying a head as in *smile* in *the smiling baby*.

Which of the three possibilities will be selected in any given case will be determined by other properties of the message to be encoded. Note that I am not implying here that such selection is consciously undertaken by the encoder; simply, that in some sense and at some level of consciousness, the human brain must be aware of what it is about to do. Whichever of these three possibilities is selected, the entire set of semantic components descriptive of the item will apply equally. That is, so far as the semantics of the item *smile* is concerned, it is not radically altered by the formal status assigned to the item in any given case. If from the total semantic description of an item any component is removed, such a removal will permit an odd or meaningless concatenation of the item in a string. Thus all strings such as *the chair smiled, the chair's smile and the smiling chair* will result from a removal of the component **process ascribed to animate participant**, while *the boy smiled the baby* and *the smiled baby* will result from the removal of the component **process limited to the ascribed participant**. The string *the baby smiled expensively* will be permitted if the component **attitudinal modification** were removed.

8.2.2   Universality of semantic description

It is perhaps evident from the above examples that the validity of the semantic description of any item depends ultimately on whether it is in accord with the facts of the language, which implies that the semantic description of an item in language A is not necessarily the same as that of its translation equivalent in a language B. In order for an item to function as the translation equivalent of some item from another language, partial overlap of meaning is sufficient. Consider for example the English lexical item *elapse*. Let us assume that somewhere in its semantic description, there will appear a component which may be formulated as: **process ascribed to temporal units**. If this component is ignored, we might get a sentence such as *the boy elapsed* (Chomsky 1965: 76–77). Compare this with the situation in Urdu. According to authoritative dictionaries[4] the nearest translation equivalent of *elapse* is *guzarnaa*. However, the component **process ascribed to temporal units** would not appear to be a part of its semantic description since the Urdu sentences[5] corresponding to the following English ones are acceptable: *much time elapsed, the boy elapsed* (= died), *that opportunity elapsed* (= was gone). One may maintain, of course, that in Urdu there is one graphic item but it has many senses, like the English graphological item *spring* (*spring* as opposed to autumn, *spring* as a specific type of jumping, *spring* as stream, *spring* as in furniture). These senses of the item *guzarnaa*, it may be claimed, are the same as that of the English items *to elapse, to die, to disappear*, but it is quite clear that such a segmentation of the meaning range covered by the Urdu item is conditioned by the fact that one's starting point was English. Were we to start with, say, Chinese, the segmentation would be different. To a speaker of English the fact seems self-evident and universally true that the processes referred to by *elapse* and *die* are conceptually different; perhaps, to the Urdu speaker it seems equally self-evident and intuitively true that the process referred to by *guzarnaa* in each of the cited examples is the same in some respect: in each case it signifies **passing out of existence mysteriously**. Thus cattle and animals may *die* as well as men, but it is only man's privilege *to elapse*. In the parody of an Urdu elegy, a line such as *alas, folks! my parrot has elapsed*[6] has at least two layers of meaning precisely because the translation equivalents of the items *to elapse* and *to die* are at once similar and dissimilar in meaning. One may grant the possibility that the total inventory of semantic components of all languages would be identical; this remains to be proved. There is however no doubt that the meaning structure of all languages is not identical; that is to say, the manner in which these components combine in a given language is not the same as in any other language.

8.2.3   How far is concept-formation independent of language?

The view that *guzarnaa* has many meanings each of which is identical with some discrete member from a list of English verbs presupposes that the area of meaning is universally the same. The foundation of the notion of universality for the area of meaning is laid upon the belief that man is everywhere capable of forming certain specific concepts and of establishing certain specific relations between phenomena around him. According to this view the faculty for the abstraction of concepts and relations is independent of language (Lenneberg 1964). Further, for a set of reasons, these universal concepts and relations will be reflected in all languages. I should like to suggest that while it is certain that a set of concepts and relations can be formed – indeed must be formed – in the absence of language, it is by no means easy to indicate just where the line between language-independent and language-modified concepts can be drawn. Consider, for example, the sentence *I am taller than myself.* Let us grant that this sentence is universally odd; one would have to think of some extraordinary situation in which it could be uttered appropriately; for example if one were standing in front of a distorting mirror one might conceivably make such a declaration humorously. Let us grant also that the source of its oddity lies in the faulty generalization conveyed by the statement. A somewhat parallel non-verbal realization of such a faulty generalization would be the efforts of a small child to fit two objects of the same shape, size and volume into one another. A universal rule may be postulated that no entity may be compared with itself in terms of one single property. So *the moon is brighter than the moon* is universally odd for the same reasons as *I am taller than myself.* However, sentences such as *I am taller than I used to be* and *the August moon is brighter than the December moon* are not odd linguistically, irrespective of whether they are factually correct or not. The propositions conveyed by these two sentences are obviously not in violation of the universal rule postulated above. If we analyse these propositions we shall find that so far as language is concerned, the entities being compared are not the same. For the purposes of language, *I-now* and *I-then* as well as *August moon* and *December moon* constitute distinct entities. One might reasonably expect that the concept referred to by the first person pronoun *I* can be formed independent of language; what seems doubtful is that any specific modification of the concept can take place independent of language. Here it might be pertinent to add that in her research on the syntactic peculiarities of the language of the congenitally deaf (being carried out at University College, London), Maris Sheppard finds that all elements of 'modality' are used either scantily or incorrectly by her subjects. Thus the use of the 'modals' such as *can, must,* the selection of 'attitudinal adverbs' such as *luckily, unfortunately,* etc. are either rare or nonsensical in the texts. Her sample consists of nearly 6,000 clauses (a clause is roughly equivalent to a simple sentence). If it is accepted that 'modality' is that component of language through which the speaker's self and attitude are made accessible to his listener (Halliday 1970), then the implication of Sheppard's findings could be that in some sense the concept of self in the normal speaker is so modified by the availability of language that it makes little sense to compare it with that concept of self which is fashioned without the aid of natural language, as in the case of the congenitally deaf.

A consideration of the two examples of comparison raises at least two questions: first, what qualifies as the same entity so far as language is concerned; and second, if the boundaries of the entities recognized in language are created by language itself, in what sense may any concept involving any entity be regarded as free of the influence of language? It may be noted in passing that the notion of co-referent cannot be used to explain why *I am taller than myself* is odd while *I am taller than I used to be* is not. Some other notion is needed to show that *I* and *myself* in our example refer to the same linguistically defined entity while the two *I*'s do not. The referent of these pronouns is not the concrete person, the speaker, in the real world, but some abstraction therefrom. Nor is this relation the same as that of synonymy. Compare *occulists are generally better trained than eye-doctors* (Chomsky 1965: 77) with *occulists are better trained than themselves,* of which only the latter will be regarded as odd by all speakers of English, whereas it is possible to interpret the former as a definition of *occulists* by comparison with *eye-doctors.* Parallel examples would be *windows are larger than casements, lads are heftier than boys, ladies are more refined than women.* It does not matter if the definitions are false; sentences presenting factual inaccuracy of the instantial kind cannot be shown to be odd linguistically (Ellis 1966: 92, note 27). Perhaps the very factor which allows the encoding of factually inaccurate messages forms the basis of that characterizing flexibility in human language which allows it to cope with all conceivable situations (cf. Marshall 1971; Morton 1971). I would go so far as to claim that factual misrepresentation of even universally acknowledged facts cannot qualify a sentence as odd, or else we would be in the absurd position of maintaining that *the earth is flat* is an odd sentence. The examples of definitions presented above are linguistically acceptable because as Lyons points out (Lyons 1963: 74; 1968) synonymy does not imply total overlap or identity of reference. *Money* and *wealth* would be regarded as synonymous by most English speakers, yet it is certainly odd to ask *have you any wealth that I could borrow?* This is not to deny that synonymous pairs are subject to certain restrictions but so are pairs related by antonymy. It is no more odd to say *my brother is an occulist and an eye-doctor* than it is to claim *my brother is fat and thin.*

A related point can be made by reconsidering *I am taller than I used to be.* This sentence must contain at least two generalizations, for the proposition conveyed by *this bottle is larger than it used to be,* literally interpreted must be universally wrong. Everywhere man must distinguish between animate organisms and inanimate objects, since the reasons that make the latter example a wrong assertion also account for the wrongness of *I am shorter than I used to be*.[7] Granted that the propositions conveyed by these sentences are universally wrong, does this also imply that they are linguistically odd? It was suggested in the last paragraph that this is not the case. When we have sentences, which when literally interpreted present an impossible proposition, as in *I shall be sorry when I am dead*, they are not counted out of hand as odd; one assigns them some interpretation which fits the possible facts of the universe of discourse as known to us. Thus given the lines of a popular song *But I was so much older then; I am younger than that now*, the native speaker does not treat them as a set of wrong propositions. The exclusion of such sentences from language is not only a misrepresentation of the facts of language as known to the native speaker; it also has the effect of reducing language to what Weinreich (1966: 399) described as 'humourless, prosaic, banal prose'. One would be closer to accounting for the native speaker's intuition, if following Bernstein (1971), one said that the lines in question convey an 'individuated' meaning – a meaning that is highly specific. In such instances the encoder combines the known and old mechanisms of language in such a way that they convey a new concatenation of meaning. Herein lies the source of most of the rhetorical figures of speech as well as of art in literature (Hasan 1970a).

8.3   Semantics and form

It was claimed above that the levels of grammar and lexis stand in a representation relation to the semantic level. As levels of linguistic description, grammar and lexis are thought of as complementary to each other, so much so that the two could be seen as the two end-points of a continuum (Halliday 1961: 247; Lyons 1968: 153). For this reason they are sometimes referred to as 'demi-levels' (Ellis 1966: 80) belonging to the formal level. Formal level in this sense may be equated roughly with the lexemic stratum in Stratificational grammars (Lamb 1966a: 18–27) as well as with the syntactic component in Transformational grammars. The need for recognizing grammar and lexis as two separate levels arises from the fact that there comes a point in the total description of language where relations of different kinds have to be postulated to account for the pattern formations. An obvious manifestation of such a fundamental difference between the two levels is expressed in a statement such as: 'in grammar one can make a relatively small number of statements to cover a great many things, while in lexicon one has to record as many individual facts as there are lexical items' (Chao 1968: 57). It would be inaccurate, though, to suggest that no generalizations may be made at the lexical level. Within the level of grammar can be recognized two kinds of relations: the syntactic and the morphological. The difference between the two can be made clear by reference to the notion of 'rank' (Halliday 1961). The concept of rank is needed to account for the fact that there are units of different sizes in language. Since this notion is basic to that of structure, no matter what one's linguistic model, most linguists make use of the concept either explicitly or implicitly. Syntax may be defined as that body of relations which specifies the conditions under which units of a smaller size are concatenated to form the structure of a bigger unit. For example 'phrase' is an instance of a unit of smaller size than 'clause', and part of the syntax of a language is concerned with stating the relations which allow the concatenation of, say, a nominal 'phrase' and a verbal 'phrase' in the structure of a clause. Morphology has traditionally been regarded[8] as the grouping of members of units of the same size on the basis of some similarity in their own form *or* in the manner of their operation in surface structures. Thus morphological groups as such are not semantically motivated; for example noun declensions in Latin are morphological as also gender in French and Urdu. This point is discussed in some detail below.

8.3.1   Semantics and lexis

It is often not accepted that both the levels of grammar and lexis stand in the same general relation to the semantic level. This might well be because the reference of lexical items is often thought of as a simple 'thing-sign-for-thing' relation, leading one to the false conclusion that the categories of the lexical level do not lend themselves to statements of formal relations. One consequence of holding this view is that whatever in language cannot be described grammatically is then relegated to the level of semantics, so that 'linguistic description minus grammar equals semantics' (Katz and Fodor 1963: 483). Semantics thus becomes largely an account of the lexicon of a given language. This view can be quite easily refuted by comparing the semantics of the two clauses *the boy loves the girl* and *the girl loves the boy*. The lexical items in the two clauses are identical; the difference in the semantic description of the two can be shown only by reference to the syntactic functions assigned to the items. A distinction is made sometimes between 'being meaningful' and 'having meaning' (Lyons 1968: 412). It is said that a word always has meaning whereas a sentence is meaningful; that is, in the case of the sentence the possibility is allowed that it may not be meaningful, so that being meaningful is not a prerequisite of a sentence but it is a prerequisite of a word. The assumption is that faced with, say, *slithy* an English speaker will not recognize it as a word, but faced with, say, *the chair smiled* he will recognize it as a sentence though perhaps commenting that it has little or no meaning. This distinction seems to me to be spurious.

An important fact regarding lexical items[9] is that a majority of them realize a concatenation of semantic components syncretically. For example supposing that the semantic components **human, female, young, peer** are realized by the lexical item *girl*, there is no specific part of the item which could be said to realize discretely any particular semantic component. Compared with this the majority of sentences realize sets of concatenations of semantic components discretely, with the result that whichever part of the semantic input is encoded correctly (i.e. follows realizational statements attached to the semantic components), that part of the sentence conveys some meaning while other parts do not. So *the chair smiled* is like *the baby smiled*; both are statements regarding a participant to whom a process of reaction is ascribed. To the extent that the realizational statements attached to the semantic description of *smile* are not followed, the sentence is odd and ungrammatical. Note that it is uncommonly difficult to find a one-word sentence which has no meaning. Where we have a lexical item in which some discrete part realizes some discrete semantic component, we can have the same types of defect in it as are possible in a sentence. For example, consider the item *discap* which is faulty in the same way as *the chair smiled*. It may be noted that the mistake in *discap* cannot be explained morphologically or syntactically, since neither syntax nor morphology has any means of predicting where *dis* can be selected as opposed to *un* as a prefix; only a consideration of the formal patterns at the lexical level will provide a reason for such a decision. The order of the elements of word structure that is prefix ^ root, is observed just as in the sentence *the chair smiled* the order of subject ^ predicate realizing the category 'declarative' is observed. A string of lexical items which does not realize any of the semantic components specific to any sentence-type will not be perceived as a sentence by any speaker. Thus *has flat who been in frying fish this?* (= *who has been frying fish in this flat?*) will not be recognized as a sentence by any speaker of English. Similarly, a speaker will correct *discap* to *uncap* but a sequence such as *cdaips* will be a nonlexical item to him, similar to our scrambled non-sentence. There seems to be no reason for making a distinction between having meaning and being meaningful, since in the last resort these characteristics of the lexical item and the sentence arise from our own mode of defining them. It seems to be a part of our definition of the lexical item that it should correctly realize some correct concatenation of semantic components; otherwise there is no reason why *slithy* could not be regarded as a lexical item having little or no meaning. If we build the same kind of requirement into our definition of sentences, then, *ipso facto*, we would not get a sentence which has little or no meaning. Thus it is neither an accident nor an immanent fact that lexical items are always meaningful.

A consideration of the source of error in *discap* will throw some light on some of the formal relations that obtain between units of the lexical level. In English, we have a lexical set some of whose members may be listed as: *cap, button, clasp, cover, close, fold, wind, tie,* etc. Let us refer to this as lexical set 1. A lexical set may be defined at the primary level of delicacy as a grouping of items which have the potentiality of realizing at least one semantic component in common. The more delicate the lexical set, the greater the number of semantic components common to the description of the members of the set. This largely forms the basis for their collocability (i.e. privilege of co-occurrence) with items from other lexical sets. For example, in the semantic description of set 1, there must appear a component which may be formulated as **process of bringing together to form one body**, and all members of the set will collocate with items from sets 2–5, whose typical items could be stated as 2. *material*, 3. *clothing*, 4. *parcel*, 5. *string*. Set 1 is not syntactically defined; there does not appear to be any syntactic category such that it could be realized by some member of set 1 but not from set 6: *cut, slice, snap, shred, mince*, etc. A general statement regarding set 1 may be made: that when the reversal of the process referred to by any member of it is required, the prefix *un-* can be attached to the item. This explains the difference between *she uncovered the baby's head* and *she discovered the baby's head* (!!). It also explains why one may *uncap a bottle* but the *uncapping of stories* is not permitted. Since deverbal adjectives can only have the prefix *un-*, if required, both *unbuttoned* and *unsliced* are permissible items. However, the semantics of *un* in the two items is different: *unsliced* bread is bread that has never been sliced while an *unbuttoned* coat is a coat which must have been buttoned. The cover verb for the reverse processes of set 1, is *undo*, so that one can *undo* what one has *wound, tied, bundled, buttoned*, etc., but one may not *undo* what one has *sliced, shredded, cut, minced*, etc. It is hoped that this discussion, although brief, shows that there is no inherent reason for denying that formal categories and relations can be established for units at the lexical level and that this level stands in the same general relation of representation to semantics as does syntax.

8.3.2 Semantics and syntax

It is somewhat paradoxical that syntax, where the deep categories have been shown to be semantically motivated (Fillmore 1968; Halliday 1967a, 1967b, 1968, 1969a; Lamb 1966a, 1966b; Lyons 1967, 1968) is often excluded from consideration in the discussion of semantics while lexis (where this notion has not been postulated) is quite frequently equated with semantics. Sometimes the question is asked with reference to a given sentence: is this sentence unacceptable semantically or syntactically? with the possible implication that the two are in opposition. As I have endeavoured to show, purely semantic unacceptability is indeed rare for the simple reason that given the right environment an acceptable string will be assigned a meaningful interpretation, no matter how odd its literal meaning may appear to be in isolation. The formal oddity of a string can be shown if one has access to a delicate description of language. Consider our sentence *the chair smiled*. According to the systemic model[10] the oddity of this sentence can be explained syntactically. A brief word first about some aspects of syntactic description in the systemic model. The syntax of a language is here presented in the form of a network of systems. The idea basic to systems is that of environmentally determined choice, so that the point where one starts, determines the range of choices available. Briefly, a system is a grouping of some syntactic features of a given language such that they are mutually exclusive. So, given that one's starting point is the unit clause (a clause is roughly the same as a simple sentence), the range of choices available is to be found in the set of systems applicable to the unit, such as those of 'mood', 'transitivity' and 'theme' to mention but three. Now the primary terms of the system of 'mood' are 'indicative' and 'imperative': no clause may at once have both these features. Supposing a clause has the feature 'indicative', there is then the possibility that it may either have the feature 'declarative' as in *the chair smiled* or 'interrogative' as in *did the chair smile*? Each systemic feature is related to some semantic component; the more delicate the system, the more specific the semantic component related to its terms. Thus the semantic component related to the feature 'indicative' may be labelled **discourse unit** while those related to 'declarative' and 'interrogative' may be labelled **statement** and **question** respectively, both these being more specific than the label **discourse unit.** Attached to each term of the system is a realizational statement, which specifies the form of the surface structure realizing the syntactic features. For example in the case of the feature 'declarative', the realizational statement requires that the elements subject and predicate be placed in that order in sequence. So, *the chair smiled* is a declarative clause whose surface structure is $S^\wedge P$, where S is represented by *the chair* and P by *smiled*. One component of the meaning of this clause is precisely this: as stated earlier it is a statement, as is *the baby smiled* or *all those people who objected to the decision taken by the board walked out.* So far as the system of 'mood' is concerned *the chair smiled* is a well-formed clause; to this extent it is also non-odd.

The source of its oddity lies in that the realizational statements attached to certain features from the system of 'transitivity' are not followed accurately. This system deals with process-participant relations.[11] Process may be regarded as the pivot of 'transitivity' choices, for the process type determines what participant roles may be selected within the clause. If the feature 'reaction' is selected, it is essential not only that the verb realizing the predicator of the clause be a member of the class which refers to processes of reaction, but also that a particular participant role be selected. This participant role, following Halliday (1968: 185ff), may be labelled 'affected'. The definition of the term 'affected' is purely syntactic (which is not to deny that it has a semantic value as well). The 'affected' is that participant, realized typically by an animate nominal phrase, without which an 'indicative active' clause with the feature 'reaction' would be meaningless or unacceptable. This 'transitivity' function may be mapped onto the subject or the (conventional) object or complement in the surface structure of the clause. This depends on some other syntactic feature(s) of a given clause. Thus in *the baby smiled, the baby* is the 'affected' while both in *the dog frightened the boy* and *the boy loved the girl, the boy* has the function of 'affected'. Note that it is possible to say *the boy loved with a passion almost fanatical in its fervour.* It is beside the point for the definition of the term 'affected' that the latter clause will always imply *loved someone*; the relevant point to our discussion is that the last example above is acceptable while *loved the girl with a passion almost ...* etc., unless elliptical, will be regarded as unacceptable. In clauses with the feature 'reaction' the participant 'affected' can be realized only by an animate nominal phrase; wherever this requirement is not met, we will have an odd clause. Thus the reason for the oddity of the clause *the chair smiled* and *the dog frightened the wall* is the same: both are odd because the 'affected' participant *the chair* and *the wall* happen to be inanimate nominal phrases. Moreover both are odd both syntactically and semantically.

8.4   Syntactic categories are semantically motivated

Syntactic peculiarity results in semantic peculiarity because, as claimed earlier, syntactic categories are semantically motivated. They do not come to have some semantic value by accident; as Bazell (1964) has implied, one cannot squeeze out more from a category than one puts into it in the first place. This claim is not tantamount to the statement that meaning determines a syntactic category. If that were the case the clauses *I don't like apples* and *I dislike apples* would have to be regarded as representing the same syntactic category; moreover, one would really be in a quandary since one would not have any criterion for deciding which of the components of the meaning of a given item determines its syntactic status, there being no reason for regarding any particular component of the meaning of that item as the crucially defining one in any given instance. Although both *I don't like apples* and *I dislike apples* have the semantic component **negation** in common (along with some others), only the former is an instance of the syntactic category 'negative'. This asymmetry between syntactic categories and semantic components arises from the fact that a given semantic component may have alternate formal means of realization, while a given syntactic category has only one given typical semantic value. So, the semantic component **negation** can be realized either by the syntactic category 'negative' or by the selection of a lexical item in whose semantic description appears the component under focus. A total one-to-one correspondence does not exist between the units of semantics and the units of form; otherwise one could do without one of the levels. The realization of some given semantic component is, therefore, a necessary but insufficient requirement for the definition of any syntactic category. This requirement (that every syntactic category should have a typical semantic value) arises from the fact that language is a code; in the absence of this characteristic not only would the syntactic symbols of the code defy decoding but it would also be impossible to describe the grammar of any language, at least in the sense in which the term 'grammar' has been traditionally used. The point regarding the typical semantic value of a syntactic category can be illustrated quite easily: thus typically, the syntactic category 'negative' realizes **negation**; 'declarative', **statement**; 'interrogative', **question**; 'imperative', **order**; and so on. I would suggest that there are at least two additional requirements for the definition of a syntactic category. In the first place, if the typical semantic value of a category is modified it should be possible to state explicitly the environment in which such a modification is possible; moreover it should be possible to make such a statement in terms of some formal property to be present in the item under focus. This condition would hold constant for all instances of the given category. For example, consider the category 'negative', whose typical semantic value has been stated as **negation**. However, when we have a clause such as *I don't dislike apples*, the semantic value of the category 'negative' is modified; this value may now be labelled **reserved negation**. The environment in which the negative category will have such a semantic value can be stated in terms of the formal properties of the process in the item: if the process of the clause is realized by a verb in whose semantic description the component **negation** occurs, the negative category will always have the value 'reserved negation'. Other examples of this type are: *they don't distrust John, they did not disarm the country, he never disagrees with anything.* It is often maintained that double negation is tantamount to absence of negation. Note, however, that **reserved negation** is neither identical with **negation** nor with its absence; *I don't dislike apples* does not mean *I like apples*, as is evident from the fact that one may have sentences such as *I don't dislike apples but I don't like them either.* Again, the typical semantic value of 'declarative' is **statement**, but when we have a clause such as *politicians are clever?* with a high-level followed by a high-rise intonation, the semantic value of the category 'declarative' is modified to that of **question**. There is however a difference between **questions** realized by the 'interrogative' and **questions** realized by a 'declarative' with such an intonation: the former is an **unmarked question**, simply calling for some information; the latter also presupposes some specific attitude on the part of the interlocutors. The distinctions of meaning to which attention is being drawn here are admittedly very delicate, but a competent speaker of English must be aware of these distinctions, otherwise the two pairs of clause types would not be used in a regular manner. The fact that the typical semantic value of a syntactic category may be modified in formally stateable environments does not prove that semantics is irrelevant to the definition of categories of syntax; rather it allows us to extend and make explicit the area of formulable distinctions in meaning available to the patterns of a given language. Strangely enough, it was Bloomfield who remarked upon the fact that the meanings conveyed by the categories of natural language are 'far more accurate, specific and delicate' than any that can be conveyed by nonlinguistic means (Bloomfield 1933; quoted from Sol Saporta 1961:

242). The accuracy, specificity and delicacy of meanings conveyed by natural languages is possible largely because the semantic values of categories in language can be modified.

The second additional requirement, and probably the strongest, for the definition of syntactic categories may be formulated as follows: a syntactic category **A** should be systematically relatable to another syntactic category **B**. Ultimately this systematic relation between two (or more) categories arises from an inherent relation obtaining between the typical semantic values of such categories under focus. As an example, we may consider the categories 'volitional' and 'causative' in Urdu (Hasan 1970b) instances of which would be *the cook weighed the rice* and *the master made the cook weigh the rice*,[12] respectively. The typical semantic value of the former category can be stated as **process capable of being voluntarily undertaken**, while that of the latter is **process instigated by some participant other than actor**. It is clear that only clauses which are instances of the 'volitional' category can also be 'causative'. The Urdu clause, *this year, excessive rainstorms caused the crops to ruin*,[13] despite mentioning a cause, is not syntactically 'causative', just as despite **negation**, the clause *I dislike apples* is not 'negative'. Unless a process can be undertaken voluntarily, the possibility of causing it to be undertaken does not exist. It is for this reason that *they made him come across an advertisement* is odd. Such relationship between the syntactic categories allows the syntax of a language to be presented as a network of systems where some category functions as the environment in which some other categories constitute a possible range of choices. This relationship also forms the basis of transformations and arrangement of items into agnate sets.[14]

8.5 Universality of syntactic categories

It scarcely needs to be pointed out that this kind of relationship between two (or more) semantic components of a given language does not arise from the language itself. It is a matter of extra-linguistic reality that a process, capable of being undertaken voluntarily, is also one which can be caused to be undertaken. This might encourage the belief that if syntactic categories are semantically motivated … as they must be if they are deep … then it follows that such categories are universal. Such a belief would be correct only *if* all languages were of necessity bound to reflect in their semantic structure the same set of relations between extra-linguistic phenomena *and if* there were no others means but syntax of realizing such sets of relations.

However, languages vary in what relations between their semantic components would be realized lexically or syntactically, nor is it to be taken for granted that they all reflect the same set of relations between extralinguistic phenomena. In the description of languages, quite often the same pair of labels is attached to a pair of categories in two distinct languages. This, it turns out, is a matter of convenience and does not furnish an adequate reason for concluding that the relation between the members of the pairs so labelled is identical. The reasons for using the same labels are not always the same. In Urdu, the verb capable of realizing a causative process has a specific form; thus *khilaanaa pilaanaa* are the causative forms of *khaanaa* (to eat) and *piinaa* (to drink). Consequently in the surface structure of an Urdu causative clause, there is only one non-discontinuous verbal phrase realizing the predicator as in *maalik nee baavarcii see caval tulvaaee* (the master made the cook weigh the rice) where *tulvaaee* realizes the predicator. In English the majority of verbs do not have a distinct causative form. Consequently, even if *make ... weigh* is regarded as one predicator, the surface structure of the English clause will be said to contain either one discontinuous verbal group or two discrete ones, depending on which analysis one favours. The clauses in the two languages would seem to be labelled 'causative' primarily because of their semantic value. On the other hand, the label 'agentive passive' is applied to the English clause *the window was washed by John*, as also to the Urdu clause *jon see khiRkii dhoii gaii*. This labelling, it would appear, is based on the peculiarities of the surface structure of the two clauses. The semantic value of 'agentive passive' in the two languages is different: for English it may be stated as **the actor of the process constitutes new but not unexpected information** (Halliday 1967b: 217); for Urdu the value of the category is the **potentiality of the process being carried out**, so that the translation equivalent of the Urdu clause in English is not the agentive passive *the window was washed by John* but *John was able to wash the window* (Hasan 1970b; Kachru 1966). Moreover in English the category 'passive' presupposes that of 'transitive'; that is to say, no clause which is not 'transitive' may be 'passive'. This requirement does not hold for Urdu; here a clause may be 'passive' irrespective of whether it is 'transitive' or not. So, a clause such as *beecaree buuRhee see itnii duur na calaa gayaa* (*the poor old man was not able to walk that far*) is an 'intransitive agentive passive' clause. It follows from the semantic value of the agentive passive in Urdu that it presupposes the category 'volitional', so that a passive clause such as *LaRkii see baRii Galtiyããa ki gaĩi* (*the girl was able to make many mistakes*) is odd while in English *many mistakes were made by the girl* is not. The comparison of the

English and Urdu passive[15] also provides an illustration of what was meant by the statement that not all languages reflect in their syntax the same set of relations between extra-linguistic phenomena. It may or may not be true that a certain set of relations between and abstractions from extralinguistic phenomena will be universally reflected somewhere in all languages. I am inclined to think that this claim as such is of no great interest to the description of individual languages unless it were also claimed that each such specific abstraction and relation will universally have the same formal mechanism for its realization. The latter is, quite patently, not the case and there is no reason for suggesting that the deep categories of syntax are by definition universal, much less that the syntax of languages is universal.

Universality does not form part of the definition of a syntactic category, the crucial criteria being the three in conjunction: that (a) it should have a typical semantic value; (b) its typical value should be modifiable only under certain stateable formal conditions; and (c) that it should be systematically related to some other categories of the same level. These criteria are in consonance with the statement that syntactic categories are semantically motivated. This is the ultimate basis of the distinction between syntax and morphology. Purely morphological categories are not semantically motivated, which is one of the reasons why they are not mastered as easily as other parts of the language. Two-year-old Jonathan insisted on *foots*; when corrected consistently to *feet*, he compromised at *feets*. An instance of a morphological category in Urdu is 'gender'; as in French, all nouns in the language are either 'masculine' or 'feminine'. The value of this pair of terms for these two languages is however different from that which they have for English. Thus an Urdu masculine noun is not one which is **animate** and **male**; such disparate items as *box, pamphlet, man, pillowcase, pen* and *formality* are masculine (the Urdu items for these are *Dabba, resaala, aadmi, Galaaf, qalam* and *takkaluf,* respectively). Thus the items labelled masculine in Urdu do not share any particular semantic component in common; what determines their status as masculine is the manner of their operation in surface structure. Depending on what syntactic function is assigned to an item labelled masculine or feminine, certain items of the surface string will have a certain specific form: thus *laRkaa aayaa* (the boy came), *laRkii aaii* (the girl came); *kitaab kaa safa* (the page (masculine) of the book (feminine)), *aadmi ki kitaab* (the man's (masculine) book (feminine)); *aadmi nee eek Dabba xariidaa* (the man (masculine) bought a box (masculine)), *aadmi nee eek Dibiya xaridi* (the man (masculine) bought a little-box (feminine)), and so on. It is of interest here to note that often what may be regarded as a purely morphological category, upon consideration turns out to be a category which can be defined by reference to deep lexis or syntax. Such an example would be the lexical set I discussed earlier. Again, the set of verbs in English to which the suffix *-able* can be attached so that the resultant item can function as an epithet as in *admirable* can be specified by reference to syntax. Very simply this suffix *-able* can be used with that set of verbs which can realize the process 'reaction' in an active transitive clause where two participants are required but where the role 'affected' can be mapped only onto the subject. Thus the epithets formed from *love, admire, like, enjoy* and *detest* are *lovable, admirable, likeable, enjoyable* and *detestable*. The clause type specified above can be exemplified by *he loved/admired/liked/enjoyed/detested it*, where *he* is the affected participant. This explains why one may say *Jim is a likeable fellow* but not *Jim is a puzzleable fellow*. Such findings indicate that we are yet very far, indeed, from having explored the depth of the syntax of even a language so well described as English.

Notes

1   For a fuller discussion of the concept 'participant' see Halliday (1967a, 1967b, 1968, 1970) and also Fillmore (1968). Roughly, participant roles are such as actor, affected, causer, beneficiary, etc. of a process. An example presenting all these participant roles would be *Marmaduke made Alison sew a dress for his daughter*, where *Marmaduke* has the function of causer; *Alison*, of actor; *a dress*, of affected and *his daughter*, that of beneficiary.

2   For a demonstration of how realizational statements bridge the gap between deep grammar and surface structure see Halliday (1969a). Linear ordering of elements within a unit, realizing a syntactic category, is specified by such statements. 'Order' is therefore a matter of deep syntax, a view that has been held by linguists in this country at least since Firth. Some relevant comments will be found in this paper.

3   The element 'predicator' is always realized by a verbal phrase; it has the function of realizing the process of a clause. Thus the element predicator is realized by the verbal phrases *smiled* and *has been sewing* in the clauses *the baby smiled* and *Alison has been sewing a dress*.

4   The dictionaries consulted were *Standard English-Urdu Dictionary* by Maulvi Abdul Haq (Anjuman Press, Karachi) and *Ferozson's EnglishUrdu Dictionary* (Ferozson's, Lahore).

5   The Urdu sentences corresponding to the English ones are as follows: *bahot waqt guzar gayaa, laRkaa guzar gayaa, mauqaa guzar gayaa*, respectively.

6   The line comes from an anonymous parody in Urdu and reads: *afsos ke logo, meraa totaa guzar gayaa*.

7 It has been pointed out to me that old people do grow shorter as they grow older, but I let the example stand since this information does not materially alter the general point being made here.

8 I must accept full responsibility for the definition of morphology being presented here; in particular, the assertion that 'similarity in the manner of their operation in surface structures' characterizes morphological groupings is my own interpretation of how the term was used, in effect, in traditional grammars. An illustration of this point is provided in this chapter. Further, one may consider such English items as *toast* and *underwear* whose assignment to the category 'mass noun' (nouns which may not be modified by a numerical such as one, two, three, ...) is purely morphological. This does not mean that the label 'mass' is therefore morphological, simply that the grouping *toast* and *underwear* with *water* is a matter of morphology, not of syntax. Since morphological groupings are not semantically motivated, they are much more difficult to predict and therefore much more difficult to learn. I still find myself wanting to say *one toast* or *a couple of underwears*. Now, there is nothing in the surface structure of the items *toast* and *underwear* which could be said to be similar except the fact that they both 'behave' as if they were mass nouns; but to maintain that *this* is the similarity in their surface structure is, to go round and round in a circle. Rather it is the manner of their operation in the nominal phrase coupled with the fact that no motivation for such behaviour can be found which will explain both cases that makes their grouping morphological. It may be objected that in interpreting syntax and morphology thus, I am substantially re-defining the terms; this may be true but the re-definition presented here seems to me to have the merit of being closer in spirit to how the terms were employed, than a literal interpretation of the terms would be.

9 It is useful to make a distinction between what constitutes a graphological word, or a grammatical word, and the lexical item. Despite a large degree of overlap, the three are not identical. Thus the item *spring* in English represents one graphological word while it represents at least four lexical items (cf. comments above). Again it may be desirable to regard *man* as one grammatical word belonging to the class *noun*, though lexically a distinction may be made between *man* in *the man came yesterday* and in *man, did you notice what she was wearing*? Thus, 'lexical item' as used in this paper is not the same as 'lexical item' or 'lexical entry' as used in transformational grammars (Katz and Fodor 1963: 495; Katz and Postal 1964: 17; Chomsky 1965: 166), where most often the terms can be equated with graphological word, as in the treatment of *bachelor* by Katz and Fodor, which is said to be *one* lexical item with many meanings.

10 The discussion of syntax and syntactic categories presented in this paper presupposes the systemic model (Halliday 1961, 1966a, 1967a, 1967b, 1968, 1969a, 1969b, 1970; Huddleston 1965; Hudson *et al.* 1968). The systemic model takes a functional view of language (Halliday 1970), maintaining that for the theoretical description of language, the distinction between

performance and competence is trivial in the sense that no aspect of performance can be theoretically described unless it is systematic and no systematic performance is independent of competence. Irrespective of their validity on other counts, most traditional descriptions of language are not descriptions of unsystematic performance. There is no opposition between competence and performance in language in any interesting sense, unless by performance were meant the motor and neurological processes involved in the production of speech, when it would be a matter of one's definition of the scope of linguistics to decide whether such processes form an integral part of the description of language. The systemic model is thus concerned with the systematics of the use of language. The discussion of the syntax and of particular systems in this paper is of necessity both brief and over-simplified; in particular I have used certain terms for ease of communication which do not appear in the system networks of English. Some examples of such terms are 'active', 'passive', 'transitive' and 'intransitive'. I am fully responsible for the interpretation of the model as well as for all views expressed on syntax and semantics in this paper.

11   A detailed discussion of the system of transitivity for English may be found in Halliday (1967a, 1967b, 1968).

12   The Urdu sentences corresponding to the two here are *baavarcii nee caval tolee* and *maalik nee baavarcii see caval tulvaaee*, respectively.

13   The corresponding clause in Urdu would be *is saal, baarish aur tuufaan fasl ko barbaad karnee kaa mujib huee* or less formally *is saal, baarish aur tuufaan ki wajeh see fasl barbaad ho gaii.*

14   An agnate set is a grouping of items which are syntactically related and differ from each other in a regular manner that can be specified syntactically. Thus active and passive form an agnate set.

15   For a more detailed discussion of the semantic values of the different types of passive in Urdu, see Hasan (1970b) (this volume).

9 The meaning of 'not' is not in 'not' [2011]

9.1 Introduction

For human beings, the world certainly turns on the exchange of meaning. Even a casual observation of daily life reveals the active participation of language in a wide range of human social practices – which means that much of our practical life is beholden to acts of meaning. As the discourse here[1] develops (Section 9.2.2), it will become obvious that this foregrounding of meaning is not designed to underplay the importance of 'syntax' or 'expression',[2] but in a very real sense the *raison d'être* for syntax and expression is their role in bringing about the 'sens-ible'[3] manifestation of meaning. We might argue quite rightly that without them meaning could not be accessed, but by the same token, without meaning the being of these phenomena – if they had any – would have no bearing on human life – and certainly not on language: meaning, literally, is the essence of language, on which more later.

Meaning in the popular sense of the word – that is, not necessarily linguistic but by any means – has been central to all major aspects of human life. This was true in the early stages of the evolution of the human species, and it is true today when thanks to woefully limited ideas about progress we might be approaching the end of that long drawn drama. Since the claim about the centrality of meaning to human life may sound exaggerated, I will briefly introduce some evolutionary and developmental perspectives based on research in such branches of the human sciences as archaeological anthropology, neuroscience, psychology, sociology and last and most pertinent, one particular approach to the study of language, which treats linguistic meaning as the essence of humanity, viz., systemic functional linguistics.

9.1.1 Meaning in social life: Archaeological anthropology

The traditional view in narrating 'The Human Ancestor's Tale' (with apologies to Dawkins 2005) had presented tool making as one of the most basic steps in the evolution of the human species. However, today research in archaeological anthropology (e.g. Noble and Davidson 1996; Davidson 2007) places social interaction at the centre of this process, arguing that the production of tools logically presupposes the existence of some form of communication for *Homo sapiens*. With hindsight, the image of a group of early 'ancestors' crafting their tools, each in his own 'bubble' of silence does strike one as somewhat absurd, especially when evidence suggests that the tools were used collectively and became, in fact, a commodity for exchange fairly early in our history. What was being exchanged in the interactions was significant in two senses: it was significant for the community's survival through a direct management of the material environment, and it was significant as a step in facilitating the development of acts of meaning as an evolving mode of human existence. Whatever its modality, social exchange consists in message-ing, and the point of a message is its meaning. The importance of meaning thus predates those anatomical changes which, by facilitating auditory modes of meaning became a milestone in human cultural evolution (Marwick 2005) and which, as the precursor to the 'meaning-sound' conjunction, have been long celebrated in linguistics as a crucial property of human language. In the next few subsections, however, the concern will be with the popular sense of meaning in communication irrespective of the means by which it is effected: in the game of evolution language arrived later than many other means.

9.1.2 Meaning making mind: Neuroscience

Archaeological anthropology also provides cogent ground for discarding the Cartesian mental myths as relics of the past; it suggests, instead, that the human brain has evolved to its present state in response to a complex set of evolutionary pressures (Noble and Davidson 1996; Davidson 2003, 2005), in the midst of which there had continued the typically human motif of action and interaction, so that material action and communication moved in parallel; which implies in turn that both the physical and the mental resources were simultaneously involved in the process of evolution. The emergence of symbolic behaviour and verbal language are milestones not only in the evolution of language, but also in that of the human brain. This phylogenetic perspective on the making of mind foregrounds the dialectic that holds social practices, acts of meaning, and the physical and functional evolution of the brain in a mutually evolving relation – a **dialectic** whereby the history of any one is part of the history of the other two.

Recent research in neuroscience appears to support this evolutionary view. The findings it offers concerning the trajectory of the brain's structural and functional development apply to the entire human species. As *Homo sapiens*, we are inordinately proud of the **faculties** of our brain, treating them as independent of its 'physique': the clear distinction made between the two has thus given rise to the widespread duality of brain and mind, as two distinct phenomena. Modern neuroscience explodes this myth: it describes mind, though cautiously, as a '**personalized brain**' (Greenfield 1997, 2008). Attempting to explain why human brains are not 'robotic' – why we do not act as clones of each other – the researchers suggest that each individual brain is shaped by the experiences it encounters in the living of life. For a variety of reasons, the latter are not – indeed, *cannot be* – identical for every member, and the ways in which different individuals encounter and 'deal with' the different experiences in different ways creates what Jean Lave (1997) has called 'habits of the mind'. Thus each individual brain develops specific ways of being, doing and saying – a mental disposition towards recognizing aspects of experience as relevant information: it is these processes that we call 'mind'. And a large part of the experience of living is the experience of 'language-ing': meaning thus spans the social universe extending from a community's lifestyle to its members' ability to act as social agents, a significant part of their identity.

9.1.3   Meaning, mind and culture: Semiotic mediation

To ask how mind is shaped by experience is to ask with Bernstein (1990) how the 'outside' becomes the 'inside'. Gregory Bateson once humorously remarked (1972) that inside the brain there are no monkeys or coconuts: experience, *per se*, does not get transplanted in the brain/mind. On the basis of modern research on the brain, and of our first-person experience of experiencing, we may claim with some confidence that to be internalized all experience must be both sensi-ble and 'intellig-ible' (Russell 1940); it must be sensuous, impinging on (some of) the five senses, and, at the same time, the brain must somehow 'make sense' of it, must 'absorb' its essence, that which gives it a 'point' in the life of the experiencing being. This is where we turn to Vygotsky's concept of '**semiotic mediation**'. This is best seen as a 'hinge concept' capable of connecting nature to nurture, phylogeny to ontogeny, community to individual and the material to the semiotic.

To present a highly simplified account: archaeological anthropology is an enquiry into the communal history of *Homo sapiens*, and neuroscience is an exploration of the structure and functioning of the brain in the members of this species; in both cases the orientation is phylogenetic; neither research is concerned with the developmental trajectory of single members of the community, which must always display some variation. But the riddle of the transformation of some outside experience into the habits of particular 'personalized brains' can be resolved only by a close look into the relationship of single human organisms to the community to which they belong: in other words the perspective has to be **ontogenetic**. Vygotsky (1978; Wertch 1985a, 1985b) solved this riddle with his concept of semiotic mediation. He postulated a continuity between the **biogenetic** foundation of the neonate's activities and the **socio-genetic** foundation of its activities as it moves through life becoming an individual. Initially culture has little hand in creating or shaping these biogenetic activities. However, many of these activities are assigned some significance by the *caregiver who is always already acculturated*: this is where **sociogenesis** sets in. It is this assigning of significance by an already socialized individual that forms the basis of continuity between the bio- and the sociogenetic, for indeed the baby grows with the growing habit of meaning (Halliday 1975; Hasan 2001): little wonder none of us can remember when meaning first became meaningful to us. In this way, Vygotsky in fact re-wrote the prefix 'onto-' as 'socio-' in the context of human development; there is very little that is *onto*genetic in human behaviour that did not begin as a communally recognized social activity, whether material or semiotic. For each mind, the internalized significance of these experiences is individuated because each history of experience is in some ways unique: what is being experienced is unique; the experiencing, internalizing brain is unique, thus *each new internalization of sociogenetic experience by an individual is at once irrevocably social, and indisputably individual*.

A distinctive feature of Vygotsky's notion of mediation was its openness to various classes of experience. For Vygotsky, developmental psychology was not about how nature designed the brain to function once for all, but rather about how the naturally designed brain of a human being has the potential for extending itself in absorbing the relevant aspects of the universe presented socially. Thus, for example, the infant absorbs the significance of the caregiver's uptake of a gesture, which links a material event to meaning; with the introduction of a material tool, the worker's earlier relationship to his work changes in grasping the significance of the tool in the performance of that task; it is however *with the arrival of linguistic meanings that the character of semiotic mediation changes qualitatively*: talk between participants of some activity does more than act as an instrument – it encourages analysis; the newcomer to the school learns concepts, their interrelations, forms of reasoning and other strategies, all mostly through the abstract tool of language. This acts as the basis for the **formation of higher mental functions**. Though there is much more to semiotic mediation,[4] the above narrative indicates clearly the central place of meanings in creating minds – and human minds[5] are the true force behind the social agents whose actions create, maintain and change human societies.

9.1.4 Bernstein and social variation: From interaction to ideology

There is a great deal of convergence between Vygotsky, Bernstein and Halliday (Hasan 2005a). Both Vygotsky and Bernstein take the social environment as critical in shaping human development, assigning a central importance to social interaction, and within that, centrally to language. However, in Vygotsky's work, society appears somewhat monochromatic, as if all types of social interaction were equally within reach of all social agents (Hasan 2005a). With a keen awareness of the systematic relationship between **social structure**, agents' **social positioning** and forms of interaction, Bernstein's research (1990, 2000) attempted to show that experience of interaction for social agents was varied from one social group to another; and that it was not simply a source of information, it also defined the participant's orders of relevance: *different forms of interaction produced different forms of consciousness*. This was not a statement about mental 'development' *per se*: it pointed to the social genesis of that mental disposition which acts as the principle for selecting some particular sets of **values and beliefs** and the principles of their **legitimation** in their immediate community, which obviously vary across the various groups in a society. Thus for Bernstein, orientations to meaning *are* **ideological orientations** which act for and against cultural continuity/change, maintaining and fighting the persistence of social hierarchy: this I take to be the essence of Bernstein's '**coding orientation**'.

9.1.5 Beyond the 'things in heaven and earth': From protolanguage to linguistic meaning

Although in the work of both Vygotsky and Bernstein, linguistic meaning is assigned an important role, it is Halliday who in his research (1975) focused on a sociogenetic theory of not only the **ontogenesis of language** in individuals but also what linguistic meaning does for the growing child.[6] Simplifying a good deal, I present here the gist of his enquiry under two headings: (1) continuities from material action to linguistic interaction (2004b: 9); and (b) the significance of becoming a language user (1975, 1980). That the exchange of meanings in the wider sense of the word predates linguistic meaning has been implied throughout this discussion. Figure 9.1 represents Halliday's view of the significant steps in this journey from the material to the semiotic where very early 'bodily actions (including ... movements of the limbs and ... movements of the vocal organs) ... get co-opted ... as symbolic expressions' (Halliday 2004b: 9).

The view presented by Halliday categorizes communication by reference to their **modes of meaning**: (a) **pre-semiotic move** expressed as some bodily act, for example, a yell – if the yell is seen as significant it is thanks to the receiver; (b) **isolated symbol** manifested as bodily action, but unmistakably[7] vested with significance; (c) a **primary semiotic system** – Halliday (1973; 1975) refers to this as **protolanguage**[8] – manifested as vocal symbols, each with a specific import; contextual evidence about the baby's communicative intent is palpable, though the expression, albeit vocal, is still 'alien' to the acculturated adult; there is no syntax in the early stages, though the function of the message in context is obvious to caregivers; and, finally, (d) the onset of the **higher order semiotic**, that is, language, where expression and meanings in the utterance come increasingly to bear systematic relationship to the caregiver's language. This classification of the different kinds of acts of 'meaning exchange' foregrounds on the one hand the enormously varied nature of that to which we refer as 'meaning' in popular usage, and on the other, the compatibility between the evolutionary and the developmental trajectories.

Figure 9.1: Moving and meaning (source: Halliday 2004b: 9)

moving [material action]	agitate limbs; cry	→	reach & grasp [directed movement]	→	roll over [shift perspective]	→	sit up [world as landscape]	→	crawl [move vantagepoint]	→	walk upright
meaning [semiotic action]	exchange attention	→	yell [directed cry]	→	"!", "?" [express wonder]	→	signs as isolates	→	protolanguage [primary semi- otic system]	→	language [higher order semiotic system]

It is not easy to describe quickly the significance of a child becoming a language user: Halliday captures the enormity of this enterprise in '*Three aspects of children's language learning: learning language, learning through language, learning about language*' (1980). The appreciation of the multiple domains of human experience captured within these three descriptive nominal groups depends on how one conceptualizes language. With Halliday's functional approach the logical implication is that what language is and what language can do for its speakers are not unrelated phenomena. So far as the potential of language for meaning is concerned, there is no exaggeration in the claim that it is limitless: it can go beyond what Hamlet referred to as the 'things in heaven and earth', covering past, present and future, concrete and abstract, real and imaginary: the limit of meaning in language is the limit of its speakers' imagination. Not surprisingly, its contribution is central in shaping individuals from their infancy – the nature of the universe they internalize, their ideological orientations, their ways of being, doing and saying, the habits of their minds, the points of departure for their imagination. Halliday's functional approach has enabled researchers to shed some light on *how linguistic interaction is transformed into ideological orientation* through habitual exchanges of meaning (Cloran 1994; Williams 1995; Hasan 2009a). Vygotsky and Bernstein give us a sociogenetic theory of the development of mind and mental disposition; Halliday's linguistics has the means of revealing the potential that, at least in theory, is available to every language user. As the model of language as meaning potential, it has the power to deconstruct the essence of any ideological orientation whatever – both as content and as process. We need to ask: What gives this powerful potential to linguistic meanings for shaping human minds, and thus human lives?

9.2   Meaning: Here, there and everywhere

The word 'meaning' in its popular sense (especially as used in Sections 9.1.1–9.1.3) may be paraphrased as 'making sense' or 'deriving significance' – in short, 'interpreting': obviously, in this perspective, any phenomenon 'has' meaning so long as it is open to interpretation. This open-ended view of meaning may appear chaotic to those who like their data neat and tidy; nonetheless, in light of first-person experience, it has to be granted that human beings do make sense of an immense range of phenomena – for example, the house one lives in, the garden that adds to its status – or not, as the case may be – the clothes one wears, the fabric, the design;

one's comportment, aloof, reserved or out-going; and a myriad of such phenomena – all 'say something' to those who encounter them. Making sense seems to be an imperative of the brain: it is impossible to state with certainty what, if anything, can *not* be interpreted; what seems certain is that *the brain is a naturally designed interpreter*: so long as it is not dozing, not drunk, not deranged, not dead, it must make a 'reading'. I am tempted to suggest that the habit in human beings to (un-/sub-)consciously interpret the elements of their environment is biogenetic – perhaps a naturally evolved disposition: the survival value of such a capacity to the species can hardly be disputed.[9]

9.2.1 Semiology, multimodality and meaning

That meaning in the above sense is so ubiquitous is primarily an outcome of how we define sign/symbol: if the sign/symbol 'is' simply 'anything that, by custom or convention, stands for something else' (Noble and Davidson 1996: 5),[10] then inevitably the entire world turns into a set of symbols, for the fact is that things, persons, processes and what not, can all 'stand for something else', and typically do. Meaning in this all-embracing sense is a meaningful concept, as argued above. But from the point of view of devising an integrated framework for its description, it poses some interesting problems. To put it mildly, it is a challenge to Saussure's 'science of semiology',[11] and by the same token to the burgeoning trade of multimodality: with this conception of sign, semiology as a 'science' (cf. Saussure 1966: 16) would need to study all those elements of the universe that have the potentiality of 'standing for something else'. To the best of my knowledge, the principles governing the identification of such signs and the goal(s) of their study have so far remained rather unclear. This line of argument opens a huge debate; and in the interest of 'science' it must be conducted sometime. A careful pursuit of this kind would be a significant contribution to the study of communication in culture. However, I propose to side-step these issues by restricting myself to linguistic meaning, in order to throw some light on the source of its power.

As a preface to what follows, note that underlying the description and identification of linguistic meaning is the weight of an entire theory of language, but the various linguistic theories are not in agreement on what it means to say 'linguistic meaning'. This is true of even varieties of what is seen as 'the same' theoretical framework, viz., Systemic Functional

Linguistics. The approach presented here is grounded in my interpretation of Halliday's SFL (henceforth, SFL).[12]

9.2.2 Concepts for meaning in language: (a) Stratification and realization

This is not the place for presenting details about the theory as a whole. However, we do need to introduce a few fundamental theoretical concepts, particularly relevant to the explication of 'meaning in language'. The first of these concerns **stratification,** which logically leads us to **realization**. Figure 9.2 shows how the two are related.

The inner ellipse in Figure 9.2, which is divided by a prominent horizontal line into two halves, represents a language-internal view of stratification. Following Hjelmslev (1961), the top half of the ellipse is called **content**, the lower half, **expression**: this is **primary stratification** with 'minimal coding'; it presents a picture of language as a symbolic system, as the term is used above (Section 9.2.1). Halliday (1961) and before him Firth (1957) see language as a **multiple coding system**; as Figure 9.2 shows the primary strata are divided[13] further into two strata each[14]: content is reconceptualized as **semantics** and **lexicogrammar** – that is, (linguistic) meaning and wording, respectively – while the expression level is re-stratified as **phonology** and **phonetics**. It is important to note here the abstractness of content, and the materiality of expression: both meaning and wording *per se* are 'invisible' in the sense that they cannot be 'accessed' by any of the senses and are therefore not available for any mental process without the intervention of phonology and phonetics which (like orthography) are

Figure 9.2: Strata in a functional theory of language

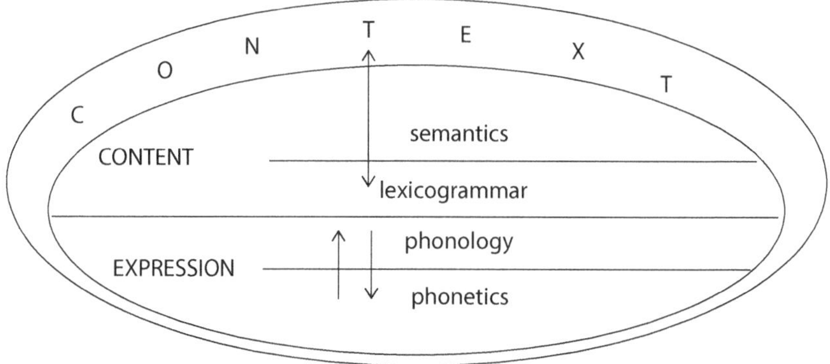

'visible' in the sense that they impinge on the human senses. The outer surround of the ellipse represents the communal environment of language, namely **context**, which, despite being language-external, bears an inherent relationship to language. For this reason *it must form an integral part of any adequate theory of language*. In SFL it is taken to represent the fifth theoretical stratum. Figure 9.2 is iconic of the fact that context of culture bears a stronger relationship to the two strata of meaning and wording, and a considerably weaker one to phonology and phonetics.

Stratification separates out each aspect of the overall organization of the linguistic theory, individuating each by virtue of the kind of abstractions each is capable of describing: to give very simple examples, the application of **true/false** or **appropriate/inappropriate** are relations valid only at the level of context – there are no false or inappropriate meanings or wordings, much less phonological or phonetic units; **synonymy/antonymy** are semantic relations; the other strata have little to say about them; **declarative/interrogative** or **hypotaxis/parataxis** are categories at the level of lexicogrammar – the units at the other strata do not contract such relations, despite the fact that we might talk of someone as having a 'declarative style' – an idiomatic usage, not to be confused with technical terminology; **homophony** is applicable to phonological objects, not to wording; **bi-labial/dental** describe qualities of phonetic units. Stratification, thus, represents a principle for the division of labour in the realm of linguistic description. This is not to claim that there are no categories based on inter-stratal relations, but simply to insist that each stratum is concerned with a distinct order of abstraction.

Obviously, the separation of strata is an artefact of analysis. In actuality, language always occurs in some social context, presenting itself as a seamless flow of meaning-wording-sound, which typically functions in harmony with the social occasion of talk. **Realization** (Halliday 1992; Hasan 1995, 1996, 2009b, 2009c; Matthiessen 2007a; Butt 2001, 2008) is that theoretical concept which specifies the inherent connections among the linguistic strata whereby the perception of their seamless unity is maintained: it is *the* most fundamental concept for examining inter-stratal relations. I have sometimes remarked (e.g. Hasan 1996, 2009b) that realization is a hard worked concept: it has been made to do many different kinds of thing, two of which are particularly relevant to the present discussion. First, consider realization as it works in primary stratification: in Figure 9.2, the bold horizontal line, dividing the ellipse into two halves, represents the Saussurean **line of arbitrariness**. Hjelmslev's content and expression, in fact, closely correspond to Saussure's **signified** and **signifier**, respectively. Saussure's sign, a two-part entity, is a conjunction of the two – a conjunction without any logical basis: the signified, an abstract phenomenon, accessible to mental activity alone; the signifier, an acoustic shape with materiality, impinging on the senses, makes the meaning it signals accessible to mental processing. Saussure described the basis of their conjunction as **arbitrary**, rooted in **convention**. This is the relation that holds between the primary strata of content and expression: units of expression 'stand for' units of content, or 'signal' them; to sum up, the realization relationship of phonetics-phonology as two strata of expression to semantics-lexicogrammar as two strata of content is characteristically arbitrary.

However, so far as the three strata above the stratum of phonology are concerned, their mutual relationship is different. Halliday (1988) has referred to the realization relation between lexicogrammar and semantics as **natural**. What this means is not that nature has granted us a biological facility for the perception of specific pairings of semantic and lexicogrammatical units, but rather that linguistic meaning is un-knowable without lexicogrammar; and one might add: the process of meaning is impossible without context. This points to a qualitatively different kind of work done by the realization relation across context, meaning and wording – it is not arbitrary but **dialectical**, so that the relationship logically locks the three together in such a way that the absence of one from this triad would leave the other two impotent: the recognition of all three working together is necessary for doing *adequate* linguistics. Based entirely on communal convention, the arbitrary realization relation of phonology to 'worded-meaning-in-context' is quite unlike the dialectical realization relation which is based in necessity – a necessity that arises from the internal logic of language not by communal convention. If language is to function as system and process 'in the living of life' (Firth 1957), this internal logic must hold. Note the double headed arrows linking the three upper strata of context, semantics and lexicogrammar: they point to the **bi-directionality** of this dialectical realization, which is motivated by the need to recognize two reciprocal perspectives essential to the maintenance and evolution of language. The 'downward' move from context to semantics to lexicogrammar is the **encoding view**, the 'upward' move 'is' the **decoding view**: the two indicate respectively the speaker and addressee position *vis-à-vis* the 'speech event' (Firth 1957). To put it more simply, in producing an utterance, the issue is the speaker's sense of the relevant context which identifies the relevant semantic domains. This enables the selection of meanings to be meant in this instance, and that leads to wording choices.[15] No matter how problematic it may seem to subscribe to this view, it would be far more problematic to reject it out of hand. It does not seem subject to doubt that, in the universe of semiotic activity, meaning comes 'before' wording in some sense of the word; let me, however, add immediately that in this locution, 'before' cannot refer to some temporal phenomenon; witness, however, the awareness of 'slips of the tongue', searching for 'that word' ('which word?' 'Well, the one whose meaning the speaker needs to encode here and now!'); saying: 'I don't know what to say', does not mean: 'I happen to have forgotten the formal structures of this language', but simply that the situation defies the possibility of choosing some appropriate meaning: the occasion is 'breath-taking'. For the receiver, however, meaning cannot come first,[16] no matter how instantaneous its grasp is in everyday use of language: what allows the addressee to get to the speaker's meanings is the speaker's wording.[17]

Realization works somewhat differently in the two directions. In the encoding view, it is an **activation** of some possible choice at the next lower level: thus *in the production of an utterance, context activates meaning, meaning activates wording*. By contrast, in the reception of the utterance, realization is **construal** of the relevant choice at the higher level: thus *in decoding an utterance, the choice in wording construes meaning, the choice in meaning construes context*. It is relevant to note here that in SFL, the **definition criteria** for a category are said to be located at the level above it (Halliday 1988): for example, it is the context of the utterance 'Join the navy and see the world' that alerts us to the fact that despite 'being' worded as coordinated imperative clauses, the utterance is not a set of **orders**; it is an advertisement in the form of exhortative invitation supplemented by a condition. By contrast, the lower level category furnishes **recognition criteria** for the category at the above stratum: thus the clause 'Do it now!' is an imperative clause which overwhelmingly functions as recognition criterion for – that is, construes – the semantic category DEMAND; GOODS/SERVICES, unless there is good reason for doing otherwise, as in the above advertisement. **Meta-redundancy** (Lemke 1984) often invoked in the discussion of meaning and metaphor is a technical label that refers to precisely the relations just paraphrased. The fact that realization between strata does *not* display a 1:1 relationship is a critical feature ensuring the semogenic power of language (further discussion in Section 9.3.1). Further, if the relationship between the categories on two strata were universally biunique, there would be no ground for the recognition of two distinct strata (Halliday 1988). By the same token, in an important respect, it would reduce the semiotic system of language to the same level of semological complexity as that found in the systems of traffic lights. Hjelmslev (1961) suggested wisely that a necessary condition for recognizing separate strata is their **non-conformality**.

Although the difference between the arbitrary and dialectical realization relation has not been made explicit in SFL, Firth's (1957: 33) distinction between **major** and **minor 'functions' of meaning** interestingly does suggest a division between the strata which seems to bear a close resemblance to the suggestion I have made here: Firth treats phonetics as the minor function[18] of meaning, and 'lexical, morphological, and syntactical (…), and the function of a complete locution in the context of situation …' as the major functions of meaning.[19] Firth does not offer an explicit justification for his division between the major and minor functions of meaning. My discussion of the special kind of solidary relation between context, meaning and wording, clearly assigns the triad an important role in the process of meaning, while the arbitrary relation between the triad and the strata at the expression level is a good reason for thinking of the latter as not having the same importance for making meaning: their function is, rather, the relay of worded meaning.

By focusing on the triad as central to the meaning process, I do not mean to imply that expression is altogether irrelevant to the process of meaning; in fact, both in production (activation) and in reception (construal), the expression strata of phonology and phonetics act as the point where the sign's *materiality works as the initial gateway for entry to the levels of wording and meaning* which would otherwise remain inaccessible. In this sense they do have a function in the encoding and decoding of meaning, but that function is, as pointed out by Firth, a minor one. For, if we leave **prosodic** phonology (Halliday and Greaves 2008) out of this discussion, it is obvious that **segmental** phonology and phonetics play little or no part in the construal of wording (hence of meaning) in the sense in which the term 'construal' is being used here. The expression strata simply **signal** the presence of a sign unit but even this signalling is not always unambiguous.[20] Their function is thus not content-forming; it is simply content-expressing. This is the price paid for arbitrary realization. However, the uncertainty thus created is constrained by the second property of sign identified by Saussure, that is, **linearity**. By supporting the syntagm, linearity gives us the invaluable **co-text** or Firth's **serial context**; not many complete speech events consist of one morpheme, leave aside one phoneme. In normal use of language phonemes occur in each other's company, so do syllables, morphemes, words, clauses, questions and responses; they thus create the 'linguistic context' or become the co-text for each other. In doing *real* linguistics, isolated linguistic categories[21] – along with the man from Mars – should be banished as irrelevant to linguistic explanation.

9.2.3 Concepts for meaning in language: (b) System and instance

The **langue** v. **parole** dichotomy is as old in linguistics as the modern discipline itself. The two have been viewed as irreconcilable; thus 'langue' – a code or system – was taken as 'a fixed set of rules' – sometimes essentially innate, and 'parole', its instance, as an unpredictable flow of signs, mercurial, and governed only by the individual's will; the former **synoptic**, the latter **dynamic**. However, *the problem with language as system is that it needs to be both stable/synoptic and changing/dynamic*: it must remain in use to stay alive,[22] and that is possible only if it changes along with the changing conditions for its use (Butt 2004b; Hasan 2009b). The SFL concept of **instantiation** resolved this seeming paradox: Halliday (1987, 1999) argued that a system and its instance are 'the same thing' seen from different perspectives; their behaviour displays deep **complementarity** (Halliday 2008). While the possibility of speakers moving beyond the system, whether by variation or innovation, is empirically evident, it is equally obvious that instances allow speakers some view of the system. Nor is there any doubt that the system is the resource by which parole as instance is interpreted (Hasan 1984a, 2009b, 2009c). It is in and by the production of the instance that both conformity and innovation play their significant roles in maintaining and renewing the system. If synchronic variation and diachronic change in language are related phenomena (Labov 1972; Fasold and Schiffrin 1989; McMahon 1994), then we may have to concede that the view of system as synoptic and of process as dynamic needs careful reconsideration. This debate is also relevant to semantic change, which does not always go hand in hand with lexicogrammatical change, as evident from the history of items such as *host, silly, condescension* and others where the primary categorization of the items does not change but the meaning does. Neither is it clear whether such semantic changes in meaning are responsive to some contextual changes; if so what they are, and what is the nature of the process of such responsive changes. Figure 9.3 captures Halliday's (1999: 8) view of the complex relationships between systems and instances.

The different stages of the development of this relationship are discussed in Halliday (1987, 1999, 2002, 2008), Hasan (1984a, 1995, 2009a), O'Donnell (1994), Matthiessen and Nesbitt (1996), and Matthiessen

Figure 9.3: Two systems and their relationships: Realization and instantiation

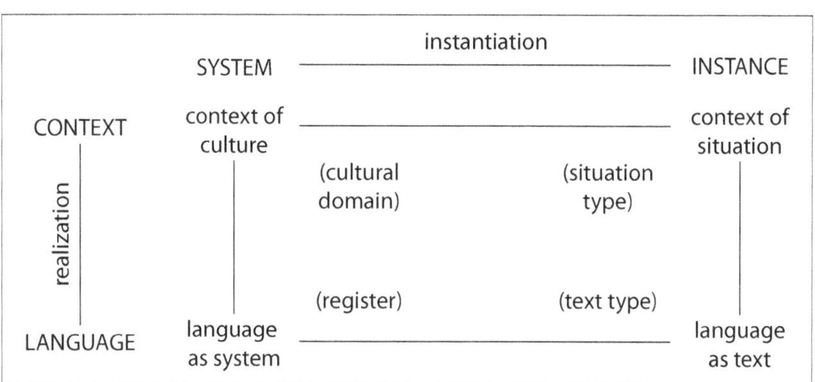

(2007a). In terms of current sociology, reflection on Figure 9.3 leads to a *theory of the social reproduction of language* (Hasan 2009a): the social permeates both text as instance, which realizes its context of situation, and language as system which realizes (aspects of) its context of culture, thus supporting the hypothesis of linguistic functionality as an inherent aspect of the organization of content – that is, the strata of meaning and wording (Halliday 1972; Hasan 1995, 2005b, 2009b). The SFL view of complementarity between system and instance bears relevance to a good many important issues; however, I will single out only the following two for discussion here: (a) the description of the semantic stratum; and (b) validation of linguistic description.

9.2.4   Concepts for meaning in language: (c) Representing the potential

Saussure's Course in General Linguistics is an evolving discourse: having described the sign as a two-part entity – the signified and the signifier – he is at pains in Part Two to describe the complex nature of each part, insisting that the **identity** and **value** of each unit of signified and signifier is forged by its relations to other units. Characteristically, Saussure produces a binary system of relations: one based on **combination** or **syntagm** 'supported by linearity' (ibid, p. 123) later also referred to as the **syntagmatic bond**, the other based on **opposition** or **association**, later referred to as the **associative bond**. Halliday's **chain** and **choice** (1963) resonate well with this Saussurean pair, though it is Hjelmslev's **syntagm** and **paradigm** (1961) that are the prevalent terms for referring to the relations essential for defining the identity and value of a sign. Since units must be identified at every stratum of language, it follows that the syntagmatic and paradigmatic axes apply to all language internal strata.

Linearity is a feature of discourse: instances are linear, thus relations postulated between the units of parole are **in praesentia**. By contrast, paradigmatic relations are supported by associative bonds (relations of differentiation): these relations, not evident in units within a discourse, are **in absentia**. Pertaining to a whole paradigm, the associative bonds are closer to the system aspect of language. Since it is system that acts as the potential, the idea of choice is clearly critical to its description. *In SFL, the potential for each linguistic stratum is represented in the form of system networks,*[23] which are in effect an account of the oppositional/associative relations that are significant to the value and identity of the categories of that stratal unit which acts as the **point of origin** for that particular system network. Thus the system network of MOOD species categories of the unit *clause* at the lexicogrammatical stratum, and so on. Each traversal of the system that is valid in terms of the logic of that system network constitutes a **selection expression** (SE) of the set of choices made from it: the SEs instantiate the system network, and are themselves realized as structures of some kind. Again much has been written in SFL about system networks,[24] so no further details will be presented here.

I begin with the assumption that given the status of semantics as a stratum of language, its units too can be described paradigmatically to represent their potential, as demonstrated by Halliday (1972), and later by Hasan (1983), Cloran (1994) and Williams (1995). However much one might disagree with the basic premises of componential semantics (Katz and Fodor 1963; Bierwisch 1970; Leech 1974), there is, in that literature too, suggestive evidence of paradigmatic organization at the semantic level. When, in some of his writing, Firth (1957) dissolves semantic description into a series of contextualizations of some specific instance, the implication is that there is nothing left to describe; there is, in other words, no stratum of meaning so that from Firth's context we move directly into 'lexical, morphological and syntactic' categories: in my view the suggestion lacks validity. First, in accepting this suggestion, we would have to reject the postulate of a stratum of linguistic meaning; for indeed a stratum without any units is an anomaly; and the recognition of units entails some existing or feasible description of their paradigmatic relations calling for some system networks. However, if there are no defined categories of meaning, talking about Firth's 'semantic' phenomena is fraught with problems; it would be impossible, for example, to say which meanings are at risk where, because we have already abolished by fiat the need for a language of description (Bernstein 2000) for semantic categories. One might suggest that semantics is interpretative: thus it will make use of semantically sensitive lexico-grammatical categories whose value is established by their place in some system networks. Against this too, there are some objections: as soon as every semantic unit – but what is that? – can be unequivocally paired with some delicate lexico-grammatical category, the justification for postulating both the level of semantics and of lexicogrammar will disappear. And even assuming that we can produce a semantically sensitive grammar which: (a) is not in a 1:1 relation with the semantic categories, and (b) is also sensitive to the semantic contribution of the syntagmatic environment (cf. discussion of 'Join the navy and see the world'), we are still left with problems: how to refer to that category of meaning which we are attempting to match? If the semantic category is itself 'notional', that is, has no basis in any principled description, then is our semantically sensitive grammar open to being treated as a 'notional grammar'? In any event, grammar must come to an end somewhere! It is difficult to imagine a lexicogrammar whose units are capable of describing larger semantic units such as **text** and **rhetorical unit** (Cloran 1994): neither texts nor rhetorical units can be described in terms of the largest lexicogrammatical unit, viz., the clause complex. Even if these problems can be surmounted, one basic issue remains unresolved: How desirable is that modelling of language which would allow the interpretation of utterances without enabling their production? For the fact remains that for the speaker the perception of meanings relevant to the context of discourse is the starting point for an utterance. I conclude that an adequate linguistic theory must allow the possibility of both activation and construal – of production and of interpretation – of meaning.

But is there a unit scale at the semantic stratum? Hasan (1996) suggested a scale of four units: proceeding from the largest to the smallest, they are **text, rhetorical unit** (RU), **message** and **message component** (MC).[25] Like all postulated unit scales on the different linguistic strata, the units here too are in a constituency relation: thus a text consists of one or more than one RUs, an RU consists of one or more than one message, a message consists of one or more than one MC. The best paradigmatically described semantic units are message (Hasan 1983;Williams 1995) and RU (Cloran 1994): both have been represented as a set of system networks at the level of semantics (Hasan *et al.*, 2007). Figure 9.4 presents a fragment of message semantics which describes semantic options in demanding goods/services: the realization statements for the entire network require too much space (for some indicative statements, Hasan 2009a, Chapter 7: Table 1:A–C:

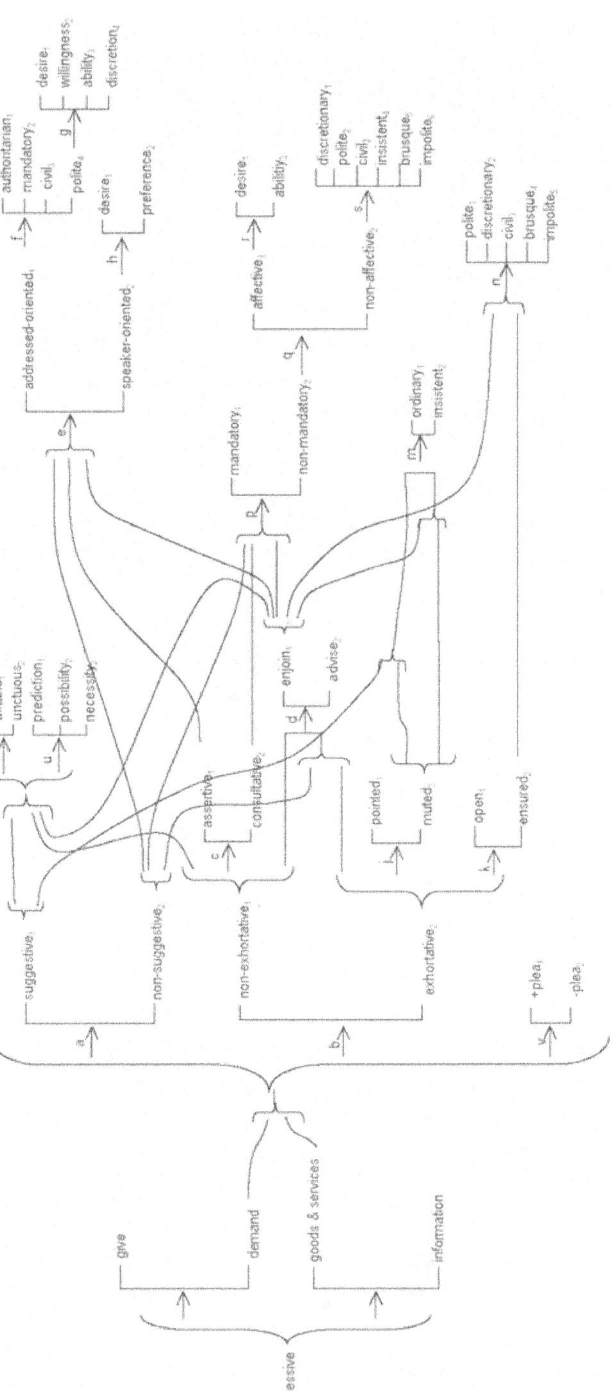

Figure 9.4 : Simplified system network of options in demanding goods/services

284). The options in the network activate some choice(s) from the MOOD system network at the lexicogrammatical stratum. Further discussion of options from Figure 9.4 will be presented in following sections.

9.2.5 Concepts for meaning in language: (d) Validating description

To sum up the Saussurean position: the identity and value of any unit at any linguistic stratum is the function of the paradigmatic and syntagmatic relations the unit enters into. This is what it means to say, as Saussure did, that there are no pre-existing categories: it is the point of view from which the facts of language are described which creates the categories we recognize. This makes the activity of description appear rather subjective; but if the description itself is governed by some explicit principles and while following those principles yields a picture of language that has observational and explanatory adequacy, then the point of view is proved to be one which may be treated as a valid modelling of that language[26] for continuing further into its description. We therefore need a device which explicitly states the conditions for treating a description as valid. Halliday's **trinocular perspective** is one such device: this involves *consulting the relations of the category under description from three relevant perspectives*, viewing relations at the *stratum above* – that is, what the category realizes; viewing relations at the *stratum below* – that is, what realizes the category; and viewing the relations at the *same stratum* – that is, where the category under description is positioned with regard to other categories of its kind; these indicate its paradigmatic relations (its associative bonds). I offer here an illustration of how these perspectives function by reference to the semantic option[27] SUGGESTIVE (see Figure 9.4: path a1:b1...) which is one possible element of meaning in the unit message: PROGRESSIVE: DEMANDING; GOODS-&-SERVICES: the message type identified construes contextual acts of commanding, requesting, persuading, cajoling, humouring someone into doing something the speaker specifies.

Looking *above the semantic level*, the contextual 'reality' which the option SUGGESTIVE realizes – or signifies – is an element of the tenor of discourse: the speaker's RHETORICAL STANCE, whereby s/he appears to place the addressee under some pressure without using physical or symbolic violence so as to get the addressee to do something by representing herself/himself as complicit in that action (e.g. saying to someone who is about to carry something fragile: 'let's be careful in lifting this', or a mother instructing her child: 'let's not tease the pussy cat, darling!'). At least two questions need to be asked: Do speakers naturally utter messages of this kind or is it simply a figment of the linguist's imagination? Second, is there any evidence that on listening to a command type utterance with the semantic feature SUGGESTIVE, the addressee would ratify the above contextual interpretation of this feature by some action or locution? A negative response to either of these questions should send the analyst back to the workbench, but for obvious reasons, such a response to the first question is more troublesome than to the second. The former would invoke doubt as to the existence of the option itself, the latter simply points to an error in description. On the assumption made by many well-known linguists (among them, Firth 1957) that a difference in linguistic 'form' equals a difference in meaning, all that is needed is to consult corpora and observe human interaction in many different contexts to establish the interpretation of the semantic element that differentiates commands such as 'let's be careful in lifting this' v. 'do be careful in lifting this' v. 'would you be careful in lifting this', v. 'I'd like you to be careful in lifting this', 'better be careful in lifting this', and so on.

Looking *at the same level*, the most immediate category in an oppositional relation to the option SUGGESTIVE, is NONSUGGESTIVE, which refers to the contextual fact of the projected action being presented as the responsibility of the addressee alone albeit under instruction, as in 'lift this carefully', 'better lift it carefully', 'could you lift it carefully', and so on. This semantic option too is realized along with most of the others described by Figure 9.4 by some choice(s) in the MOOD system network. But looking at the same stratum cannot be reduced to simply noting its difference to the other term(s) within the same individual system.[28] Two points need to be clearly stated with regard to viewing the facts at the same stratum: first, what this means, in effect, is examining the over-arching system network the options of which act as the systemic description of the unit that served as its point of origin, for example, in this case message PROGRESSIVE as opposed to PUNCTUATION (Hasan 1996). There are certainly other units on the semantic stratum (Section 9.2.4), but for checking on the validity of the description of some element of a message, the categories of the unit message itself are more relevant than those of a lower or higher unit. At the same time, there are many different message types: one way of identifying a primary type is by focusing on the least delicate oppositional features. In Figure 9.4, these primary oppositional systems of options are placed within the first right facing open brace. Although we are concerned here with the message type DEMAND; GOODS-&-SERVICES (the primary systemic options in Figure 9.4), more specifically, the option SUGGESTIVE applies to any message type one of whose primary semantic choices is GOODS-&-SERVICES: more simply *the giving* OR *demanding of goods-&-services is the environment in which the choice between SUGGESTIVE v. NON-SUGGESTIVE has significance*. Thus the system SUGGESTIVE v. NON-SUGGESTIVE will also form part of the systemic description of messages functioning as offers and invitations whose primary options are GIVE; GOODS-&-SERVICES (Hasan 1986b), and in this network too, the terms will refer to the same contextual tenor-related facts. Second, the value of SUGGESTIVE/ NON-SUGGESTIVE is determined by their positioning *vis-à-vis* the other terms within the network as a whole: for example it is significant that although the options may be freely co-selected with the systemic options ASSERTIVE v. CONSULTATIVE they are not freely co-selected when it comes to the options that depend on EXHORTATIVE and the more delicate options in the system network are not available to those messages which have the feature SUGGESTIVE. Thus we do not find messages such as 'we'd like us to be quiet' (SPEAKER-ORIENTED: DESIDERATIVE) and options dependent on the feature ADDRESSEE-ORIENTED are logically impossible with the option SUGGESTIVE.

Finally, looking at the stratum below, that is, at lexicogrammar, reveals how the semantic option(s) are realized. Simplifying somewhat, the realization statements may take different shapes depending on the logic of the network. The system SUGGESTIVE/NON-SUGGESTIVE is concurrent with two others, so the realization statements will differ according to what terms are co-selected. At message rank, two kinds of realizational statement are typical: (a) choice of an option from a clause rank lexicogrammatical system

Table 9.1: Lexicogrammatical realization statements for some semantic options

Semantic options	*Realization statements in terms of lexicogrammar*
demand; goods-&-services	enter MOOD system network
non-exhortative	↘ indicative
assertive	↘ declarative
consultative	↘ interrogative
exhortative	↘ imperative
suggestive	↘ insert Subject
	↘ Subject preselects Thing
non-suggestive	↘ Subject implied/present refers to addressee
suggestive; non-exhortative	↘ Thing at Subject preselects item *we*
suggestive; exhortative	imperative: inclusive
	↘ Thing at Subject preselects item *let's*

network; and/or (b) statement of pre-selection(s) at some clausal element including its category identification and/or realization. Table 9.1 illustrates some cases with a few semantic options from Figure 9.4; the options are in column 1 of the table, and the realizations in column 2.

Choices in the system network at the stratum of lexicogrammar entail the formation of structural information. Thus to say that something is realized as *declarative* is to say that a structure needs to be formed with the elements *Subject* and *Finite* in that order, represented formulaically as *S^F*. The default realization of element Subject is by a nominal group; that of Finite is by an auxiliary verb functioning either as primary tense (e.g. 'is, was, will be') or as a modal auxiliary (e.g. 'can, may, would, should, have to, must ...'). The pre-selecting realization is used when the option can be realized by some unique element of structure and/or linguistic item. A realization statement such as 'Subject preselects Thing' can be rephrased as 'Subject must be realized as a nominal group which "has" the element Thing in it'; in other words an elliptical nominal group such as in 'those two' is not allowed.[29] The preselecting realization statement can also call for a unique item or specify the selection of some item from a paradigm with a particular feature, for example, 'Thing at Subject preselects item *we*' may be worded as 'a clause realizing these semantic elements must have the element Subject and Subject must be the item *we*', as for example in 'we have to be very quiet' whose semantic description is represented in the SE below:[30]

[demand;goods/services:nonexhortative:assertive;suggestive:affable;necessity]

Strictly speaking, naming unique items such as 'you/we' is a short cut: for example, underlying 'we', are the word rank lexicogrammatical options for the category *pronoun* as shown below (after Halliday and Hasan 1976: 44):

[person:interactant:speaker:inclusive]

and it is this lexicogrammatical 'reality' that is arbitrarily signalled by the sound structure represented in writing as 'we'. Of course the realizational path should be pursued right through to the expression level, but enough has been said to establish that the description of SUGGESTIVE as presented here is explicit, and likely to be valid in matching the 'facts'. But how about explanatory adequacy?[31]

To me it seems that explanatory adequacy in the description of language calls for at least three kinds of evidence: (a) **global** evidence that the language internal description is not only adequate for one variety of some one *état de langue* but also offers principled path(s) within the theoretical framework for granting the potential for variation; at the same time, there is the possibility of productive movement across the many varieties which correlate with spatiotemporal phenomena as both time and space 'reshape' while language responds to the many social demands in the living of life in society; (b) evidence of **exotropic connections** whereby the modelling and description of language is such as to entertain the findings of modern research about the interconnections between **language, culture and consciousness**: this chapter began with a description of the ways in which language has been central to the evolution of persons and cultures; a theory with explanatory adequacy should be able to show what aspects of language are instrumental in playing this part, and how this comes about;[32] and (c) **local** evidence: description of language explaining the significance of the instance in the linguistic systems and its relation to context of culture and situation. The discussion here has pertained largely to this third aspect.

9.3 The meaning of grammar and the description of meaning

In the description of the semantic feature SUGGESTIVE as presented above, the trinocular perspective focuses primarily on the paradigmatic relations of that category; thus the inter-stratal relations between semantics and lexicogrammar are observed largely in terms of systemic choices. If context has not participated in this celebration of the paradigmatic here, this is only because SFL so far does not have any developed contextual networks easily accessible for such use. Note, however, Saussure's suggestion that the identity and value of a unit is the function of the relations the unit enters into *both* paradigmatically *and* syntagmatically. Of course, some syntagms were mentioned above, for example, in the realization statement regarding the option *declarative*, but they were realizationally entailed and so form part of the syntax. Significantly Saussure adds that there is more to syntagm than syntax (ibid, p. 123, note 5). This makes sense: syntax is unit-internal, and even the largest lexicogrammatical unit has a limit, recursion notwithstanding. The syntagmatic axis is not bound by any such constraints – especially if 'syntagm' is viewed simply as a flow of signs within some specifiable social environment, it would represent the textual environment for those patterns/units one might choose to examine. This is not the place to develop a critique of the predilection in linguistics for peering simply inside the bounds of a single unit isolating it from all else to find 'objective' evidence of the validity of some proposed description. Firth pointed out half a century ago that words are known by the company they keep; perhaps this generalization should be extended to most linguistic units; the trick is to establish the principles of consistency in deciding what counts as 'company'.

I pointed out in Section 9.2.2 that there can be no 1:1 realization relation between linguistic strata. Ample proof of this will be found in the very few realization statements presented in Table 9.1. For example, *imperative* clause is generally regarded as that lexicogrammatical category which realizes DEMAND; GOOD-&-SERVICES, that is, a 'proposal' of some kind. Considered as a probabilistic statement, this is very likely the default position. Nonetheless, neither is every proposal an imperative, nor is every imperative a proposal. And this statement could be extended to all primary categories of MOOD. Thus a demand for goods and services may be ASSERTIVE realized as *declarative* (e.g. 'you must not shout') or CONSULTATIVE realized as *interrogative* (e.g. 'could you do my shoe laces, Mum?'). Faced with such descriptions, the suggestion has been to treat these as some kind of **interpersonal grammatical metaphor**. This is not the place to go into this debate; the problems in this solution are many and certainly some of them appear to threaten the concept of grammatical metaphor itself, which has proved so useful in the analysis of discourse (Halliday and Martin 1993). In any event, what seems to clinch the matter is the fact that this solution may not be possible for all lexicogrammatical categories. The category **negative polarity** is one such. In the following sections, I will discuss what semantic options the category of negative polarity is able to realize in just one semantic context, namely, DEMAND; INFORMATION. First, a brief description of the category negative.

9.3.1 'Not' as a lexicogrammatical category

The **system of polarity**, with the options *positive* v. *negative*, is well known in SFL as a part of the interpersonal description of the English clause. It is thus positioned within the MOOD system network, with the clause itself having a function in role exchange. The functional element Mood is central to the description of the categories used for role exchange (Halliday 1994): potentially *Mood* expands into the elements *Subject* and *Finite*, the former realized as some nominal category, the latter by the first *auxiliary* of a finite verbal group, which will either select for *tense* or *modality*. What happens actually by way of expansion – for example, are both elements there? if so, in what order of sequence? If not, which may be assumed where and on what evidence? – all this is realizationally relevant to the identification of the categories of role exchange. Mood is the element that according to Halliday (1994: 71) is 'tossed back and forth' in a series of conversational moves, for example, 'he is, is he'? The Subject is the element on which the validity of the rhetorical move rests, while the Finite ties down each such move to some specific point in space and time by reference to the utterance act (for discussion, Halliday 1994: 68ff; Halliday and Matthiessen 2004: 106ff). The system of polarity is considered 'an essential concomitant of finiteness' (Halliday and Matthiessen 2004: 116) since 'for something to be arguable it has to be specified for polarity: either it is so or it isn't so' (Halliday 1994: 75). Figure 9.5 presents a simplified system network for MOOD with 'cryptic' realization statements.

9.3.2 Options in polarity: From grammar to meaning

In Figure 9.5, the realization of the option negative is not stated fully: 'not/ n't' are certainly the most frequent realizations of negative polarity but there are quite a few other items, such as 'neither/nor', 'never', and in some

Figure 9.5: A simplified system network of options in MOOD

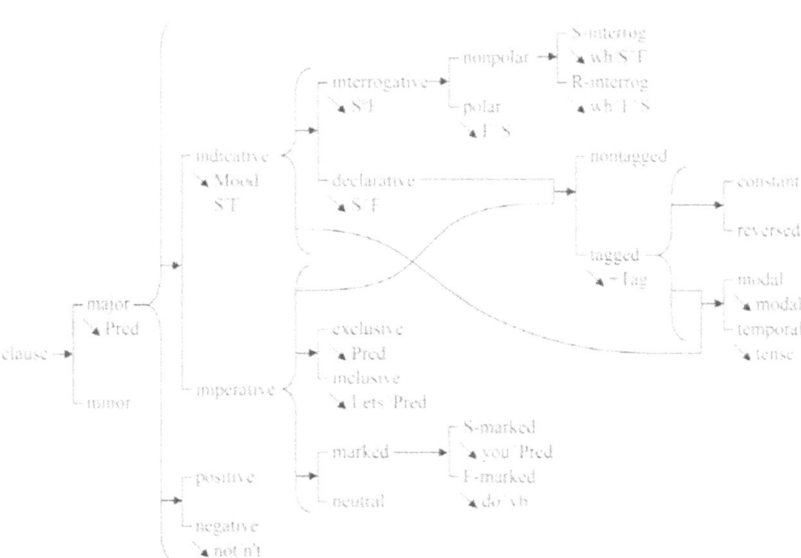

contexts even items such as 'hardly, scarcely, seldom', and so on, though they have not been thought of as realizing negative polarity.[33] However these latter items construe some meaning that 'modifies' the negation: in other words, they go beyond the default meaning of negative polarity. But what exactly is that meaning? In their descriptions, both Halliday and Matthiessen – indeed, most SFL practitioners, including myself – not only show the value and identity of the lexicogrammatical unit under description, they also give some statement about its 'function'. These concern the default construal of meaning by that unit, and form part of what 'looking above' means in the trinocular perspective. With regard to polarity, Matthiessen (1995: 487) suggests that:

> the choice between positive and negative … is clearly interpersonal … the speaker in principle chooses negative if s/he judges that s/he has to cancel what the addressee believes or will do. The choice of polarity thus depends on the speaker maintaining and revising a model of the relationship between himself/herself and the addressee: what is the semiotic distance between them in their construal of experience and their readiness to act? – what is the balance between consensus and conflict?

According to Halliday (1994: 89):

> In a proposition, the meaning of the positive and negative poles is asserting and denying: positive 'it is so', negative 'it isn't so'. … In a proposal, the meaning of the positive and negative poles is prescribing and proscribing: positive 'do it', negative 'don't do it'.

The default meanings of positive/negative polarity suggested by Halliday here are also echoed by most dictionaries, for example, Chambers, Collins Cobuild, Macquarie and others. The description certainly captures the meaning of positive/negative polarity in the context of the default realization of proposition and proposal. These meanings are actually category specific; thus denial is the meaning construed by negative polarity with statements; prescribing and prohibiting are specific to commands. However, the accounts by the grammarians and the lexicologists make two outstanding omissions, viz., neither is there an interpretation of negative in DEMANDING INFORMATION, that is, in questions, nor in GIVING GOODS/ SERVICES, that is, offers. But of course there too, the choice of polarity makes a difference to the meaning of the realizing clause. In the following sections I shall discuss the function of negative polarity in DEMAND;

INFORMATION, that is to say, in questions. Time and space will not allow a similar review of GIVING GOODS/SERVICES, that is, making offers or in DEMAND GOODS/SERVICES, that is, the command family.

9.3.3 The uses of not/n't in demanding information

Table 9.2 presents the functions of polarity suggested above by Halliday together with one naturally occurring example of each category. To this account I have added an interpretation for both negative interrogatives and imperatives: the former is typically a question with an attitude and the latter ceases to be an offer.

As Table 9.2 shows, interrogatives with negative polarity construe the semantic feature ASSUMPTIVE. Contextually the feature is related to the tenor

1:	Mother:	didn't you see me go out
	Karen:	no!
	Mother:	you must be blind!
2:	Mother:	wasn't that a big fishy?
	Pete:	yeah
	Mother:	it was a whopper!
3:	Mother:	you aren't tired?
	Donna:	nope
	Mother:	what! After all that running around

Table 9.2: The meaning of polarity with some primary MOOD options in English

Proposition	Positive	Negative
Demand	meaning: asking a question did you see me go out?	meaning: assumption re response didn't you see me go out?
information		
Give	meaning: telling the water's getting too cold	meaning: rejecting some thesis no, it isn't for me
Proposal	**Positive**	**Negative**
demand	meaning: prescribing do as you're told!	meaning: proscribing don't tell me 'no' all the time!
goods/services		
give	meaning: offer have another piece of toast!	meaning: restriction hey, don't eat up all those nuts!

of discourse, referring specifically to the speaker's stance to her/his own question and her/his expectation of what the answer could *reasonably* be. Here are three examples from naturally occurring dialogues which substantiate this point:

Thanks to the textual syntagm, we can be quite certain that in each case the mother thought she 'knew' what her addressee's mental state should be, thus revealing one subtle aspect of her social relation to her child. In the Macquarie empirical studies of sociolinguistic variation in semantic orientation, the feature ASSUMPTIVE showed up statistically as a highly significant element of the sociolinguistic variable (Hasan 2009a). This is an impressive result in view of the fact that in a corpus based study Halliday and James (1993) demonstrated a skewed probability (9:1) for positive v. negative polarity choice; in their study covering over 1.5 million cases of finite clauses, they found 87.6 per cent occurrences of positive and only 12.4 per cent of negative, which included 'never', 'seldom' and other such items as well.

Example 3 offered above is an instance of the category 'question$_3$' in Halliday and Matthiessen (1999: 22; for discussion, Section 9.4); and its inclusion here indicates that not all questions are realized as interrogative, whatever their polarity choice. At the same time it should be noted that negative polarity does not always construe the feature ASSUMPTIVE in all kinds of questions. Figure 9.6 presents a simplified system network of options in asking English questions, while Table 9.3 shows the functions of **not/n't** in the semantic environment of DEMAND; INFORMATION along with lexicogrammatical information.

Figure 9.6: Simplified system network of options in demanding information

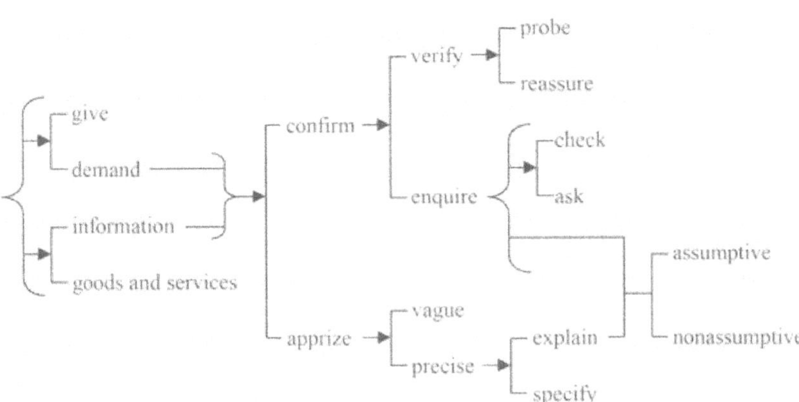

Table 9.3: The meaning of 'not' in questions: Semantic and grammatical views

Simplified semantic SEs			*Simplified grammatical SEs*
		(i) you were sad, were**n't** you?	declarative: tagged: reversed
	reassure	(ii) you do**n't** like this T-shirt, do you?	declarative: tagged: reversed
verify (A)			
	probe	(iii) you left it on the train did you?	declarative: tagged: constant
		(iv) you do**n't** like sugar, do**n't** you?	declarative: tagged: constant
confirm			
	ask: nonassumptive	(v) did you see me go out?	interrogative: polar: positive
	ask: assumptive	(vi) was**n't** that a big fishy?	interrogative: polar: negative
enquire (B)			
	check: nonassumptive	(vii) was it a big fish?	declarative: non-tagged: positive; Tone 2
	check: assumptive	(viii) you are**n't** hungry?	declarative: non-tagged: negative; Tone 2
	explain: nonassumptive	(ix) why did you say 'look'?	interrogative: non-polar: R-interrogative; positive
apprize precise (C)			
	explain: assumptive	(x) why are**n't** you hungry?	interrogative: non-polar: R-interrogative; negative

Table 9.3 is best examined in three parts by reference to the three systemic options in column 2 (A, B and C). Every entry in the table systemically 'assumes' the choices PROGRESSIVE: DEMAND; INFORMATION (see Figure 9.6). The feature VERIFY (column 2(A)) is the entry point for the systemic choice between REASSURE V. PROBE (column 3); VERIFY is itself in systemic opposition to ENQUIRE (column 2 (B)) the entry point for this system being the selection of the feature CONFIRM (column 1), the realization of which calls for an *indicative* clause. For each example, column 5 provides a lexicogrammatical selection expression from the MOOD system network, which counts as the realization of the semantic selection expression stated across columns 1 to 3. It is clear from this table that any message with the feature VERIFY would have a *declarative: tagged* clause as its lexicogrammatical realization. The semantic option REASSURE is realized by the MOOD features *tagged: reversed*, irrespective of the location of the negative; thus in (i) the Tag is negative, in (ii) the declarative is. The semantic option PROBE is realized by the MOOD features *tagged: constant*, which for most varieties of English would imply a zero instance instead of (iv) in column 4 – however, (iv) is a fairly common occurrence in informal Australian English, especially where speakers are not concerned about the danger of being perceived as speaking a sub-standard dialect. Note that the negative in these two environments appears to be the converse of ASSUMPTIVE. If the feature ASSUMPTIVE implies that the speaker already knows what the 'reasonable' response is, the features REASSURE and PROBE imply that the speaker is in need of verifying something. So what is the difference between REASSURE and PROBE? It is subtle but nonetheless important as an indicator of interpersonal relationships; messages with the feature REASSURE may be paraphrased as follows: 'I think something is the case, and I believe you do, too; is that so?', whereas those with the option PROBE are actually probing for 'correct' information: so, for example (iii) may be paraphrased as: 'I understand you left it on the train. Is that what happened?' We can see why questions with the feature REASSURE would be relevant to what Bernstein (1971) called 'sympathetic circularity' which is a form of interaction only among people with intimate relationship – as an aspect of tenor relation, it has been described as construing minimal social distance between the interactants (Hasan 1973, 1985d); by contrast, messages with the feature PROBE could not have this contextual significance; the relationship here is not as close as in the previous case.

The option ENQUIRE (B) is the entry point for two simultaneous systems, ASK V CHECK and also NON-ASSUMPTIVE V ASSUMPTIVE (see Figure 9.6). The choice of negative polarity in a clause realizing ENQUIRE will always construe the semantic feature ASSUMPTIVE. We note that ASK is realized by an interrogative clause and CHECK by declarative + Tone 2. But what difference does this make to their semantic character? A message with the feature ASK is a yes/no question without any strings attached – what is sometimes referred to as a 'straight' question; CHECK, on the other hand, is not a 'crooked' question – it is simply one with additional information about some attitude on the part of the speaker regarding that question: this may be surprise, disappointment, doubt, enthusiasm – the exact nature is realized by the choice in the system of key (Halliday and Matthiessen 2004; Halliday and Greaves 2008).

This leaves us with the option PRECISE (C in column 2). As Figure 9.6 shows, the option APPRIZE is in systemic contrast to CONFIRM: unlike the latter it does not construe a yes/no-question, but what is known as a *wh*-question: it thus seeks some specific element of information, and is lexicogrammatically realized as a non-polar clause. In questions which have the feature PRECISE, the query point is explicitly realized by the preselection of a *wh*- word as *Theme*, such as 'why, who, what, when, where', etc. The option PRECISE is the entry point for a choice between EXPLAIN and SPECIFY. The feature EXPLAIN is realized by an *interrogative* clause in which 'why/what for' would be preselected as *Theme*. As Figure 9.6 shows, the option EXPLAIN is one of the entry points into the system whose choices are ASSUMPTIVE and NON-ASSUMPTIVE (note in Figure 9.6 the disjunct entry condition, one of which leads from EXPLAIN to the systemic choice between ASSUMPTIVE and NON-ASSUMPTIVE, while the other entry conditions is ENQUIRE. Further details concerning the realization of other options in Figure 9.6 will be found in Hasan 2009a; Hasan *et al.* 2007; Cloran 1994; Williams 1995). The feature *R-interrogative* mentioned in the realization of EXPLAIN (last two lines of column 3) stands for Residue-interrogative; in a clause with this feature some *Residue* element forms the query point, as in 'what did you eat'?, 'when/where did you go?', 'what did you do?' and so on. This feature is in systemic contrast with *S-interrogative* (see Figure 9.5 for this system) which stands for Subject-interrogative; in a clause with this feature *wh*-element conflates with Subject as, for example, in 'who/what/which was it?' As is obvious from the examples, the structural realization of S-interrogative is distinct from that of R-interrogative: the structure of S-interrogative is Subject/Wh – ˆFˆPred as in 'who said that?' (which resembles a declarative except for its *wh*-element) while that of R-interrogative is Adjunct or Complement/wh – ˆFˆSˆPred as in 'when did he say that?' or 'what did he say?', which are 'typical' of the structure associated with interrogative, that is, FˆS.

Table 9.4: The meaning of 'not' with demand information .... apprize: specify

Semantic options	Positive polarity	Negative polarity
Global	What's going on?	What's not going on?
	What happened?	What didn't happen?
Particpt: circs	Where have you been?	Where haven't you been?
	When did you visit Rome?	When didn't you visit Rome?
	With whom did you go there?	With whom didn't you go there?
	What were you talking about?	What weren't you talking about?
Particpt: event	What did you do then?	What didn't you do then?
Particpt: actant	Who was calling you?	Who wasn't calling you?
	What did you eat?	What didn't you eat?

The most relevant characteristic of messages with the feature SPECIFY is their 'resistance' to the selection of negation, as Table 9.4 attempts to show. It is not that the selection of negative polarity in clause types that realize messages with the semantic option SPECIFY is necessarily 'ungrammatical', simply that the right context for them is not easy to imagine, and in many cases it seems to shift the rhetorical stance of the message. Compare, for example, 'what didn't you do then?' with 'what didn't you do to stop that kid from smoking!' It seems appropriate to suggest that the syntactic 'conditions' on the selection of negative polarity in such interrogatives could benefit by the kind of semantic research underlying networks such as presented here in Figures 9.4 and 9.6. Both pertain to the interpersonal metafunction and are realized by some feature of the system of MOOD, but the meanings pertaining to all four metafunctions can be described in a similar way (e.g. Hasan 1983).

9.3.4   The meaning of 'not' is not in 'not'

The above account of the meaning of 'not' in English is both condensed and incomplete. For example, time does not allow a discussion of the choice of negative polarity in the context of DEMANDING or GIVING GOODS AND SERVICES. Reversing the meaning construal in many types of commands, negative polarity in offers is more often than not polite, precisely because it insists as in 'do have some more, won't you?' But it seems clear on the basis of the evidence offered here that categories of wording are typically multivalent. Their semantic identity and value become evident only on an examination of the range of their paradigmatic and syntagmatic relations: this is what I have attempted to show by a case study of the meanings of 'not/n't' in the above discussion. This particular category of wording is not exceptional in having such a varied set of meanings: on the basis of the semantics of lexicogrammatical categories such as declarative, interrogative and imperative, we may safely conclude that the meanings of a category of wording are not in that category itself; they take particular shape in the specific environment in which the wording occurs, and significantly, this environment is most parsimoniously identified by reference to the semantic level. To extend a Firthian claim, the meaning of not only lexical categories but most probably of all linguistic categories is known by the company the category keeps.

9.4   Concluding remarks

I accept without reservation the claim that it is impossible to mean any meanings without lexicogrammar: both making meaning and reading meaning depend to a very large extent on lexicogrammar. This, however, does not imply that the only approach to meaning has to be 'from below', concerned only with how sets of lexicogrammatical categories are to be interpreted. True, that a metafunctional lexicogrammar will be semantically oriented: this follows logically from the genesis of metafunctions in contextually situated discourse (Halliday 1972; Hasan 2005b, 2009a); but reflection on the acts of speaking and 'hearing' will suggest that the two outermost strata of language are in a systematic relation to these two aspects of the activity of languaging. To present a full account of meanings, we need to know not only how lexicogrammar construes meanings but also what meanings are construable in a given language variety, when, and by whom, and how they become accessible to the listener. If the trinocular perspective on the validity of semantic description links context to lexicogrammar via semantics, treating the latter as an interface between the two, this clearly implies that the point of origin for the speaker's meaning is not specifiable by reference to lexicogrammar, much less phonology or phonetics: the origin is found in the speaker's perception of the occasion of talk, which entrains a complex of social factors, a meeting of mental dispositions typically shaped by the culture that is instantiated in that context of situation, whose 'reading' is the identifier of the meanings at risk, and for the speaker to get to this point is to be half way into the lexicogrammar. To account both for the speaker's choice of meanings and the addressee's interpretation of speaker's wordings both the construal and the activation of meaning are equally important issues for a functional linguistics. From this perspective, one question that demands immediate attention is what criteria are to be used for identifying that point in the descriptive enterprise where it is maximally productive to draw the line between a 'most delicate lexicogrammar' and a systemic semantics capable of representing the potential for meaning.

In the course of lexicogrammatical description, we often encounter statements regarding a category's default meaning. These, however, cannot be treated as more than excursions into semantics; I say 'excursions' because such statements typically do not – and *cannot* – state the complete meaning potential of any lexicogrammatical unit[34] for reasons presented above. The non-default meanings of a category are many and just as important as the default ones; I hope the discussion of 'not' has indicated that looking up into semantics from lexicogrammar provides a different view into the meanings of some category from that which is presented when the main concern is with categories of semantic systems, because it is here that one asks: What possibilities of meaning are available for realizing some feature of the context of discourse: the focus is on 'what possible meanings are pertinent to this semantic unit', not 'what are the meanings of this category of wording'. This is a subtle and important difference. For example, in SFL following Halliday (e.g. 1966–1968) the systemic choices of MOOD have been widely regarded as construing speech role exchange and certainly they do that, but as the above discussion has shown options from this system network are capable of doing far more than just speech role exchange: they act as a rich resource for creating, maintaining and changing social distance between the interactants by varying the nuances of a speech act thus revealing subtle aspects of speaker attitude to the addressee(s).

Theoretically, SFL is committed to the idea of language as an ever-renewing system: innovation, change, developments of different kinds are phenomena inherent in language use. In accounting for linguistic change, both diachronic linguistics and dominant sociolinguistics have largely been concerned with the expression level. By contrast, Halliday's concept of **semogenesis** has developed in the context of the description of wording and meaning (Halliday 1985), that is, in reflection on the content level: an over-arching concept, embracing different dimensions of human history (Halliday and Matthiessen 1999), semogenesis refers to essential processes whereby the dynamic nature of language as system is able to be maintained.

In their illuminating discussion of the process of semogenesis with specific reference to the level of content, Halliday and Matthiessen (1999: 21–22) draw attention to 'the dissociation of associated features in the wording' whereby over time the 'map' of wording and meaning in English has been changed. The two associated features of wording they consider are those from the system of MOOD and of KEY: the Mood of an English interrogative is 'known by' the Mood configuration F^S with Rising Tone; the default interpretation of the pattern is DEMANDING INFORMATION. The dissociation of the features of Mood and Key and their 're-configuration' expands the total meaning-wording potential of the language, giving the speaker three different ways of saying and meaning by way of asking questions:

> Here again one meaning has been replaced by three: we now have (say) question₁ ↘ interrogative x rising tone; question₂ ↘ interrogative x falling tone; and question₃ ↘ declarative x rising tone, e.g., is she cóming? Is she còming? She's cóming? (Halliday and Matthiessen 1999: 22)

Semantic networks of the type presented here appear to be ideally suited to describe the paradigmatic relations of the different semantic categories as well as their lexico-grammatical realizations which treat systems of MOOD and of KEY as simultaneous, thus allowing the possibilities of dissociating those choices of the two which represent their default association at some given *état de langue* while permitting their innovative reconfigurations. Note also that it is not easy to find a rational basis for insisting on the one hand that the lexicogrammatical patterns F^S/Tone 2, F^S/Tone 1 and S^F/Tone 2 should be accommodated in their full detail within the description of that stratum while also maintaining that the expansion of Mood F^S must be treated as the only pattern capable of construing the 'meaning proper' DEMANDING INFORMATION. As I see it, there are only three options: (a) subscribe to the absence of bi-uniqueness, implying that semantic functions such as DEMANDING INFORMATION may be construed by more than one lexicogrammatical pattern, all of which are paradigmatically related but distinct from each other in some way; (b) insist that the ideal language system is bi-unique in respect to meaning-wording relation, which poses serious problems in accounting for empirical data which clearly contradict that position; or (c) wherever bi-uniqueness is demonstrated to be absent, explain the fact away as some kind of grammatical metaphor, implying that grammatical metaphor is something other than a part of lexicogrammatical description. Accepting any of these options has a payback; in the context of interpersonal role-related meanings, I have considered the first as the best solution: it stays close to the observed facts of language use, and leaves the possibility of systematic variation open, a desirable characteristic of language as dynamic system.

The outstanding characteristic of the primary modes of meaning – that is, those modes of meaning which form the object of enquiry in kinesics and linguistics – is that they have no other function in human life except that of enabling exchanges of meaning. Facial, physical and vocal gestures preceded that modality of meaning which we call language: the non-linguistic modes of meaning were central to the life of our ancestors, as linguistic meanings are to that of ours. With evolving, developing and differentiating cultures, human life today is infinitely more complex, discourse is more diverse, communications, more complex. Although 'body language' remains in use – in fact, cannot be eschewed – and although secondary modes of meaning such as images, graphs, tables, and so on make considerable contribution to some categories of discourse, there is no exaggeration in the claim that today it is verbal language that acts as the foundation of our complex social existence. Linguistic meaning appears to surpass all other modes of meaning – primary or secondary – in its efficacy[35] precisely because of the limitless-seeming possibilities of subtle re-configurations of vast but limited variables. It is interesting to ask: How can semantic description and representation capture this dynamic quality of linguistic meaning?

Notes

1 This chapter is a revised version of the talk I presented at the Free Linguistics Conference 2008 convened by Ahmar Mahboob and Naomi K. Knight on 11–12 October at the University of Sydney.

2 I use 'syntax' and 'expression' because these terms can be applied to a large variety of 'signing'/'symbolic' phenomena; by contrast, 'wording' and 'sound' are restricted to language.

3 I use here Russell's (1940) distinction between the 'sens-ible' and the 'intelligible', the former refers to sensing acts and the latter to acts of intellection.

4 The literature on semiotic mediation is vast, and opinions vary on the interpretation of the expression 'semiotic mediation'. For some discussion see Lucy (1987); Mertz and Parmentier (1991); Wertsch (1985b, 1997). On Vygotsky in an SFL perspective, see Hasan (2005a).

5 'Meaning' is thus coming to acquire another meaning, namely, 'the representation/trace of experience in the human brain'.

6   Of course Vygotsky talked about the relationship between language and the development of higher mental functions in individuals, but Vygotsky was chiefly concerned with specialized concepts dear to official pedagogy (Hasan 2005a). Halliday's concern is with the growing child as a social agent living and developing in a society, who needs higher mental functions for coherently handling the logic of both the ideological and the interpersonal.

7   Although we may attribute communicative intent to such symbols, it may not be possible to offer objective criteria for the claim.

8   Halliday's use of protolanguage is qualitatively different from its use in formalistic linguistics, such as Bickerton's (1990).

9   From this point of view, a review of experiments in psychology concerning the ability to recall will most probably provide support in the finding that a meaningful series is significantly easier for humans to 'internalize' than a 'meaningless' one: to the digital machine meaningfulness makes no difference.

10   It is convenient to quote this often voiced 'definition' of sign/symbol, but in fairness to Noble and Davidson (1996) I must point out that their subsequent discussions of the linguistic sign go far beyond the claim quoted here.

11   Saussure's linguistic 'sign' is in fact much more carefully defined; it is perhaps the textual organization of this intricate discourse that tempts infelicitous interpretations.

12   From now on in this chapter, SFL will refer to Halliday's SFL as interpreted by me, without any implication that Halliday is necessarily in agreement everywhere with my interpretation. For further discussion, see Halliday 1996; Halliday and Matthiessen (2004, Chapter 1).

13   Hjelmslev (1961) recognized more delicate distinctions in each of his primary strata: his 'content substance' and 'content form' approximate Halliday's 'semantics' and 'lexicogrammar', as also 'expression form' and 'expression substance' approximate 'phonology' and 'phonetics'; there are however some significant differences (for some discussion, see Hasan 1995).

14   To be more precise, up till quite recently, expression was seen in SFL as monostratal, with phonology subsuming phonetics. Recent developments (Halliday and Matthiessen 2004; Halliday and Greaves 2008) have led to the recognition of a separate stratum of phonetics.

15   This is what gives us the licence to say that registers are defined by the 'meanings at risk' in some context.

16   Let me emphasize again that despite the use of these 'serial/sequential' expressions, I am not suggesting at all that the units of the various strata appear in temporal sequence. I am tempted to cite Firth (1957: 147) on this issue:

The utterance happens in time. The stream of speech with all its items integrated unrolls itself … on the *time track* of occurrence. But the systemic abstraction which we isolate in language systems are not limited by the time track dimension of the utterances from which they are taken. *The statement of the systems when we talk or write about them have their own time track, since they are speech events* (last emphasis mine, RH).

17   Though our concept of discourse in context is capable of handling this complexity (Hasan 2005a, 2005b), in the interest of saving space, we assume here that the occasion of talk does not involve **semantic distance** (Hasan 2004).

18   Sadly phonology does not figure in this list, but by reference to his co-text, we may conclude that Firth recognizes the contribution of prosodic phonology to meaning and is referring here simply to the minor function of segmental phonology and phonetics (for some supporting discussion by Firth, see 1957: 192).

19   I agree with the spirit of this division but take issue (Section 9.2.3) with the 'absence' of semantics itself from the list: although Firth is not consistent in this practice, often in his writing, semantics is dissolved into a 'comprehensive description of a speech event', which seems to be a move lacking in validity.

20   Space does not allow discussion of examples, but the potential of segmental phonology and phonetics as a recognition criterion for categories of wording is highly varied from near 1:1 conventional association with strong lexical items to near nil with 'fully grammatical' ones. One is safe in venturing a semantic gloss on 'honesty' without looking for its co-text or context, but it would be foolhardy to suggest one single gloss for such phonetic units as the suffix '-s' in 'walks', or '-ing' as in 'painting' or even for the item 'not' as I propose to show in Section 9.3, and 'not' is not alone – we have to think of words such as 'see, turn, give, have, can' and many others. Contra formalistic grammarians, fully grammatical items *do* make a contribution to the meaning of the utterance by virtue of realizing a grammatical relation, though the nature of this relation can only be determined by what is going on up above in worded meaning in context.

21   Always excepting the bright linguist's imagination, who when it suits him can turn the exception into a rule.

22   In fact this may be a feature of all social systems; numerals do not get 'archaic' but words, and social practices do.

23   I do not wish to imply that the description of the potential of each unit in terms of such paradigmatic relations is anywhere near complete for each stratum. Such description in SFL is most developed for lexicogrammar; much less so for the strata above or below it. Further, as I see it, this is one of the points where models such as Fawcett's (2000) or Martin's (1992) differ from Halliday's SFL. For the former there are no systems at any other stratum than that of what he calls semantics; for the latter, either there is no system network applicable to semantics as a whole, or it is to be represented by taxonomies of already identified semantic units.

24   For example, to name a very few: Fawcett (1980, 1988, 2000); Halliday (1961, 1966, 1969a, 1973, 1975, 1979); Hasan (1983, 1987, 1989, 1996, 2009a); Martin (1992); Matthiessen (1995, 2007a).

25   A fifth unit lower than MC would be **seme**, with categories such as entity, process, quality, and so on. However until some description is attempted, it is

going to be difficult to decide whether this unit is needed at the semantic level: it is just possible that lexis as delicate grammar can describe such units more economically without residual problems for semantics.

26 This would neither be claimed as 'God's Truth' nor as a 'Hocus Pocus' theory of language: simply a pro-tem 'real picture of language', offering an account of some unit that may be said to possesses 'descriptive adequacy', until proven wrong.

27 Semantic options are presented in small capitals to distinguish them from the ordinary and non-technical uses of the same orthographic shape.

28 I make a consistent distinction between system and system network: a system network is a logically related set of two or more individual systems. Individual systems are viewed as 'forming' a system network as soon as two or more individual systems are logically related by concurrence and/or dependence. The complexity of the system network increases as the relations of dependence and/or concurrence multiply.

29 Subject ellipsis may occur but *only* if an option explicitly calls for it.

30 The semantic description has two options not discussed before: AFFABLE which contrasts with UNCTUOUS. Compare 'we have to be very quiet' (AFFABLE) with 'we have to be very quiet, don't we?' (UNCTUOUS); and NECESSITY AS OPPOSED TO POSSIBILITY as opposed to PREDICTION. These options are realized by choices in the system of modality.

31 Note the absence of 'descriptive adequacy': the reason is simple. Descriptive adequacy is what is being established by showing that the description has observational and explanatory adequacy.

32 This clearly leads us into the issue of 'appliable linguistics' (Halliday 2005) – a linguistic theory that is able to explain the efficacy of language in human life.

33 However, see Halliday and James (1993). Hardly, scarcely and other such items do not easily co-occur with 'not/n't' (? 'He was not hardly happy') though it is fine to say 'he was hardly not happy' with two 'negatives' making a positive (= 'he was certainly happy').

34 It seems likely that we can go furthest within grammar perhaps in 'lexis as most delicate grammar' (Hasan 1987; Matthiessen 1995; Tucker 1998) but discourses are not a series of lexical items, and encountered in a syntagm, even lexical meaning is likely to display 'shifts' from its default meaning.

35 In fact it might be better to talk about 'effectivity' rather than 'efficacy'; the latter, with its 'purr' connotations gives the impression that the power of language is benign. This is not necessarily the case: its power is neutral as to creation or destruction; it can accomplish both equally effectively.

IV
BRIEF EXCURSIONS INTO URDU GRAMMAR

10 Some Clause Types in Urdu

10.1

The aim of this paper is to describe some of the transitivity choices applicable to some Urdu clauses. The description presented here is based on the Systemic Model of Grammar, where the deep structure of a language is stated in a series of 'system networks'. The origin for each system network is a constituent type; thus in Urdu, there will be one set of system networks for clause, one for group and another one for word, but none for the sentence since so far it has not been possible to establish sentence as a constituent type. Every individual system is built up of mutually exclusive features, each feature being related to some semantic distinction. Provided a member of a given constituent type satisfies the entry condition to the system, one and only one of its terms *must* be selected in the item. For example the entry condition to the system of transitivity in Urdu is that the item be a member of the constituent type 'major clause'; the terms of this system cannot be selected in any clauses other than major ones, nor in any other constituent type such as group or word. 'Major' may be defined systemically by reference to the other systems the terms of which are applicable to the clause or by reference to the surface structure of the item. Since the surface structure of an item can be fully predicted by its systemic selections, these two ways of defining an entry condition are, in fact, two ways of looking at an entry. Thus systemically the term 'major' for Urdu clauses can be defined as a clause to which the system of 'mood' is applicable; structurally a clause is complete if it has a P(redicator) element in it. The word 'has' does not mean 'necessarily present in substance'; so, for example in a sentence such as *rashiid kaafi rahaa thaa aur zaid caae*, (=Rasheed was drinking coffee and Zaid tea), both clauses are considered to be major, inspite of the fact that in *zaid caae* there is no item in substance which represents the P element.

10.1.1

A system network is built up gradually. Once a given item satisfies the first entry condition to a system network, the environment for entry into all subsequent individual systems is wholly or partially stated within the network itself. Thus while all major clauses in Urdu must either have the feature 'intensive' or 'extensive', only a major clause which has the feature extensive satisfies the condition for entering into the systemic choice whose terms are 'effective' and 'non-effective'. In other words, the systemic choices formalized in a system network are 'ordered'; the selection of all subsequent features is dominated by the selection of some other preceding selection(s). Therefore each subsequent individual system in any given network represents a move in 'delicacy'. It provides a new parameter for distinguishing between two or more items which in all other respects may be the same. The presence of a given feature may constitute sufficient condition for entry into two systems which are simultaneously applicable. Where this is the case, each such individual system represents the same degree of delicacy. For example in Urdu, the presence of the feature extensive permits selections at least from two simultaneous systems: the features of one of these systems are 'effective' and 'non-effective' while those of the other one are 'defective' and 'non-defective'. The systemic description of a clause as 'extensive: effective' is at the same degree of delicacy as that of another as 'extensive: defective'. The entry condition into any system may be disjunctive, i.e., the system may be applicable to any item which has either the feature a or b. For instance if an Urdu clause has either the feature non-defective or resultative, it may enter that system whose terms are 'causative' and 'non-causative'. The entry condition is said to be compound if an item has to have both the features a and b to enter into a systemic choice. For instance, in order to select from among the features 'mediary' and 'non-mediary', an Urdu clause must have both the features 'non-benefactive' and 'causative', since this choice is not open to all those clauses which have only the feature 'causative'. The disjunctive and the compound conditions for entry into a given system x may combine; thus the choice of the terms 'mediary' or 'non-mediary' is not only open to those clauses which have the features 'effective: non-benefactive/causative' but also to those which have the features 'non-effective/causative'. The terms used in this section are elaborated in the paper. The notational conventions employed in building the transitivity network below are presented in appendix I while the conventions used to transcribe Urdu sentences in

Roman script are generally those used by Harter, Choudry, and Budhraj in their Hindi Basic course (Units 1–18, reprinted by The Center for Applied Linguistics, Washington 1960). A capital G is used instead of ɣ as in *Gaalib* to represent the voiced velar fricative sound; instead of *oo*, only *o* is used to signify the vowel in *do* (= two), *sh* is used to signify the voice-less palatal fricative as in the word *shaam* (= evening).

10.2

The transitivity system network is set up to formalize the mutual relationships of the process expressed in the clause and the participants, attributes and circumstances involved in the process. 'Process', 'attribute', 'participant' and 'circumstance' are all used here in the same sense as in Halliday (1967). According to this use, process 'subsumes both action or "doing", including perception and ascription, or "being", including description and identification'. Participants may be animate or in-animate, abstract or concrete; attribute subsumes both qualitative and identificative attributor. Circumstance here refers only to those circumstantial factors which are obligatory with a certain type of process, *as klaas mẽe* in a clause such as *woh klaas mẽe hai*. S(ubject), P(redicator) and A(djunct) are all elements of clause structure which are arrived at by reference to some other system network than that of transitivity. The element C(omplement) is needed specifically for the choices made in the transitivity network. As will be seen later, the P can express different kinds of process; if one wishes to signify this in the structural statement of the clause one can add superscripts to this element to show the difference. On the other hand, if the systemic selection statement regarding a given item is complete there is no need to add the superscripts to the elements since not only the order of the elements but also their function can be derived from the 'systemic selection expression'. A systemic selection expression regarding a given item is complete only if all the selections from all the system networks applicable to it have been stated.

10.2.1

The process expressed by the P of any major clause may be described in the first instance by reference to two simultaneous systemic choices. Consider the following clauses:

1. rashiid nee kitaab paRhi.
    (= Rasheed read (the) book.)
2. kitaab paRhi gaii.
    (= (The) book was read.)
3. ustaad nee rashiid ko mehntii samjhaa.
    (= (The) teacher thought Rasheed hardworking.)
4. rashiid mehnti samjhaa gayaa.
    (= Rasheed was thought hardworking.)

A different set of pairs can be made out of these four clauses according to which systemic choices we are interested in describing. Thus 1 and 2 form a pair in opposition to 3 and 4. The process in the first two is of the non-ascriptive type and can be described as a goal-directed process, the goal in both 1 and 2 being represented by the item *kitaab*. The process of the last two clauses can be described as ascriptive: an attribute *mehntii* is being ascribed to an attribuant *rashiid* in both the clauses. This, then, is one meaningful distinction between the two pairs. Another set of pairs can be made by putting 1 and 3 together in opposition to 2 and 4. Both in 1 and 3 the doer of the action is present in the clause as a participant. In both the doer function is associated with the element S of the clause. More specifically in 1, the doer is the 'actor' of the action while in 3 the doer may be described as the 'attributor' (one who attributes, ascribes). In 2 and 4 the elements S is not associated with actor or attributor: the goal participant to which the action is directed is associated with S in 2 and the attribuant to whom the attribute is assigned is associated with the element S in 4. The above is, as it were, an informal statement regarding some of the semantic differences between the opposing pairs. The participant functions that we have so far found it necessary to recognize are then as follows: actor, goal, attributor, attribuant, attribute. The process types distinguished so far are: ascriptive, non-ascriptive. In stating the difference between the pair under focus, not only the distinction between process type is to be taken into consideration but also what participants can be involved with the process and what elements of the clause structure they are to be associated with. Members of the pair 1 and 3 are alike in that the doer function is assigned to the S element; members of the pair 2 and 4 are alike in that the element S is associated with the participant towards whom the process is directed. The grammatical terms to be incorporated in the system network are as follows: 'extensive' = process type non-ascriptive, 'intensive' = process type = ascriptive, 'operative' = doer of process associated with element S, 'receptive' = a participant function other than that of doer associated with element S. This set of systemic choices can be built into a network as follows:

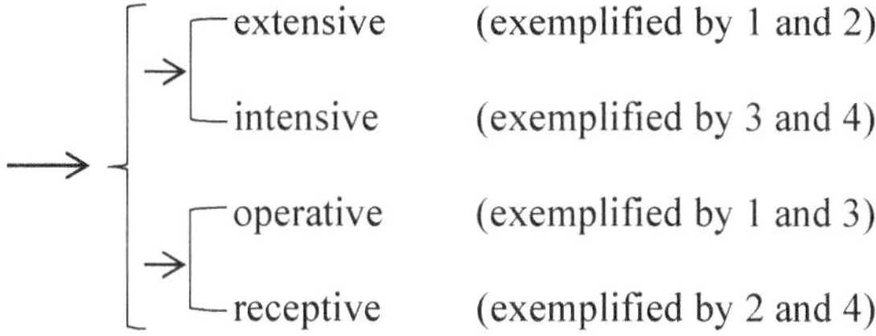

10.2.2

Not all non-ascriptive processes are as goal-directed as may be seen from the following examples:

5. rashiid kuudaa.
    (= Rasheed jumped)
6. kuudaa gayaa
    (= Jumping took place)

This implies that two clauses with the feature extensive may differ from one another only in one respect as is the case with 1 and 5, and 2 and 6; the process in 1 and 2 is goal-directed while that in 5 and 6 is non-directed. The selection of the feature extensive, therefore, constitutes the environment for a subsequent systemic selection, the terms of the system being 'effective' and 'non-effective'. 1 and 2 are clauses with the feature effective: the process in both is goal-directed; 5 and 6 have the feature non-effective: the process in both is non-directed. The feature extensive then 'dominates' the selection of the features effective v. non-effective. Therefore if a clause is said to have the feature effective, this also implies that it must have the feature extensive; and if it is said to have the feature extensive, this implies that it must either have the feature effective *or* non-effective. This systemic choice can be built into the above diagram as follows:

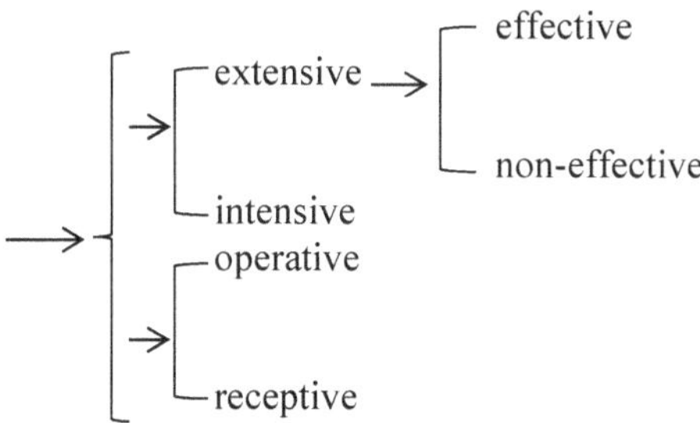

10.2.3

The systemic description of the six clauses so far presented will be as follows in terms of the network above:

1.   ((extensive: effective) / operative)
2.   ((extensive: effective) / receptive)
5.   ((extensive: non-effective) / operative)
6.   ((extensive: non-effective) / receptive)
3.   (intensive / operative)
4.   (intensive / receptive)

Compare this with the surface structure of the items which are:

1.   S C P
2.   S P
3.   S C C P
4.   S C P
5.   S P
6.   P

As is obvious, no distinction can be made between 1 and 4 on the one hand and 2 and 5 on the other merely on the basis of the selection and concatenation of elements. When the surface structure is considered with reference to the underlying selection expression the distinction between these pairs is made immediately apparent. Thus with the selection expression given for 1, the system of transitivity must associate the element S with the participant role 'actor' while for 4 it must be associated with the role of 'attribuant'; for 1 C must be associated with the participant role 'goal' while for 4 it must be associated with 'attribute'; given the feature selections of 1, its P should not only express goal-directed action but also it should be represented by an active verbal group while the selections of 4 make it necessary that the P here expresses an ascriptive process and at the same time be represented by a verbal group which is passive. Since the underlying selection expression specifies the specific function of each element, it is not necessary to build the distinctions into the structural notation.

10.3

Two participant roles have so far been established for the effective clauses. However, an effective clause may have more than two participants. Consider:

   7.   rashiid nee zaid ko kitaab bheejii.
        (= Rasheed sent Zaid (a) book)

Two of the participants in this clause have already been identified; 'actor' associated with the subject *rasheed* and 'goal' associated with the complement *kitaab*. *Zaid* in some grammars would be described as an indirect object. It can be semantically characterized as a participant who 'benefits' from the process of the clause, and as such may be given the label 'beneficiary'. It is however not the case that all effective clauses can have such a participant. A clause such as **rashiid nee zaid ko khaanaa khaayaa* is unacceptable. If the process of an effective clause benefits a participant we may say that the clause has the systemic feature 'benefactive'; when this is not the case the clause may be said to have the systemic feature 'non-benefactive' as in *rasheed nee khaanaa khaayaa*.

In Urdu there is a small list of verbs whose process is always not only goal-directed but also benefactive. But it is not the case that the beneficiary can be selected only in those clauses whose process is expressed by such a verb. Consider the following pair:

   8.   saliima nee eek kurtaa rãgaa.
        (= Saleema dyed (a) shirt.)
   9.   saliima nee apnii bahan kee liyee eek kurtaa rãgaa
        (= Saleema dyed (a) shirt for her sister.)

Semantically, *apnii bahan* has the same participant function here that has been assigned to *zaid* in 7; it benefits from the process. However, one must also take into account the difference between *ko* and *kee liyee*, it being unacceptable at least in my dialect to say **saliima nee apnii bahan ko kurta rãga*. In fact, *kee liyee* like many 'post-positions' is a multivalent item, i.e. it has different functions in different environments, since there is a clear distinction between 9 and

   10. laRkii nee shaadii kee liyee nayee kapRee siee.
        (= The girl sewed new clothes for the marriage.)

This distinction between 9 and 10 can be made most conveniently by considering *apnii bahan* as a beneficiary participant associated with the element C so that *kee liyee* is a function marker in the same way as *ko* and *nee* while *shaadii kee liyee* can be considered as an Adjunct of cause. In all those clauses where the beneficiary participant can be introduced *only* with the structure marker *kee liyee* can be said to have an optional benefactive feature. Thus 9 is a clause which has the features 'benefactive: optional'. This, however, leaves one problem unresolved: 8 must be distinguished from:

11. rashiid nee khaanaa khaayaa.
    (= Rasheed ate his dinner / lunch.)

since it is neither possible to have *rashiid nee zaid ko khaanaa khaayaa* (Rasheed ate Zaid his lunch/dinner) nor *rashiid nee zaid kee liyee khaanaa khaayaa* (= Rasheed ate his dinner/lunch for Zaid). *khaanaa* comes from a list of verbs which always express a non-benefactive process, whereas *rãgnaa* belongs to a list, members of which have the option of expressing a benefactive process. This is in direct contrast to verbs such as *bheejnaa* as can be seen from a comparison of 8 and 9 on the one hand and 7 and 11 on the other:

11. rashiid nee kitaab bheejii.
    (= Rasheed sent (the) book.)

The difference between 7 and 11 can be handled by ellipsis; a beneficiary is present in substance in 7 but only implied in 11. With 8, however there is no justification for thinking that a beneficiary is implied. The presence in substance of an item to realize the beneficiary role is crucial to the description of 9 as an optional benefactive. By setting up the opposition 'optional' v. 'obligatory' we can describe the difference in the process type expressed by *rãgnaa* and *bheejnaa*. The difference between *rãgnaa* and *khaanaa* has been taken care of by describing the former as an optional benefactive type. One must, however, distinguish between 8 and 9. The process in 8 has the potential for becoming benefactive, whereas that in 9 is actually benefactive. We could then say that both clauses 8 and 9 have the features 'benefactive: optional' but that 8 has the feature 'potential' while 9 has the feature 'actual' in addition to the other features that they have.

10.3.1

Let us now go back to 7 and 11, clauses which have the features 'benefactive: obligatory'. We have here a set such as the following:

7.   rashiid nee zaid ko kitaab bheejii.
     (= Rasheed sent (a) book to Zaid.)
11. rashiid nee kitaab bheeji.
     (= Rasheed sent (a) book.)
12. rashiid nee umar kee liyee zaid ko eek kitaab bheejii.
     (= Rasheed sent Zaid a book for Umar.)
13. rashiid nee umar kee liyee eek kitaab bheeji,
     (= Rasheed sent a book for Umar).

If we accept that the absence in substance of *zaid ko* in 11 and 13 can be taken care of through ellipsis, then the distinctions we have to account for are those between 7 and 12, and 12 and 13. It would appear that all inherently benefactive processes can involve two beneficiary participants. The beneficiary always demanded by such a process is marked by the structure marker *ko*. We could describe such beneficiary participants as 'intermediary beneficiary' since 7 does not necessarily mean *rashiid nee zaid ko zaid hii kee liyee kitaab bheejii* = (Rasheed sent Zaid a book for Zaid). In 12 and 13, *umar (kee liyee)* represents the 'real beneficiary'. Since the intermediary beneficiary is always involved in the process, 7 and 11 may be said to have the feature 'intermediate' while 12 and 13 have the feature 'direct'. For the realization of the feature 'direct' the selection of a real beneficiary participant (marked by *kee liyee*) is obligatory; if the clause has the feature direct, such an item must be present in substance; if such an item is not present in substance, the clause has the feature intermediate.

10.3.2

The benefactive system (which forms a part of the transitivity network) raises an interesting question where the intensive clauses are concerned. Given the definition of the term 'benefactive', it may well be argued that 3 and 4 have this feature, since the attribuant in each of these clauses 'benefits' from the process of ascription. And it may be argued that the benefactive system applies to intensive clauses as well. This however would be undesirable for the simple reason that so far as the intensive clauses are concerned there is really no option.

An ascriptive clause may have a process which either ascribes an attribute to an attribuant or an identity to an identified. The attribute or the identity may be stated as 'found present' in the attribuant or it may be stated as the result of a process. Consider the following examples:

3. ustaad nee rashiid ko mehntii samjhaa.
    (= Tutor considered Rasheed hard working.)
14. DaakTar nee rashiid ko acchaa kiyaa.
    (= The doctor made Rasheed well i.e. cured him)
15. rashiid nee zaid ko sosaaiTi kaa preesiDenT samjhaa.
    (= Rasheed thought Zaid the president of the society i.e. took
    him to be the president of the society)
16. rashiid nee zaid ko sosaaiTi kaa preesiDenT banaayaa.
    (= Rasheed made Zaid the president of the society)

In 3 and 14 an attribute is being ascribed to the attribuant whereas in 15 and 16 an identity is being assigned to the identified. The first two clauses are said to have the feature 'attributive' while the last two have the feature 'identificatory'. In 3 and 15 the attribute and the identity are stated as found present by the ascriber; in 14 and 16 they result from the process which can be described as that of 'creating' an attribute or identity. 3 and 15 are said to have the feature 'depictive' while 14 and 16 have the feature 'resultative'.

In all these clauses both the attribuant and the identified may be said to benefit from the process of ascription. There is however no intensive clause in which the attribuant or the identified may not benefit from the process in this sense. The case of the intensives is thus somewhat parallel to that of the non-effectives: the process of the non-effective clause does not benefit any participant other than the actor just as the process of the intensive clauses does not benefit any other participant but attribuant or identified. If it were the case that in some clauses it could be shown that the actor (in non-effective) and the attribuant or the identified (in intensive) do not benefit from the process (in this limited sense of the word 'benefit'), then there would be a real option which would correspond with some difference in meaning. In the present situation, however, it is sufficient to build this information into the participant function 'actor' for non-effective and for 'attribuant' and 'identified' for the intensive. In order to set up a systemic option a v. b, it is necessary that two items having, say, the feature x may differ from one another only with respect to a and b, one of the items having the features 'x:a', the other having the features 'x:b'. If all items with the feature x must necessarily have the feature a, there is obviously no real option for them and as such there is no systemic choice.

The systemic choices so far described can be built into the network as follows:

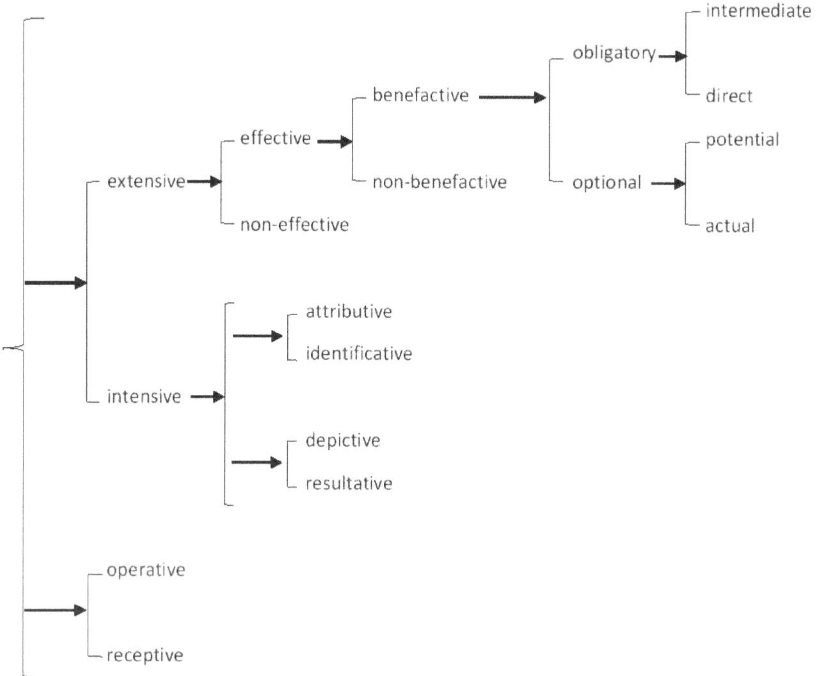

If we say that a clause has the feature 'potential' this implies that it must also have the features 'optional', 'benefactive', 'effective' and 'extensive'. It is in this sense that all subsequent systems in a network are said to be 'ordered' with respect to the preceding related systems.

10.4

It has been said that the process of the clause is expressed by the P of the clause. However, there are a large number of clauses in Urdu in which the verb is, as it were, 'empty', as in the following clause:

17. rashiid nee zaid ko takliif dii.
    (= Rasheed gave Zaid discomfort)

Here if we regard only *dii* as representing the P element of the clause, then all the information we derive from it is regarding tense, aspect and other systemic choices applicable to the verbal group together with the fact that it must be goal-directed. The range of the process remains unknown until we take the word *takliif* into consideration. In most traditional Urdu grammars such verbs are described as 'majhool' i.e. verbs whose meaning is not clear. Unfortunately, among the majhool verbs are included such verbal auxiliaries as *saknaa, deenaa, leena, paRnaa, cahnaa,* and *honaa.* The defect in this treatment is that the difference between 17 and

18. rashiid nee kitab paRh lii.
    (= Rasheed has read the book. (aspect perfective))

is not made clear, whereas in *paRh lii* both the words are verbs, in *takliif dii* it would be difficult and probably unjustifiable to regard *takliif* as a word belonging to the verb class. Also it would be desirable to distinguish *takliif deenaa* and *muqqarar kernaa.* The latter is a compound lexical verb since it is not possible to use the word *muqqarar* except in conjunction with *kerna.* A clause such as *zaid see rashiid ki takliif na deekhii gaii* is acceptable but it is unacceptable to say **zaid see rashiid ki/ka muqqarar na deekhii/aa gaii/aa.* (= Rasheed's worries could not be seen (were not bearable for) by Zaid, and Rasheed's appointment could not be seen by Zaid, respectively). The nominal form for *muqqarar kerna taqqarrurii* such as *zaid see rashiid ki taqqarrurii na deekhii gaii* (= Rasheed's appointment could not be seen by Zaid i.e. he was jealous of Rasheed's appointment) is acceptable.

We suggest that the nominal with such majhool verbs should be regarded as a participant that specifies the extent of the process. Thus its status is that of a secondary goal like the beneficiary. Most goal functions are associated with the element C in operative clauses, as such *takliif* in 17 would be said to represent a C element in the clause. The systemic feature that a clause such as 17 may be said to have selected could be described as 'defective'; and for the semantic characterization of the defective the process should be described as one which is not fully expressed by the P of the clause and always involves the presence of a specifying participant. Such processes are not restricted to effective clauses alone since we have:

19. Rashiid nee takliif uThaai.
    (= Rasheed bore inconvenience; Rasheed was inconvenienced)

Thus the systemic choice 'defective' v. 'non-defective' is applicable to all extensive clauses. In other words this systemic choice is simultaneous with the systemic choice of effective v. non-effective.

10.4.1

The function of *takliif* in 17 and 19 has been stated. What can be said about *rashiid ko* in 17? It would appear that 17 resembles a clause such as *rashiid nee zaid ko kitaab dii* (= Rasheed gave Zaid a book.) in that in both cases *rashiid ko* has the function of a beneficiary as it undoubtedly 'benefits' from the process. But this may be because of the selection of the verb *dee-naa*, since in a pair such as:

> 20. rashiid nee zaid ko D̃aaTaa,
>   (= Rasheed scolded Zaid.)
> 21. rashiid nee zaid ko laanat malaamat kii.
>   (= Rasheed did scolding to Zaid i.e. he scolded him.)

It is obvious that *rashiid ko* in 20 must be treated as a goal – the process is directed to him; he may be said to benefit no more from the process than *meez* in a clause such as:

> 22. rashiid nee eek meez banaai.
>   (= Rasheed made a table.)

This being the case there does not appear any underlying reason to distinguish between 20 and 21 so far as the participant function of *rashiid ko* is concerned. Both clauses are effective; the only difference between them is that while 20 is non-defective 21 is defective.

10.5

When an extensive clause has the feature non-defective, this constitutes sufficient condition for entry into another systemic selection. Consider:

> 1. rashiid nee kitaab paRhii.
>   (= Rasheed read the book.)
> 21. ustaad nee rashiid ko kitaab paRhaai.
>   (= The teacher made Rasheed read a book).

22. darzii nee kapRee siee.
    (= The tailor sewed clothes).
23. Saliima nee darzii see kapRee silaee.
    (Saleema made the tailor sew some clothes)
24. ghoRaa dauRa.
    (= The horse ran.)
25. rashiid nee ghoRee ko dauRaayaa.
    (= Rasheed made the horse run.)

Clauses 1, 22 and 24 can be described by reference to the system network presented above (section 10.3.2), but for 21, 23 and 25 we have to enquire into the process type and the various participant roles. To take 21 first, here the participant function of *rashiid* is that of actor as in 1. There is however a difference: in 1 *rashiid* is not only the actor but also the 'initiator' of the action. It is irrelevant whether in the extra-linguistic situation his process was a voluntary one or not. So far as 1 is concerned he is presented as an actor who is also the initiator of the action. In 21, however, the function of initiator is fulfilled by *ustaad*. The process in this clause is expressed by a verb which demands that the roles of initiator and actor be distributed to different participants, i.e. they cannot be conflated. The situation for 21 holds true for 23 and 25 as well, thus in 23 *saliima* is the initiator while *darzii* is the actor and in 25 *rashiid* the initiator and *ghoRee* (*ko*) the actor. We could say then that clauses with the feature non-defective can vary in respect to this one difference in the process type: the process type may demand discrete actor and initiator participants, or it may not. In the former case the clause may be said to have the feature 'causative' in the latter 'non-causative'. Where a clause with the feature defective is concerned, such an option is not available since a clause such as **zaid nee rashiid ko takliif dilwai* (= zaid made *x* give inconvenience to Rasheed) is unacceptable.

10.5.1

The systemic choice of causative v. non-causative also applies to those intensive clauses which have the feature resultative. Consider:

26. rashiid nee baccee ko chup kiya.
    (= Rasheed did the child silent i.e. silenced the child)
27. saliima nee rashiid see baccee ko chup karayaa.
    (= Saleema got Rasheed to silence the child.)

28. zaid nee rashiid ko preesiDenT banaayaa.
    (= Zaid made Rasheed president.)
29. umar nee zaid see rashiid ko presiDenT banvaayaa.
    (= Umar got Zaid to make Rasheed president.)

The proportion that exists between 1 and 21 also exists between 26 and 27, and 28 and 29. All clauses have the feature resultative. A clause with the feature depictive has no option with reference to the terms causative v. non-causative. It would therefore be unacceptable to say *zaid nee ustaad see rashiid ko mehntii samjhvaayaa* (= Zaid got the teacher to consider Rasheed hardworking).

10.5.2

In some cases when a clause has the feature causative it may enter into another systemic choice. Consider the following:

21. ustaad nee rashiid ko kitaab paRhaai.
    (= The teacher made Rasheed read a book.)
30. waaldain nee ustaad see rashiid ko kitaab paRhwai
    (= The parents got the teacher to make Rasheed read a book.)
25. rashiid nee ghoRee ko dauRaayaa.
    (= Rasheed made the horse run.)
31. zaid nee rashiid see ghoRee ko dauRvaayaa.
    (= Zaid got Rasheed to make the horse run.)

In 30 and 31 we have an additional participant role which we have not come across in the earlier example. Both in 21 and 30, *rashiid* remains the actor of the action. However, in 21 *ustaad* is the initiator of the action while in 30 *waaldain* fulfils this function; the function of *ustaad* in 30 can be described as that of 'mediary': he neither initiates the action nor is its actor; he simply functions as a participant who mediates between the initiator and the actor.

It has been said above that this choice is open to only some causative clauses. More specifically, this choice is available only when the clause has the feature non-effective or the features effective:non-benefactive; (it is obvious that in both cases the clause must also have the feature causative). Thus if we have a set of clauses such as:

23. saliima nee darzii see kapRee silaae.
    (= Saleema made the tailor sew some clothes.)
32. saliima nee darzii see kapRee silwaae
    (= Saleema made the tailor sew some clothes.)
27. saliima nee rashiid see baccee ko chup karaayaa.
    (= Saleema got Rasheed to silence the child.)
33. saliima nee rashiid see baccee ko chup karvaayaa.
    (= Saleema got Rasheed to silence the child.)

the difference in the verb form is a surface difference. The proportion that exists between *paRhaayaa* and *paRhvaayaa* does not exist between *silaayaa* and *silvaayaa*. As a proof consider the following:

34. kitaab paRhwaai ?
    (= Did you get the book read?)
35. kapRee silvaayee ?
    (= Did you get the clothes sewn?)
36. kaam karvaayaa ?
    (= Did you get the work done?)

The process of 34 needs the participants initiator, mediary and actor in addition to goal so that the clause will be interpreted as *did x get y to make z read the book?* Consequently even if the clause were written as *ustaad see kitaab paRhvaai?* or as *rashiid ko kitaab paRhvaai?* it would still be elliptical with respect to two participant functions, just as *ustaad see rashiid ko kitaab paRhvaai?* would be with respect to one such function. With 35 and 36 only two other participants are required for the complete interpretation of the clause. While both *darzii see kapRee silvaayee?* and *saliima nee kapRee silvaayee?* are elliptical, a clause such as *saliima nee darzii see kapRee silvaayee?* is fully non-elliptical.

10.5.3

The fact that all non-effectives and only those effectives which are also non-benefactive have the option between 'mediary' and 'non-mediary' raises an interesting question. It may be recalled that the non-effective clauses do not enter the systemic choice benefactive v. non-benefactive since the beneficiary participant is never discretely selected. That the beneficiary role is conflated with the actor is true both for the non-effective and the non-benefactive clauses as can be seen from considering the following clauses:

1.   rashiid nee kitaab paRhi.
5.   rashiid kuudaa.

One may then enquire whether it is not the case that clauses of the type such as 21 and 25 are not in fact a variant form of benefactive selection. This position, it would appear cannot be held if we consider the participants to whom the role of a discrete beneficiary has been assigned. In all clauses so far described as having the benefactive process, the beneficiary participant is always a 'passive agent'; he is not an actor and even when the clause has the feature receptive as in the following this remains true. Consider:

37.   rashiid ke liyee kurtaa siyaa gayaa.
      (= A shirt was sewn for Rasheed.)
38.   rashiid ko kitaab bheejii gai.
      (= Rasheed was sent a book.)
39.   rashiid ko zaid ke liyee kitaab bheejii gaii
      (= Rasheed was sent a book for Zaid,)

There is therefore no reason to consider clauses such as 21 and 25 as a variant realization of the feature benefactive.

To sum up the discussion in this section, all extensive:non-defective clauses and all intensive:resultative clauses enter into the systemic choice of the term causative v. non-causative; only those causative clauses which are either non-effective or effective: non-benefactive may enter into the subsequent systemic choice of the term mediary v. non-mediary. The distinction between the two forms *paRhaanaa* and *paRhvaanaa* is meaningful; it reflects an underlying distinction in meaning i.e. the processes expressed by the two forms vary from each other in a certain respect. The distinction between *silaanaa* and *silvaanaa* does not reflect any distinction in this particular respect though it is likely there is some other distinction to be made by the use of these differing forms.

10.6

All those clauses which have the features benefactive:optional and receptive enter into a further systemic choice. Consider the following:

40. saliima nee kurtaa siyaa.
    (= Saleema sewed a shirt.)
41. kurtaa si gayaa
    (= the shirt got sewn.)
42. kurtaa siyaa gayaa.
    (= the shirt was shown.)

41 and 42 differ from 40 in that both the former are clauses with the feature receptive whereas 40 is operative. But there is a distinction between 41 and 42. 41 is a clause in which the process is stated as if it were independent of the actor; it is as if the process is thought of as taking place of its own accord. There is a proportion between the above set and the following:

43. saliima nee kursii toR dii.
    (= Saleema broke the chair.)
44. kursii TuuT gai
    (= The chair broke)
45. kuursii toRii gai.
    (= the chair was broken (by someone).)

The clauses 41 and 44 could be described as having the feature 'stative'; the process of such a clause is stated as if it could have happened of its own accord. This is not a semantic-characterization of the nature of the process as such but rather of the way that the speaker looks at the process: the process in all the above examples is goal-directed; the way of looking at the process differs. Compare the following:

46. rashiid kitaab lee aayaa.
    (= Rasheed brought the book.)
47. kitaab aai.
    (= The book came / arrived.)
48. kitaab laai gai.
    (= The book was brought.)
49. zaid rashiid ko lee aayaa.
    (=Zaid brought Rasheed (with him))
50. rashiid aayaa.
    (= Rasheed came.)
51. rashiid laayaa gayaa.
    (= Rasheed was brought.)

The difference between 46 and 49 is that while in the former *rashiid* is both the actor and the initiator of the process with *kitaab* representing the goal, in 49 *zaid* is the initiator of the action and *rashiid* only the actor. 46 is an operative clause with the features effective:non-causative whereas 49 must be regarded as an operative clause with the features noneffective:causative. It is a clear that while for 47 we must imagine the presence of an initiator and actor other than *kitaab*, for 50 there is no doubt that *rashiid* is both the initiator and the actor of the action signified by the verb. In 47 the speaker treats the process as if it were capable of taking place of its own accord whereas in 50 there is no choice; not only is the process taking place of its own accord but it cannot be regarded as one which could be otherwise viewed. 48 and 51 have the same relationship to 46 and 49 respectively: the process is viewed as one to which actor and initiator in 48 and initiator in 51 is relevant.

It is significant that just as we can say *rashiid nee khaanaa xud see khaayaa* (= Rasheed ate lunch/dinner of his own accord), we can also say *kursii xud see TuuT gai* (= The chair got broken of its own accord) or even, given the right extra-linguistic context *kurtaa xud see sil gayaa* (= the shirt got sewn of its own accord). But it makes no sense to say *kurtaa xud see siyaa gayaa* (= the shirt was sewn of its own accord) or *xud see aayaa gayaa*. Where we have a clause such as *xud see to kurtaa siyaa nahii jaataa kapRee ko ilzaam deetee hai* (= the shirt cannot be sewn by himself and he blames the material, i.e. he is himself incapable of sewing the shirt and he blames the material for it), the item *xud see* does not refer to the goal but to the actor. Thus in fact, clauses with the feature stative are halfway between the operatives and the receptives of the type exemplified by 42 and 45 and by 48 and 51. In the latter the speaker's way of looking at the process is as one which cannot take place of its own accord but must be 'actor/+initiator oriented'. These latter clauses could be said to have the feature 'agentive'.

10.6.1

The systemic choice between stative and agentive is not limited to only those clauses which are effective and non-defective. An effective defective clause may also vary from another effective defective clause only in this respect. Consider the following:

17. rashiid nee zaid ko takliif dii
52. zaid ko takliif hui.
    (= to Zaid discomfort happened i.e. Zaid was in some discomfort)

53. zaid ko takliif dii gai
    (= Zaid was given discomfort)

It is tempting to suggest that the choice presented here is applicable also to the non-effective defective clauses for it seems that the proportion of the above is the same as that of the following:

54. zaid nee takliif uThaai.
    (= Zaid bore discomfort)
55. zaid ko takliif thii.
    (= to Zaid was discomfort)
56. zaid see takliif uThaai gai.
    (= discomfort was borne by Zaid)

It would seem then that the two forms of *honaa* (i.e. *hai, thaa/ii* as opposed to *hua/i*) are selected somewhat consistently in the effective and the non-effective stative clauses respectively, to show the effective v. non-effective distinction. This comment by no means implies that the problem of the analysis and description of the verb *honaa* in Urdu is exhausted: it only states one difference in a given systemic environment.

10.6.2

The verb *honaa* (as opposed to the auxiliary *honaa*) is however associated with the stative clauses. In intensive clauses where the choice of stative v. agentive applies, *honaa* with a few exceptions is the verb used to signify the stative process. Consider:

3.   ustaad nee rashiid ko aqalmand samjhaa.
57. rashiid aqalmand thaa.
    (= Rasheed was clever.)
58. rashiid aqalmand samjhaa gayaa.
    (= Rasheed was thought clever.)

In 57 the ascription is as if it could take place of its own accord and does not need an ascriber. The verb selected is a form of *honaa*; in the following clause:

59. rasheed acchaa hua.
    (= Rasheed became well.)

Again the verb selected is a form of *honaa*. It would appear that for all resultative intensive clauses the stative process is expressed by this form of *honaa*, whereas for the depictive ones the verb form *hai thaa*, etc. are selected. With some verbs there may be a choice; consider:

60. zaid nee rashiid ko preesiDenT banaayaa.
    (= Zaid made Rasheed (the) president.)
61. rashiid preesiDenT hua/banaa.
    (= Rasheed became president.)
62. rashiid preesiDenT banaayaa gayaa.
    (= Rasheed was made president.)

It is significant that where the choice of retaining the lexical verb of the operative is permissible in the stative, there is always the possibility of employing the resultative form of *honaa* as is indicated in 61; the meaning of 61 remains the same whether we use *banaa* or *hua*.

10.6.3

The systemic choices of causativity are not applicable to any clauses with the feature stative. Thus while we have clauses such as:

63. kurtaa rãgaa gayaa.
    (= The shirt was dyed.)
64. kurtaa rãgvaayaa gayaa.
    (= The shirt was got dyed.)
65. dauRaa gayaa.
    (a receptive form of the verb *run*)
66. dauRvaayaa gayaa.
    (= was got run)

there are no such clauses as **kurtaa rãgayaa* to correspond with the stative *kurtaa rãgaa*.

10.7

The account presented here of the transitivity network of Urdu is not exhaustive. I have not dealt with various types of clauses such as *woh tak-liif mẽe hai, woh kamree mẽe hai, woh diiwaar kuudaa, us nee khaanaa acchaa pakaayaa* and undoubtedly a host of other clause types. As such the analysis presented here must be taken as tentative, until all the distinctions made through the transitivity network have been exhaustively built into the network.

It may perhaps be felt that the description presented here is not that of the syntax of Urdu but of its semantics. Space does not permit me to demonstrate the relationship of the systemic choices to the structure of the clauses in any detail though an effort has been made to indicate how the systemic selections of any item are inevitably related to the structure. This would not be surprising considering that structure is only a mechanism for carrying meaningful distinctions between given items of a language.

Appendix: Notes on conventions used

Diagram	Explanation
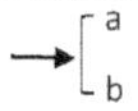 a / b	there is a system of features a/b (either a or b must be selected, if the entry condition is satisfied.)
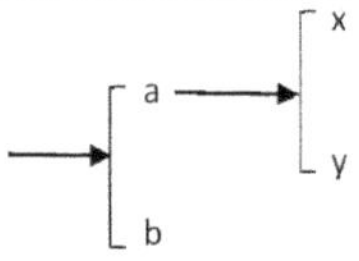 a → x/y, b	system (1), features a/b, and system (2), features x/y are ordered in delicacy such that a in system (1) is the entry condition for system (2): (if a is selected either x or y must be selected)
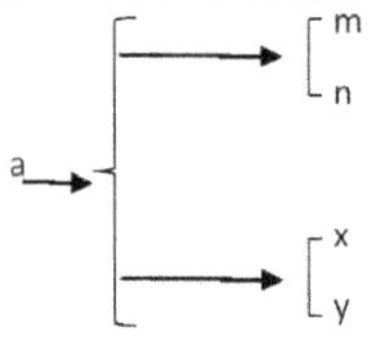 a → m/n, x/y	systems m/n and x/y are simultaneous (if a is selected then either m or n must be selected *and* also either x or y must be selected.)
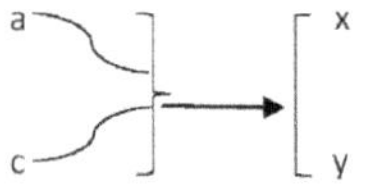 a, c → x/y	the entry condition for system x/y is compound, being the intersection of a and c (if both a and c are selected then either x or y must be selected.)
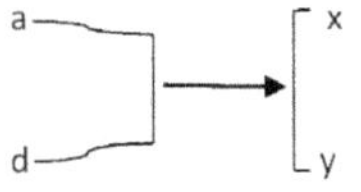 a, d → x/y	system x/y has two possible entry conditions: (if either feature a or d is selected then either x or y must be selected.)
( )	encloses a selection expression or a set of simultaneous features within a selection expression.
m/x	m and z are simultaneously selected features.
a:x	x is ordered with respect to a
(a:(n/x))	Selection expression in which n is simultaneous with x, both being dominated by a

Note: the above convention are derived from Halliday 1967.

11 The verb 'be' in Urdu[1] [1970]

11.1

The aim of this paper is to provide a description of the semantics of the Urdu verb *honaa* (to be). Although my examples will be taken from the educated variety of Lakhnavi Urdu, the statements made here are expected to be applicable to all the social varieties of the language as spoken by the native speakers of the language in Uttar Pradesh (India). The conventions employed for the transcription of Urdu sentences in Roman script are borrowed from Harter *et al.* (1960) with the following modifications:

(i)   the letter *G* is used instead of *γ* to represent the voiced velar fricative, exemplified by the initial sound in the name of the famous Urdu poet Gaalib;

(ii) the symbol *o* is used, instead of *oo*, to represent that pure vowel in Urdu which is nearest to the cardinal vowel number seven (Abercrombie 1967: 154); the vowel in *lo!* (take!) exemplifies the sound;

(iii) the symbol *e* is used to represent that pure vowel in Urdu which is nearest to the second cardinal vowel (Abercrombie *ibid.*), exemplified by the vowel in *bel* (one of the forms of the verb *beelnaa*, which means 'to roll out', used mainly with reference to *dough*);

(iv) the complex *sh* is used, instead of *ʃ*, to represent the voiceless palatoalveolar fricative, exemplified by the initial sound in *shaam* (evening).

11.1.1

Examples are first presented in Roman script; they are followed by a word rank literal translation in English, where the sequence of the translated version is determined by the original. Structural markers such as *nee*, which have no word equivalent in English, reappear verbatim in the word rank translation. If an Urdu word has more than one word rank translation equivalent, only one of these appears in the translation. The decision in these cases is based upon the suitability of the item to represent an example of the type which is under focus. The word rank translation is followed by the clause rank translation.

11.1.2

The description presented here is based on the systemic model of grammar. In particular, this article makes extended reference to Halliday's 'Notes on Transitivity and Theme in English' (Parts 1, 2, and 3) and presupposes the technique of grammatical description as expounded there, naturally without taking over all the details of the systemic networks, since these were set up with specific reference to English. Each clause is viewed here as realizing certain systemic options; each of these systemic options can be related directly to the semantics of the clause. The implication is that if two given clauses realize the same set of systemic options then their semantic description cannot vary except by virtue of the lexical choices. The term 'feature' is used interchangeably with 'systemic option'.

11.2

The verb *honaa* is a multivalent item; that is, it may have different functions. Thus grammatically it may function as an auxiliary or it may function as the lexical verb, signifying the process of the clause. Both these functions of the verb are recognized by traditional Urdu grammars, which assign the item simultaneously to two different sub-classes of verb. Thus it is a member of the class of verbs labelled *feel-ee-imdaadi* (auxiliary) along with such items as *saknaa* (can, be able to) and *cuknaa* (to finish, e.g. in *jab woh khaanaa khaa cukaa* = when he food ate finished = when he finished eating the food); at the same time, *honaa* is listed as a member of the class of verbs labelled *feel-ee-asl* (real verb, i.e. lexical verb) along with items such as *sonaa* (to sleep), *jaanaa* (to go), *paanaa* (to find), etc.

The translation equivalents of the lexical verb *honaa* are as follows: *to be, to exist, to have, to own, to become,* and *to happen.* Examples of each are provided below:

(1) laRki xuubsurat hai.
    girl   beautiful   is
    the girl is beautiful.

(2) kariim sadar   hai.
    Kariim president is
    Kariim is the president.

(3) xudaa hai
    God   exists
    God exists.

(4) kariim kee do   bahẽe   hãĩ.
    Kariim of   two sisters has
    Kariim has two sisters.

(5) rafta rafta kariim   tandrust huaa.
    gradually Kariim   healthy   became
    gradually Kariim became healthy.

(6) Kariim sadar   huaa.
    Kariim president   became
    Kariim became president.

(7) kal shaam   shahar mẽe balwaa huaa.
    last evening city   in   riot   happened
    Last evening a riot took place in the city.

11.2.1

Grammatical and lexical multivalence is not unique to the verb *honaa*.
Items such as *jaanaa* (to go) and *rahnaa* (to live, to stay) can function
either as auxiliary or as lexical verb as is evident from the following pairs:

(8) (a) woh kal   shaam   landan   gayaa.
        he   last   evening London   went
        He went to London last evening.

    (b) meeraa santraa kaun khaa gayaa?
        my   orange who   ate   went
        who ate up my orange?

(9) (a) woh yahãa sirf   caar din   rahaa.
        he   here   only four days lived
        he stayed here only for four days.

    (b) bacca saari raat   rotaa rahaa.
        child whole night cries lived
        the child kept crying the whole night.

As examples of lexical multivalence elsewhere one may cite items such as *phuulnaa* (to swell, to blossom), *rakhnaa* (to own, to put), *samajhnaa* (to understand, to think, to consider). It is of course true that where two or more formal items have the same graphological or phonological realization, there may exist some historical relationship between the formal items, but this is by no means always necessary. Thus it cannot be maintained that at some stage in the history of Urdu the verb *honaa* was univalent (i.e. had only one function) and that the various meanings are historically derived from this original one. Even if two formal items are historically related it cannot be argued that their synchronic description at a given stage will be identical. Indeed the very fact that they are perceived as two distinct formal items suggests that the description of one is going to be different from that of the other in some respect. In the following sections an attempt has been made to show in what respects the different senses of *honaa* differ from one another and in what respects they are alike; at the same time the relationship of clauses (1)–(7) to other clause types has been explored with a view to determining the place of these *honaa*-clauses in the transitivity system network.

11.3

In traditional Urdu grammars clauses (1)–(2) and (5)–(6) would be described as *jumlaa xabariyaa* (clause with news); the verb *honaa* in all four would be regarded as belonging to the category *naaqis* (defective). Thus Maulvi Abdul Haq in his *Qawaaid-ee-Urdu* (Grammar of Urdu) makes the following comments:

> *feel* (verb) is that from which appears (i.e. is signified, R.H.)[2] the existence or performance of anything …
> With regard to meaning verbs can be subdivided into three categories:
>
> 1. laazim[3]
> 2. mutaaddi
> 3. naaqis.
>
> *feel laazim* is that through which the doing of some action may be signified, but its (the verb's, R.H.) effect may be limited to the actor of the action, i.e. *faael*[4] (subject) and no more. Example: *ahmad aayaa* (Ahmad came).

feel mutaaddi is that whose effect reaches the *mafuul*[5] (object or complement) via the *faael*; (*mafuul* is that on which the action takes place). Example: *ahmad nee xat likhaa* (Ahmad wrote a letter). Here *likhaa* is *feel*, *ahmad* its *faael* and *xat* (on which the *feel* of *likhnaa* takes place) is its *mafuul*.

feel naaqis is that which does not affect anything/anyone but signifies an effect. Example: *ahmad biimaar hai* (Ahmad is ill). In this clause the *feel* signifies not an action but existence; *ahmad* which is *faael* here is not an actor but an effect-bearer (patient) of the *feel* and *biimaar* provides *xabar* (news) regarding his state (*Qawaaid-ee-Urdu*: 119).

In addition to (1)–(2) and (5)–(6), clauses such as *woh baRaa beewaquuf niklaa* (he big idiot turned-out = he turned out a big idiot) and *maĩ nee us ko beewaquuf samjhaa* (I nee he to idiot considered = I considered him an idiot) would also be regarded as *jumlaa xabariyaa*, with the implication that the verbs in these clauses belong to the category *naaqis*. Three of the implications of such an analysis could be stated as follows: (1) *feel naaqis* is considered to be in contrast with *laazim* and *mutaaddi*; according to this analysis no Urdu clause may be labelled simultaneously as *xabariyaa* and *mutaaddiyaa* or *xabariyaa* and *laazmiyaa*. However, since *maĩ nee us ko beewaquuf samjhaa* is a *jumlaa xabariyaa*, the validity of such a position may be questioned. (2) If the latter clause is regarded as a *jumlaa xabariyaa*, it follows that the transitivity functions associated with the subject of the *xabariyaa* clauses vary, since clearly *maĩ* in the latter clause and *laRki* in (1) do not have the same functions. (3) The verb class *naaqis* contains, besides *honaa*, other verbs such as *paanaa* (to find), *mannaa* (to regard, to acknowledge), *samajhnaa* (to consider, to think, to regard), *lagnaa* (to seem), *qaraar deenaa* (to acknowledge), and so on.

One might ask, then, whether all these verbs have the same syntactic function so that what is said about one will also hold true of the others or whether there are any grounds for further distinctions.

11.3.1

I shall assume that as for English, so for Urdu, it is not valid to contrast *feel naaqis* with *laazim/mutaaddi* (Halliday 1967a, 1968), and will simply concentrate on the characteristics of clauses labelled *jumlaa xabariyaa*. As is clear, *feel naaqis* and *jumlaa xabariyaa* may be seen as mutually defining labels; whatever clause can be labelled *xabariyaa* must in its predicator have a lexical verb of the *naaqis* class; whatever verb can be labelled *naaqis* must occur only in the predicator of a *xabariyaa* clause. If we take some lexically multivalent items such as *maannaa, paanaa* and *samajhnaa* which may function either as a *naaqis* verb or as a non-*naaqis* one, it will be possible to throw some light on the defining characteristic of the *xabariyaa* clause; consider:

(10) (a) maĩ nee us ki baat sahi   maani.
         I   nee he of talk   correct considered
         I considered his comments correct.
     (b) maĩ nee us ki baat maani.
         I   nee he of talk   accepted
         I agreed with his comments.
(11) (a) maĩ nee laRki ko xuubsurat paayaa.
         I   nee girl   to beautiful   found
         I found the girl beautiful.
     (b) maĩ nee laRki ko kamree mẽe paayaa.
         I   nee girl   to room   in   found
         I found the girl in the room.
(12) (a) maĩ nee un kaa sawaal   beejaa   samjhaa.
         I   nee he of   question inappropriate thought
         I thought his question inappropriate.
     (b) maĩ nee un kaa sawaal   samjhaa.
         I   nee he of   question understood
         I understood his question.

The member (a) of each of these pairs would be regarded as a *xabariyaa*, whereas member (b) would be regarded as non-*xabariyaa*. It would appear then that the characteristic of the *naaqis* verb is that it signifies a relational process: more specifically the relation it establishes can be only of intensional type (Halliday 1967a: 62–63; Lyons 1968: 454); thus the two 'things' intensionally related must form an integral part of the clause where the verb is *naaqis*. It is not the case that in members (b) the process does not relate the participants to each other, but here the relation is extensional (Halliday 1967; Lyons 1968: 454). I shall now refer to the clauses of type (a) as 'relational'. The verb *honaa* in one of its senses is then like the other verbs used in this clause type in that it can be used for the realization of an intensional relation. It does not need to be pointed out that the lexically multivalent verbs when used in a relational clause have a different meaning from that which they have when used in extensional clauses.

11.3.2

In Urdu at least two types of relational clauses can be recognized; these are exemplified by (1) and (2). In (1) *laRki xuubsurat hai* the two related 'things' are *laRki* and *xuubsurat*; such clauses may be called 'attributive' in that the intensional relationship exists between an attribuand *laRki* and an attribute *xuubsurat*. In (2) *kariim sadar hai* the two related things are *kariim* and *sadar*; such clauses may be called 'equative' in that the relationship exists between an identity[6] *sadar* and an identified *kariim* which are equated. *xuubsurat* and *sadar* may be regarded as 'circumstance' of participant whereas *laRKi* and *kariim* may be regarded as the participants of a process. It is necessary for all relational clauses to have one element in their structure which realizes the circumstance and another which realizes the participant to whom the circumstance is ascribed.

11.3.3

It is not the case that circumstance can be selected only in relational clauses. Thus it is possible to say:

> (13) darzi nee kurtaa choTaa siyaa.
> tailor nee jumper small   sewed
> the tailor sewed the jumper small (i.e. sewed it so that it was small).
> (14) laRki nee kapRee gandee paaee.
> girl   nee clothes dirty   found
> the girl found the clothes dirty.
> (15) maĩ nee caar   rupyaa jurmaanaa diyaa.
> I   nee four   rupees fine   gave
> I paid four rupees as fine.

In these clauses, the attribute-attribuand relationship may be said to exist between *choTaa* and *kurtaa* in (13) and *gandee* and *kapRee* in (14); the identity-identified relationship may be said to exist between *jurmaanaa* and *caar rupyaa* in (15). These clauses are not regarded as relational on the ground that the circumstance is not a 'necessary' part of the clause in the sense that if it is removed from these clauses the clauses still remain grammatical and the relationship of the process to the remaining items does not change; moreover the participants stand in the same relation to each other in which they stand when the circumstance is present in the clause. Thus consider:

> (13a) darzi nee kurtaa   siyaa.
>   tailor nee jumper sewed
>   the tailor sewed the jumper.
> (14a) laRki nee kapRee paaee.
>   girl   nee clothes found
>   the girl found the clothes.
> (15a) maĩ nee caar rupyaa diyaa.
>   I   nee four rupees gave
>   I paid four rupees.

If we compare the pairs here with the pairs (10)–(12), it will be clear that circumstance is an obligatory element in a relational clause, so that if circumstance is removed the clause may no longer be regarded as relational; further the meaning of the process-signifying item undergoes a change and often (if the verb is not multivalent or if some other restrictions on the selection of the verb exist) the resultant clause would be regarded as ungrammatical; thus consider *naqqaad nee un kahaaniyõ ko muxrib-ee-ixlaaq maanaa* (critic nee those stories to immoral regarded = the critic regarded those stories as immoral) and **naqqaad nee un kahaaniyõ ko maanaa* (the critic regarded those stories). Thus although circumstance may be selected in nonrelational clauses and it may be related to one of the participants in the clause, this relationship is not crucial to the clause in the same way as it is to the relational clause; this is because the process of the nonrelational clause is not itself relational in the intensional sense. The fact that there are multivalent lexical verbs and that circumstance may be selected in non-relational clauses accounts for the ambiguity of certain clauses in the language. Consider (14), which may be decoded as a relational clause or as a non-relational one; as a relational clause it will be decoded as *laRki nee paayaa ke kapRee gandee thee* (girl nee found that clothes dirty were = the girl found that the clothes were dirty) while as a non-relational clause it may be decoded as *laRki nee kapRee paaee aur kapRee gandee thee* (girl nee clothes found and clothes dirty were = the girl found the clothes and the clothes were dirty).

11.3.4

The systemic option of relational vs. non-relational is applicable to all major clauses in Urdu; that is, any given major clause will either have the feature relational or non-relational. So far in the discussion of the relational clauses only those elements have been considered which are intensionally related. In clauses such as (10a) *maĩ nee us ki baat sahi maani*, there is yet another participant to be considered, namely *maĩ*. The function of *maĩ* in this clause is that of 'attributor'; where the relational clause is equative, the function of the corresponding participant may be labelled 'identifier', e.g. in *maĩ nee kariim ko sadar samjhaa* (I nee Kariim to president thought = I thought Kariim president, i.e. took him to be president), *maĩ* would have the function of identifier.

Traditional Urdu grammars recognize the fact that *kurtaa* in (13a) has a different transitivity function from that of, say, *laRki* in (11a). They also assign the attribute and the identity a transitivity function in the clause, and do not regard *xuubsurat honaa* or *sadar honaa* as compound verbs with the items *xuubsurat* and *sadar* as part of the verbal group. (However, see notes 11 and 34.) Thus in a clause such as *ahmad biimaar hai* (see the quotation from Abdul Haq, cited above, Section 11.3) the verb is *hai* and not *biimaar hai*. The grammars agreed unanimously in labelling 'circumstance' as *xabar* (report, news); thus the term *xabar* is less delicate than the labels 'attribute' and 'identity', and should be considered as an adequate translation equivalent of 'circumstance' but not of the other two as such. Opinion was divided as to the best suited label for the participant which has here been labelled 'attribuand' in the attributive, and 'identified' in the equative clause. A summary of the arguments could be presented in the words of Maulvi Fateh Mohammad Khaan (1945):

> In Arabic there are two kinds of nominal clauses.[7] First, that in which there is absolutely no verb and such a clause must consist of at least two nominals e.g. in *zaidun qaaeemun* (Zaid standing = Zaid is standing); second, that in which there is a verb but it is *naaqis* e.g. in *kaana zaidun qaaeemun* (was Zaid standing = Zaid was standing). In clause type one, they call the *musnad ileha*[8] (topic) *mubteedaa*[9] (initiating item) and *musnad*[10] (comment) *xabar*, while in clause type two they call the *musnad ileha, ism* (noun) and *musnad, xabar*. But neither Persian nor Urdu has clause type one; that is to say, a clause may not be made up of two nominals only. In Persian not only should there be a *musnad ileha* and a *musnad* but also another word, namely

hast or *ast*, whether it is overt or covert ... Similarly in Urdu *hai* is obligatory,[11] whether (it occurs, R.H.) overtly or covertly ...

As you see from these examples, where in Arabic only two words were sufficient, there in Urdu and Persian three are required. Most grammarians of Persian and Urdu following the grammars of Arabic, have labelled the *musnad ileha, mubteedaa* and the *musnad, xabar* and have regarded *ast/hast* and *hai* as *harfee-rabt*[12] (connecting word), but so far as we are concerned these are not connecting words; they are verbs ... (Vol. 2, pp. 21–22.)

Those who consider *hai* as a connector, regard *mahmuud* as *mubteedaa* and *aalim* as *xabar* in a clause such as *mahmuud aalim hai* (Mahmuud learned is = Mahmuud is learned), but we would ask why in *mahmuud aalim thaa* (Mahmuud learned was = Mahmuud was learned) they do not consider *mahmuud mubteedaa* and *aalim xabar*. If we consider *hai* as a connector, we wonder what reasons could be provided for a distinction between *hai* and *thaa* ... (ibid., p. 27.)

If *hai* is a connector why is *thaa* not a connector? No one describes *thaa* as a connector and yet there is no difference between *hai* and *thaa* except that through *hai* is signified present tense and through *thaa* past tense. (ibid., p. 27.)

Now, as to the question whether the *musnad ileha* of *hai* should be called *mubteedaa* or *ism*, it needs to be pointed out that the grammarians of Arabic refer to *mubteedaa* as *mubteedaa* because it is the initial item in the clause. If it were the case that in clauses with verbs too the *faael* was the initial item, there would be no ground for calling *mubteedaa mubteedaa*. But in Urdu, *faael* too occurs clause-initially,[13] hence no specific value can be attached to this fact where the *musnad ileha* of a nominal clause is concerned. For this reason we hesitate to refer to the *musnad ileha* of a nominal clause as *mubteedaa* on the only criterion that it occurs clause-initially. So far as we are concerned we would prefer to refer to this (element, R.H.) as *ism*. (ibid.)

The various strands running through this argument can be stated as follows: the label *mubteedaa* is rejected by Fateh Mohammad because: (a) it is not applied consistently to all clauses with the verb *honaa* in them but only to those which have the present tense form of the verb; (b) in Arabic this label is applied only to the *musnad ileha* of what Fateh Mohammad classifies as clause type one, in which there is 'absolutely no verb'; this clause type 'does not occur' in Urdu since some form of the verb *honaa* is required for the realization of some feature of the clause; and, lastly, (c) the very meaning of the term *mubteedaa* is unsuited for making a distinction between the grammatical subject of clauses whose process is signified by *honaa* as opposed to those whose process is signified by some other verb; the sequential criterion does not apply.

It has to be granted that taken individually these three arguments put forward by Fateh Mohammad Khaan are valid, yet his resolution of the problem has been generally ignored. The reasons for this are as follows. The distinction between *hai* and *thaa* pointed out by Fateh Mohammad Khaan seems to have been abandoned by the Urdu grammarians. In fact, it has not been possible for me to trace a grammar of Urdu, in which *honaa* is assigned to two different primary classes of word according to whether it is in the present tense or in the past tense. There seems to be a tacit agreement, therefore, that *honaa* in one of its senses is a lexical verb no matter what tense may be signified by any given form of it, from which it followed that there were no clauses in Urdu which replicated clause type one of Arabic (at least in their surface manifestation). The labels *ism* and *mubteedaa*, as labels for transitivity function in the clause, could therefore not be distinguished from one another so far as Urdu was concerned. Here only one label was needed. *ism*, both in Arabic and Urdu, was employed to label a word class, i.e. noun; *mubteedaa* was therefore less confusing and seems to have been universally adopted. The motivation for the choice of this item as a label in Arabic might very well have been the one cited by Fateh Mohammad Khaan; it would however be absurd to think that the sequence criterion was regarded as the defining one by Urdu grammarians: no grammarian faced with a string such as *xuubsurat laRki hai laRkaa nahĩ* (beautiful girl is boy not = it's the girl who is beautiful not the boy) would consider *xuubsurat* as carrying the function of *mubteedaa*, even though the item occurs clause-initially. An even more interesting example would be a particular type of relational clause exemplified by, say, *rashiid ko kariim beewaquuf lagtaa hai* (Rashiid to Kariim idiot seems is = Kariim seems an idiot to Rashiid), in which the function of *mubteedaa* is assigned to *Kariim* and not *rashiid*. It is therefore safe to assume that in Urdu grammars the term *mubteedaa* came to mean not 'that which constitutes the beginning of the clause' but 'that participant to which some circumstance is ascribed'. Again, like *xabar*, the term *mubteedaa* is less delicate than either attribuand or identified, since it subsumes both. A comparable term in English would be 'ascribed participant'.

11.4

If the relational clause is characterized as one whose process signifies intensional relation and 'calls for' two elements one of which carries the function of 'ascribed participant' and the other that of 'circumstance ascribed', then the following may be regarded as an agnate set of such clauses:

> (16)   laRkee nee laRki ko xuubsurat paayaa.
>   boy   nee girl   to beautiful found
>   the boy found the girl beautiful.
>
> (16a) laRki xuubsurat paai   gai.
>   girl   beautiful   found   was
>   the girl was found beautiful.
>
> (16b) laRki xuubsurat lagi.
>   girl   beautiful   seemed
>   the girl seemed beautiful.
>
> (16c) laRki xuubsurat thi.
>   girl   beautiful   was
>   the girl was beautiful.

While most Urdu grammars have explicitly stated the relationship existing between clauses (16) and (16a), I have not found any account of how the remaining two clauses are to be treated so far as their relationship to the other two clauses is concerned. There is only an agreement regarding the basic fact that they should all be treated as *jumlaa xabariyaa* (relational clause). However, some indication can be found in the treatment of the non-relational paradigm such as the following:

> (17)   naukar nee caaval tolee.
>   servant nee rice   weighed
>   the servant weighed the rice.
>
> (17a) caaval tolee   gaee.
>   rice   weighed   was
>   the rice was weighed.
>
> (17b) caaval tulee.
>   rice   got-weighed
>   the rice got weighed.

Both (16) and (17) would be regarded as active clauses, the definition of the active being 'that clause the actor of whose process is known'. In our terminology, the actor in the non-relational and the 'ascribing participant' in the relational clause are 'known' in an active clause and these transitivity functions are associated with the grammatical subject of the clause. Both (16a) and (17a) would be regarded as passive clauses, the definition of the passive being 'that clause the actor of whose process is not known'.[14] This definition of the passive for Urdu is more accurate than has been realized by some recent grammarians of Urdu and Hindi. It has been assumed that as in English, the actor of the process (the grammatical subject of the active clause) may be inserted into the passive as an 'agentive adjunct'.[15] This observation is correct only to the extent that a clause such as *naukar see caaval tolee gaee* (servant by rice weighed was = the rice was weighed by the servant) is not ungrammatical but it is doubtful whether it could be regarded as a passive agnate of (17). The insertion of the agentive adjunct in clauses of the type (17a) has the effect of introducing an element of potentiality into the clause; that is to say, the clause cited last should be translated idiomatically as *the servant was able to weigh the rice* and not as *the rice was weighed by the servant*. So far as (16a) is concerned the insertion of the agentive adjunct is totally unacceptable here,[16] since there is no such clause in Urdu as **laRkee see laRki xuubsurat paai gai* (boy by girl beautiful found was = the girl was found beautiful by the boy). The restriction on the selection of the feature 'potential' can, however, not be explained by the clause being relational since a relational clause such as *laKki see kamraa saaf kiaa gayaa* (girl by room clean done was = the room was made clean by the girl) is acceptable. Instead this restriction has to be explained by reference to another primary system which is applicable to all major clauses in Urdu. The terms of this system are 'volitional' and 'non-volitional'; every major clause in Urdu must have one of these features in addition to the feature relational or non-relational. Consider the following examples:

(16) laRkee nee laRki ko xuubsurat paayaa.

(17) naukar nee caaval tolee.

(18) laRki nee kamraa saaf kiyaa.
      girl nee room   clean did
      the girl made the room clean.

(19) naukar nee eek baks paayaa.
      servant nee one box found
      the servant came across a box.

A volitional clause[17] may be characterized semantically as one the process of which is such that it could be undertaken voluntarily; (17) and (18) are examples of such clauses. The non-volitional clause may be semantically characterized as one the process of which is such that it could not be undertaken voluntarily; rather it is a process that 'happens' to some one/thing; (16) and (19) are examples of such a clause.

Since the process of the non-volitional clause is one that happens to some one and is not undertaken voluntarily, we find that the selection of the feature causative is not permitted to such clauses. The feature causative for Urdu may be characterized generally as 'causing some one to undertake an action' from which it follows that the process of the clause is to be of the volitional type if external causation is to be introduced. Thus it is possible to say *maalik nee naukar see caaval tolvaayee* (master nee servant by rice caused-to-weigh = the master made the servant weigh the rice) and *maã nee laRki see kamraa saaf karvaayaa* (mother nee girl by room clean causedto-do = the mother made the girl make the room clean) while both **maalik nee naukar see eek baks pavaayaa* (master nee servant by box caused-tocome-across = the master made the servant come across a box) and **maã nee laRkee see laRki ko xuubsurat pavaayaa*[18] (mother nee boy by girl to beautiful caused-to-consider = the mother made the boy consider the girl beautiful) are unacceptable. Given the characterization of the causative and the non-volitional process, it must follow that verbs which signify the latter process may not be selected in imperative clauses. So while both *caaval tolo!* (rice weigh = weigh the rice) and *kamraa saaf karo!* (room clean do = make the room clean) are possible grammatical clauses, both *laRki ko xuubsurat paao!*[19] (consider the girl beautiful) and *baks paao!* (come across a box) are unacceptable. It is suggested here that the feature volitional also controls the selection of the feature 'potential'; only those clauses can have the feature 'potential' which also have the feature 'volitional'. The reasons for the unacceptability of **laRkee see laRki xuubsurat paai gaii* (the boy was able to find the girl beautiful) are the same as those which account for the unacceptability of clauses such as **laRkaa laRki ko xuubsurat paa sakaa* (the boy was able to find the girl beautiful), **hawaa patta hilaa saki* (the wind was able to move the leaf), **laRki ghabraa saki* (the girl was able to get confused), **aadmi mar sakaa* (the man was able to die), etc.

On the basis of these observations it would appear to me that the characterization of passives such as (16a) and (17a) as clauses in which the actor remains unknown is correct. I shall refer to passives of this type as 'nonagentive passive'.

11.4.1

Clauses of the type (17b) *caaval tulee* have sometimes been described as active intransitive clauses. Such an analysis would not distinguish (17b) from:

(20) bacca soyaa.
      child   slept
      the child slept (i.e. went to sleep).

There are, however, grounds for doubting whether the points of dissimilarity between (17b) and (20) are not just as important as – or, perhaps more important than – the points of similarity. It is true that every active volitional clause, whether 'transitive' or 'intransitive', may be seen as standing in a causal relation to an agnate causative. Thus we have pairs such as:

(17i) maalik nee naukar see caaval tulvaayee.
(17) naukar nee caaval tolee.
(20i) maã   nee baccee ko sulaayaa.
      mother nee child   to caused-to-sleep
      the mother caused the child to sleep.
(20) bacca soyaa.

It is possible to think of (17) and (20i) as sharing a certain similarity in the sense that both can be interpreted as *x nee kuch kiaa jis kaa asar y par paRaa* (*x* did something the effect of which fell upon *y*); in (17) *x* would be *naukar* and *y caaval*; in (20i) *x* would be *maã* and *y bacca*. From this it would follow that (17b) *caaval tulee* stands in the same relation to (17) as (20) does to (20i), so that (17b) and (20) would both be regarded as active non-causative and intransitive. To be sure some differences between the clauses would be noticed, but these would be explained by the fact that there exists an animate vs. inanimate distinction between the grammatical subjects of the clauses, and this would explain why, for instance, we may say *bacca sonee par majbuur huaa* (child to sleep on obliged became = the child was obliged to sleep) but not **caaval tulnee par majbuur huee* (the rice was obliged to get-weighed).

There is, however, a defect in this reasoning. The distinction of animate vs. inanimate grammatical subject is certainly relevant to the syntactic organization of the language but at this particular point this distinction does not appear to me to be the crucial one. Consider a clause such as:

(21) ma͠a   nee baccee ko piiTaa.
mother nee child   to beat
the mother beat the child.

This clause could be interpreted in the same general way as (20i) and (17); ma͠a *nee kuch kiaa jis kaa asar baccee par paRaa* (the mother did something the effect of which fell upon the child), therefore a clause such as *bacca piTaa* should stand in the same relation to the above as the two pairs considered above. Since the grammatical subject of the latter clause is animate it should be possible to say **bacca piTnee par majbuur huaa* (the child was obliged to get-beaten); but this clause is unacceptable. The clauses *bacca piTaa* and *caaval tulee* are more like each other than the clauses *bacca piTaa* and *bacca soyaa*. Since the verbs *tolnaa, sulaanaa* and *sonaa* as well as *piiTnaa* all signify a volitional process, these verbs can be selected in imperative clauses independently or in an embedded form. Thus we have a set such as the following:

(17ii) caaval tolo.
rice   weigh
weigh the rice.

(17iii) naukar see kaho kee woh caaval tolee.
servant to say   that he   rice   should-weigh
ask the servant to weigh the rice.

(20ii) baccee ko sulaao
child   to cause-to-sleep
cause the child to sleep.

(20iii) ma͠a   see kaho kee woh baccee ko sulaaee.
mother to say   that she child   to cause-to-sleep
ask the mother to cause the child to sleep.

(22ii) baccee ko piiTo.
child   to beat
beat the child.

(22iii) ma͠a   see kaho kee woh baccee ko piiTee.
mother to   say   that she child   to should-beat
ask the mother to beat the child.

The verb *sonaa*, as is evident from the above examples, is more like *tolnaa* and *piiTnaa* than it is like *piTnaa* or *tulnaa*. There are no such clauses as **naukar see kaho kee woh caaval ko tulee* or ** ma͠a see kaho kee woh baccee ko piTee* nor is it possible to say *tulo* or *piTo* as an imperative (see note 19).

In the preceding section it has been pointed out that the feature imperative may be selected only if the clause has the feature volitional. It is however not true that all volitional clause types can have the feature imperative; consider that it is impossible to say **caaval tolaa jaao* (to be weighed the rice) or **soyaa jaao* (to be slept). The feature imperative may be selected only if the clause is both volitional and active; thus both (17ii) and (22ii) are acceptable. Both these clauses are active transitive; the rule however applies to intransitive clauses as well, thus to correspond to (20) we have an imperative clause *so-o!* (sleep). And here, again, we find *sonaa* more like *tolnaa* and *piiTnaa* than like *tulnaa* and *piTnaa*.

In Urdu, all major clauses whether they are volitional or non-volitional, relational or non-relational, transitive or intransitive have the option of active vs. non-agentive passive. So that in addition to (16a) and (17a), we have the following clauses:

(18a) kamraa saaf   kiyaa gayaa.
         room   clean done was
         the room was made clean.

(19a) baks paayaa gayaa.
         box   found was
         a box was found.

(20a) soya gayaa.
         slept was
         was slept (i.e. sleeping was done).

If *sonaa* and *tulnaa* are both treated as intransitive verbs, we would expect to find a corresponding passive for *tulnaa* in the manner of *sonaa*. There, however, does not exist any such passivized form of the verb, the item *tulaa gayaa* or *piTaa gayaa* being unacceptable.

The above reasons seem to me to be sufficient for emphasizing the dissimilarity between clause types (17b) and (20). In fact, some traditional Urdu grammars recognize this distinction. Thus Haq points out that there are certain verbs in the language which in their 'shape' resemble the intransitive but are in their meaning, in fact, passive. To quote him:

Consider *aaTaa tulaa* (the flour got weighed). It is clear that the flour cannot get weighed by itself; the weigher must be some other entity. So how can *aaTaa* be regarded as the *faael?* In fact the clause was (meant, R.H.) *aaTaa tolaa gayaa* (the flour was weighed); similarly (we have, R.H.) *kapRee silee* (the clothes got sewn), *rupyee baTee* (money got distributed) and *darwaaza khulaa* (the door got opened), *lakRi gaii* (the wood went) etc. etc. (*ibid.*, p. 143).

In all these examples the grammatical subject would be referred to by the label *qaaem-muqaam-ee-faael* (standing-place-of-actor, i.e. officiating actor) on the assumption that *faael* is to be interpreted as performer of the process. This same label is used to refer to the grammatical subject of (17a) and (19a), the grammatical subjects of (16a) and (18a) being referred to as *mubteedaa*.

The solution of regarding (17b) as a type of passive appears to me to be more attractive since it immediately makes explicit the relationship of the clause to (17) and also distinguishes it from (20), which as has been pointed out is necessary if what we are interested in is a semantically motivated grammar of the language. I shall refer to this type of passive as 'processive passive'. The processive passive may be informally characterized as 'a clause the process of which is seen as taking place independent of the actor, attributor or identifier'. The grammatical subject of such clauses, therefore, carries the transitivity function of affected, attribuand or identified.

11.4.2

From the above characterization it follows that clause (16b) *laRki xuubsurat lagi* and (17b) *caaval tulee* can be regarded as the processive passive related to (16) and (17) respectively; the process in these clauses is seen as independent of actor and attributor as if *tulnaa* were a process capable of taking place without a participant other than *caaval* and *lagnaa* were a process which could take place without a participant other than *laRki*. The processive passives related to (18) and (19) would be:

(18b) kamraa saaf   huaa.
      room   clean became
      the room became clean.
(19b) eek baks milaa.
      one box   got-found
      a box got found.

The use of the lexical verb *honaa* in the sense 'to become' is realizationally related to the selection of the feature processive in relational clauses which have the feature volitional. Thus we have clauses such as *kariim sadar huaa* (example (7)) and *bacci taiiyaar hui* (little-girl ready became = the little girl got ready). Traditionally, the verb *honaa* with the meaning *to become* has been regarded as one which could occur in an intransitive active clause. The reasons for this are easy to understand: like (20) *bacca soyaa*, a clause such as:

(23b) bacci taiiyaar hui.

may be seen as one which is only potentially related to an active clause such as:

(23) kisi   nee bacci   ko taiiyaar kiyaa.
     somebody nee little-girl to ready   made
     somebody made the little girl ready.

in the same manner as *bacca soyaa* is only potentially related to a causative *m͂aa nee baccee ko sulaayaa*. Semantically, it is possible to view both (20) and (23b) as clauses in which causation external to *bacca* and *bacci* is not needed. Consequently we may say *bacca xud see soyaa* (the child slept by himself) and *bacci xud see taiiyaar hui* (the little girl got ready by herself). There are however certain differences between (20) and (23b). If the latter is a relational clause, no active member of it will be acceptable without the attributor. The examples of active relational attributive clauses so far presented in this paper will bear witness to this fact; however, in all these examples the two participants selected are distinct entities, since this is the unmarked case. It should be noted however that it is by no means necessary that they be two distinct entities (extra-linguistically). There is a well-defined category[20] of transitive clauses in which the affected participant may be realized by a reflexive pronoun, e.g. *aurat nee xud ko tolaa* (the woman weighed herself). The attribuand is a special case of affected and may be realized by such a pro-noun, as in:

(23i) bacci   nee xud   ko taiiyaar kiyaa.
      little-girl nee herself to ready   made
      the little girl made herself ready.

It is, however, not possible to say *baccee nee xud ko sulaayaa* (the child made himself sleep) or *bacci nee xud ko dauRaayaa* (the little girl made herself run) for the obvious reason that there is no affected participant to be realized in the clause. The following clause:

(23a) bacci taiiyaar ki gaii.
       the little girl was made ready.

will be invariably regarded as the non-agentive passive agnate of the active
clause (23) but not of (23i). I would suggest that the non-agentive passive
agnate of the latter clause would be *xud taiiyaar huaa gayaa* (herself ready
become was = herself was got ready). Note the similarity between *laRki
see kamraa saaf kiyaa gayaa* (cf. (18a)) and *bacci see xud taiiyaar huaa
gayaa* (little-girl by herself ready become was = herself was got ready by
the little girl). In both cases the attribuand function is associated with the
grammatical subject of the clause and the attributor is signified through
the agentive adjunct; further, in conformity with all volitional intransitive
passive clauses with agentive adjunct, the feature of potentiality is relevant
to the semantics of the clause.

If the above suggestion is accepted, then *honaa* in the sense 'to become,
to get' would always be associated with the selection of the feature passive
in relational volitional clauses. If such a clause is non-reflexive, the verb
would be associated only with the processive passive as in (18b); if the
clause is reflexive, it would be associated both with the non-agentive and
processive passive, since the processive passive agnate of (23i) would be
the clause (*bacci*) *xud taiiyaar hui* ((little-girl) herself got ready). Unlike
(23b) *bacci taiiyaar hui*, this clause is totally unambiguous; it could be
related to (23i) only, not to (23).

11.4.3

It will be seen from the examples discussed so far that if a clause is active
and non-causative, then the actor of the non-relational and the attributor
and identifier of the relational clause share certain syntactic potentialities.
From now on, I shall refer to all these three functions by a less delicate
term 'the dynamic participant'. In effect, the dynamic participant function
is always associated with the grammatical subject of such clauses. The
non-agentive passive is characterized by the fact that the dynamic participant of the process remains unknown; in the case of volitional clauses
there exists a clause type which in its surface structure resembles the
non-agentive passive except that here the dynamic participant can be signified through the agentive adjunct. This clause type is the passive agnate
of an active clause with the feature 'potential'. These categories have been
exemplified by the following clauses:

(17a) caaval tolee gaee.
the rice was weighed.
(18a) kamraa saaf kiyaa gayaa.
the room was made clean.
(23ia) xud taiiyaar huaa gayaa.
herself was got ready.
(17ai) naukar see caaval tolee gaee.
the servant was able to weigh the rice.
(18ai) laRki see kamraa saaf kiyaa gayaa.
the girl was able to clean the room.
(23iai) bacci see xud taiiyaar huaa gayaa.
the girl was able to get ready by herself.

The first three of the above examples are non-agentive passive without the feature potential; the last three have the feature potential. All six have the features volitional, transitive and passive.

The processive passive is characterized as one in which the process is viewed as if it could take place without the intervention of the dynamic participant, although extra-linguistically this is not the case. The type may be exemplified by:

(16b) laRki xuubsurat lagi.
the girl seemed beautiful.
(17b) baks milaa.
a box got-found.
(18b) caaval tulee.
the rice got weighed.
(19b) kamraa saaf huaa.
the room got clean/became clean.

In all four clauses the process in fact 'requires' a participant other than the one associated with the grammatical subject of the clauses, while in the active intransitive clauses of the type *bacca soyaa* (the child slept) and *buD-Dhaa maraa* (the old man died) there is no such obligatory 'requirement'.

The reasons for making a distinction between the active intransitive and the passive processive have already been offered (see Section 11.4.1 above). It is, however, not the case that two distinct syntactic categories have to be totally distinct semantically. Thus the active and the passive members of a paradigm share certain semantic similarities while the caus-ative and the transitive clause types may be seen as having one similar semantic component in the sense that in both causation is external to the affected participant.[21] As a matter of fact, one may maintain that the move from causative to noncausative is in some way similar to the move from transitive to intransitive, just as the move from active to passive is in some way similar to the move from volitional to non-volitional. If the non-volitional process is a process that happens to someone without any volition on his part, then those processive passive types for which there exists no option 'reflexive' can be seen as somewhat close in their meaning to non-volitional intransitive active clauses such as *buDDhaa maraa* (the old man died). Examples (16b)–(19b) belong to this type of processive passive. If, on the other hand, we look at the volitional processive passive type for which there exists the option 'reflexive', this may be seen as close in its meaning to volitional intransitive active clauses such as *bacca soyaa* (the child slept) since one component of the meaning of the latter clause is the same as that in *bacci xud see taiiyaar hui* (the little girl got ready by herself). This seems reasonable since reflexive causation (using causation in its most general sense) is equal to no external causation and since the absence of external causation can in general be related to intransitivity.

11.4.4

It has been pointed out that so far as the 'true' non-agentive passive is concerned, it has no mechanism for signifying the dynamic participant of the agnate active (see Section 11.4). The same holds true for the volitional non-reflexive clauses of the processive type; thus if we have a clause such as (cf. (17b)) *naukar see caaval tulee* (the rice got weighed by the servant) and (cf. (18b)) *laRki see kamraa saaf huaa* (the room got made clean by the girl), these clauses have the same element of meaning in them which has been related to the feature 'potential'. As for the non-agentive passive so here too, the non-volitional clauses show a difference from the volitional ones: in the non-volitional processive type the dynamic participant of the agnate active may be signified through an adjunct without entailing any sense of potentiality; thus we may say (cf. (16b)) *laRkee ko laRki xuubsurat lagi* (the girl seemed beautiful to the boy) and (cf. (17b)) *naukar ko eek baks milaa* (a box got found to the servant).

The position implicitly taken in this rather lengthy discussion is that *honaa* in the sense 'to become' is in some respects syntactically like the verbs *tulnaa,lagnaa* and *milnaa*; in these said respects, then, the semantics of *honaa* is like that of the last three verbs. That there is a regular phonetic similarity between *tolnaa* and *tulnaa* but not between *karnaa* and *honaa* seems to me to be irrelevant in the context of this discussion.

11.4.5

If the passive for Urdu is generally defined as a clause in which the dynamic participant of the agnate active may not be associated with the grammatical subject, then a clause such as (16c) *laRki xuubsurat thi* presents some interesting problems. There is no doubt that the grammatical subject here is *laRki*; the question that may be debated is whether or not it also carries the transitivity function of dynamic participant. The view may be taken that this is a subcategory of non-volitional relational active clause; if so it could at once be related to:

  (16) laRkee nee laRki ko xuubsurat paayaa.
  (24) buDDhaa maraa.

so that (16) and (16c) would resemble each other by virtue of the fact that both have the features non-volitional and relational; to distinguish the two we would have to maintain that (16) is a clause in which the relational process can be more delicately described as 'perception', whereas this would appear to be not true of (16c). The latter clause would resemble (24) by virtue of the fact that, in both, the process happens to the participant associated with the grammatical subject of the clause; the two could be distinguished from each other on the ground that (16c) is relational, whereas (24) is not. Further we would have to maintain that if a clause is non-volitional there exists another option namely that it may either have the feature 'existential' or 'actional', so that at a certain degree of delicacy both (16) and (24) would have the feature actional whereas (16c) would have the feature existential.

If, however, the comments made earlier regarding the points of semantic similarity between distinct syntactic categories (see Section 11.4.3) are conceded, it may be maintained that the relational use of *honaa* in clauses of the type (16c) and (19c) *kamraa saaf thaa* are in fact maximally passive so that they share one component of the meaning of the non-volitional; at the same time since relational clauses may not be 'causative' this clause type ((16c) and (19c)) is also the least causative of the clause types, and thus shares one component of the meaning of 'intransitive'. The advantage in regarding (16c) as a member of the paradigm (16)–(16b) would be that the clause could be still regarded as related to a clause of perception, for in fact it is not true that (16c) has no element of perception in it. We have to assume that in the deep grammar of the clause the feature of perception is 'present' in order to account for the unacceptability of the following sentence:

> (25) *kariim rashiida ko xuubsurat paataa hai magar kariim kee liyee
>   Kariim Rashiida to beautiful finds is   but   Kariim for
>   rashiida xuubsurat nahĩ hai.
>   Rashiida beautiful not is
>   Kariim finds Rashiida beautiful but for Kariim Rashiida is not
>   beautiful.

The anomaly here is of the same nature as in *mãã nee baccee ko piiTaa magar bacca nahĩ piTaa* (the mother beat the child but the child did not get beaten); if the active clause is true then the other clause must be false and vice versa. When we have a sentence such as *laRki koi xaas xuubsurat nahĩ magar laRkee ko xuubsurat lagti hai* (the girl is not particularly beautiful but she seems beautiful to the boy), this clause can be treated as not anomalous only on the assumption that for some other perceiver/ attributor the *laRki* is not beautiful but so far as *laRkaa* is concerned he perceives her as beautiful. Such clauses as *aap kee liyee to har laRki koh-ee-qaaf ki pari hai* (for you every girl is a fairy from the Caucasian mountains) and *karnee walee kee liyee har kaam aasaan hai* (for one who wishes to act every action is easy), *xudaa kee liyee Gariib amiir baraabar haĩ* (for God the rich and the poor are equal), *meeree liyee tum aaj bhi baccee ho* (for me you are still a child) are all frequent and acceptable utterances in the language and for all these clauses the nominal with the post-position *kee liyee* can be shown to be the same as the dynamic participant of the active agnates of these clauses. In view of this close relationship between clause types (16) and (16c) it appears desirable to regard the latter as a member of the same paradigm as that to which (16) belongs. Let us now tentativily suggest that (16c) is a 'stative passive' [22] agnate of (16); the process of a stative passive may, in this context, be characterized generally as the process of existence in a perceived state. The verb *honaa* in the sense 'to be' is the only verb in the language which may be used for signifying the process of a clause with the set of syntactic options 'non-volitional, relational and stative passive', and as such its meaning may be exhaustively stated by reference to these options. The verb *honaa* (to be) signifies a process which happens to someone (cf. option non-volitional); it signifies a process that is relational so that basically in its semantics it 'needs' the ascribing participant, the ascribed participant, and the circumstance ascribed; being realizationally related to a stative passive, it is at the furthest remove from active, so that the process is least causal in character; in the manner of other passives, the process appears as if it required no dynamic participant (of which ascribing participant is a special case) but simply pertains to the affected one (of which ascribed participant is a special case).

11.4.6

Clauses of the type (16c) are in fact statements of opinion, either personal, e.g. in *laRki xuubsurat hai* (the girl is beautiful) or general, e.g. in *laRkiyaã sharmiili hoti haĩ* (girls are usually shy) or technical, e.g. in *Tinkcar aayo-Diin zahriilaa hotaa hai* (tincture iodine is poisonous). The post-position *kee liyee* (for) can also be used in volitional benefactive clauses to signify the 'beneficiary', e.g. in *naukar nee baavarci kee liyee caaval tolee* (the servant weighed the rice for the cook); when *kee liyee* occurs in clause type (16c) the nominal to which it is attached does not have the function of beneficiary. Since the basic contextual function of this clause type is to make a statement, the phrase *in the opinion of + attributor* (attributor *ki raaee meẽ*) may be substituted for *for + attributor* (attributor *kee liyee*) without leading to any change in the relationship of the participants of the clause. Thus the clauses *laRkee kee liyee laRki xuubsurat hai* and *laRkee ki raaee meẽ laRki xuubsurat hai* have the same transitivity selection. Note that it is impossible to have a clause such as **laRkee ki raaee meẽ laRkee kee liyee laRki xuubsurat hai* (in the opinion of the boy the girl is beautiful for the (same) boy) while the clause *baavarci ki raaee meẽ naukar nee usi kee liyee caaval tolee* (in the opinion of the cook the servant weighed the rice for him (the cook)) is acceptable. The following discussion will throw some light on the selection of *kee liyee* in stative passive clauses.

It is now tentatively assumed that (16c) *is* a member of the non-volitional relational paradigm. Are its characteristics shared by (18c) *kamraa saaf thaa*? It has been shown that sentence (25) is unacceptable; it is however perfectly possible to say:

(26) laRki nee saaree din kamraa saaf kiyaa magar phir bhi
     girl   nee whole day room   clean did   but   even then
     kamraa saaf   nahĩ thaa.
     room   clean not   was
     the girl had been making the room clean all day but even then
     the room was not clean.

Unlike (25), the above example has no illogicality or anomaly; both the clauses of the sentence may be true at once. Now if (16) and (18) are compared, it will be found that in the former the attribute is perceived as if it were 'present in the attribuand'; that is, it is impossible for a perceiver to 'find' an attribute in an attribuand and yet not to regard it as existing in the attribuand. In (18) the attribute is not seen as existing in the attribuand but as one which the attributor's action makes the attribuand acquire. We may refer to these two kinds of attribute as 'depictive' and 'resultative' respectively. The attribute in volitional relational clauses is always of the latter type; in accordance with its semantics only non-durational adjectives (i.e. those which signify a non-permanent quality) may function as attribute in such clauses.[23] The semantics of the resultative attribute also accounts for the acceptability of (26); it is logically possible to undertake the process of making an attribuand acquire an attribute without actually achieving this end. On the other hand, the achieving of this end will always imply that for some attributor *now* the attribute is 'present in the attribuand'. Thus clauses of the type (18c) genuinely face in two directions; they may be shown to be implicationally related to the volitional relational clause or to the non-volitional non-relational clause. So we may construct a set of clauses such as the following:

(18)   laRki nee kamraa saaf kiyaa.
(18a) kamraa saaf kiyaa gayaa.
(18b) kamraa saaf huaa.
(18c) kamraa saaf thaa.
(18d) kamraa saaf milaa.
(18e) kamraa saaf paayaa gayaa.
(18f) kisi nee kamraa saaf paayaa.

It has been pointed out that clauses of the type (18f) are ambiguous (cf. example (14), Section 11.3.3 above), because of the lexical multivalence of the verb which may be interpreted as 'consider' or 'come across'. When it has the former meaning the processive passive verb corresponding to it is *lagnaa* or *maaluum honaa* (to seem); in the latter sense the processive passive verb is *milnaa*. (18f) is used here as an example of a non-volitional non-relational clause which may be paraphrased as *kisi nee kamraa paayaa aur kamraa saaf thaa* in the same manner as *naukar nee baks TuuTaa paayaa* may be paraphrased as *naukar nee baks paayaa aur baks TuuTaa thaa* (the servant found the box and the box was broken). One component of the meaning of a non-volitional non-relational clause with attribution can be readily seen as follows: to the dynamic participant a process happens which involves an affected participant and the latter is perceived by the former participant as 'having an attribute'. Thus attribution in a non-volitional non-relational clause may be regarded as depictive; by contrast in volitional non-relational clauses attribution is generally resultative, so that if we have *darzii nee kurtaa choTaa siyaa* (the tailor sewed the shirt small) the clause may be paraphrased as *darzii nee kurtaa is tarah siyaa kee woh choTaa ho gayaa* (the tailor sewed the shirt so that it became small). Strictly speaking the attribute *choTaa* in the preceding example combines both result and manner. I shall ignore this complication for the time being and concentrate only on the resultative part of the meaning of the clause.

It has been pointed out that certain volitional clauses may have the feature benefactive and the beneficiary participant has usually the postposition *kee liyee* attached to it, e.g. *naukar nee baavarci kee liyee caaval tolee* and *darzii nee kisi kee liyee kurtaa siyaa* (the tailor sewed the shirt for some one) where *baavarci* and *kisi* have the function of beneficiary. On the same analogy it is possible to say:

> (27) laRki nee kisi   kee liyee kamraa saaf kiyaa.
> girl   nee somebody for   room   clean did
> the girl made the room clean for some one.

(27) differs from (18) only in one respect: the former has the feature benefactive whereas the latter does not have such a feature. Consequently a clause such as *kisi kee liyee kamraa saaf hai* (the room is clean for some one) is potentially ambiguous; it may mean that *kisi ki raaee mee~ kamraa saaf hai* (in somebody's opinion the room is clean) or *kamraa kisi kee isteemaal kee liyee saaf hai* (the room is clean for somebody's use). In the non-volitional relational clause where the selection of the option benefactive is not permissible (there being no such clauses as *the boy found the girl beautiful for somebody*) *laRki kisi kee liyee xuubsurat hai* cannot be regarded as ambiguous; the phrases *attributor kee liyee* and *attributor ki raaee mee~* are interchangeable.

11.4.7

Two facts follow from the above discussion: (a) clause type (18c) is related to clause type (18); and (b) by indirect implication it is also related to clause type (16); hence if we say:

(28) laRki nee kamree ko saaf samjhaa magar laRki ki raaee
     girl nee room   to clean thought but   girl of opinion
     mẽe kamraa saaf nahĩ thaa.
     in room   clean not   was
     the girl considered the room clean but in the girl's opinion the
     room was not clean

we are faced with the same kind of illogicality which was encountered in
(25). Thus it appears that those stative passive clauses in which the attribute is realized by a non-durational adjective can be seen as simultaneously related to non-volitional relational clauses, to the volitional relational
clauses and to the non-volitional non-relational attributive clauses. Thus if
we are interested in the derivational history of a clause *laRki xush thi* (the
girl was happy), it matters very little, it would seem, whether we claim it
to be derived from *kisi nee laRki ko xush samjhaa* (some one thought the
girl happy) or from *kisi nee laRki ko xush paayaa* (somebody found the
girl happy) or from *kisi nee laRki ko xush kiyaa* (somebody made the girl
happy). I would maintain that if we make an effort to consider the clause
as derived chiefly from one of these three types, we will be distorting some
facts about it. It is suggested that clauses of the type (18c) may be seen
as a type in which certain features get neutralized, which to a large extent
explains why they have not been traditionally shown as related to specific clause paradigms of the language. Thus while if we relate (18c) to the
non-volitional relational clause of perception the attribute may be viewed
as depictive, if we relate it to the volitional relational one it may be viewed
as the result of an activity.

11.5

So far for the volitional non-relational clause of the type (17) *naukar nee
caaval tolee* a paradigm has been set up which in general terms corresponds to the paradigms for (16), (18) and (19). The question arises if the
option of stative passive is available to clause type (17). Let us consider:

(17c) caaval tulee   huee   haĩ.
      rice   weighed   become are
      the rice is weighed.

It is suggested that (17c) is different from:

(20iv) bacca soyaa huaa   hai.
      child slept become is
      the child is still sleeping.

This difference lies in the function of *tulee huee* and *soyaa huaa*. Other examples of the type (17c) would be *kurtaa rãgaa huaa hai* (the shirt is dyed), *kursi TuuTi hui hai* (the chair is broken), *duudh ublaa huaa hai* (the milk is boiled), *farsh dhulaa huaa hai* (the floor is washed) and so on; examples of the type (20iv) would be *laRki leeTi hui hai* (the girl is still lying down), *naukar baRi deer see gayaa huaa hai* (the servant has been gone for a long time), and so on. The items *tulee huee, rãgaa huaa, TuuTi hui,* etc. may be regarded as having the function of an attribute in the clause type (17c), so that it is possible to co-ordinate these items with a situationally appropriate adjective with the entire adjectival complex functioning as attribute in the clauses *caaval tulee huee aur saaf hãi* (the rice is weighed and clean), *duudh taazaa aur ublaa huaa hai* (the milk is fresh and boiled), *kursi TuuTi hui aur gandi hai* (the chair is broken and dirty); items such as *soyaa huaa* and *gayaa huaa,* etc. cannot be co-ordinated with any adjectives in clause type (20iv); thus clauses such as **bacca thakaa aur soyaa huaa hai* (the child is tired and still sleeping) or **laRki leeTi hui aur biimaar hai* (the girl is still lying down and ill) are unacceptable.

11.5.1

Three points emerge from a consideration of type (17c): (a) if the clause *caaval saaf hai* (the rice is clean) is regarded as a relational attributive clause, then there is reason to consider (17c) as a clause having the same features; (b) if (17c) is regarded as a relational attributive clause, the attribute *tulee huee* would be like the attribute in (18c): both result from the undertaking of a volitional process; and (c) if *caaval tulee huee hãi* is a relational attributive clause and is still regarded as a member of the paradigm of (17), then we have a case where by the time we arrive at this particular member of the paradigm, the features of the paradigm as a whole no longer apply to it. While (17)–(17b) are volitional (17c) may not be regarded as having such a feature; while (17)–(17b) are non-relational, we have shown that (17c) may be regarded as relational; and finally while (17)–(17b) are non-attributive the type under focus has to be regarded as attributive.

11.5.2

It can be readily seen that the above is, in fact, the inevitable logical result of the approach taken in the discussion of (18c) with reference to (18f) and (18e), where, it might be recalled, (18c) was treated as a relational clause while the types (18f) and (18e) were considered to be nonrelational. Further it was pointed out that a particular category of the stative passive type is, as it were, the genuine meeting ground for many different paradigms (see Sections 11.4.6–11.4.7 above). The ground is now clear to take a further step: if it is the case that a particular type is related to so many basically different types, then it is also the case that it is not related specifically to any one particular type. The clauses which have been labelled stative passive may then be regarded as the most neutral type of clause in the language; that is to say, they represent a category for the semanticization of which such basic options as causative vs. non-causative, volitional vs. non-volitional, transitive vs. non-transitive, active vs. passive and relational vs. non-relational are, in fact, somewhat irrelevant. A given instance of such a category will no doubt be relatable to a given permissible set of the above options, both by sharing some of the syntactic potentialities of the clause type which has the said set of systemic features and by showing a constant logical implicational relationship to it. The instances which could be most readily related to other clause types would be marked neutral clauses, i.e. marked in respect to some feature which is exclusively related to a particular category. Thus given *caaval baavarci kee liyee tulee huee haĩ* (the rice is weighed for the cook) it is possible to relate it to a volitional benefactive such as *kisi nee baavarci kee liyee caaval tolee* (some one weighed the rice for the cook). The systemic option of relational vs. non-relational is said to be irrelevant to the neutral clause type because such clauses do not in fact have an 'option': each instance of this type may be treated as relational if intensional relation is not confined to the specific types discussed above, namely that of attribute-attribuand and identity and identified; in other words if it could be extended to include such relations as location-localized and possession-possessed, then all the following would be instances of relational clause:

(29) laRki   xush   hai.
     girl   happy   is
     the girl is happy.

(30) woh   DaakTar   hai.
     he   doctor   is
     he is a doctor.

(31) baks kamree me͂e hai.
     box room in is
     the box is in the room.

(32) laRki kee paas eek baks hai.
     girl of near one box is
     the girl has a box.

It is in this sense that *honaa* 'to be' may be regarded as a connecting word (or as 'copula') in that its primary function in these cases is to relate the circumstance ascribed to the ascribed participant. It is immaterial that *hai* in (32) has to be translated as *has* in English; in all four cases the semantics of *honaa* for the Urdu clauses is identical: it is an item which signifies the process of existence which is predicated of the ascribed participant and of the circumstance ascribed: both exist and both exist in a given relationship to each other.

11.6

Examples (29)–(32) are instances of the neutral type of clause. They are distinguished from each other by having a distinct feature. Thus (29) is attributive, (30) is equative, (31) is locative and (32) is possessive; of these the first two categories have been discussed in some detail. One might question whether it is valid to set up a systemic option for the neutral clause type whose terms are attributive, equative, locative and possessive so that if the clause is attributive it may not be equative and if it is either, then it may not be locative and if it is any of the latter three categories then it may not be possessive. It might be argued that since we have:

(33) laRki landan me͂e xush hai.
     girl London in happy is
     the girl is happy in London.

(34) haamid kee paas laahaur me͂e kaii makaan haı̃.
     Haamid of near Lahore in many houses are
     Haamid has many houses in Lahore.

(35) woh haspataal me͂e sab see qaabil DaakTar hai.
     he hospital in all of able doctor is
     he is the ablest doctor in the hospital.

the option locative should not be regarded as being in contrast with the options attributive (cf. (33)) or possessive (cf. (34)) or equative (cf. (35)). It is suggested that such a view could be taken only if the semantic function of *landan mẽe, laahaur mẽe* and *haspataal mẽe* is not taken into consideration; in other words they could be regarded as having the function of the locative if we were defining locative only by reference to the post-position *mẽe, par,* etc. The locative may be characterized as that phrase which signifies the place in some relation to which the process takes place; the specific relation is, in general, signified by the post-position attached to the place-signifying noun, thus in *bacca kamree mẽe soyaa* (the child slept in the room) the process of sleeping takes place in the room, with *mẽe* signifying the specific relation of the process to the place signified by the noun *kamraa*. Similarly in *woh kamree mẽe see niklaa* (he came out of the room), *mẽe see* signifies the specific relation in which the process of *nikalnaa* stands to the location *kamraa*. If so defined, the function of the locative is simply to signify a localization relation; it may not signify condition or part-whole relations. In (33), however, we find that *landan mẽe* has precisely the function of signifying condition, so a near paraphrase of the clause may be *cũkee laRki landan mẽe hai is liyee xush hai* (because the girl is in London therefore she is happy). If the verbal group of the clause had a modal construction *hoti hai* (usually is) signifying a 'habitual occurrence' then we could have paraphrased it as *jab laRki landan mẽe hoti hai to xush hoti hai* (when the girl is in London, she is happy), whereas even if we have a clause such as *bacca kamree mẽe sotaa hai* (the child usually sleeps in the room) we may not interpret it as *when the child is in the room, he sleeps*. The function of *landan mẽe* in (33), if the verbal group has a modal construction, is the same as that of *javaani mẽe* in the following:

> (36) javaani mẽe gadhaa bhi   xuubsurat hotaa   hai.
>   youth   in   donkey too beautiful usually-is
>   even a donkey is beautiful in youth.

It may be noted here that in a clause such as *kisi nee laRki ko kamree mẽe xaamosh paayaa* (somebody found the girl silent in the room), the clause is paraphrased as *kisi nee laRki ko kamree mẽe paayaa aur woh xaamosh thi* (somebody found the girl in the room and she was silent) and not as *kisi nee laRki ko paayaa aur woh kamree mẽe xaamosh thi* (somebody found the girl and she was silent in the room). Thus the domain of the locative in the last clause mentioned above does not extend over the attribute.

The interrogative locative employed in non-polar interrogative clauses is *kahãa* (where). However, in the written form the following is an ambiguous clause:

(20) (v) bacca kahãa soyaa?
        child where slept
   (i) where did the child go to sleep?
   (ii) the child has certainly not gone to sleep.

In interpretation (i) the function of the item *kahãa* is that of an interrogative locative; it calls for a specification of place of action. *kahãa* alone is the 'new' part of the message; the other elements of the message are known. Consequently in speech *kahãa* is the item that would carry the greatest amount of prominence; that is to say, it will function as a 'tonic' syllable.[24] This is a constant characteristic of the interrogative locative. Usually an interrogative locative immediately precedes the verbal group; this is the unmarked order of occurrence for an interrogative locative, as shown by the above example as well as by *laRki nee kitaab kahãa paRhi?* (where did the girl read that book?). Again, if *kahãa* functions as an interrogative locative in the latter clause, it will carry the tonic. In interpretation (ii) of (20v) the tonic will be carried by some other item than *kahãa*. If it is carried by *bacca*, the implication is that some one else has gone to sleep but not the child; if it is carried by *soyaa*, the implication is the child is doing something else, not sleeping. In the latter case, the information may also be carried by reversing the sequence of the verbal group and the item *kahãa*, so that the clause would read *bacca soyaa kahãa*. But here another distinction operates: if the tonic is carried by *soyaa* the implication is that by contrast the child did something else; if it is carried by *kahãa*, no contrast is intended so that there is only emphatic negation regarding the process. When *kahãa* signifies emphatic and/or contrastive negation, its place in sequence can be varied in many ways in agreement with what part of the message is being negated and/or is contrastive. This is not true of the interrogative *kahãa*. When *kahãa* signifies emphatic and/or contrastive negation, it may or may not carry the tonic according to whether it is functioning contrastively or not. It stands to reason therefore that when *kahãa* has the most unmarked place in sequence as in *laRki nee kitaab kahãa paRhi* (girl nee book where did-read), the distinction in the two meanings of the clause is made through the selection of the tonic. So that if *kahãa* is tonic, the clause is locative interrogative, if some other item is tonic then the clause is contrastive, negative and emphatic. Thus:

> (37) laRki nee kitaab *kahaã* paRhi?
> *where* did the girl read the book?
> (38) laRki nee *kitaab* kahaã paRhi.
> the girl certainly did not read the *book*.

are distinct in their meaning. Now consider the following pair:

> (33a) laRki xush *kahaã* thi.
> (33b) laRki *xush* kahaã thi.

The distinction in meaning here is not parallelled by the distinction between (37) and (38). (33a) may be translated as *the girl certainly* wasn't *happy* with the tonic on the verbal group, so that there is an emphatic negation of the process here as would be the case if the tonic had been carried by *paRhi* in (37) or (38). (33b) may be translated as *the girl certainly wasn't happy*, with the tonic on the attribute, so that there is a contrastive emphatic negation and we may interpret the clause as 'whatever else the girl might have been she certainly wasn't happy'. In fact *kahaã* in its interrogative locative meaning may not be used in clauses of the type (33). This discussion provides us with well-motivated reasons for the statement that if a neutral clause type has the feature attributive, it may not have the feature locative; these features are mutually exclusive and can therefore be regarded as terms in the system. When in clause type (33) there occurs a phrase which in its structure contains a place name, its function is to specify (by indirect means) the time during which a said attribuand had a specific attribute. That is why it is difficult, if not impossible, to find an appropriate context for a clause such as *laRki landan meẽ zahiin thi* (the girl was intelligent in London). This is not to deny that the place-name phrase may have other functions in such a clause type, e.g. in *is mulk meẽ laRkiyaã xuubsurat hoti haĩ* (in this country girls are usually beautiful) where *is mulk meẽ* has the function of modifying *laRkiyaã* so that it is possible to say *is mulk ki laRkiyaã*. My purpose is not to go into the detailed description of the environments in which such place-name phrases have different functions, but simply to point out that a locative feature does not co-occur with the feature attributive in the neutral clause type.

11.6.1

That the equative and the attributive features are mutually exclusive is probably demonstrated sufficiently in the discussion of the relational clauses. In *kariim qaabil DaakTar hai* (Kariim is a capable doctor), *qaabil* and *DaakTar* do not have two separate functions, so that the clause may not be paraphrased as *kariim qaabil hai aur kariim DaakTar hai* (Kariim is capable and Kariim is a doctor) but rather as *kariim DaakTar ki haisiyat see qaabil hai* (Kariim is capable as a doctor). The function of *qaabil* is to modify the (identity) noun *DaakTar* and the entire group *qaabil DaakTar* functions as the identity ascribed to the identified. Thus it is justifiable to regard equative and attributive features as terms in the same system.

11.6.2

The question that arises at this point is whether the feature locative and equative are also mutually exclusive so that in (35) *woh haspataal mẽe sab see qaabil DaakTar hai* (he is the ablest doctor in the hospital) the place-name phrase *haspataal mẽe* can be shown to be not locative. Unlike (33), the clause here may not be paraphrased as *cũkee woh haspataal mẽe hai is liyee sab see qaabil DaakTar hai* (because he is in the hospital therefore he is the ablest doctor) or *jab woh haspataal mẽe hotaa hai to sab see qaabil DaakTar hotaa hai* (when he is in the hospital he is the ablest doctor). Indeed, if the latter were a possible paraphrase, it would be also possible to say that when he comes out of the hospital he is no longer the ablest doctor in the hospital which would be manifestly absurd. In fact then we have to regard *haspataal mẽe* as a modifying phrase; it constitutes a part of the complex group *haspataal mẽe sab see qaabil DaakTar* and the entire group has the function of identity, despite the fact that the item may occur discontinuously, e.g. in *haspataal mẽe woh sab see qaabil DaakTar hai* (in the hospital he is the ablest doctor). It is clear that the relationship here is not that of location-located but that of part-whole. This relation of part-whole is internal to the nominal group functioning as identity and does not dominate the clause. Thus a possible close paraphrase of (35) is *woh haspataal ka sab see qaabil DaakTar hai* (he is the ablest doctor of the hospital). It is not the case that the locative relation 'gets converted into' part-whole relation through the process of nominalization. Thus given (31) *baks kamree mẽe hai*, its nominalization will not be *kamree kaa baks* but *kamree mẽe kaa baks* (*box of the room* and *box of in the room*, literally). Other examples of the type (35) would be *woh hamaaree halqee mẽe hardil-aziiz shaaer hai* (he is a popular poet in our circle), *woh is kaalij mẽe lekcarar hai* (he is a lecturer in this college), *woh kisi shahar mẽe jaj hai* (he is a judge in some city), and so on.

In the manner of (33), the possibility of introducing an interrogative locative[25] in clause type (35) does not exist; here too the item *kahaã* could be used to signify emphatic and/or contrastive negation. Thus if the feature equative 'appears' in the deep grammar of the neutral clause, this will imply that neither the feature attributive nor locative may be 'present'. One means of making this environmental restriction explicit is to say that the features attributive, equative and locative form terms in the same system so that the selection of one option in the clause restricts the selection of the other two options.

11.6.3

If the locative is a phrase which signifies the place in some relation to which a process occurs, then (34) *haamid kee paas laahaur mẽe kaii makaan haĩ* may not be regarded as a clause with the feature locative in it, since the process of possession is independent of the locational relation signified by *laahaur mẽe*. In other words it is not the case that *haamid laahaur mẽe nahĩ hai magar haamid kee paas laahaur mẽe kaii makaan haĩ* (Haamid is not in Lahore but Haamid has many houses in Lahore) is either illogical or false, while a sentence such as *haamid kee paas laahaur mẽe kaii makaan haĩ magar woh makaan laahaur mẽe nahĩ haĩ* (Haamid has many houses in Lahore but those houses are not in Lahore) is clearly illogical and one constituent clause of the sentence must be false if the other is true. Thus in (34) the domain of *laahaur mẽe* is seen to extend only over *kaii makaan*; note that the clause may be paraphrased as *haamid kee paas kaii makaan haĩ jo kee laahaur mẽe haĩ* (Haamid has many houses which are in Lahore). The location-localized relation therefore is clearly group-internal; that is to say it is not at the rank of clause that the locative has been selected but at the rank of that group which has the function of 'possession' in the clause. A comparable situation exists in the clause *woh baRaa mehnti laRkaa hai* (he is a hard-working boy) where the relation of attribute-attribuand in *baRaa mehnti laRkaa* is group-internal; the clause itself is equative, not attributive.

As in (33) and (35), so here too, the possibility of introducing an interrogative locative[26] in the clause does not exist; the item *kahaã* when used in such a clause type signifies emphatic and/or contrastive negation. The source of the ambiguity in clauses such as *aap kee biwi bacce kahaã haĩ* (your of wife children where are) is discussed below (see Sections 11.8–11.8.1).

11.6.4

If the arguments put forward in Sections 11.6–11.6.3 are accepted, clauses (29) and (33) would be regarded as having the feature attributive, (30) and (35) would be regarded as having the feature equative, (32) and (34) as having the feature possessive; (31) *baks kamree mẽe hai* alone would be a clause with the feature locative. The domain of the locative here extends over the entire clause. No such paraphrases are possible as *jab baks thaa to kamree mẽe thaa* (when the box existed then was in the room), *cũkee baks thaa is liyee kamree mẽe thaa* (because the box existed therefore was in the room), *baks thaa jo kee kamree mẽe thaa* (the box existed which was in the room) or *kamree kaa baks thaa* (the box of the room existed).

In fact the reason for regarding the neutral clause type[27] as essentially relational is precisely this: the ascribed participant and the circumstance ascribed in such a clause cannot be 'separated' from each other, as if the predication of existence without the 'state of existence' were totally impossible. Thus (29) *laRki xush hai* does not mean *laRki hai* (a girl exists) and *xush hai* (happy is), nor does (32) mean *eek baks hai* (a box exists) and *laRki kee paas hai* (the girl has). Logically or extra-linguistically it may be a fact that an ascribed participant has to exist in order for it to be in a state, but so far as Urdu language and its syntax is concerned, this logical extra-linguistic 'fact' is of no consequence. That being the case, what is the description of *kariim hai* (Kariim is), or *baks hai* (a box is), etc.? The answer, in my opinion, is that such clauses are always elliptical and such ellipsis is decoded either by reference to the co-text or to the immediate context of situation. Thus the clause *kariim hai* may function as an answer to such questions as *kaun biimaar hai?* (who is ill?), *kamree mẽe kaun hai?* (who is (there) in the room?) and *kaun DaakTar hai?* (who is the doctor?), etc., where both for the encoding and decoding of the clause *kariim hai*, the items *biimaar, kamree mẽe*, and *DaakTar* are relevant. In other words for the deep grammar of the clause, one of the four terms from the system just discussed will always be relevant. A question like *kariim hai?* is not to be decoded as *does Kariim exist?* but rather as *is Kariim here?* in which case the tonic would be carried by the verb *is* (hai); or as *is it Kariim who is ill/a doctor?* in which case the tonic would be carried by *kariim*. If for *kariim* we substitute an inanimate noun (or any noun that can function as 'possession' in the language) such as *baks hai* it may function as an answer to a question with the feature locative, attributive, equative or possessive; equally, given the right intonation it may function as a question with one of these features. One could maintain that in Urdu there exists no verb with the scope of the verb *exist* in English. This raises a question regarding the clause *xudaa hai* (God exists).[28] I suggest that the peculiarity of this clause arises from the selection of the item *xudaa*. This item, as is perhaps befitting given the belief of the speech community, overrides all syntactic distinctions that can be made so that we have clauses such as *xudaa nee kariim ko do beeTee diyee* (God gave Kariim two sons), *xudaa nee murdee ko jilaayaa* (God caused the dead (person) to live) and even *xudaa kee hukm see laRkee nee laRki ko xuubsurat paayaa*[29] (according to the will of God, the boy found the girl beautiful), and so on. It would be somewhat pointless to make rules for the description of these clauses as also for *xudaa hai;*[30] one rule suffices, namely that in Urdu *xudaa* is capable of anything and everything.

11.7

The neutral clause type has been characterized as one which can be potentially related to different clause types. This was exemplified in the discussion of the attributive and the equative neutral clauses. Does this characterization also hold true of the possessive and the locative? Let us first examine the possessive neutral clause.

The characterization of the possessive clause as one in which there exists a possessor-possession relation is highly generalized since it is possible to establish at least four subtypes of relation as exemplified by the following clauses:

    (39) kariim kee eek bhaai   hai.
          Kariim of   one brother is
          Kariim has a brother.
    (40) kariim kee baRi   daulat hai.
          Kariim of   lots-of wealth is
          Kariim has a lot of wealth.
    (41) kariim kee do   aãkhẽe haĩ.
          Kariim of   two eyes   are
          Kariim has two eyes.
    (42) kariim kee aql   hai.
          Kariim of   intelligence is
          Kariim has intelligence.

In (39) the relation between *kariim* ('possessor') and *eek bhaai* ('possession') may be more specifically described as kin-to-kin relation. In (40), the relation between kariim ('possessor') and *baRi daulat* ('possession') may be more specifically regarded as owner-property relation. In (41), the relation between *kariim* ('possessor') and *do aakhee* ('possession') may be described as a whole-part relation, while in (42) *kariim* and *aql* may be seen as standing in a qualified-quality relation. Of these only (40) is alienable possession, the remaining are all 'inherent' or 'in-alienable' possession. The possessor in all the above cases is an animate noun; when the possessor is animate the post-position *kee/kee paas* (of, of near) occurs as the marker of this transitivity function. Both post-positions are multivalent, that is, they may function as markers in other structures either at clause rank or at group rank (see Section 11.8.1 below). All four specific types of possession exemplified above are available to clauses in which the possessor is animate; if, however, the possessor is inanimate only the whole-part and qualified-quality relations are available, as can be exemplified by the following:

> (43) is   kamree mee do   khiRkiyaa haĩ.
>   this room   in   two windows   are
>   this room has two windows.
> (44) is   kapRee mee kuch aib   hai.
>   this material in   some defect is
>   this material has some defect (in it).

(43) is like (41) a clause in which there exists a whole-part relation; (44) is like (42) a clause in which there exists qualified-quality relation. If our concern was only to describe (41)–(44), without relating them to any other clause types in the language, then it would be possible to view all four as cases of whole-part relation. (44) and (42) are however relatable to the attributive clause so that (42) may be regarded as giving more or less the same information as is conveyed by *kariim aqlmand hai* (Kariim is intelligent) while (44) stands in the same relation to *yee kapRaa aibdaar hai* (this material is defective), whereas neither (41) nor (43) can be related to an attributive clause. Such clauses as *yee gaaee dumdaar hai* (this cow is with-a-tail) and *kariim do aakhõ waalaa hai* (Kariim is with-two-eyes) or *yee kamraa khiRki waalaa hai* (this room is with-a-window) are perceived as odd, if not totally ungrammatical.

As can be seen from (43) and (44), the post-position *mee* (in) occurs as the marker of possessor function. *mee*, needless to say, is multivalent and in addition to this function, it may be used either to signify the locational function of a noun or the time function, e.g. in *kamree mee* in (31) and *din mee* in a clause such as *is kaarxaanee mee din mee baRaa shor hotaa hai* (there is a lot of noise in this factory during the day), where the first occurrence of *mee* signifies location and the second time duration. It is easy to see how the surface similarities of (43) and (31) may be construed as implying a deep grammar similarity between the locative and the possessive (see note 31).

11.7.1

Clauses (39)–(42) may be potentially related to a non-volitional non-relational active clause type, as is exemplified by the following:

(39i) kariim   eek   bhaai   rakhtaa hai.
Kariim   one   brother   owns   is
Kariim owns a brother.

(40i) kariim   baRi   daulat   rakhtaa hai.
Kariim   lot-of   wealth   owns   is
Kariim owns a lot of wealth.

(41i) kariim   do   aakhee   rakhtaa hai.
Kariim   two   eyes   owns   is
Kariim owns two eyes.

(42i) kariim   aql   rakhtaa hai.
Kariim   intelligence   owns   is
Kariim owns intelligence.

It is irrelevant that the English translations of these clauses sound 'odd'; in Urdu given the right context, these clauses are used without any perception of 'oddity' about them. Thus when we have *laRkaa eek nahĩ chee bahnee rakhtaa hai; aisee laRkee ko laRki deenaa munaasib nahĩ* (the boy owns not one but six sisters; it is not right to give a girl (in marriage) to such a boy) or *ai bahan! aakhee rakhti ho yaa baTan jo tumhee kuch nazar hi nahĩ aataa* (O sister! do you own eyes or buttons that nothing ever gets seen by you) or *tum bhi to aql rakhtee thee; apni aql see kaam liyaa hotaa* (you too owned intelligence! you should have used your own intelligence), none of the clauses with the feature possessive in these sentences is seen as 'odd'. That clause types (39i)–(42i) do not occur very frequently is not being denied; simply the point is being made that they are all grammatical and acceptable and that there is no oddity in their use, and that they are related to (39)–(42).

11.7.2

It has been suggested that a clause such as:

(45) kariim kee paas eek kitaab hai.
     Kariim of near one book   is
     Kariim has a book.

is potentially related to a benefactive clause[31] such as:

(46) kisi   nee kariim ko eek kitaab di   hai.
     somebody nee Kariim to one book   gave is
     somebody has given Kariim a book.

Certainly there exists a constant logical relationship of implication (effect/result-cause) between (45) and (46). However it is doubtful whether the benefactive feature as such is at the basis of such a relation. (45) can still have a result relation with a non-benefactive clause such as:

(47) kariim nee kutub-xaanee see   eek kitaab curaai hai.
     Kariim nee library   from one book   stolen is
     Kariim has stolen a book from the library.

Similarly the pair *kariim nee musiiqi par eek kitaab xarridi hai* (Kariim has bought a book on music) and *kariim kee paas musiiqi par eek kitaab hai* (Kariim has a book on music) are potentially related as cause and effect, and there seems no reason to think that the benefactive is the only clause type which could stand in a causal relation to the possessive.

Like (40), the possessive relation in (45) can be regarded as that of owner property. Whereas it is true that some benefactives can be related to such a clause type, it is not true of the other possessive types, unless we thought of *xudaa* or some item signifying supernatural power as the benefactor. Thus while both (40) and (45) may be potentially related to (40ii) and (46) respectively:

> (40ii) kariim kee waaldeen nee kariim ko baRi   daulat di   hai.
>   Kariim of parents   nee Kariim to a-lot-of wealth gave is
>   Kariim's parents have given Kariim a lot of wealth.
> (46)   kisi nee kariim ko eek kitaab di hai.

the benefactive is in general not a feature which would be related to (39), (41) and (42). If clauses (39)–(42) are all regarded as cases of possessive type, then the case for the benefactive being related to the feature possessive cannot be argued successfully, at least so far as Urdu is concerned.

11.7.3

Taking (39)–(44) as the various sub-types of the possessive neutral clause one may enquire about each: what other clause types are these potentially related to? (39) which is a kin-to-kin relationship can only be related to a clause such as (39i). We ignore *xudaa nee us ko eek bhaai diyaa hai* (God has given him a brother) as not very relevant since it does not reflect a general syntactic tendency in the language; that is, it is not the case that benefactive clauses as such are related to (39). A very small sub-category of these in which the benefactor participant has to be characterized by its lexical properties may be so related; there is no such clause as *mãa nee us ko eek bhaai diyaa hai* (the mother has given him a brother). It is perhaps justifiable to maintain that clauses with kin-to-kin relationship form a special category in most languages; thus while in English *he has a brother* may be seen as related by its meaning to some such clause as *his mother has two sons*, it is not clear how this meaning relation can be formalized in the syntactic description of the language, except through the interrelationship of the kinship items as elements of lexis in the language. In Urdu too, it is probably not true that (39) can be potentially related to paradigms of different clause types. To relate (39) to *us ki mãa kee eek beeTaa huaa* (a son was born to his mother) we would have to set up a body of ad hoc rules – ad hoc in the sense that the kind of syntactic and implicational relationship postulated in this case would probably not be reflected anywhere else in the syntax of the language.

11.7.4

As has been indicated by the discussion in Sections 11.7.1–11.7.2, for a clause type with the owner-property relation both volitional and non-volitional clauses are relevant. Although the feature benefactive is by no means necessarily related to such a clause, in a given case it may be so related, as is shown by the examples above. A non-benefactive volitional clause potentially related to (40) may be cited: *kariim nee baRi daulat banaai hai* (Kariim has made a lot of wealth) would be such a clause; like (40ii), it has the implication *kariim has a lot of wealth*, but unlike (40ii) it does not have the feature benefactive.

The volitional non-benefactive clause *kariim nee baRi daulat banaai hai* stands in a cause relation to the volitional relational clause *kariim kee baRi daulat hui* (kariim of a-lot-of wealth became = kariim came to have a lot of wealth). This cause-effect relationship also exists between *laRki nee kamraa saaf kiyaa* (the girl made the room clean) and *kamraa saaf huaa* (the room became clean). However, the resemblance between the two pairs is partial: while both members of the latter pair have the relational feature, in the former pair this feature is present only in the processive passive *kariim kee baRi daulat hui* (Kariim came to have a lot of wealth). On the other hand, the relationship existing between *kariim nee baRi daulat banaai hai* and *kariim kee baRi daulat hai* (Kariim has a lot of wealth) is very closely paralleled by that obtaining between *naukar nee caaval tolee haĩ* and *caaval tulee huee haĩ* (the servant has weighed the rice and the rice is weighed, respectively). Members of both pairs stand in cause-effect relation; the active member (the cause) in both cases is non-relational, while the neutral type clause in both pairs, related as result to the active one, has the relational feature. Finally the surface structure shows certain similarities: the affected participant in the neutral type in both pairs is associated with the grammatical subject of the clause, namely, *baRi daulat* and *caaval*.

11.7.5

Clause type (41) resembles (39) in that it can only be shown to be related to the type (41i) or to a benefactive in which the benefactor participant is some supernatural power. It has been pointed out that (41) and (43) can both be regarded as whole-part relation, the distinction being simply that in (41) the possessor is animate while in (43) it is inanimate. Even if we were to grant that a small specific subcategory of the benefactive can be shown to be related to (41), this is in fact not true of (43); the latter clause is not related to a benefactive clause. It can however stand in a cause-effect relation to:

> (48) kisi   nee kamree mẽe do khiRkiyãa lagaai haĩ.
>   somebody nee room   in   two windows fixed is
>   somebody has fixed two windows in the room.

The latter is a volitional non-benefactive clause; *kamraa* may not be regarded as a beneficiary participant here any more than it may be so regarded in a relational volitional clause such as *laRki nee kamraa saaf kiyaa* (the girl made the room clean). It is significant, perhaps, that the verbs *deenaa* (to give) and *bheejnaa* (to send), equivalents of which in most languages may be regarded as signifying an inherently benefactive process, when used in a clause type represented by (48) lead either to ungrammaticality or to a meaning which can be readily perceived as having no overt selection of the beneficiary in it; thus consider:

> (49) *kisi   nee kamree mẽe do khiRkiyãa di   haĩ.
>   somebody nee room   in   two windows   gave is
>   somebody has given two windows in the room.
> (50) *kisi   nee kamree mẽe do khiRkiyãa bheeji haĩ.
>   somebody nee room   in   two windows   sent   is
>   somebody has sent two windows in the room.

The unacceptability of (49) and (50) does not arise from the selection of the post-position *mẽe*; one may maintain at least for these cases that the ungrammaticality arises because of covert selection of beneficiary in an environment where ellipsis is not permissible. If however one uses the post-position *ko* (to) which is normally associated with beneficiary function of a specific kind, the clauses become even more ungrammatical in that there would then exist more than one reason for their ungrammaticality. In the following:

> (51) maĩ nee darwaazee ko dhakkaa diyaa.
>   I   nee door   to push   gave
>   I gave the door a push.

the verb *deenaa* is used as a pro-verb, with *dhakkaa* functioning as process-range. It has been shown[32] that an item functioning as action-range may not be replaced by a *wh*-interrogative item without changing the pro-verb. Thus for *I gave the door a push,* the non-polar interrogative is not **what did you give the door* but *what did you do to the door?* This observation also applies to (51); in Urdu we cannot say **aap nee darwaazee* *ko kyaa diyaa* (which corresponds to the former of the clauses above) but rather *aap nee darwaazee kee saath kyaa kiyaa* (what did you do with reference to the door?). Other arguments may be offered to show that neither (51) nor (48) could be regarded as benefactive; consider:

(48i)　*jo mai͂ nee kamree me͂e lagaayaa woh yeh khiRkiyãa thĩ.
　　　　 what I fixed to the room were these windows.
(48ii)　*jo mai͂ nee us laRkee ko diyaa woh yeh kitaab thi.
　　　　 what I gave that boy was this book.
(48iii) jisee mai͂ nee woh kitaab di woh yeh laRkaa thaa.
　　　　 the one to whom I gave that book was this boy.
(51i)　*jo mai͂ nee darwaazee ko diyaa woh dhakkaa thaa.
　　　　 what I gave the door was a push.

(48iii) which is the only clause above with the feature benefactive is related to a clause such as *mai͂ nee woh kitaab is laRkee ko di thi* (I had given that book to this boy); that in some sense *kitaab* in this clause and *khiRkiyãa* in (48) are alike is shown by the fact that both (48i) and (48ii) are unacceptable. Let us then assume that (43) is not even potentially related to a volitional benefactive clause; rather it is related to a volitional relational clause such as (48). The clause is considered to be relational because the process here 'requires' at least three participants, *kisi* (actor), *kamraa* (possessor: whole) and *khiRkiyãa* (possession: part), so that in *khiRkiyãa lagaa di gaĩ?* (Have the windows been fixed?) the implication is that they were fixed *to* something and that somebody was doing the fixing.

I would suggest that although (43) itself is ambiguous (see Section 11.8 below) (48) may not be regarded as ambiguous with reference to the features possessive and locative. It is in fact an accident that the process stands in the *in* relation to the noun *kamraa* for the simple reason that it is a place noun. The following clause representing the type (48) is not ambiguous:

(52)　kisi nee baks me͂e Dhaknaa lagaayaa.
　　　 somebody fixed the lid to the box.

It would be absurd to suggest that (52) is a locative clause, in the sense in which the term locative is being used here.

The whole-part type of possessive may be seen as (a) not locative and (b) as not related to a benefactive; instead it is related to a volitional relational non-benefactive clause (e.g. (48), (52)) to which it stands in a result relation in somewhat the same way as *caaval tulee huee hai͂* is related to *kisi nee caaval tolee haĩ.* In certain cases, type (43) may also be seen as related to a nonvolitional clause. Consider the following pair:

> (53) masjid meẽ caar miinaar hotee haĩ.
>   a mosque has usually four minarets.
> (53i) aap har masjid meẽ caar miinaar paaeẽ gee.
>   you will find four minarets in every mosque.

It is probably the case that such a relationship exists often if the neutral clause type has a verbal group which signifies 'habitual occurrence'.

11.7.6

(42) and (44) are distinct in their deep grammar only by virtue of the fact that in (42) possession involves an animate possessor whereas in (44) it involves an inanimate one. As already indicated these clauses are closely related in their meaning to the relational attributive clause. Thus the following:

> (42i) maĩ nee kariim kee zaraa bhi aql nahĩ paai.
>   I did not find Kariim to have any intelligence.
> (42ii) maĩ nee kariim ko zaraa bhi aqlmand nahĩ paayaa.
>   I did not find Kariim intelligent in the least.

may be regarded as fairly close in their meaning for the obvious reason that the quality-qualified relation is very close to the attribute-attribuand relation. A significant fact here is that in type (42) the quality noun is one which signifies a durational (hence often 'inherent') quality. There are no such clauses as *laRki kee Gam hai* (the girl has sorrow) or *laRki kee xushi hai* (the girl has happiness). (However, see Section 11.9 below.) This being the case these clauses can be related only to the relational non-volitional ones such as (42i) and (42ii). In the former case the type may be regarded as having the features non-volitional, relational, possessive (qualified-quality); in the latter case the clause has the feature attributive instead of the feature possessive.

The clause type (44) too is related to a relational clause such as:

> (44i) maĩ nee us   kapRee meẽ aib   paayaa.
>   I   nee that material in   defect found
>   I found some defect in that material.

(44ii) maĩ nee us kapRee ko aib-daar samjhaa.
    I nee that material to defective considered
    I considered that material defective.

As can be seen whenever the neutral clause type is related to a non-volitional relational clause the implicational relationship is not that of effect and cause, but simply that in the latter case (i.e. (42i), (42ii), (44i) and (44ii)) the commentator whose opinion is presumably also expressed in the neutral clause, is selected overtly with the function of dynamic participant in the clause whereas in the latter (i.e. (42), (44)) this is not made explicit.

There is however a difference between (42) and (44); if the quality noun in (44) is of the type that may be described as 'transient' (i.e. it is a quality which may be acquired and/or lost) then the clause may be seen as standing in a cause relation to a corresponding neutral type. Consider:

(54) is kamree mẽe baRi xushbu hai.
    this room in big perfume is
    there is a beautiful perfume in this room.[33]

(54i) kisi nee is kamree mẽe baRi xushbu ki hai.
    somebody nee this room in big perfume done is
    somebody has made the room have a beautiful perfume.

Here (54) may be seen as standing in a result relation to a volitional clause (54i). This relationship is not possible for a neutral clause type such as *gulaab mẽe baRi xushbu hoti hai* (the rose has a beautiful perfume) for obvious reasons. Other clauses of the type (54) would be *kamree mẽe and-heeraa hai* (it is dark in the room), *kaii Galaafõ par dhabbee thee* (there were stains on many covers), *is baalTi mẽe cheed hai* (there is a hole in the bucket) and so on. All these can be related to a volitional clause and all will stand in the result relation to such a clause.

11.7.7

The neutral locative type may again be seen as related to both the volitional and the non-volitional clause types. Consider:

(55) kisi nee kamree mẽe eek baks paayaa hai.
    somebody nee room in one box found is

somebody has found a box in the room.

(56) kisi   nee kamree meẽ eek baks rakkhaa hai.
somebody nee room   in   one box put   is
somebody has put a box in the room.

The relationship of the locative to clause type (56) (which is volitional) has already been pointed out by Lyons (1968). That (55) and (31) *kamree meẽ eek baks hai* (there is a box in the room) are related may perhaps be shown by the illogicality of a sentence such as *baks kamree meẽ nahĩ thaa magar kisi nee kamree meẽ eek baks paayaa hai* (there was no box in the room but somebody has found a box in the (same) room). This relationship cannot be attributed to the selection of the locative in the two clauses of the sentence since it is perfectly logical to say *us nee kamree meẽ baks nahĩ paayaa leekin usi kamree meẽ woh baks thaa* (he did not find the box in the room but the (same) box was in that (same) room). *To find* (paanaa), *to come across* (paanaa), *to spot* (deekhnaa) all imply a locative just as much as the verb *to put* (rakhnaa) does. There seems no *a priori* reason for thinking that whatever is somewhere *was put* or *was sent* there by someone unless that category of someone includes the supernatural powers. It appears to me that once we include such supernatural powers as 'actors', the case for *put* type clause (i.e. volitional ones) becomes somewhat weaker, since the relationship postulated between a put-clause and the neutral locative is, truly speaking, no longer of sufficient significance. The verbs *put, come, go, throw,* etc. may be regarded as forming a subset of that class of verbs which signifies volitional process. Without the postulation of some supernatural power as actor, it is not easy to see how a volitional clause with these verbs would be related to locatives such as *suraj aasmaan kee nisf par hai* (the sun is at the zenith (of the sky)), *hindustaan tibbat kee junuub meẽ hai* (India is to the South of Tibet), *tumhaaree piichee tumhaari parchaaĩ hai* (behind you is your shadow), *landan meẽ kaii hazaar DaakTar haĩ* (there are thousands of doctors in London). Thus while it has to be granted that there are cases of the neutral locative, which are potentially related to a volitional clause, there are also neutral locatives which cannot be so related in any significant sense. On the other hand, most neutral locative clauses may be related to non-volitional clauses, with verbs such as *to spot* (i.e. to see accidentally), *to come across, to find,* etc. These non-volitional verbs are at least as 'inherently' locative as are the volitional ones cited above; further there is the extra-linguistic fact that whatever is somewhere has not always been *put* or *sent* there though it is true that whatever is *spotted* somewhere always must have been there at the time of being *spotted,* etc.

11.7.8

My conclusion, then, is that for most neutral clause types there exists the possibility of establishing some constant implicational relationship with more than one paradigm. The details of the relationship may vary from type to type but where it does exist, it shows a constant syntactic similarity apart from the meaning relation. It is probably this characteristic that baffles all efforts made to establish the neutral type as the member of one given paradigm alone. Perhaps what we require is a grammar in which simultaneous relationships may be built in without causing any inconsistencies in the description, since it would appear that in most languages we shall encounter some type which will show this particular characteristic of the neutral clause type in Urdu. I would suggest that a description in which the deep grammar of an item under focus is based upon its syntagmatic characteristics will handle this aspect only poorly.

11.8

In this section two clause types are examined which are, in fact, ambiguous though often treated as simply a possessive or a locative. The two clauses are:

(43) is kamree me͞e do khiRkiya͞a hai͞.
(57) aap kee biiwi baccee kaha͞a hai͞.

(43) is potentially ambiguous; it may be interpreted as: (a) there are two objects in this room and these objects are 'windows'; or as (b) the windows form part of this room. In the first case it resembles a locative such as (31); in the second case it resembles a possessive such as (41). The fact that in isolation (43) would most often be interpreted as having a possessive meaning implying part-whole relation is yet another indication of how much extralinguistic information goes into the interpretation of language. One makes use of one's knowledge that very few people are in the habit of keeping windows (the objects that have not been fixed to any place yet) while probably every room has at least one window as a part of it. But were we engaged in the construction of a house, it would be not too far-fetched to say to our assistant *us kamree me͞e do khiRkiya͞a hai͞, unhe͞e uThaa laao!* (there are two windows in that room, fetch them here!). Such a sentence would be absurd if the clause (43) were always to be interpreted

as a possessive type and could not be interpreted as a locative in certain environments.

In Urdu for certain number words we have a corresponding 'inclusive' number, e.g. *do* (two), *donõ* (both); *tiin* (three), *tiinõ* (all three); *caar* (four), *caarõ* (all four). The difference between *do kursiyaã uThaa laao!* (bring two chairs) and *donõ kursiyaã uThaa laao!* (bring both the chairs) is that in the latter case the objects signified by the nominal group are known (definite) whereas in the former case they are not known (indefinite). When the noun signifies an unknown single entity, the modifier *eek* (a, an) precedes it and often, in accordance with the function of *eek*, we find a complex modification *eek koii* (a some) as in *eek koii laRki saRak par cali jaa rahi thi* (some girl was walking along the street); when the noun signifies a single known entity the modifier *eek* can only be selected as a numeral *one* (contrasting with *two, three*, etc.) or to show contrast (one as opposed to the other). In both cases *eek* will carry the tonic. Thus we have the following clauses:

> (58) (i)   kamree mẽe *eek* baks thaa (do nahĩ).
>   there is *one* box in the room (not two).
> (ii)   *eek* baks kamree mẽe hai (duusraa kahĩ aur hai).
>   *one* box is in the room (the other is somewhere else).
> (iii) kamree mẽe eek *baks* hai.
>   there is a box in the room.

(58iii) represents the unmarked sequence of the indefinite located *vis-à-vis* the location. The unmarked sequence of the definite located *vis-à-vis* location is as represented by (31) *baks kamree mẽe hai* with the tonic carried by the item *kamree* (or more accurately by the first syllable of it). When therefore we have a clause such as:

> (59) meez par *kitaab* hai.

the clause is to be interpreted as *the* book *is on the table* and has a contrastive feature. Corresponding to (31) we have a clause:

> (59i) donõ baks kamree mẽe haĩ.
>   both the boxes are in the room.

And corresponding to (59) we would have a clause *meez par donõ kitaabẽe haĩ* (both the *books* are on the table), where the tonic would be carried by the second syllable of *kitaabẽe*; the clause has the same kind of contrastive information as in (59). Accordingly if corresponding to (43) we have:

(43a) kamree mẽe donõ khiRkiyãa haĩ.

with the tonic carried by some part of *khiRkiyãa*, this implies that both the windows are there but something else is not.

The use of the inclusive number as a modifier for a noun in a nominal group functioning as possession at clause rank is not permissible, so that neither (43a) nor (43b) would be ambiguous:

(43b) donõ khiRkiyãa kamree mẽe haĩ.
      both the windows are in the room.

The unmarked sequence of possessor-possession at the clause rank is as exemplified by (43) in one of its senses, i.e. the possessor precedes the possession. When the sequence is reversed, the clause has a contrastive implication. These two facts account (a) for the unacceptability of:

(60)   *kariim kee donõ ãakhẽe haĩ.
       Kariim has both eyes (or both the eyes).
(60i)   *kursi mẽe donõ hatthee haĩ.
       the chair has both the arms.

(b) they account for the distinction in meaning between:

(60ii) caar laRkiyãa kariim kee haĩ hamiid kee nahĩ.
       it is Kariim who has four daughters not Hamiid.
(60iii) dum jaanwar kee hoti hai insaan kee nahĩ.
       it is animals who have tails not human beings.

and the unmarked possessives such as *kariim kee caar laRkiyãa haĩ* (cf. (60ii) above: Kariim has four daughters) and *jaanwar kee dum hoti hai* (cf. (60iii): animals have tails). (43) being ambiguous has all the forms available to the locative as well as those available to the part-whole possessive.

11.8.1

The ambiguity of (57) *aap kee biiwi baccee kahãa haĩ* arises from the multivalence of *kahãa* and *kee*. It may be interpreted either as a locative interrogative or it may be interpreted as an emphatic and/or contrastive negative. *kahaa* has been discussed earlier (see Section 11.6); it may mean either *where* or *(but) surely not*. The possessive relation can be selected either at the clause rank as exemplified in the above discussion, or it may be selected at the group rank as in *meeree bhaaii ki beeTi* (my brother's daughter). At the group rank, except for the pronominals *maĩ* and *tum* (*I* and *you* in its familiar function), all items having the function of possessor must have a post-position; the post-position shows number gender concord with the possession so that we have *kariim ki biiwi* (Kariim's wife; the marker *ki* in concord with singular feminine noun '*wife*') *kariim kaa beeTaa* (Kariim's son; the marker *kaa* in concord with singular masculine noun) and *kariim kee bhaai bahan* (Kariim's brother and sister; the marker *kee* in concord with group complex, gender mixed, i.e. one group masculine one feminine); *kariim kee beeTee* (Kariim's sons; *kee* in concord with plural masculine) and *kariim ki beeTiyaã* (Kariim's daughters; *ki* in concord with plural feminine). So far as the discussion here is concerned the three uses of *kee* are relevant; it may now be seen that the *kee* in (57) can be interpreted in two ways: either it signifies a possessive relation at the clause rank in which case *kahaã* has a non-locative function as in the sentence *aap kee biiwi baccee kahaã haĩ itnaa baRaa makaan lee kee kyaa kareẽ gee* (but you *don't* have wife and children what are you going to do with such a big house), or it signifies a possessive relation at the group rank (where the group functioning as possession is of a complex structure with a feminine and a masculine noun co-ordinated) as in the sentence *aap kee biiwi baccee kahaã haĩ bahot dinõ see un see mulaaqaat nahĩ hui* (where are your wife and children, I haven't met them for a long time). Clauses in which possession noun is singular are unambiguous in this respect whether the possession relation obtains at the group rank or at the clause rank. *aap ki laRki kahaã haĩ* (where is your daughter?) would be interpreted unambiguously as a locative interrogative clause with the possessive relation obtaining at the group rank; by comparison *aap kee laRki kahaã hai* (but you *don't* have a daughter) will be interpreted as an emphatic negative possessive clause (i.e. here the possession relation obtains at the clause rank). The same applies respectively to *aap kaa beeTaa kahaã hai* (where is your son?) and *aap kee beeTaa kahaã hai* (but surely you don't have a son). If the possession is a plural but feminine noun, then again this ambiguity would not take place, e.g. in *aap ki beeTiyaã kahaã hai* (where are your daughters?) which is locative interrogative with possession obtaining at the group rank and *aap kee beeTiyaã kahaã haĩ* (but surely you don't have daughters), which is emphatic negative with possession obtaining at the clause rank. In the remaining cases the ambiguity of the type exemplified by (57) will exist and would be resolved, in speech by reference to the phonological pattern of the clause, in writing by reference to the co-text. The characteristic of these clauses may be taken as yet another indication of the fact that at clause rank the features possessive and locative are not selected within the same clause in the neutral type.

11.9

There are at least two other categories in which the verb *honaa* is regularly used; in fact no other verb is available except some form of *honaa* (with some specific meaning) to this category. Two examples are presented here:

(61) keraaee-daar ko takliif   hui.
       tenant   to inconvenience happened
       the tenant suffered inconvenience.
(62) keraaee-daar ko takliif   hai.
       tenant   to inconvenience is
       the tenant faces inconvenience.

Both (61) and (62) may be seen as related to *kisi nee keraaee-daar ko takliif di* (somebody caused the tenant inconvenience). In general 'verbs' such as *takliif deenaa* (to cause inconvenience), *ummiid rakhnaa* (to keep hope, i.e. to hope), *shor karnaa* (to make a noise), *balwaa karnaa* (to cause riot), etc. have been regarded as *feel-ee-murrakkab* (compound verbs).[34] I would argue that in all these cases we have a complex of process-range+pro-verb, where the process-range is realized by the nominal 'bit' and the pro-verb by the verbal 'bit'. This is not to deny that there are compound verbs in the language such as *muqarrar karnaa* (to appoint), *qaraar deenaa* (to consider), *maaluum karnaa* (to discover), and so on.[35] The genuine compound verbs, such as represented by the latter list all have this in common: the two bits of the group may not appear without the other; moreover the first word of such compound verbs cannot be assigned to any known class of word, since they do not function as nouns, adjectives or adverbs, etc. By contrast the item realizing process-range can function as noun and may accept modification and qualification in the manner of other nouns, e.g. *aap ki takliif ki xabar sun kar mujhee baRaa afsos huaa* (I was sorry to hear the news of your trouble) or *guzishtaa saal kee balwee mee bahot log maree* (many people died in last year's riot).[36]

The difference between the two is also apparent at the clause rank. In general it is the case that verbs of the former category have in their paradigm a member such as (62), whereas this is not the case with the latter set. Below are provided some tentative suggestions regarding three sub-types of clauses with pro-verb and process+range selection in them.

11.9.1

There is a certain process type in Urdu which always requires an animate affected participant. Examples would be *kisi nee kisi ko takliif di hai* (somebody has caused somebody inconvenience), *kisi nee kisi ko DãaTaa* (somebody scolded somebody), and *kisi nee kisi ko tassali dilaaii* (somebody consoled somebody); in all these cases *kisi ko* may not be replaced by *kisi ciiz ko* (to something); that is to say, the affected participant has to be animate.[37] I shall refer to this type of process as 'complex process type'; *takliif deenaa* (to cause inconvenience), *DãaTnaa* (to scold) and *tassalli dilaanaa* (to console) signify such a process type. When the process of the clause is of this type and the verb selected belongs to the category pro-verb as in *takliif deenaa* and *tassalli dilaanaa* (to console), then the paradigms of such clauses will have, apart from the active and the non-agentive passive, two members corresponding to (61) and (62), where for the type (61) we may retain the term processive passive and for (62) may be used the term stative passive. Clauses such as *laRki ko Gam hai* (the girl has sorrow) (see Section 11.7.6), *laRki ko xushi hai* and *laRki ko tassalli hai* all represent type (62) and are related to the clause type mentioned above, to which they stand in a result relation. In their meaning such clauses are close to the qualified-quality possessive type, since the process range is usually realized by some abstract noun involving some perception. To this set may also be related clauses such as *laRki takliif mẽe hai* (the girl is in trouble), *laRki inteezaar mẽe hai* (the girl is waiting) and so on.

11.9.2

Not all clauses with a pro-verb and process-range have the complex process type. One set has the function contextually of verbalization (Halliday 1968); verbs of this category are usually *rakhnaa* and *karnaa* (*to keep* and *to do*) and the process-range is potentially a verbalizing noun, e.g. *ummiid, xwaahish* (desire), *tammannaa* (wish). The verbalized may be a rankshifted clause functioning as an immediate constituent of the matrix clause or of a nominal group. Examples of each are presented below:

(63) laRki ko ummiid thi kee woh kaamyaab ho gi.
       the girl had hoped that she would succeed.
(64) laRki ko apni kaamyaabi ki ummiid thi.
       the girl had the hope of her own success.

Both (63) and (64) may be shown to be related to either of the two clause types below:

(63i)   kisi nee laRki ko ummiid dilaaii thi kee woh kaamyaab ho gi.
         somebody had given the girl to hope that she would succeed.
(63ii) laRki nee ummiid ki thi kee woh kaamyaab ho gi.
         the girl had hoped that she would succeed.

The process of the first clause here may be seen as a complex transitive type, that of the second as intransitive; in both cases it is of the type verbalization. (63i) is not a benefactive clause except in that general sense in which all complex process type clauses may be seen to be benefactive. The clause type (63) and (64) may be seen to be related to the relational attributive clause type; only two rules suffice for the mechanical conversion of one into the other, if one were interested in carrying out such mechanical conversion. These are: (a) delete *ko*; (b) for the process-range nominal substitute a lexically related adjective (i.e. instead of *ummiid* write *ummiidwaar*; instead of *xwaahish* write *xwaahishmand*; instead of *itmiinaan* write *mutmaiin*, and so on and so forth). When these rules are followed we have the following:

(63a) laRki ummiidwaar thi kee woh kaamyaab ho gi.
        the girl was hopeful that she would succeed.
(63b) laRki apni kaamyaabi ki ummiidwaar thi.
        the girl was hopeful of her own success.

where the matrix clause *laRki ummiidwaar thi* is essentially like *laRki xuubsurat thi*. (63a–b) may also be seen as closely related to the qualified-quality type of possession; this is not surprising since the latter is itself easily relatable to a relational attributive. The motives for assigning different labels to:

 (65i) kariim kee samajh hai.
    Kariim has maturity (mental).
 (65ii) kariim samajhdaar hai.
    Kariim is mature.
 (66i) kariim ko xwaahish hai...
    Kariim has the wish ...
 (66ii) kariim xwaahishmand hai...
    Kariim is desirous ...

are to my mind primarily syntactic; semantically the two members of each are very close to each other.

11.9.3

If one considers the clauses:

 (62i) kisi nee keraaee-daar ko takliif di.
    somebody caused the tenant inconvenience
 (63i) kisi nee laRki ko ummiid dilaaii...
    somebody gave the girl to hope...
 (63ii) laRki nee ummiid ki...
    the girl did hope...

in one respect they are all like (51) *maĩ nee darwaazee ko dhakkaa diyaa*; the active nonpolar interrogative corresponding to all of these will have the pro-verb *karnaa* (i.e. some of it); moreover, the post-position *kee saath* would be attached to the affected participant *keraaee-daar* (62i) *laRki* (63i) and *darwaazaa* (51) in all such non-polar interrogative clauses. Thus we have *kisi nee keraaee-daar kee saath kyaa kiyaa* (what did somebody do to the tenant), *kisi nee laRki kee saath kyaa kiyaa* (what did somebody do to the girl). In (63ii) where *laRki* must be regarded as a dynamic participant the postposition *kee saath* cannot be attached to it. The non-polar interrogative would be *laRki nee kyaa kiyaa?* (what did the girl do?). The interesting point here is that if one postulates that the latter clause is a non-polar interrogative corresponding to (63ii), one is faced with the fact that the question would in all probability never get the response (63ii) except in a grammar, which fact may be attributed to the grammarian's great passion for symmetry.

If now we compare (63ii) with:

(67) baccõ nee kamree mẽe baRaa shor kiyaa.
      the children made a lot of noise in the room.

we find that (67) may stand as a probable response to a question:

(67i) baccõ nee kamree mẽe kyaa kiyaa?
       what did the children do in the room?

just as *laRki nee kyaa kiyaa* may get the response:

(68) laRki nee eek kurtaa siyaa.
      the girl sewed a shirt.
(69) laRki nee eek meez banaaii.
      the girl made a table.

One of the things that is in common to both the last-mentioned clauses here is that the process may be seen as one of creation, where the affected participant may more delicately be labelled 'effectum' (Fillmore 1968). If the process is creative, the effectum may not be thematized in the following manner:

(68i) *jo laRki nee siyaa woh *kurtaa* thaa.
       what the girl sewed was a shirt.
(69i) *jo laRki nee banaaii woh *meez* thi.
       what the girl made was a table.

(67) is similar to (68) and (69), the following clause being unacceptable:

(67ii) *jo baccõ nee kiyaa woh *shor* thaa.
        what the children made was a noise.

Since (68) and (69) are transitive clauses, it may be thought that (67) too is a transitive clause, with *shor* functioning as effectum. But now consider:

(68ii) jo kurtaa laRki nee siyaa woh yeh waalaa thaa.
        the shirt that the girl sewed was this one.
(69ii) jo meez laRki nee banaaii woh yeh waali thi.
        the table that the girl made was this one.

But we cannot say **jo shor baccõ nee kiyaa woh yeh waalaa thaa* (the noise that the children made was this one). It might be rightly thought that since *shor* is not a count noun it cannot be replaced by *waalaa*, but the clause **jo shor baccõ nee kiyaa woh yeh thaa* (the noise that the children made was this) is also ungrammatical. The ungrammaticality of the clause does not stem, it would appear, from the fact that the effectum *shor* is abstract. The clause *jo baat laRki nee kahi woh yeh thi* (the comment that the girl made was this) is grammatical; equally it is possible to say *jo raaee laRki nee di woh yeh thi* (the opinion that the girl gave (i.e. expressed) was this). One of the differences between *shor* and *baat/raaee* is that while the former is a mass noun, the latter two are count ones; they are both abstract. However *ummiid* and *takliif* are like *baat* and *raaee*; both are abstract count nouns. We may, however, not say:

(70) *jo ummiid laRki nee ki woh yeh thi.
       the hope that the girl did was this.
(71) *jo takliifẽe kisi nee keraaee-daar ko dĩ woh yeh thĩ.
       the inconveniences that somebody caused the tenant were these.

It would appear that *shor* is at once like *kurtaa* and *meez* in (68) and like *ummiid* and *takliif* in (62i) and (63ii); it functions as process-range hence it cannot be thematized like *baat* or *kurtaa* but behaves like *ummiid* and *takliif*. Both (62) and (63ii) are related to a transitive with complex process such as:

(62i) kisi nee keraaeedaar ko takliif di.
(63i) kisi nee laRki ko ummiid dilaaii.

but if the process-range is such that it may be described as the 'creative' one then whether a complex process clause corresponding to it exists or not, it is possible to have a stative passive of the type exemplified by (67). Thus while we have:

(72) kisi nee bacci see rozaa rakhwaayaa.
       somebody caused the girl to keep fast (i.e. to fast).
(72i) bacci nee rozaa rakkhaa.
       the girl kept fast (i.e. fasted).

There is no such clause as *rozaa hai* (fast is = there was a fast). But clauses such as *shor thaa* (there was a noise), *balwaa thaa* (there was a riot), *miilaad thaa* (there was a religious gathering) are all possible. In such passives the dynamic participant of the corresponding active clause need not appear and since there is no affected participant (unless *shor* is regarded as one, the arguments against which have been provided above), the nucleus of the clause may be considered to be composed of process-range+*honaa* (the pro-verb). Such clauses, however, always seem to imply a locative. So *baRaa shor thaa* (there was a lot of noise) implies *there was a lot of noise somewhere* and *miilaad thaa* implies *kahĩ miilaad thaa* (there was a religious gathering somewhere) and so on.

11.9.4

In general the meaning of *honaa* associated with the processive passive of the type discussed in this section such as *keraaeedaar ko takliif hui* (the tenant was faced with a lot of inconvenience), *laRki ko ummiid hui* (the girl came to have the hope), and *shor huaa* (noise took place) may be stated as 'some process took place and is stated as if it took place of its own accord without intervention from any participant', the meaning of the stative passive such as *keraaeedaar ko takliif thi, laRki ko ummiid thi* and *baRaa shor thaa* may be stated as 'the predication of the existence of whatever the processrange signifies such that the latter is always in relation to some participant or circumstance'.

No doubt the meanings offered here for *honaa* are highly generalized, but it is to be doubted if the meaning derived from the syntactic categories is ever of very specific nature, except in the case of structure markers.

11.10

The clause types with the verb *honaa* discussed in this article (which incidentally do not exhaust all possible uses) are as follows:

(73)	laRki xuubsurat hai.	(cf. examples (1) and (16) – (16c))
(74)	kamraa saaf hai.	(cf. examples (18) – (18f))
(75)	kamraa saaf huaa.	(cf. examples (18) – (18f))
(76)	kariim sadar hai.	(cf. examples (18) – (18f))
(77)	kariim sadar huaa.	(cf. examples (18) – (18f))
(78)	caaval tulee huee haĩ.	(cf. example (17))
(79)	kariim kee eek bhaaii hai.	(cf. example (39))
(80)	kariim kee baRi daulat hai.	(cf. example (40))
(81)	kariim kee baRi daulat hui.	(cf. example (40))

(82) kariim kee do aākheẽ haĩ.   (cf. example (41))
(83) kariim kee aql hai.   (cf. example (42))
(84) is kamree meẽ do kursiyaā haĩ. (cf. example (43))
(85) is kapRee meẽ kuch aib hai.   (cf. example (44))
(86) baks kamree meẽ hai.   (cf. example (31))
(87) xudaa hai.   (cf. example (31))
(88) kariim hai.   (cf. example (31))
(89) aap kee biiwi baccee kahaā hai. (cf. example (57))
(90) keraaeedaar ko takliif thi.   (cf. example (62))
(91) keraaeedaar ko takliif hui.   (cf. example (61))
(92) laRki ko ummiid thi.   (cf. example (63))
(93) laRki ko ummiid hui.   (cf. example (63))
(94) shor huaa.   (cf. example (67))
(95) shor thaa.   (cf. example (67))

Wherever these clauses are related to any paradigm,[38] it would appear that either we would have to recognize two active members in the same paradigm or we would have to treat them as some form of passive.[39] Sub-groups of these 23 clauses may be made according to which feature is under consideration; thus all uses of *honaa* for which the past tense is realized by the form *huaa/hui* have the feature processive passive (i.e. this is the label used in this article); these stand in a result relation to their active agnate; clauses (73)–(75), (83), (85), (90), (92) may be seen as forming one sub-group on the ground that they could be regarded as the source for the derivation of the attribute-attribuand relation at the nominal group rank. Within this, (83), (85), (90), and (92) may be seen as closely related to each other since in some sense the possession of an attribute is implied. To go on would be tedious. Perhaps it would be appropriate to end with the Urdu sentence *jo hai so hai* (whatever is there is there) which cannot be interpreted as *whatever exists exists.*

Appendix

1. The word-class membership of *honaa* was a subject of controversy for Urdu grammarians as indicated incidentally by the quotation from Fateh Mohammad Khaan in Section 11.3.4 of this paper. In fact, it would be more accurate to say that the controversy centred round the items *hai, thaa, ho* (is, was, be), etc. rather than the form *honaa* itself. This state of affairs arose directly from the crucial

definition offered for the primary word-classes. According to traditional Urdu grammars, the words of the language could be exhaustively classified into three primary categories: particle, noun, and verb.

> A particle, to quote Fateh Mohammad Khaan, is that which conveys no definite meaning by itself. Particles are used for establishing relations between other words. You can understand nothing [of, R.H.] what the speaker wants to say from *see* (from/by/with/to), *me͠e* (in/of) …, etc., until they are used in company with some other words between which they establish some relation. (*Misbaah-ul-Qawaaid*; Part I: 20)

On the other hand both noun and verb are classes of words, any one member of which may even in isolation signify something definite.

> The difference between noun and verb is only this: the former cannot signify time, whereas the latter *must* signify some discrete time. Thus when we say *aanaa* (to come), in this word there is no definite indication of time and *that is why it is a noun*. But when we say *aayaa* (came), *aataa hai* (comes) or *aaee gaa* (come will = will come), then time is definitely and compulsorily indicated. (*ibid.*)
>
> Elsewhere Fateh Mohammad Khaan is careful to emphasize that the signifying of time is not 'accidental' to the members of the word-class verb; every member of this class, he maintains, should be potentially capable of signifying any of the three points on the time scale, namely past, present and future. Thus a noun such as *kal* (the day adjacent to today, i.e. either *tomorrow* or *yesterday*) is not a verb because it has no potentiality of signifying present, and in any given instance can signify either past or future.

2. It followed from this definition of noun and verb that the item *honaa* itself was universally regarded as belonging to a specific subclass of noun labelled *ism-ee-masdar* (noun-of-infinitive; *masdar* literally means 'that which constitutes the source' so that *ism-ee-masdar* is that sub-class of noun which functions as the source for verb). On the other hand, while the grammarians were agreed that the forms *thaa* and *ho* (*gaa*) (*was* and (*will*) *be*) belonged to the verb

class, they disagreed regarding the class-membership of *hai* (is), some of them maintaining that all derived forms of *honaa* belonged to the verb class, while others maintaining that all derived forms except *hai* (is) belonged to verb class; *hai* in their opinion was a particle (with the function of connecting two words). As pointed out by Fateh Mohammad Khaan (see quotation in Section 11.3.4 of this paper) the latter view was the result of making Urdu language fit the descriptive categories set up for the analysis of Arabic. The Arabic clause *zaidun aalimun* (Zaid learned = Zaid is learned) could be called an 'unmarked' clause following Lyons' suggestion (Lyons 1968); that is to say, it is a clause which has an unmarked selection of tense, aspect and mood. Like some other languages of the world, the unmarked relational clause in Arabic 'does not have a verb': there is no segment in the clause such that it may be said to belong to the word-class verb. Those Urdu grammarians who followed the Arabic tradition therefore refused to treat *hai* in such unmarked Urdu clauses as a verb word, preferring to label it a connector. The controversy, however did not last long; the very definition of the verb making it impossible to allow this analysis of *hai* (is). Once *hai* (is) was accepted as belonging to the word-class verb, it 'became' a fact that unlike Arabic, all relational clauses in Urdu must have a verb. The verb may be selected overtly or covertly.

3. It would be a mistake to think that Fateh Mohammad Khaan's concern with overt and covert selection of the verb is a concern with superficial matters, without any implications for the description of the language. The position taken by him may be reformulated as follows: in Urdu and Persian all relational clauses 'must have' a verb; that is to say, systemically the feature relational is 'present' and is realized partially by the selection of a suitable item from the word-class 'verb'. An item realizing a given feature may not be present in substance within the string under focus, but if the deep grammar of a language is related to its semantics, the presence of the given systemic feature and hence of the item realizing it has to be postulated. If in answer to the question (i) *who is ill?* we have a clause such as (ii) *my brother's daughter*, the latter cannot be regarded as a clause without attribute and verb except in the most superficial sense. Thus both clauses (i) and (ii) 'have' a verb, the former has it overtly, the latter covertly.

These observations are so patently obvious and so widely accepted that one seldom bothers to spell them out. However, the implications of the feature of ellipsis or 'deletion' are not equally patently obvious. It is suggested here that the environments in which ellipsis of a particular type is permissible can be stated by reference to the interrelations existing in the system network of a given language; these too form 'rules' in the integral description of the language although they may not be as obvious as the rules which prohibit a clause such as *my brother's daughter ill laughed*. Despite the fact that there is a lot in common in the description of the Arabic clause *zaidun aalimun* (Zaid (is) learned) and the Urdu one *zaid aalim* (Zaid learned) it is not a fact that both these clauses have deletion; or if we say that both of them have deletion we must mean two different things by the word 'deletion'. The view taken here is that the Arabic clause has no deletion; in accordance, mark that there is no obligation for the Arabic clause to be anaphorically related to any preceding language; this clause can constitute a text on its own. The speaker of Arabic does not have a set of rules which enumerate the environment in which alone this so-called 'deleted version' may be grammatical for the simple reason that there is no real contrast of deletion vs. non-deletion here. In the case of *zaid aalim*, we have predicate-ellipsis and it is obligatory for this clause to be anaphorically or cataphorically related to some specifiable clause forming part of the larger text in which this elliptical clause occurs; unlike the Arabic clause it may not constitute a text on its own. The speaker of Urdu has a set of rules which enumerate the environment in which a relational predicate-elliptical clause will be regarded as both grammatical and appropriate and this environment is not identical with that in which the non-elliptical version would be appropriate. There is no doubt that these rules have to be built into a grammar which rises above the description of the simple sentence. If these rules are regarded as belonging to the sphere of performance and not of competence, I can only say that I know of no instance of performance which is independent of competence except the uninteresting cases of memory lapse, etc.

4. It has been suggested by Lyons (1968) that the verb *be* may not be regarded as an element in the deep grammar of some languages, since its 'principal function' is to realize certain particular syntactic options. I would suggest that no individual lexical item of a given language may be regarded as an element in the deep grammar of that language, unless grammar is to be interpreted as 'the total description of the language including syntax, lexis phonology and

phonetics'. It appears to me that an individual lexical item is related to the deep grammar only by virtue of its realizational potentialities with reference to some syntactic option(s). In this respect *be* is not different from *eat* or *drink*. There is however a significant difference between *be* and *eat* or *drink*. If I may confine myself to Urdu and English alone, this difference may be stated as follows. At a particular degree of delicacy in the syntactic description of these languages, we arrive at a verb class which has only one member in it, namely, *be*. On the other hand, no matter how delicate a syntactic description of these languages is made, we shall never arrive at a verb class such that its only member is *eat* but not *drink*; that is to say, unless we introduce some *ad hoc* or non-syntactic grounds for sub-classification these two verbs will appear as members of the same most delicate verb class. Since the sub-categorization of a class is based upon the potentiality of the said sub-category to realize a set of syntactic options uniquely, it follows that some component(s) of the meaning of all items in a given subcategory is 'the same'. Whenever we have an item which forms a unique member class (i.e. the class contains no item but this one), the meaning of the item may be stated exhaustively by reference to the set of systemic options which the item is capable of realizing; in other words, there is no 'lexical residue' for which one must account. The reason for this is quite obvious: since the category consists of only one member and is itself based upon a set of systemic options, the question of lexical contrast does not exist as it does in the case of *eat* or *drink*. The meaning of the item can be stated solely by reference to the semantics of the set of systemic options relevant to the sub-category. It could therefore be cogently argued that the item *be*, like *a, the, this, that*, etc., which all form unique member classes at the most delicate stage of grammatical description, should not be treated as elements in the *deep lexis* of these languages and that they are far more grammatical than are items such as *eat, two, boy, girl,* etc. This position is implicit in Halliday (1966b) and Sinclair (1966).

5. It is significant that neither those Urdu grammarians who treated *hai* as a connecting particle nor those who treated it as a verb along with *thaa,* etc. ever questioned the fact that there is need to recognize at least one complete verbal paradigm derived from *honaa* which belonged to that sub-class of verb known as *feel-ee-imdaadi* (auxiliary verb). Thus arose the curious situation that while there

was disagreement regarding the class membership of *haĩ* in *yeh laRkiyaã sharmiili haĩ* (these girls are shy), no such problem arose regarding the description of *haĩ* in *laRkiyaã sharmiili hoti haĩ* (girls are (usually) shy) where it was unanimously treated as an auxiliary.

Recently it has been suggested that in many languages all occurrences of the verb *be* may be regarded as some kind of auxiliary. To quote Lyons (1966) again:

> there appears no reason to regard S (the 'copula') as a lexical class in English (or in the Indo-European languages generally). The 'verb *to be*' in sentences of the kind we are considering [the sentences under consideration are *Mary is beautiful* and *Mary is a child*, R.H.] ... may be regarded as a 'dummy carrier' of tense, mood, aspect, and number in 'surface' structure (roughly comparable with the '*do*-auxiliary' in negative, interrogative and emphatic sentences ...).

Lyons' 'dummy carrier' may be seen as in some sense corresponding to 'an item representing a unique member class, arrived at by reference to the syntactic options it may realize'. It is true, by definition, that all such items, at the most delicate stage of the description of the language are shown as belonging to a class which contains no items that may contrast with it lexically. Thus although in the first instance we may think of *a* and *the* as belonging to the same word class as other modifiers such as *frequent*, *normal* and *usual*, there comes a stage at which the former two represent two separate delicate sub-classes of the class 'modifier'. On this analogy *be* should be separated from the other lexical verbs but whether this implies that therefore it should be treated as an auxiliary seems to me to be a separate question. At least in Urdu, it is not true that *honaa* alone is a verb which represents a unique member set; in one of its senses (i.e. the possessive) the item *rakhnaa* would also constitute such a set and it would indeed pose many problems to think of *rakhnaa* in this sense as an auxiliary on the ground that its function is simply to realize certain syntactic options.

Further, so far as Urdu is concerned, the treatment of all verbs derived from *honaa* as auxiliary will pose a problem: if the fully grammatical copula *be* is regarded as an auxiliary, it would still have to be differentiated from that *be* which has traditionally been regarded as auxiliary since the syntactic potentialities of these two *be* would not be identical. The *be* copula-auxiliary will be the only auxiliary in the language that will share some potentialities of the lexical verbs of the language. Consider that while it is possible to say *laRkaa qaabil thaa aur laRki hasiin* (the boy was capable and the girl beautiful), the sentence **laRkaa khaanaa khaataa thaa aur laRki paani piiti* (the boy was eating the food and the girl drinking water) is ungrammatical. The copula-*be* may be 'deleted' in any kind of branching but the auxiliary-*be* can be deleted only in certain very restricted environments. Again the clause *thee hi kahãã itnee log* (there *were*n't many people) is grammatical but the clause **thee hi kahãã log caltee* (people *did*n't (usually) walk) is ungrammatical; it is possible to use the copula-*be* 'thematically' as the first of the last two examples shows; it is not possible to use just the auxiliary-*be* in this manner; thus it is ungrammatical to say **thee hi kahãã itnee log hotee* (there *were*n't (usually) many people). These examples show some of the differences between the auxiliary and the copula-*be*. Consider now the sentences *laRkaa qaabil thaa aur laRki hasiin* (the boy was capable and the girl beautiful) and *laRkee nee caaee pi aur laRki nee kaafi* (the boy drank tea and the girl coffee); the conditions under which the lexical verb may be deleted are the same whether the verb is copula-*be* or *piinaa* (drink). Similarly compare *thee hi kahãã itnee log* (there *were*n't many people) and *khaayaa hi kahãã us nee khaanaa* (he *did*n't eat any food); again the rules regarding the thematization of the verbal group remain the same irrespective of whether the lexical element of the verbal group is realized by a (fully) lexical verb like *khaanaa* (to eat) or by a fully grammatical one like *honaa*. These appear to me to be strong reasons for carefully examining the suggestion that all occurrences of *be* should be regarded as some kind of auxiliary; at least so far as Urdu is concerned this solution does not seem to me to carry much weight. Often characteristics are cited which are supposedly specific to the copula *be* and not shared by other 'lexical' verbs. One such characteristic is that the continuous tense would seem to be not permissible with copula *be*, clauses such as *she is/was being beautiful* being odd. This observation will apply equally to a large number of relational verbs as well as to some superventive ones, since clauses such as *the boy is/was coming across a man, the girl is/was hearing a shriek, I am/was owning a house* are all odd. Even more interesting is the case of *I am finding the girl attractive*, where it is very much open to question whether the verbal group *am finding* is to be interpreted semantically as 'process being carried out at the moment of speaking'.

Notes

1   I am deeply grateful to Michael Halliday who discussed various aspects of the syntax of Urdu with me. Although specific reference to his work is not provided here except in special cases, this article presupposes the technique of grammatical description as expounded in his 'Notes on Transitivity and Theme in English' (Parts 1–3). The responsibility for the statements made in this article is, however, my own.

2   Wherever in a translated text a bracket has my initials, this implies that such a bracket did not exist in the original text and has been introduced by me in order to make the import as clear as possible.

3   *laazim* can be literally translated as 'obligatory, compulsory'; its nearest terminological translation in English would be 'intransitive', though the two are not identical. *mutaaddi* literally means 'that which goes beyond, extends, is infectious'; its nearest terminological equivalent in English is 'transitive'. *Naaqis* may be literally translated as 'defective'; to my knowledge there is no traditional term in English which could be considered its equivalent, unless we postulated that it is nearest the copula in its meaning. Halliday's (1968) term 'relational' would however be better.

4   *faael* is often translated as subject; like subject, it is used sometimes to mean 'grammatical subject' (see the discussion of *naaqis* verb in the passage quoted from Haq in Section 11.3) and sometimes it is used as if it were determined entirely by its transitivity function of 'actor' (as is evident from Haq's definition of the item in the para). See the discussion of the term *mubteedaa* in Section 11.3.4; and note also the implications of recognizing a structural label such as *qaaem-muqaam-ee-faael* (officiating subject) discussed in Section 11.4.1.

5   *mafuul* may be translated as 'object' or sometimes as 'complement'. Again attention must be drawn to the terms *mubteedaa* and *xabar.*

6   The terms for the participants and circumstance in the equative clause here differ from those used by Halliday (1968). In the clause *John is the leader* (*ibid.*, 190–193), *John* would be regarded as having the transitivity function of 'identified', which is in keeping with my treatment of *kariim* in *kariim sadar hai* (Kariim is the president); however Halliday's label for *the leader* is 'identifier' whereas I would use the label 'identity' for *the president*, thus leaving the term 'identifier' to be used as a label for a function corresponding to 'attributor' in the attributive clause. In a clause such as *us nee kariim ko sadar banaayaa* (He made Kariim president) *he* would have the function of actor and identifier, *kariim* that of affected and identified while I would regard *president* as having the function of 'circumstance' of the type 'identity'. The

Urdu equative and attributive clauses show a great degree of similarity, as if the 'identity' were a particular kind of 'attribute' and vice versa. Thus both identity and attribute may be thematic, e.g. in *sadar kariim hai* (it is Kariim who is the president) and *xuubsurat laRid hai* (it is the girl who is beautiful); in both these cases the tonic must be carried by the identified and the attribuand. The nominal group functioning as 'identified' or 'attribuand' may be 'definite' or 'indefinite', e.g. in *ek laRkaa kahĩ taalibilm thaa* (a boy was a student somewhere) and *kahtee haĩ kee ek laRki baRi xuubsurat thi* (it is said that a girl was very beautiful); the tonic is carried here by *laRkaa* (identified) and *laRki* (attribuand), and *eek*, the non-specific deictic, is reduced. When we have an item which may function as adjective or as a noun, e.g. *biimaar* and the other element in the clause is realized by an indefinite nominal group, the tonic alone determines the transitivity functions in the clause. *biimaar koii musaafir hai* is an ambiguous clause (ill some traveller is); if *biimaar* carries the tonic then the clause is to be interpreted as *the ill man is some traveller*; if *musaafir* carries the tonic, the clause would be interpreted as *it is some traveller who is ill*. Because of these close similarities between the equative and the attributive, I have not discussed them separately in great detail.

7   I understand from Dr. Arafat (Department of Arabic, School of Oriental and African Studies, London) that in Arabic *jumlaa ismiah* (nominal clause) is used to designate all clauses which have no verb in them. If therefore *kaana zaidun qaaeemun* is regarded as a nominal clause, the underlying assumption would be that *kaana* does not function as a verb. This causes some confusion with reference to some of the statements made by Fateh Mohammad Khaan.

8   *musnad ileha* may be literally translated as 'that to which something is related'; it seems to correspond fairly closely with both 'topic' and 'grammatical subject'. Note that *musnad ileha* need not be the initial item of the clause; in *darwaazaa zaid nee kholaa* (door Zaid nee opened = it was Zaid who opened the door) not *darwaazaa* but *Zaid* would be labelled *musnad ileha*. I have used the term 'topic' for *musnad ileha* in the translation in order to keep it distinct from *faael* (subject).

9   *mubteedaa* literally means 'that which constitutes the beginning'. Its use in Urdu grammars has been discussed in some detail in Section 11.3.4.

10 *musnad* can be translated as 'that which relates to something'. If one is thinking in terms of the distinction between topic and comment, *musnad* may be translated as 'comment'. In those grammars where a stage in grammatical analysis involves a binary segmentation of the clause, that segment which in such grammars is labelled 'predicate' is closest in its meaning to the term *musnad*. The segment thus labelled, therefore, usually contains the verbal group constituent of the clause and will also contain the permissible participants and cirumstances, etc. In Urdu grammars a confusion arises when *musnad ileha* is equated with *faael* and *musnad* with *mafuul*, so that the verbal group is seen as having the function of joining the two to each other, as is implicit in this passage from Fateh Mohammad Khaan.

11 The dots indicate that some items from the original text have not been translated. The two omissions here are of examples from Persian and Urdu poetry to show what the author means by 'overt' and 'covert'. It is, however, not necessary to appeal to the poetic variety of language for the exemplification of 'covert' selection. (The significance of the emphasis Fateh Mohammad Khaan places on covert selection is discussed in some detail in the Appendix.)

12 *harfee-rabt* literally means 'word-of-connection'. The class thus labelled contains words which may most readily be associated with preposition, postposition and conjunction in English, but structure markers such as *nee, ko, kee liyee,* etc. are also referred to by this label.

13 In fact this should be taken to mean 'in clauses with unmarked theme, *faael* is always clause-initial' if the word *faael* is interpreted as grammatical subject. Any other interpretation of this statement by Fateh Mohammad would not be true in all cases.

14 I have not gone into any details concerning the syntactic similarities of the grammatical subject in types (16)–(19); in the discussion of these four types the term 'actor' is used (or 'dynamic participant') for the participant function associated with the grammatical subject of an active clause. If we were to think of the terms dynamic and passive participant as contrasting with each other, it would be seen that wherever we have the use of lexical *honaa*, the participant function associated with the grammatical subject of the clause is the 'passive' one. A detailed discussion of the implications of such an analysis would require another paper.

15 So far as I can see *agentive* is used here as in Fillmore (1968), the only difference being that I use the term *agentive adjunct* only when the dynamic participant is signified by an adjunct and is not associated with the grammatical subject, that is, I do not use 'agent' for attributor, actor, perceiver, etc., if these functions are associated with the grammatical subject of the clause.

16 The non-agentive passive agnate of type (16) and (19) is usually employed for: (a) an assertion that is habitual, e.g. in *aisi kahaaniyaã muxrib-ee-ixlaaq maani jaati haĩ* (such stories are considered immoral); and (b) an assertion that, naturally enough, takes the dynamic participant as known either through the co-text or through the immediate extra-linguistic situation.

17 A distinction of this kind is recognized by Halliday (1968). The term volitional corresponds roughly to his term 'actional' and the non-volitional to his 'superventive'. I have avoided the use of actional for the volitional type of process since according to one view a clause such as *bacca giraa* (the child fell) may be seen as one in which *bacca* is involved in some kind of activity.

18 In the deep grammar the only exception to this rule would be found if the causer was some supernatural power such as *xudaa* (God) but only if we were to regard *maalik nee naukar see caaval tolvaayee* (the master caused the servant to weigh the rice) and *maalik kee hukm see naukar nee caaval tolee* (according to the order of the master, the servant weighed the rice) as having

the feature causative at some point in their deep grammar. The non-volitional verb itself may never be causative in its own structure.

19   There are certain clauses in Urdu which in their surface structure resemble the imperative but have a non-volitional verb, e.g. jio! (live!) *xush raho!* (remain happy!) *duniyaa aur uqbaa meẽ cain paao!* (find peace in this world and in the other!). These clauses are not imperative; in fact they may be perceived as elliptical. Their contextual function is to greet or to curse, so that some such verbalizing clause as *duaa karti hũ* (I pray), *xwaahishmand hũ* (I desire), etc., are always implied. It would appear to me that the non-volitional feature and certain restrictions on imperative structures are very closely related.

20   There are restrictions on the selection of the feature 'reflexive' but the details of these need not concern us here. The main point is that although extra-linguistically the process of (23i) may not be seen as involving two distinct entities, there is a syntactic 'requirement' for a participant attribuand (or more generally 'affected') so that *bacci nee taiiyaar kiyaa* (the girl caused to be ready) will not be interpreted as (23i).

21   This point is discussed in greater detail by Halliday (1968, Section 9.1). That two different sets of systemic options may share some component(s) of meaning is interesting since it will have direct relevance to semantics and also, probably, to stylistics.

22   The term 'stative' as used here is, probably, roughly comparable with Lyons' (1968) usage, and perhaps it is as closely related to 'static'. The opposition dynamic vs. static, Lyons suggests, is relevant to the verb vs. adjective distinction (*ibid.* p. 437). The same is true of stative and action verbs (*ibid.* p. 325) '… there are certain stative verbs in English which do not normally occur in the progressive form … This aspectual difference between stative verbs and verbs of action is matched by a similar difference in English adjectives. … The possibility of free combination with the progressive aspect correlates with a number of other important features in English syntax: most notably, with the potentiality of occurrence in answer to a question like *what did she do? what is she doing?…*' If this criterion were applied to Urdu a large sub-category of the non-volitional verbs would have to be regarded as 'stative' for we may not say **laRki ciix sun rahi hai* nor may we offer the response *laRki nee eek ciix suni* (the girl heard a cry) to the question *laRki nee kyaa kiyaa?* (what did the girl do?). The same applies to the pair **laRkaa baks paa rahaa hai* (the boy is coming across a box) and *laRkee nee eek baks paayaa* (the boy found a box). For Urdu the term stative passive as used in this article means 'the predication of existence regarding some participant and/or circumstance'.

23   This should be regarded as a statement of the general tendency. One can think of grammatical clauses in which the attribute is resultative though realized by a durational adjective as in *is kriim nee bahot si aurtõ ko hasiin banaayaa hai* (this cream has made lots of women beautiful) or *rozaana ki jhak-jhak nee us ko bad-mizaaj banaa diyaa* (these daily altercations made him irritable) (!). It

would appear that the grammatical subject in such cases has to be inanimate and may be interpreted as 'cause' rather than as 'perceiver'.

24 For the terms tonic, given, new, contrastive and emphatic see Halliday (1967c).

25 Perhaps this fact is relevant to English syntax as well. A clause such as *where are you the president?* or *where are you the doctor?* is ungrammatical, whereas clauses such as *which society is he the president of?* are grammatical.

26 Again it may be noted in passing that the same applies to English; clauses like *where do you have a pen? *where do you have a brother? *where do you have eyes? *where does he have intelligence?* are all unacceptable. In Urdu since the equivalent of *where* has two functions one of which is permissible in the possessive clause, the clauses with *kahaã* are not unacceptable; they simply do not have the locative meaning.

27 That there may be clause types which can be potentially related to more than one paradigm is perhaps implicit in Halliday's (1968) treatment of nuclear clause type as well as in his discussion of the superventional and actional clauses.

28 The question that arises here is of the clause type *eek laRki thi* (there was a girl) in which the sequence of verb and noun may be reversed so that the verbal group is 'included' within the group (nominal) as in *eek thi laRki*. Both the types have generally the limited function of starting a fictional narrative. In my opinion they may not be interpreted as *a girl existed*, or *there existed a girl*. Such a clause may have a locational phrase in it as *kisi mulk meẽ eek laRki thi* or *eek thi laRki kisi mulk meẽ* (there was a girl in some country). The locational phrases which may occur with *xudaa hai* are severely limited; the following clauses represent the total of the location phrases available to it: *xudaa har iagah hai* (God is everywhere), *xudaa na masjid meẽ hai na mandir meẽ; insaan kee dil meẽ hai* (God is neither in the mosque nor in the temple; he is in man's heart) (!). This restriction does not apply to *eek laRki thi*. Second, usually the clause following the latter one in the narrative can, on the grounds of intonation, be shown to be related to it in some kind of modificational function; thus *eek laRki thi us kaa baap waziir thaa* (there was a girl; her father was a prime minister). When we have a string of clauses *eek laRkaa hai; woh mujhee rozaana pareeshaan kartaa hai* (there is a boy; he teases me every day), the clauses can be related to each other by the substitution of *jo* for *woh*. In the previous example *us* may be replaced by *jis*, without changing the meaning of the utterance in either case. It would seem to me that the use of *honaa* in these clauses is no more existential than it is in other stative passive clauses.

29 See Section 11.4.1 above for the relationship between the causative and the non-volitional clauses.

30 See Yamuna Kachru (1968): '… the verb *ho* is used as a complementless verb in only very special contexts, asserting the existence of some being or thing; the following philosophical sentence is an example of this: *iishwar hai* (God exists or God is)'.

31   Lyons (1967: 390–396); also Lyons (1968: 368); also Allen (1964: 337–343).

32   See Huddleston *et al.* (1968: 26).

33   Unlike the English clause the Urdu one is not ambiguous; the Urdu clause may
     not be interpreted as: there is an object in this room; the name of the object is
     'perfume'.

34   Haq (p. 150): 'Compound verbs are formed in two ways: (i) with the help of
     other verbs, which are called "auxiliary verb" and (ii) by "arranging" verbs
     with adjectives and nouns [in a particular order, R.H.]'. From this definition
     it is clear that Haq is contradicting his own statement regarding the *naaqis*
     verbs; secondly he is not making a distinction between a verbal group such as
     aayaa hotaa ((if) had come), a group which has the feature conditional, and
     muqarrar kiyaa (appointed) which is like *khaayaa* a simple past; further he
     makes no distinction between *waada kiyaa* (made a promise) and *muqarrar
     kiyaa*, although the syntactic potentialities of *waada* and *muqarrar* are very
     distinct. Yamuna Kachru (1966) makes a distinction between conjunct verb
     and compound verb; an example of conjunct verb for Yamuna Kachru is *band
     karnaa* (to shut; literally, shut to do) which is like *saaf karnaa* (clean to do,
     i.e. to clean). The conjunct verb is 'translatable by a one-word English verb'
     (*ibid.*: 59); example of a compound verb would be *aa gayaa* (has arrived)
     as opposed to *aayaa* (arrived) (derived from the list of examples in Yamuna
     Kachru 1966: 53). According to this approach the conjunct verbs could also
     be compound, e.g. *band kar diyaa* (has shut) as opposed to *band kiyaa* (shut
     (past)). It is clear that many confusions will arise from this.

35   More accurately one might say that the first word (of what to my mind are
     not 'compound verbs' on some superficial criterion of whether there are two
     graphic words or only one) may not appear except in company with the verb
     associated with certain choices; thus in the processive passive the verb *huaa/
     hui* (with auxiliaries or without according to the options being realized by
     the verbal group) must occur with *muqarrar* as in *woh sadar muqarrar huaa*
     (he got appointed president), *woh sadar muqarrar ho gayaa hai* (he has got
     appointed president).

36   Thus while we have *darwaazaa band karo* (shut the door) we may also have
     a group such as *band darwaazaa* (shut door, i.e. closed door); while we have
     takliif di (caused inconvenience) we also have *aap ki takliif* (your inconve-
     nience), *is tarah ki takliifee* (inconveniences of this kind). But in the case
     of the compound verb (which is distinct from compound verbal group) we
     have *is aadmi ko sadar muqarrar karo* (appoint this man president) but not
     **muqarrar aadmi* (appoint man); instead we should say *muqarrar shuda
     aadmi* (appointed become man, i.e. the appointed man) or *muqarrara waqt*
     (appointed time); nor do we have **aadmi kaa/ki muqarrar* (the man's appoint).

37   The dynamic participant in the active agnate need not be animate; consider
     in *waaqeaat nee us ko baRaa sadmaa pauhcaayaa* (these events caused him
     great sorrow), *aap ki mohabbat nee mujhee taqwiyat di hai* (your love has
     given me strength) and *is mashiin nee mjuhee baRaa aaraam diyaa* (this

machine has given me a lot of rest, i.e. it has helped me greatly). These clauses may be seen as resembling the ones quoted in note 23 above; there appears to be restrictions so far as the verb+process-range of the type discussed in Sections 11.9.2 and 11.9.3 is concerned, the details of which are too complicated to go into here.

38   That implicational relationship is in some sense reflected in syntactic relationship of items may not be questioned. There are, however, no criteria, to my knowledge, for regarding one set of implicational relations as more relevant than another. The effort to relate a clause to a given clause paradigm, it would appear, has to be based not only on the 'presence' of a particular type of implicational relation but (and, perhaps primarily), because some of the syntactic characteristics are shared by the clause under focus with the paradigm to which it is being related. I have not gone into details regarding this aspect at every point but even the surface structure of the items which I have shown to be related to each other will display the kind of syntactic similarities which may be established.

39   This finding would agree with Lyons' (1968) statement that the uses of *be* copula are 'stative'. Instead of dynamic vs. stative process as a two term opposition I have maintained here that we have a move from dynamic to stative; the active and/or causative of any paradigm is the maximally dynamic member while its stative passive is the maximally passive member, with the result that the *honaa* associated with the processive passive can at once be related to the dynamic and the stative types.

Bibliography

Aarsleff, H. (1970). The history of linguistics and Professor Chomsky. *Language, 46*. Reprinted in H. Aarsleff (Ed.) *From Locke to Saussure*. Minneapolis, MN: University of Minnesota Press, 1982. https://doi.org/10.2307/412308

Aarsleff, H. (1982). *From Locke to Saussure: Essays on the Study of Language and Intellectual History*. Minneapolis, MI: University of Minnesota Press.

Abercromie, D. (1967). *Elements of General Phonetics*. Edinburgh: Edinburgh University Press.

Allen, W. S. (1964). Transitivity and Possession. *Language, 40*, 337–343. https://doi.org/10.2307/411499

Austin, J. L. (1962). *How to Do Things with Words*. Oxford: Clarendon Press.

Bateson, G. (1972). *Steps to an Ecology of Mind*. New York: Ballantine Books.

Bazell, C. E. (1964). Three Misconceptions of Grammaticalness. *MSLL* 17, 3–9.

Benson, J. D. and Greaves, W. S. (Eds) (1985). *Systemic Perspectives in Discourse*: Vol. I Selected theoretical papers from the Ninth International Systemic Workshop, Norwood, NJ: Ablex.

Berger, P. L. and Luckman, T. (1967). *The Social Construction of Reality*. Harmonsdworth: Penguin.

Bernstein, B. (1970). A sociolinguistic approach to socialization. In J. Cumperz and D. Hymes (Eds), *Directions in Sociolinguistics* (1972). Oxford: Blackwell.

Bernstein, B. (1971). *Class, Codes and Control, Vol. I*. London: Routledge and Kegan Paul. https://doi.org/10.4324/9780203014035

Bernstein, B. (1981). Codes, modalities and the process of reproduction. *Language and Society*, 10: 327–363. https://doi.org/10.1017/S0047404500008836

Bernstein, B. (1990). *The Structuring of Pedagogic Discourse: Class, Codes and Control*, Vol. 4. London: Routledge. https://doi.org/10.4324/9780203011263

Bernstein, B. (2000). *Pedagogy, Symbolic Control and Identity*: Theory, Research and Critique (revised edition). Lanham, MD, Boulder, CO, New York and Oxford: Rowman and Littlefield.

Berry, M. (1977). *An Introduction to Systemic Linguistics, 2 Levels and Links*. London: Batsford.

Bickerton, D. (1990). *Language and Species*. Chicago, IL: University of Chicago Press.

Bierwisch, M. (1970). 'Semantics'. In J. Lyons (Ed.), *New Horizons in Linguistics*. Harmondsworth: Penguin.

Blakemore, D. (1992). *Understanding Utterances: An Introduction to Pragmatics*. Oxford and Cambridge, MA: Blackwell.

Bloomfield, L. (1933). *Language*. New York: Henry Holt and Co.

Bobrow, D. and Collins, A. (Eds) (1975). *Representation and Understanding: Studies in Cognitive Psychology*. New York: Academic Press.

Bourdieu, P. (1990). *The Logic of Practice.* (Translated by R. Nice: English translation) Cambridge: Polity Press.

Bowcher, W. (2007). Field and multimodal texts. In R. Hasan, C. Matthiessen, and J. Webster (Eds) *Continuing Discourse on Language*. London: Equinox.

Brachman, R. J. (1979). On the epitemological status of semantic networks. In N. V. Findler (Ed.) *Associative Networks: Representation and Use of Knowledge by Computers*. New York: Academic Press.

Brown. R. and Lenneberg, E. H. (1954). A study in language and cognition. *Journal of Abnormal and Social Psychology, 49*(3). Reprinted in R. Brown (Ed.) *Psycholinguistics: Selected Papers*. New York: Free Press.

Bruner, J. L. (1978). Learning how to do things with words. In J. L. Bruner and A. Garton (Eds) *Human Growth and Development*. Oxford: Clarendon Press.

Bühler, K. (1990). *Theory of Language: The Representational Function of Language.* (Translated by D. F. Goodwin) Amsterdam: Benjamins. https://doi.org/10.1075/fos.25

Butt, D. G. (1983). Ideational meaning and the mirror of nature. Paper presented at the VIII A. L. A. A. Congress, La Trobe.

Butt, D. G. (2001). Firth, Halliday and the development of systemic functional grammar. In E. F. K. Koerner (Ed.), *An International Handbook on the Evolution of the Study of Language from the Beginning to the Present*. Berlin: Walter de Gruyter.

Butt, D. G. (2004a). How our meanings change: school contexts and semantic evolution. In G. Williams and A. Lukin (Eds) *The Development of Language: Functional Perspectives on Species and Individuals*. London: Continuum.

Butt, D. G. (2004b). Parameters of context: on establishing the similarities and differences between social processes. Mimeo.

Butt, D. G. (2005). Method and imagination in Halliday's theory. In R. Hasan, C. Matthiessen and J. Webster (Eds) *Continuing Discourse on Language: A Functional Perspective*, Vol. 1. London: Equinox.

Butt, D. G. (2008). The robustness of realization systems. In J. J. Webster (Ed.) *Meaning in Context: Implementing Intelligent Applications of Language Studies*. London: Continuum.

Butt, D. and Wegener, R. (2007). The work of concepts: context and metafunction in the systemic functional model. In R. Hasan, C. Matthiessen and J. J. Webster (Eds), *Continuing Discourse on Language,* Vol. 2. London: Equinox.

Chao, Y. R. (1968). *Language and Symbolic Systems*. London: Cambridge University Press.

Chomsky, N. (1957). *Syntactic Structures*. The Hague: Mouton and Co.

Chomsky, N. (1959). Review of B. F. Skinner's 'Verbal Behaviour'. *Language*, 35: 26–58. https://doi.org/10.2307/411334

Chomsky, N. (1965). *Aspects of the Theory of Syntax*. Cambridge, MA: The MIT Press.

Chomsky, N. (1974). Noam Chomsky. In H. Parret (Ed.) *Discussing Language*. The Hague: Mouton. https://doi.org/10.1515/9783110813456-003

Chomsky, N. (1980). *Rules and Representations*. Oxford: Blackwell.

Chomsky, N. (1986). *Knowledge of Language: Its Nature, Origin and Use*. New York: Praeger.

Christie, F. and Martin, J. R. (Eds) (2007). *Language, Knowledge and Pedagogy: Functional Linguistics and Sociological Perspectives*. London: Continuum.

Christie, F. and Maton, K. (2011). *Disciplinarity: Functional Linguistics and Sociological Perspectives*. London: Continuum.

Cloran, C. (1994). *Rhetorical Units and Decontextualisation: An Enquiry into Some Relations of Context, Meaning and Grammar*. Monographs in Systemic Linguistics 6. Nottingham: Department of English, Nottingham University.

Cole, M. and Scribner, S. (1974). *Culture and Thought: A Psychological Introduction*. New York: John Wiley and Son.

Cole, M. and Gay, J. (1972). Culture and memory. *American Anthropologist*, 74: 1066–1084. https://doi.org/10.1525/aa.1972.74.5.02a00030

Collins, A. M. and Quillian, M. R. (1972). Experiments on semantic memory and language comprehension. In L. W. Gregg (Ed.) *Cognition in Learning and Memory*. New York: Wiley.

Culler, J. (1975). *Structuralist Poetics*. Ithaca, NY: Cornell University Press.

Culler, J. (1976). *Saussure*. Glasgow: Fontana/Collins.

Damasio, A. (2010). *Self Comes to Mind: Constructing the Conscious Brain*. London: Heinemann.

Davidson, I. (2003). The archaeological evidence of language origin: States of arts. In M. H. Christiansen and S. Kirby (Eds) *Language Evolution*. Cambridge: Cambridge University Press. https://doi.org/10.1093/acprof:oso/9780199244843.003.0008

Davidson, I. (2005). Beyond mysticism? Review of Jackendoff, R. (2002). *Linguistics and the Human Sciences*, *1* (2): 337–345.

Davidson, I. (2007). Scales and balances: Archaeology, cultural heritage and sustainability. *Proceedings of Australian Academy of the Humanities*. (Annual Lecture 2007): 13–143.

Davis, S. (Ed.) (1991). *Pragmatics*. New York: Oxford University Press.

Dawkins, R. (2005). *The Ancestor's Tale: A Pilgrimage to the Dawn of Life*. London: Phoenix.

Deacon, T. (1997). *The Symbolic Species: The Co-evolution of Language and the Brain*. London: Penguin Books.

Derrida, J. (1974). *Of Grammatology*. (Translated by G. C. Spivak) Baltimore, MD: Johns Hopkins University Press.

Derrida, J. (1977). *Limited Inc: a b c.* Glyph, Vol. II. Baltimore, MD: Johns Hopkins University Press.

Derrida, J. (1978). *Writing and Difference.* (Translated by A. Bass) London: Routledge and Kegan Paul.

Derrida, J. (1981). *Positions.* (Translated by A. Bass) Chicago, IL: University of Chicago Press.

Derrida, J. (1982). *Margins of Philosophy.* (Translated by A. Bass) Brighton: Harvester Press.

Dijk, T. A. van and Petöfi, S. (Eds) (1977). *Grammar and Descriptions.* Berlin: de Gruyter.

Douglas, J. D. (1971). Understanding everyday life. In J. D. Douglas (Ed.) *Understanding Everyday Life: Toward the Reconstruction of Social Knowledge.* London: Routledge and Kegan Paul.

Douglas, M. (1975). Do dogs laugh? A cross-cultural approach to body symbolism. In M. Douglas. *Implicit Meanings*: *Essays in Anthropology.* London: Routledge and Kegan Paul.

Eagleton, T. (1983). *Literary Theory: An introduction.* Oxford: Blackwell.

Eco, U. and Marmo, C. (Eds) (1989). *On the Medieval Theory of Signs.* Amsterdam: John Benjamins. https://doi.org/10.1075/fos.21

Edelman, G. M. and Tononi, G. (2000). *Consciousness: How Matter Becomes Imagination.* London: Penguin.

Eggins, S. and Slade, D. (1997). *Analysing Casual Conversation.* London: Cassell.

Ellis, J. (1966). On Contextual meaning. In C. E. Bazell, J. C. Catford, M. A. K. Halliday, and R. H. Robins (Eds). *In Memory of J. R. Firth.* London: Longmans.

Evans-Pritchard, E. E. (1973). For example, witchcraft. In M. Douglas (Ed.). *Rules and Meanings.* New York: Penguin.

Fasold, R. W. and Schiffrin, D. (Eds) (1989). *Language Change and Variation.* Amsterdam: Benjamins. https://doi.org/10.1075/cilt.52

Fawcett, R. P. (1980). *Cognitive Linguistics and Social Interaction: Towards an Integrated Model of a Systemic Functional Grammar and the Other Components of an Interacting Mind.* Heidelberg: Julius Gross and Exeter University.

Fawcett, R. P. (1983). Language as a resource. *Australian Review of Applied Linguistics*, 7 (1): 17–56. https://doi.org/10.1075/aral.7.1.02faw

Fawcett, R. P. (1988). What makes a good system network good?: Four pairs of concepts for such evaluations. In J. D. Benson and W. S. Greaves (Eds) *Systemic Functional Approaches to Discourse: Selected Papers from the 12th International Systemic Functional Workshop.* Norwood, NJ: Ablex.

Fawcett, R. P. (2000). *A Theory of Syntax for Systemic Functional Linguistics.* Amsterdam: Benjamins. https://doi.org/10.1075/cilt.206

Fawcett, R. P., Halliday, M. A. K., Lamb, S. M., and Makkai, A. (Eds) (1984). *The Semiotics of Culture and Language: Vol. 1 Language as Social Semiotic.* London: Frances Pinter.

Fillmore, C. J. (1968). The Case for Case. In E. Bach, and R. T. Harms (Eds), *Universals in Linguistic Theory.* New York: Holt, Reinhart and Winston.

Fillmore, C. J. (1977). Topics in lexical semantics. In R.W. Cole (Ed.). *Current Issues in Linguistic Theory*. Bloomington, IN: Indiana University Press.

Findler, N. V. (Ed.) (1979). *Associative Networks: Representation and Use of Knowledge by Computers.* New York: Academic Press.

Firth, J. R. (1935). The technique of semantics. *Transactions of the Philological Society*, *34*(a): 36–73.

Firth, J. R. (1951a). Modes of meaning. *Essays and Studies*, The English Association: 118–148.

Firth, J. R. (1951b). General linguistics and descriptive grammar. *Transactions of the Philological Society*, *50* (1): 69–87. Reprinted in Firth (1957a).

Firth, J. R. (1957a). *Papers in Linguistics 1934–1951*. London: Oxford University Press.

Firth, J. R. (1957b). Personality and language in society. In *Papers in General Linguistics 1934–1951*. London: Oxford University Press.

Firth, J. R. (1964). Ethnographic analysis and language with reference to Malinowski's views. In R. Firth (Ed.) *Man and Culture: An Evaluation of the Work of Bronislaw Malinowski*. New York: Harper.

Firth, J. R. (1968). A synopsis of linguistic theory, 1930–55. In F. Palmer (Ed.). *Selected Papers of J. R. Firth 1952–59.* London: Longman.

Fischer, O. and F. van der Leek. (1987). A 'case' for the Old English impersonal. In W. Koopman, F. van der Leek, O. Fischer and R. Eaton (Eds). *Explanation and Linguistics Change*. Amsterdam: John Benjamins.

Fishman, J. A. (1960). A systematization of the Whorfian hypothesis. *Behavioural Sciences*, *5* (4): 323–339. Reprinted in J. W. Berry and P. R. Dasen (Eds) (1974). *Culture and Cognition: Readings in Cross-cultural Psychology*. London: Methuen. https://doi.org/10.1002/bs.3830050407

Ghadessy, M. (Ed.) (1999). *Text and Context in Functional Linguistics*. Amsterdam: Benjamins. https://doi.org/10.1075/cilt.169

Goffman, E. (1981). *Forms of Talk*. Philadelphia, PA: University of Pennsylvania Press.

Goody, J. (1977). *The Domestication of the Savage Mind*. Cambridge: Cambridge University Press.

Goody, J. (1978). Towards a theory of acquisitions. In E. N. Goody (Ed.) *Questions and Politeness*. Cambridge: Cambridge University Press.

Green, G. M. (1996). *Pragmatics and Natural Language Understanding* (Second edition). Mahwah, NJ: Laurence Erlbaum.

Greenfield, S. (1997). *The Human Brain: A Guided Tour*. London: Weidenfield and Nicholson.

Greenfield, S. (2000). *The Private Life of the Brain*. London: Penguin.

Greenfield, S. (2008). *The Quest for Identity in the 21st Century.* London: Sceptre.

Gregg, L. W. (Ed.) (1972). *Cognition in Learning and Memory*. New York: Wiley.

Gregory, M. (1985). Towards communication linguistics: A framework. In J. Benson and W. Greaves (Eds). *Systemic Perspectives on Discourse, Vol. 1.* Norwood, NJ: Ablex.

Gregory, M. (2002). Phasal analysis within communication linguistics: Two contrastive discourses. In P. H. Fries, M. Cummings, D. Lockwood, and W. Spruiell (Eds). *Relations and Functions Within and Around Language*. London: Continuum.

Greimas, A. J. (1974). Algirdas J. Greimas. In H. Parret (Ed.) *Discussing Language*. The Hague: Mouton. https://doi.org/10.1515/9783110813456-004

Halliday, M. A. K. (1960). General Linguistics and its application to language teaching. *Etudes de Linguistique Appliqué*, Vol. 1. Reprinted in A. McIntosh and M. A. K. Halliday. *Patterns of Language*. London: Longman.

Halliday, M. A. K. (1961). Categories of the theory of grammar. *Word*, 17 (3): 241–292. Reprinted in CW Volume 1: 2002.

Halliday, M. A. K. (1963). Class in relation to the axes of chain and choice. *Linguistics*, 2: 5–15. Reprinted in CW, Volume 1: 2002.

Halliday, M. A. K. (1964). The users and uses of language. In M. A. K. Halliday, A. McIntosh, and P. Strevens (Eds) *The Linguistic Sciences and Language Teaching*. London: Longman.

Halliday, M. A. K. (1966–1968: Reprinted in full 2005). Notes on transitivity and theme in English, Parts 1–3. In J. J. Webster (Ed.) *The Collected Works of M. A. K. Halliday, Vol 7: Studies in English Language*. London: Continuum.

Halliday, M. A. K. (1966a). Some Notes on Deep Grammar. *Journal of Linguistics* 2: 56–67. https://doi.org/10.1017/S0022226700001328

Halliday, M. A. K. (1966b). Lexis as a Linguistic Level. In C. E. Bazell, J. C. Catford, M. A. K. Halliday, and R. H. Robins (Eds). *In Memory of J. R. Firth*. London: Longmans.

Halliday, M. A. K. (1967a). Notes on Transitivity and Theme in English, 1. *Journal of Linguistics* 3, 37–81. https://doi.org/10.1017/S0022226700012949

Halliday, M. A. K. (1967b). Notes on Transitivity and Theme in English, 2. *Journal of Linguistics* 3, 199–244. https://doi.org/10.1017/S0022226700016613

Halliday, M. A. K. (1967c). *Intonation and Grammar in British English*. The Hague: Mouton. https://doi.org/10.1515/9783111357447

Halliday, M. A. K. (1968). Notes on Transitivity and Theme in English, 3. *Journal of Linguistics* 4, 179–215. https://doi.org/10.1017/S0022226700001882

Halliday, M. A. K. (1969a). Options and Functions in the English Clause. *Brno Studies in English*. Reprinted in J. J. Webster (Ed.) (2005). *The Collected Works of M. A. K. Halliday, Vol 7: Studies in English Language*. London: Continuum.

Halliday, M. A. K. (1969b). Relevant models of language. *Educational Review*, *22*, 26–37. https://doi.org/10.1080/0013191690220104

Halliday, M. A. K. (1970). Language structure and language function. In J. Lyons (Ed.) *New Horizons in Linguistics*. Harmonsdworth: Penguin.

Halliday, M. A. K. (1972). Towards a sociological semantics. Reprinted in J. J. Webster (Ed.) (2003). *The Collected Works of M. A. K. Halliday, Vol 3: Language and Linguistics*. London: Continuum.

Halliday, M. A. K. (1973). *Explorations in the Functions of Language*. London: Arnold.

Halliday, M. A. K. (1974a). *Language and Social Man*. London: Longman. (Schools Council Programme in Linguistics and English Teaching: Paper Series II, Vol. 3)

Halliday, M. A. K. (1974b). M. A. K. Halliday. In H. Parret (Ed.) *Discussing Language*. The Hague: Mouton. https://doi.org/10.1515/9783110813456-005

Halliday, M. A. K. (1975/2004). Learning how to mean: Explorations in the development of language. In J. J. Webster (Ed.) *The Collected Works of M. A. K. Halliday, Vol 4: The Language of Early Childhood*. London: Continuum.

Halliday, M. A. K. (1976a). Anti-languages. *American Anthropologist. LXXVIII*: 570–584. https://doi.org/10.1525/aa.1976.78.3.02a00050

Halliday, M. A. K. (1976b). Early language learning: A sociolinguistic approach. In W. McCormack and S. Warm (Eds) *Language and Man: Anthropological Issues*. Berlin: Mouton de Gruyter.

Halliday, M. A. K. (1977a). Text as semantic choice in social contexts. In T. A. van Dijk and J. S. Petöfi. (Eds). *Grammars and Descriptions*. Berlin: Mouton de Gruyter.

Halliday, M. A. K. (1977b). Ideas about language. In *Aims and Perspectives in Linguistics. Occasional Papers I.* University of Southern Queensland, Applied Linguistics Association of Australia, Centre for Language Learning and Teaching.

Halliday, M. A. K. (1978). *Language as Social Semiotic*. London: Edward Arnold.

Halliday, M. A. K. (1979). Modes of meaning and modes of expression: Types of grammatical structure and their determination by different semantic functions. In D. J. Allerton, E. Carney, and D. Holdcroft (Eds) *Function and Context in Linguistic Analysis: Essays Offered to William Haas.* 57–79. London: Cambridge University Press. Reprinted in J. J. Webster (Ed.) *The Collected Works of M. A. K. Halliday, Vol. 1: On Grammar*. London: Continuum.

Halliday, M. A. K. (1980). Three aspects of children's language development: Learning language, learning through language, learning about language. In Y. M. Goodman, M. M. Haussler and D. Strickland (Eds). *Oral and Written Language Development: Impact on Schools*: Proceedings from the 1979 and 1980 IMPACT conferences. Newark, DE: International Reading Association. Reprinted in Halliday CW, Volume 4 (2003).

Halliday, M. A. K. (1985). *An Introduction to Functional Grammar.* London: Edward Arnold.

Halliday, M. A. K. (1987/2003). Language and the order of nature. In J. J. Webster (Ed.). *The Collected Works of M. A. K. Halliday, Vol 3: Language and Linguistics*. London: Continuum.

Halliday, M. A. K. (1988/2002). On the ineffability of grammatical categories. In J. J. Webster (Ed.). *The Collected Works of M. A. K. Halliday, Vol. 1: On Grammar.* London: Continuum. https://doi.org/10.1075/cilt.39.03hal

Halliday, M. A. K. (1992/2002). How do you mean? In M. Davis and L. Ravelli. (Eds). *Recent Developments in Systemic Functional Theory*. London: Pinter. Reprinted in Halliday, CW Volume 1: 2002.

Halliday, M. A. K. (1993). The act of meaning. In J. E. Alatis (Ed.) *Language, Communication and Social Meaning*. Georgetown University Round Table on Language and Linguistics 1992. Washington, DC: Georgetown University Press. Reprinted in Halliday, CW Volume 3: 2003.

Halliday, M. A. K. (1994). *An Introduction to Functional Grammar* (2nd revised edn). London: Arnold.

Halliday, M. A. K. (1995). On language in relation to the evolution of human consciousness. In S. Allen (Ed.) *Of Thoughts and Words: Proceedings of Nobel Symposium 92 'The Relation Between Language and Mind'*, Stockholm, 8–12 August 1994. London: Imperial College Press. https://doi.org/10.1142/9781908979681_0008

Halliday, M. A. K. (1996/2002). On grammar and grammatics. In J. J. Webster (Ed.) *The Collected Works of M. A. K. Halliday, Vol. 1: On Grammar*. London: Continuum. https://doi.org/10.1075/cilt.121.03hal

Halliday, M. A. K. (1999). The notion of context in language education. In M. Ghadessy (Ed.) *Text and Context in Functional Linguistics*, 1–24. Amsterdam: John Benjamins. Reprinted in J. J. Webster (Ed.) (2007). *The Collected Works of M. A. K. Halliday, Vol. 9: Language and Education*. London: Continuum. https://doi.org/10.1075/cilt.169.04hal

Halliday, M. A. K. (2002). Computing meanings: Some reflections on past experience and present prospects. In G. Huang and Z. Wang (Eds). *Discourse and Language Functions*. Shanghai: Foreign Language Teaching and Research Press.

Halliday, M. A. K. (2003a). Introduction: On the architecture of human language. In J. J. Webster (Ed.) *The Collected Works of M. A. K. Halliday, Vol. 3: On Language and Linguistics*. London: Continuum.

Halliday, M. A. K. (2003b). The act of meaning. In J. J. Webster (Ed.) *The Collected Works of M. A. K. Halliday, Vol. 3: On Language and Linguistics*. London: Continuum.

Halliday, M. A. K. (2003c). Syntax and the consumer. In J. J. Webster (Ed.) *The Collected Works of M. A. K. Halliday, Vol. 3: On Language and Linguistics*. London: Continuum.

Halliday, M. A. K. (2003d). Language and the order of nature. In J. J. Webster (Ed.) *The Collected Works of M. A. K. Halliday, Vol. 3: On Language and Linguistics*. London: Continuum.

Halliday, M. A. K. (2003e). *The Collected Works of M. A. K. Halliday, Vol. 4: The Language of Early Childhood* (J. J. Webster (Ed.)). London: Continuum.

Halliday, M. A. K. (2004a). On grammar as the driving force from primary to higher order consciousness. In G. Williams and A. Lukin (Eds) *The Development of Language: Functional Perspectives on Species and Individuals*. London: Continuum.

Halliday, M. A. K. (2004b). Representing the child as a semiotic being (one who means). In J. J. Webster (Ed.) *The Language of Early Childhood: The Collected Works of M. A. K. Halliday, Vol 4*. London: Continuum.

Halliday, M. A. K. (2005). On matter and meaning: the two realms of human experience. *Linguistics and the Human Sciences*, *1* (1): 59–82.

Halliday, M. A. K. (2008). *Complementarities in Language*. Beijing: The Commercial Press.

Halliday, M. A. K. (2009). Methods – techniques – problems. In M. A. K. Halliday and J. J. Webster (Eds) *Continuum Companion to Systemic Functional Linguistics*. London: Continuum.

Halliday, M. A. K. and C. M. I. M. Matthiessen (1999). *Construing Experience Through Meaning: A Language-Based Approach to Cognition*. London: Continuum.

Halliday, M. A. K. and C. M. I. M. Matthiessen (2004). *An Introduction to Functional Grammar* (3rd revised edn). London: Arnold.

Halliday, M. A. K. and J. J. Webster (Eds) (2009). *Continuum Companion to Systemic Functional Linguistics*. London: Continuum.

Halliday, M. A. K. and J. R. Martin (Eds) (1981). *Readings in Systemic Linguistics*. London: Batsford.

Halliday, M. A. K. and J. R. Martin. (1993). *Writing Science: Literacy and Discursive Power*. London: Falmer Press.

Halliday, M. A. K. and R. Hasan. (1976). *Cohesion in English*. London: Longman.

Halliday, M. A. K. and Hasan, R. (1985). *Language, Context, and Text: Aspects of Language in a Social-semiotic Perspective*. Oxford: Oxford University Press.

Halliday, M. A. K. and Greaves, W. S. (2008). *Intonation in the Grammar of English*. London: Equinox.

Halliday, M. A. K. and James, Z. L. (1993/2005). A quantitative study of polarity and primary tense in the English finite clause. In J. J. Webster (Ed.) *The Collected Works of M. A. K. Halliday, Vol 6: Computational and Quantitative Studies*. London: Continuum.

Haq, M. A. (1930). *Qawaaid-ee-Urdu*. Dehli: Taj Publishing House.

Harter, Choudhry and Budhraj (1960). *Hindi Basic Course*. Washington, DC: Center for Applied Linguistics.

Hasan, R. (1970a). Rime and reason in literature. In S. Chatman (Ed.) *Literary Style: A Symposium*. London: Oxford University Press.

Hasan, R. (1970b). The Verb 'be' in Urdu. In J. W. M. Verhaar (Ed.). *The Verb 'be' and its Synonyms*. Foundations of Language, supplementary series, 7.

Hasan, R. (1971). Syntax and semantics. In J. Morton (Ed.) *Biological and Social Factors in Psycholinguistics*. London: Logos.

Hasan, R. (1973). Code, register and social dialect. In B. Bernstein (Ed.) *Class, Code and Control, Vol. 2: Applied Studies towards the Sociology of Language*. London: Routledge and Kegan Paul. Reprinted in J. J. Webster (Ed.) (2005a). *Language, Society and Consciousness: The Collected Works of Ruqaiya Hasan, Vol. 1*. London: Equinox.

Hasan, R. (1975). Ways of saying: Ways of meaning. Paper presented at Bourg Wartenstein Symposium No. 66 on Semiotics of Culture and Language. In R. Fawcett, M. A. K. Halliday, S. M. Lamb and A. Makkai (Eds) (1984). *The*

Semiotics of Culture and Language, Vol. 1: Language as Social Semiotics. London: Frances Pinter.

Hasan, R. (1978a). The implications of semantic distance for language in education. Paper presented at 10th I.C.A.E.S., Mysore. In A. Annamalai (Ed.) (1985). *Proceedings of the Xth I.C.A.E.S.*

Hasan, R. (1978b). Text in the systemic-functional model. In W. Dressler (Ed.) *Current Trends in Text Linguistics*. Berlin: Walter de Gruyter. https://doi.org/10.1515/9783110853759.228

Hasan, R. (1979). On the notion of text. In J. S. Petöfi (Ed.) *Text vs Sentence: Basic Questions of Text Linguistics, Second Part*. Hamburg: Helmut Buske Verlag.

Hasan, R. (1983). A semantic network for the analysis of messages in everyday talk between mothers and their children. Mimeo.

Hasan, R. (1984a). What kind of resource is language? *Australian Review of Applied Linguistics*, 7: 57–85. https://doi.org/10.1075/aral.7.1.03has

Hasan, R. (1984b). Ways of saying: ways of meaning. In R. P. Fawcett, M. A. K. Halliday, S. M. Lamb and A. A. Makkai (Eds) *The Semiotics of Culture and Language Vol. 1: Language as Social Semiotic.* London: Francis Pinter.

Hasan, R. (1984c). Coherence and cohesive harmony. In J. Flood (Ed.) *Understanding Reading Comprehension*. Newark, DE: International Reading Association, Inc.

Hasan, R. (1985a). Meaning, context and text – fifty years after Malinowski. In J. D. Benson and W. S. Greaves (Eds) *Systemic Perspectives on Discourse, Volume 1*. Norwood, NJ: Ablex.

Hasan, R. (1985b). Language, context and text: Aspects of language in a social–semiotic perspective, Part B. In M. A. K. Halliday and R. Hasan (Eds) *Language, Context, and Text: Aspects of Language in a Social-semiotic Perspective*. Oxford: Oxford University Press. Geelong, Vic: Deakin University Press.

Hasan, R. (1985c). *Linguistics, Language and Verbal Art*. Geelong, Vic: Deakin University Press.

Hasan, R. (1985d). Lending and borrowing: From grammar to lexis. In J. E. Clark (Ed.). *The Cultivated Australian: Festschrift in Honour of Arthur Delbridge*. Amsterdam: Helmut Buske.

Hasan, R. (1986a). The ontogenesis of ideology. In T. Threadgold, E. A. Crosz, G. Kress, and M. A. K. Halliday (Eds). *Semiotics – Ideology – Language*. Sydney: Association for Studies in Society and Culture.

Hasan, R. (1986b). Offers in the making: A systemic functional approach. Mimeo.

Hasan, R. (1987/1996/2016). The grammarian's dream: Lexis as most delicate grammar. In R. P. Fawcett and M. A. K. Halliday (Eds) (1987). *New Developments in Systemic Linguistics, Vol. 1 Theory and Description*. London: Pinter. Also in Hasan (1996). *Ways of Saying, Ways of Meaning*. London: Cassell Academic. Reprinted in this volume, Chapter 6.

Hasan, R. (1989). The disempowerment game: Bourdieu on language in literacy. *Linguistics and Education*, 10 (1): 25–80. Reprinted in J. J. Webster (Ed.)

(2005). *The Collected Works of Ruqaiya Hasan, Vol. 1: Language, Society and Consciousness.* London: Equinox.

Hasan, R. (1995). The conception of context in text. In P. H. Fries and M. Gregory (Eds). *Discourse in Society: Systemic Functional Perspectives.* Norwood, NJ: Ablex. https://doi.org/10.1075/cilt.118

Hasan, R. (1996). Semantic networks: A tool for the analysis of meaning. In C. Cloran, D. Butt, and G. Williams (Eds). *Ways of Saying, Ways of Meaning: Selected Papers of Ruqaiya Hasan.* London: Cassell.

Hasan, R. (1999). Speaking with reference to context. In M. Ghadessy (Ed). *Text and Context in Functional Linguistics.* Amsterdam: Benjamins. https://doi.org/10.1075/cilt.169.11has

Hasan, R. (2001). Wherefore context? The place of context in the system and process of language. In S. Ren, W. Guthrie and I. W. R. Fong (Eds). *Grammar and Discourse: Proceedings of the International Conference on Discourse Analysis.* Macau: University of Macau Publication Centre.

Hasan, R. (2004). Reading picture reading: A study in ideology and inference. Reprinted in J. J. Webster (Ed.) (2005). *The Collected Works of Ruqaiya Hasan, Vol. 1: Language, Society and Consciousness.* London: Equinox.

Hasan, R. (2005a). *The Collected Works of Ruqaiya Hasan, Vol. 1: Language, Society and Consciousness.* London: Equinox.

Hasan, R. (2005b). Language, society and consciousness: Transdisciplinary orientations and the tradition of specialisation. In J. J. Webster (Ed.). *The Collected Works of Ruqaiya Hasan Vol. 1: Language, Society and Consciousness.* London: Equinox.

Hasan, R. (2005c). The disempowerment game: Bourdieu and language. In J. J. Webster (Ed.) *The Collected Works of Ruqaiya Hasan Vol. 1: Language, Society and Consciousness.* London: Equinox.

Hasan, R. (2005d). Society, language and mind: The metadialogism of Basil Bernstein's theory. In J. J. Webster (Ed.). *The Collected Works of Ruqaiya Hasan Vol.1: Language, Society and Consciousness.* London: Equinox.

Hasan, R. (2009a). *The Collected Works of Ruqaiya Hasan, Vol. 2: Semantic Variation: Meaning in Society and in Sociolinguistics* (J. J. Webster (Ed.)). London: Equinox.

Hasan, R. (2009b). Wanted: A theory for integrated sociolinguistics. In J. J. Webster (Ed.). *Semantic Variation: Meaning in Society and in Sociolinguistics: The Collected Works of Ruqaiya Hasan, Vol. 2.* London: Equinox.

Hasan, R. (2009c). On semantic variation. In J. J. Webster (Ed.). *The Collected Works of Ruqaiya Hasan Vol. 2: Semantic Variation: Meaning in Society and in Sociolinguistics.* London: Equinox.

Hasan, R. (2009d). Rationality in everyday talk: From process to system. In J. J. Webster (Ed.). *The Collected Works of Ruqaiya Hasan Vol. 2: Semantic Variation: Meaning in Society and in Sociolinguistics.* London: Equinox.

Hasan, R. (2009e). The place of context in a Systemic Functional Model. In M. A. K. Halliday, and J. Webster (Eds). *Continuum Companion to Systemic Functional Linguistics*. London: Continuum.

Hasan, R. (2010). The meaning of not is not in not. In A. Mahboob and N. Knight (Eds). *Appliable Linguistics*. London: Continuum.

Hasan, R. (2011). English process, English tense: Foreigner learner, foreign teacher. In J. Webster (Ed.). *The Collected Works of Ruqaiya Hasan, Vol. 3: Language and Education: Learning and Teaching in Society.* London: Equinox.

Hasan, R. (2012). A view of pragmatics in a social semiotic perspective. *LHS* 2009, 5 (3): 251–271.

Hasan, R. (2013). Choice, system and realisation: Describing language as meaning potential. In. L. Fontaine, T. Bartlett and G. O'Grady (Eds). *Systemic Functional Linguistics: Exploring Choice*. Cambridge: Cambridge University Press. https://doi.org/10.1017/CBO9781139583077.018

Hasan, R. (2014). Linguistic sign and the science of linguistics. In Y. Fang and J. Webster (Eds). *Developing Systemic Functional Linguistics: Theory and Applications.* London: Equinox.

Hasan, R. (2016). Towards a paradigmatic description of context: Systems, meta-functions and semantics. In J. J. Webster (Ed.). *The Collected Works of Ruqaiya Hasan, Vol. 4: Context in the System and Process of Language*. London: Equinox.

Hasan, R., Cloran, C., Williams, G., and Lukin, A. (2007). Semantic networks: The description of meaning in SFL. In R. Hasan, C. Matthiessen and J. J Webster (Eds). *Continuing Discourse on Language, Vol. 2: A Functional Perspective*. London: Equinox.

Hasan, R., Matthiessen, C., and Webster, J. J. (Eds) (2005). *Continuing Discourse with Language: A Functional Perspective, Volume 1*. London: Equinox.

Hasan, R., Matthiessen, C., and Webster, J. J. (Eds) (2007). *Continuing Discourse on Language: A Functional Perspective, Volume 2*. London: Equinox.

Hjelmslev, L. (1961). *Prolegomena to a Theory of Language* (translated by F. J. Whitfield). Bloomington, IN: Indiana University Press.

Hjelmslev, L. (1969). *Prolegomena to a Theory of Language* (translated by F. J. Whitfield) Revised English edition. Madison, WI: The University of Wisconsin Press.

Hoijer, H. (1954). The Sapir-Whorf hypothesis. In H. Hoijer (Ed.). *Language and Culture*. Chicago, IL: The University of Chicago Press.

Hood, S. and Martin, J. R. (2007). Invoking attitude: The play of graduation in appraising discourse. In R. Hasan, C. Matthiessen, and J. J. Webster (Eds). *Continuing Discourse on Language, Volume 2*. London: Equinox.

Huang, Y. (2007). *Pragmatics*. New York: Oxford University Press.

Huddleston, R. (1965). Rank and Depth, *Language, 41* (4): 574–586. https://doi.org/10.2307/411525

Huddleston, R. D., Hudson, R., Winter, E. O., and Henrici, A. (1968). *Sentence and Clause in Scientific English.* London: University College London, Communication Research Centre.

Jakobson, R. (1985). Sign and system of language: A reassessment of Saussure's doctrine. In K. Pomorska and S. Rudy (Eds). *Verbal Art, Verbal Sign, Verbal Time*. Oxford: Blackwell.

Kachru, Y. (1966). A*n Introduction to Hindi Syntax*. Urbana, IL: University of Illinois, Department of Linguistics.

Kachru, Y. (1968). The Copula in Hindi. In W. M. V. John (Ed.). *The Verb 'Be' and Its Synonyms.* Foundations of Language, 6.
https://doi.org/10.1007/978-94-017-3496-7_2

Katz, J. A. and Postal, P. M. (1964). A*n Integrated Theory of Linguistic Description.* Cambridge, MA: MIT Press.

Katz, J. J. and Fodor, J. A. (1963). The structure of a semantic theory. In J. A. Fodor and J. J. Katz (Eds). *The Structure of Language: Readings in the Philosophy of Language.* Englewood Cliffs, NJ: Prentice-Hall. https://doi.org/10.2307/411200

Khaan, M. and Fateh, M. (1945). *Misbaah-ul-Qawaaid,* Part I, II. Rampur: Barqi Press.

Labov, W. (1968). The reflection of social processes in linguistic structures. In J. A. Fishman (Ed.). *Readings in the Sociology of Language.* The Hague: Mouton. https://doi.org/10.1515/9783110805376.240

Labov, W. (1969). The logic of non-standard English. *Georgetown Monographs on Language and Linguistics, Vol. 22.* Washington, DC: Georgetown University Press.

Labov, W. (1972). *Sociolinguistic Patterns.* Oxford: Basil Blackwell.

Laguna, G. A. de. (1927). *Speech: Its Function and Development.* Bloomington, IN: Indiana University Press.

Lamb, S. M. (1964). A sememic approach to structural semantics. *Transcultural Studies in Cognition, 66,* 57–77.

Lamb, S. M. (1966a). *Outline of Stratificational Grammar.* Washington DC: Georgetown University Press.

Lamb, S. M. (1966b). Epilegomena to a theory of language. *Romance Philology, 19,* 531–573.

Lashley, K. S. (1951). The Problem of Serial Order in Behaviour. In L. A. Jeffress (Ed.). *Cerebral Mechanism in Behaviour.* New York: John Wiley.

Lass, R. (1987). Language, speakers, history, and drift. In W. Koopman, F. van der Leek, O. Fischer, and R. Eaton (Eds). *Explanation and Linguistics Change.* Amsterdam: John Benjamins.

Lave, J. (1997). Learning, apprenticeship, social practice. *Journal of Nordic Educational Research, 3,* 140–151.

Leech, G. N. (1974). *Semantics.* Harmondsworth: Penguin.

Leech, G. N. (1983). *Principles of Pragmatics.* London: Longman.

Lemke, J. L. (1984). Semiotics and Education. Toronto Semiotic Circle Monographs. Working Papers and Pre-publications. Toronto: Victoria University.

Lenneberg, E. H. (1964/1967). A biological perspective of language. In E. H. Lenneberg (Ed.). *New Direction in the Study of Language.* Cambridge, MA:

M.I.T. Press. Reprinted in R. C. Oldfield and J. C. Marshall (Eds) (1967). *Language.* Penguin Books.

Lenneberg, E. H. (1975). Language and cognition. In D. D. Steinberg and L. A. Jakobovits (Eds). *Semantics.* London and New York: Cambridge University Press.

Levinson, S. C. (1983). *Pragmatics.* London: Cambridge University Press. https://doi.org/10.1017/CBO9780511813313

Lucy, J. A. (1987). Vygotsky and Whorf: A comparative analysis. In M. Hickman (Ed.). *Social and Functional Approaches to Language and Thought.* London: Academic Press.

Lyons, J. (1963). *Structural Semantics.* Publication of the Philogical Society XX. Oxford: Basil Blackwell.

Lyons, J. (1966). Towards a 'Notional' Theory of 'Parts of Speech'. *Journal of Linguistics, 2* (2): 209–236. https://doi.org/10.1017/S0022226700001511

Lyons, J. (1967). A note on possessive, existential and locative sentences. *Foundations of Language 3*, 390–396.

Lyons, J. (1968). *Introduction to Theoretical Linguistics.* Cambridge: Cambridge University Press. https://doi.org/10.1017/CBO9781139165570

Lyons, J. (Ed.) (1970). *New Horizons in Linguistics.* Harmondsworth: Penguin.

Lyons, J. (1977). *Semantics Vols. 1 and 2.* Cambridge: Cambridge University Press. https://doi.org/10.1017/CBO9781139165693

Malinowski, B. (1923/66). The problem of meaning in primitive communities. Supplement in C. Ogden and I. A. Richards. *The Meaning of Meaning.* London: Routledge ad Kegan Paul.

Malinowski, B. (1935). An ethnographic theory of language. *Coral Gardens and their Magic.* Vol. 2 Part IV. London: Allen and Unwin.

Mann, W. (1985). An introduction to the Nigel text generation grammar. In J. Benson and W. Greaves (Eds) *Systemic Perspectives on Discourse, Vol. 1.* Norwood, NJ: Ablex.

Mann, W. C., Matthiessen, C. M. I. M. and Thompson, S. A. (Eds) (1992). Rhetorical structure theory and context analysis. In W. C. Mann and S. A. Thompson (Eds). *Discourse Descriptions: Diverse Linguistic Analyses of a Fund-Raising Text.* Amsterdam: Benjamins.

Mann, W., and Matthiessen, C. M. I. M. (1983). *Nigel: A Systemic Grammar for Text Generation* (Chapter 2). ISI/RR.

Marshall, J. C. (1971). Can Humans Talk?. In J. Morton (Ed.) *Biological and Social Factors in Psycholinguistics.* London: Logos.

Martin, J. R. and Veel, R. (Eds) (1998). *Reading Science: Critical and Functional Perspectives on Discourse of Science.* London: Routledge.

Martin, J. R. (1985). On the analysis of exposition. In R. Hasan (Ed.) *Discourse on Discourse.* Sydney: Applied Linguistics Association of Australia, Publication No. 7.

Martin, J. R. (1987). The meaning of features in systemic linguistics. In M. A. K. Halliday and R. P. Fawcett (Eds) *New Developments in Systemic Linguistics. Vol. 1*. London: Pinter.

Martin, J. R. (1992). *English Text: System and Structure*. Amsterdam: Benjamins. https://doi.org/10.1075/z.59

Marwick, B. (2005). The interpersonal origins of language: Social and linguistic implications of an archaeological approach to language evolution. *Linguistics and the Human Sciences, 1* (2): 197–224.

Mathesius, V. (1964). On the potentiality of the phenomena of language. In J. Vachek (Ed.) *A Prague School Reader in Linguistics*. Bloomington, IN: Indiana University Press.

Matthiessen, C. M. I. M. and Nesbitt, C. (1996). On the idea of theory-neutral descriptions. In R. Hasan, C. Cloran, and D. Butt (Eds) *Functional Descriptions: Theory in Practice*. Amsterdam: John Benjamins. https://doi.org/10.1075/cilt.121.04mat

Matthiessen, C. M. I. M. (1995). *Lexicogrammatical Cartography: English Systems*. Tokyo: Internal Language Science Publishers.

Matthiessen, C. M. I. M. (2004). The evolution of language: A systemic functional exploration of phylogenetic phases. In G. Williams and A. Lukin (Eds). *The Development of Language: Functional Perspectives on Species and Individuals*. London: Continuum.

Matthiessen, C. M. I. M. (2007a). The architecture of language according to systemic functional theory: Developments since the 1970s. In R. Hasan, C. Matthiessen, and J. J. Webster (Eds). *Continuing Discourse on Language*, Vol. 2. London: Equinox.

Matthiessen, C. M. I. M. (2007b). Lexicogrammar in systemic functional linguistics: Description and theoretical developments in the IFG tradition since the 1970s. In R. Hasan, C. Matthiessen, and J. J. Webster (Eds). *Continuing Discourse on Language*, Vol. 2. London: Equinox.

Matthiessen, C. M. I. M. (2012). Tenor. Plenary presented at the Symposium on Register and Context: Social Context and the Enactment of Tenor, convenors. A. Lukin and A. Moore, 6–8 February 2012, Macquarie University, Sydney.

McMahon, A. M. S. (1994). *Understanding Language Change*. Cambridge: Cambridge University Press. https://doi.org/10.1017/CBO9781139166591

Mead, G. H. (1910). What social objects must psychology presuppose? *The Journal of Philosophy, 7*. Reprinted in T. Luckman (Ed.). *Phenomenology and Sociology*. New York: Penguin.

Mertz, E. and R. J. Parmentier. (1991). *Semiotic Mediation: Sociocultural and Psychological Perspectives*. New York: Academic Press.

Mey, J. L. (1993). *Pragmatics: An introduction*. Oxford: Blackwell.

Mey, J. L. (Ed.) (1998). *Concise Encyclopedia of Pragmatics*. Amsterdam: Elsevier.

Mitchell, T. F. (1975). *Principles of Firthian Linguistics*. London: Longman.

Morton, J. (Ed.) (1971). *Biological and Social Factors in Psycholinguistics*. London: Logos.

Newson, J. (1978). Dialogue and development. In A. Lock (Ed.). *Action, Gesture and Symbol: The Emergence of Language*. London: Academic Press.

Noble, W. and Davidson, I. (1996). *Human Evolution, Language and Mind: A Psychological and Archaeological Inquiry*. Cambridge: Cambridge University Press.

O'Donnell, M. (1994). *Sentence analysis and generation: a systemic perspective*. Unpublished PhD thesis, Department of Linguistics, University of Sydney.

Ogden, C. K. and Richards, I. A. (1923). *The Meaning of Meaning*. London: Kegan Paul.

Painter, C. (1984). *Into the Mother Tongue: A Case Study of Early Language Development*. London: Pinter.

Painter, C. (1989). Learning language: A functions view of language development. In R. Hasan and J. R. Martin (Eds) *Language Development: Learning Language, Learning Culture*. Norwood, NJ: Ablex.

Peirce, C. S. (1878/1960). Consequences of four incapacities. *Journal of Speculative Philosophy, 2*. Reprinted in C. Hartshorne and P. Weiss (Eds) (1960). *Collected Papers of C.S. Peirce Vols. V and VI*. Cambridge, MA: Harvard University Press.

Peirce, C. S. (1955). *Philosophical Writings of Peirce*. Selected and edited by J. Buchler. New York: Dover Publications, Inc.

Pratt, M. L. (1987). Linguistic utopias. In N. Fabb, D. Attridge, A. Durant, and C. McCabe (Eds) *The Linguistics of Writing: Arguments between Language and Literature*. Manchester: Manchester University Press.

Putnam, H. (1975). The meaning of meaning. *Mind, Language and Reality*. London: Cambridge University Press.

Rorty, R. (1979). *Philosophy and the Mirror of Nature*. Princeton, NJ: Princeton University Press.

Rorty, R. (1980). Pragmatism, relativism and irrationalism. *Proceedings of the American Philosophical Association, LIII*. Reprinted in R. Rorty (1982). *Consequences of Pragmatism*. Minneapolis, MN: University of Minnesota Press. https://doi.org/10.2307/3131427

Rorty, R. (1981). Method, social science and social hope. *The Canadian Journal of Philosophy, XI*. Reprinted in R. Rorty (1982). *Consequences of Pragmatism*. Minneapolis, MN: University of Minnesota Press.

Rorty, R. (1982). *Consequences of Pragmatism*. Minneapolis, MN: University of Minnesota Press.

Royce, J. R. (1964). *The Encapsulated Man*. Princeton, NJ: Van Nostrand Co.

Russell, B. (1940/1962). *An Enquiry into Meaning and Truth*. London: Allen and Unwin. Reprinted in 1962. Harmondsworth: Penguin Books Ltd.

Salusinszky, I. (1983). Intellectual war. *Times Literary Supplement*, 28 October 1983.

Saporta, S. (1961). *Psycholinguistics*. New York: Holt, Reinhart and Winston.

Saussure, F. de. (1916/1959/1974). *A Course in General Linguistics*. (Tr. by W. Baskin) English edition. London: Fontana.

Saussure, F. de. (1966). *Course in General Linguistics*. C. Bally, A. Sechehaye and A. Riedlinger (Eds) (Tr. and introduced with notes by W. Baskin). New York: McGraw-Hill Book Company.

Saussure, F. de. (2006). *Writings in General Linguistics*, S. Bouquet and R. Engler (Eds) (T. C. Sanders and M. Piers). Oxford: Oxford University Press.

Schank, R. (1972). Conceptual dependency: A theory of natural language understanding. *Cognitive Psychology, 3* (4): 552–631.
https://doi.org/10.1016/0010-0285(72)90022-9

Schank, R. (1975). The structure of episodes in memory. In D. Bobrow and A. Collins (Eds). *Representation and Understanding: Studies in Cognitive Psychology*. New York: Academic Press.
https://doi.org/10.1016/B978-0-12-108550-6.50014-8

Schank, R. and R. Abelson. (1977). *Scripts, Plans, Goals and Understanding*. Hillsdale, NJ: Lawrence Erlbaum Associates.

Schmidt, J. (1985). *Maurice Merleau-Ponty: Between Phenomenology and Structuralism*. London: Macmillan. https://doi.org/10.1007/978-1-349-17869-8

Searle, J. R. (1969). *Speech Acts: An Essay on the Philosophy of Language*. London: Cambridge University Press. https://doi.org/10.1017/CBO9781139173438

Shotter, J. (1978). The cultural context of communication studies: Theoretical and methodological issues. In A. Lock (Ed.). *Action, Gesture and Symbol: The Emergence of Language*. London: Academic Press.

Sinclair, J. McH. (1966). Beginning the study of Lexis. In C. E. Bazell, J. C. Catford, M. A. K. Halliday, and R. H. Robins (Eds) *In Memory of J. R. Firth*. London: Longmans.

Skinner, Q. (1981). The end of philosophy (Review of R. Rorty: Philosophy and the Mirror of Nature) in *The New York Review of Books* (March 19).

Strang, B. M. H. (1970). *A History of English*. London: Methuen.

Thibault, P. J. (1977). *Re-reading Saussure: The Dynamics of Signs in Social Life*. London: Routledge.

Torr, J. (1997). *From Child Tongue to Mother Tongue* (*Monographs in Systemic Linguistics*, No. 9). Nottingham: University of Nottingham, Department of English Studies.

Trevarthen, C. and Hubley, P. (1978). Confidence, confiding and acts of meaning in the first year. In A. Lock (Ed.). *Action, Gesture and Symbol: The Emergence or Language*. London: Academic Press.

Trevarthen, C. (1979). Communication and cooperation in early infancy: A description of primary intersubjectivity. In M. Bullowa (Ed.) *Before Speech: The Beginnings of Interpersonal Communication*. London: Cambridge University Press.

Tucker, G H. (1998). *The Lexicogrammar of Adjectives: A Systemic Functional Approach to Lexis*. London: Cassell.

Vachek, I. (1966). *The Linguistic School of Prague*. Bloomington, IN: Indiana University Press.

Van Valin, R. D. Jr and LaPolla, R. J. (1997). *Syntax: Structure, Meaning and Function*. Cambridge: Cambridge University Press. https://doi.org/10.1017/CBO9781139166799

Verscheuren, J. (1995). The pragmatic perspective. In J. Verscheuren, J. Östman, and J. Blommaert (Eds). *Handbook of Pragmatics: Manual*. Amsterdam: John Benjamins. https://doi.org/10.1075/hop.m.prag

Verscheuren, J., Östman, J. and Blommaert, J. (Eds) (1995). *Handbook of Pragmatics: Manual*. Amsterdam: John Benjamins. https://doi.org/10.1075/hop.m

Vygotsky, L. S. (1978). *Mind in Society: The Development of Higher Psychological Processes*, M. Cole, V. John-Steiner, S. Scribner, and E. Souberman (Eds). Cambridge, MA: Harvard University Press.

Webster, J. J. (Ed.) (2009). *Meaning in Context: Implementing Intelligent Applications of Language Studies*. London: Continuum.

Weinreich, U. (1966). Explorations in semantic theory. In T. A. Sebeok (Ed.) *Current Trends in Linguistic Theory*. Hague: Mouton and Co.

Weinreich, U., W. Labov and M. I. Herzog. (1968). Empirical foundations for a theory of language change. In W. P. Lehmann and Y. Malkiel (Eds). *Directions for Historical Linguistics: A Symposium*. Austin, TX and London: University of Texas Press.

Weiss, P. (1952). The logic of creative process. In P. P. Weiner and F. H. Young (Eds). *Studies in the Philosophy of C. S. Peirce*. Cambridge, MA: Harvard University Press. https://doi.org/10.4159/harvard.9780674862906.c16

Wertsch, J. V. (1985a). *Vygotsky and the Social Formation of Mind*. Cambridge, MA: Harvard University Press.

Wertsch, J. V. (1985b). *Culture, Communication and Cognition: Vygotskian Perspectives*. Cambridge: Cambridge University Press.

Wertsch, J. V. (1997). Collective memory: Issues from a sociohistorical perspective. In M. Cole, Y. Engeström, and O. Vasquez (Eds). *Mind, Culture and Activity*. Cambridge: Cambridge University Press.

Whorf, B. L. (1940). Science and linguistics. *Technological Review, 42*. Reprinted in J. B. Carroll (Ed.) (1956). *Language, Thought and Reality*. Cambridge, Massachusetts: M.I.T. Press.

Whorf, B. L. (1941a). The relation of habitual thought and behavior to language. In L. Spier (Ed.). *Language Culture and Personality: Essays in Memory of E. Sapir*. Menasha, WI: Sapir Memorial Publication Fund. Reprinted in J. B. Carroll (Ed.) (1956). *Language, Thought and Reality*. Cambridge, MA: M.I.T. Press.

Whorf, B. L. (1941b). Language and logic. *Technological Review, 32*. Reprinted in J. B. Carroll (Ed.) (1956). *Language, Thought and Reality*. Cambridge, MA: M.I.T. Press.

Whorf, B. L. (1942). Language, mind and reality. *Theosophist*, January–April. Reprinted in J. B. Carroll (Ed.) (1956). *Language, Thought and Reality*. Cambridge, MA: M.I.T. Press.

Whorf, B. L. (1956a). A linguistics consideration of thinking in primitive communities. In J. B. Carroll (Ed.). *Language, Thought and Reality*. Cambridge, MA: M.I.T. Press.

Whorf, B. L. (1956b). *Language, Thought and Reality: Selected writings of Benjamin Lee Whorf*, J. B. Carroll. (Ed.). Cambridge, MA: M.I.T. Press.

Wilkes, Y. (1978). Making preferences more active. *Artificial Intelligence, 11*: 197–223. https://doi.org/10.1016/0004-3702(78)90001-2

Williams, G. (1995). *Joint Book Reading and Literacy Pedagogy: A Socio-Semantic Examination*. Unpublished PhD thesis. Department of Linguistics, Macquarie University.

Wittgenstein, L. (1958). *Philosophical Investigations* (2nd edition). (Tr. by G. E. M. Anscombe) Oxford: Basil Blackwell.

Young, D. J. (1980). *The Structure of English Clauses*. London: Hutchinson.

Index

CPSIA information can be obtained
at www.ICGtesting.com
Printed in the USA
BVHW040824310119
539106BV00001B/1/P